son and Religion

REM B. EDWARDS

AN INTRODUCTION TO THE
PHILOSOPHY OF RELIGION

ason
and
igion AN INTRODUCTION
TO THE PHILOSOPHY
OF RELIGION

Reason
and
Religion
AN INTRODUCTION
TO THE PHILOSOPHY
OF RELIGION

Rem B. Edwards
UNIVERSITY OF TENNESSEE

Harcourt Brace Jovanovich, Inc.

NEW YORK   CHICAGO   SAN FRANCISCO   ATLANTA

To Charles Hartshorne
who helped me to love God
with all my mind

Cover photo: Harbrace

ISBN: 0–15–576002–5

Library of Congress Catalog Card Number: 72–80882

Printed in the United States of America

gogical point to this. It is common to put a selection of questions for discussion at the *end* of textbook sections, and thus to relegate them somewhat artificially to the realm of optional "exercises," but I have chosen instead to incorporate such questions into the body of the text itself so that they can be considered immediately.

I have attempted to deal with most of the standard problems of the philosophy of religion, as a glance at the chapter titles will indicate. It may appear, however, that some familiar and important issues—the problem of evil and theodicy and the problem of immortality—have been neglected. But this is not the case; the treatment of evil and theodicy is integrated into other discussions, primarily the discussions of the nature of religion in Chapter 1, the concepts of God in supernaturalism and panentheism in Chapters 7 and 8, and the teleological argument in Chapter 9. Immortality and experience after death are considered in Chapters 1 and 14. Religious language receives even more thorough treatment than is indicated by the fact that the main title of Chapters 12, 13, and 14 is "Religious Language and Experience," since problems of religious language are treated *throughout* the book. Also, the empiricist-positivist critique of religion is given more attention than one might surmise, being treated in Chapter 5 under the heading "The Elimination of 'Subject Matter' from Both Philosophy and Theology: Logical Positivism"; in Chapters 9, 10, and 11 in connection with objections to the ontological, cosmological, and teleological arguments; and throughout Chapters 12, 13, and 14, especially in connection with the introductory discussion of "Language and Experience" in Chapter 12. Finally, brief discussions of the "death of God" theology appear where relevant in many places in the book.

I have tried to write the book in language that the average college junior and senior can readily understand, with a minimum of cumbersome technical jargon. I have also tried to arrange the material so that the discussion of one topic leads naturally into the discussion of the next, a sequence that at the same time proceeds from less difficult to more difficult themes. From my own experience in teaching this material, I am convinced that none of the topics covered is beyond the powers of an intelligent college student, though some may be a significant challenge to him. It may not be possible to cover all this material in a single quarter or semester, so the instructor may have to exercise some selectivity.

Many people have contributed significantly to the writing of this book. I cannot mention or thank them all, but I would especially like to thank my wife and children, who had to live with me during the difficult writing period; my students at Jacksonville University and at the University of Tennessee, on whom I first tried out many of the presentations that appear in this book; several of my colleagues at the University of Tennessee who read and criticized most of the material; Monroe Beardsley of Temple University, Robert L. Ferm of Middlebury College, and Charles Hartshorne of the University of Texas, whose reviews of the manuscript were very helpful; my departmental chairman, John W. Davis, who made many helpful criticisms and comments and who permitted me to mimeograph, at departmental expense, the various sections of the book so that they could be subjected to classroom testing and consequent revision; Mrs. Dolores Scates, our departmental secretary, for her superb assistance in preparing the mimeographed version of the manuscript; the University of Tennessee for a reduced teaching load during the period of writing; and Cecilia Gardner and Michelle Daly of Harcourt Brace Jovanovich for their exceptionally able editorial assistance.

I should also like to thank the editors of the journals and the publishers of the books from which I have quoted for permission to reproduce their copyrighted material. The first footnote for each quoted source should be interpreted as an acknowledgment of indebtedness to the copyright holders. The discussion of the fallacy of composition and the cosmological argument in Chapter 10 is a considerably revised version of my article "Composition and the Cosmological Argument," which appeared in *Mind,* Vol. LXXVII, January 1968, pp. 115–17; my thanks to Gilbert Ryle, the editor of *Mind,* for permission to use this material.

REM B. EDWARDS

Contents

Four The Relation of Philosophy and Theology:
SOME EXTREME POSITIONS

Five The Relation of Philosophy and Theology:
SOME MODERN ALTERNATIVES

Six The World Without God:
NATURALISM AND HUMANISM

Seven God and the World:
SUPERNATURALISM

Eight God and the World:
PANENTHEISM

Reason
and
Religion

AN INTRODUCTION
TO THE PHILOSOPHY
OF RELIGION

what is uniquely religious about all these things? In other words, what do such terms as *religious* or *religion* mean?

Before we attempt to answer this question, let us first ask what the difference is between the philosopher of religion and the theologian. Both are concerned with the uniquely religious features of reality, knowledge, and value; but the philosophy of religion is a different enterprise from that of theology. Philosophers do not usually wish to be called theologians, nor vice versa! Again, as the relation between the two is traditionally conceived, the philosophy of religion is differentiated from theology by the method that each employs of arriving at fixed beliefs. In the definition of *philosophy* given above, it is the final phrase, "relying exclusively on the use of human intelligence," that provides the difference between philosophy and theology: Whereas the philosopher of religion makes use of whatever methods of inquiry are generally available to unaided human intelligence in formulating and justifying his conception of the uniquely religious features of reality, knowledge, and value, the theologian relies ultimately on a faith response to a supposed revelation or to revelatory events in arriving at his conception of the uniquely religious features of reality, knowledge, and value. Thus theology, as the systematic conceptual elaboration of the faith response to revelation or revelatory events, is not the same thing as the philosophy of religion. Ideally, the philosophy of religion is the systematic elaboration of what human intelligence can discover all by itself about such religious issues as the existence of God, the characteristics of God, the problem of evil, the relation of man to God, and the religious destiny of man. Those who rely on special inspiration have provided us with many and diverse accounts of these matters, but what can human intelligence alone discover about them? This is the large and difficult province that the philosopher of religion chooses for himself, and as in other areas of human knowledge, we must allow for the possibility that those who operate within this province have made use of the available methods of inquiry with varying degrees of thoroughness and effectiveness. We must also bear in mind the possibility that this traditional way of differentiating between theology and the philosophy of religion might prove untenable, and we shall return to this theme once more in chapter five.

Now, what is *religion?* This is one of the most difficult and complicated questions to be answered by the philosophy of religion. In religious literature, whether philosophical or theological, we find an incredible variety of answers, ranging all the way from simply "a belief in God" or "a belief in the supernatural" to "the opiate of the people."

One thing we must realize in searching for the meaning or definition of a concept is that not all definitions are of the same type. Definitions are offered to accomplish many diverse ends: to report the meaning attached to certain words in some established natural language such as ordinary English or ordinary German; to initiate a connection between a symbol and its meaning when the symbol is being introduced; to call special attention to one of the several legitimate meanings attached to a symbol in some established language; to draw sharper boundaries around the meaning of a symbol than are usually drawn in an established language; to attempt to tell us in Platonic fashion what a symbol "really means" irrespective of the conventions of any established language; to persuade us to reinforce or alter our values. And this is only a partial list of the uses of definitions! So we must decide what kind or kinds of definition of *religion* we want, and then perhaps we can bring some order out of the initial chaos of meanings with which we are first confronted when we ask, What is religion?

It will be a very fruitful beginning if we can arrive at some understanding of the meanings ordinarily attached to *religion* and *religious* in everyday language, and then go on to examine some of the other uses to which definitions of these concepts have been put. If we do not begin here, then when we go on in later chapters to discuss particular "religious problems," we shall in all likelihood not be discussing any religious problems that any of us in fact have, and our "solutions" to these problems may not be solutions to any religious problems that have ever perplexed us. In particular, we shall examine three approaches to defining these concepts, the first two of which will help us to understand the meaning that we ordinarily attach to *religion* in our everyday discourse, and the third of which might help us to see the multifarious ways in which definitions of *religion* have been offered in order to influence and alter our religious attitudes and values.

We shall call these approaches, first, *the search for a common essence,* second, *the search for family resemblances,* and third, *the offering of persuasive definitions.*

The Search for a Common Essence of Religion

Is there some essential property or set of characteristics that a thing must have before we will call it religious or a religion? Many people have searched for such an essence of religion, and some have even thought they have found it. What method might we use to guide our search for such an essence? We might first draw up a list of things that we ordinarily call religions or to which we ordinarily apply the adjective *religious.* Then we might examine the items in our list to identify the features that each has in common with all the rest and that are lacking in things not ordinarily called religions. A procedure such as this can be and often has been used in an attempt to discover the "pure essence" of our ordinary concept of religion—that is, in an attempt to discover those features that are both common to and distinctive of all the objects to which the concept is usually applied. Let us examine this procedure in some detail.

The attempt to find a common essence of religion is not as easy as it may seem. It is easy to show in Socratic fashion that many of the popular, unexamined answers given to our question will not work. For example, if we say that religion is "a belief in God," we are confronted with the fact that many of the great world religions such as early Buddhism, Zen Buddhism, and the Hinayana Buddhism that prevails today in southeastern Asia are completely atheistic. Or if we say that religion is "a belief in the supernatural," we are confronted with the fact that many versions of pantheism, such as those developed by the Stoics, by Spinoza, Schelling, and Schleiermacher, and by some of the religions of the Orient, tend to identify God with nature and allow no place at all for the supernatural. As H. Richard Niebuhr has pointed out, some men worship Jesus' God, some worship country, and some worship Yale.[1] But not all religious men are devotees of the supernatural.

The search for a common essence of religion is complicated still further by the fact that humanism has become a "religion" for some people and so has Communism for others; but whereas these may provide answers to the question of the meaning of life or the meaning of history, neither makes a place for such traditional religious concerns as the supernatural or life after death. Moreover, we often find ourselves saying that some acquaintance has "made a religion" out of success or wealth or golf or fishing. What do these things have in common with the great world religions such as Christianity, Judaism, Islam, Hinduism, and Buddhism? Where is our "common essence"? Is there anything distinctive that all these "religions" have in common? Such initial difficulties as these have caused some to give up the search for a common essence of religion, but we should not regard the cause as hopeless until we have examined some more sophisticated attempts.

TILLICH'S DEFINITION OF RELIGION

One thing we must recognize from the outset is that the result of any attempt to find a factor common to and distinctive of such diverse concepts as Christianity, Communism, and golf must necessarily be extremely diluted, diffuse, abstract—a minimal definition incorporating only the lowest common denominator. Paul Tillich has made such a definition, one that has gained wide acceptance among both philosophers and theologians:

> Religion is the state of being grasped by an ultimate concern, a concern which qualifies all other concerns as preliminary and which itself contains the answer to the question of the meaning of our life.[2]

In Tillich's sense of *religion* both the great and small religions of man seem to qualify, for the men who belong to them find themselves grasped by an ultimate concern. They find themselves in possession of some ultimate value or set of values that forms the focal point of their existence, that gives meaning and unity to the whole of their lives, and to which all other values and interests are somehow related and subordinated. Certainly one thing that we ordinarily mean when we call Christianity, Islam, Hinduism, Buddhism, and others religions is that men find in them such an ultimate set of values, but this also applies to such lesser "religions" as Communism, Nazism, humanism, fishing, and golf. The man who has made a religion out of wealth is the man who has made his money-making activities the very center of his life, and all his other interests and activities are subordinated to and somehow made significant by his ultimate concern. These are among the last values he would be willing to sacrifice, and for these values he would be willing to sacrifice all others; he loves them with all his heart and soul and mind and strength.

There are problems involved in Tillich's definition of *religion,* however. Some of these seem to spring from the inconsistent ways in which Tillich applies his own concept, some from his choice of words, and some from the inclusiveness of the definition itself. Let us see whether there is a remedy for these difficulties.

Does Tillich Apply the Word Ultimate Consistently?

In the definition as we have discussed it thus far, Tillich uses the adjective *ultimate* to modify the noun *concern,* but sometimes he applies it to the object of that concern, so that *religion* seems to mean "ultimate concern about an ultimate object." [3]

For our purposes, the strength of Tillich's definition lies in its capturing a common and distinctive essence for most of the things that we commonly call religions. As he first presents it, this essence resides not in religious beliefs or religious objects, but in the human response to them. There is no attempt to find a single *belief* or *object of devotion* common to all the religions of man. This is the great advantage of Tillich's definition: It gives us as a common essence the human response to these objects while at the same time allowing for the great multitude of such beliefs and objects of devotion, which vary so widely from culture to culture and even from person to person. *Any* belief or object of human interest can become the focal point of a religion, as Tillich first defines the concept. It seems that any adequate definition of *religion* must allow for such diversity. At the same time, Tillich gives us a clue that enables us to distinguish religious from nonreligious beliefs, objects, and practices—the depth and breadth of the human response to and involvement with them. We thus have a rule that most speakers of English would be willing to accept for extending the concept of religion to circumstances that may never have been called religions before. The ultimacy of human concern seems to be at least common to and perhaps even distinctive of all religions, for (with some reservations to be expressed later) we are and would be willing to call anything a religion in which this quality appears.

Tillich seems to complicate unnecessarily this beautiful picture by attempting to distinguish "true religion" from "idolatry" or "quasi-religion," stating that:

> The more idolatrous a faith the less it is able to overcome the cleavage between subject and object. For that is the difference between true and idolatrous faith. In true faith the ultimate concern is a concern about the truly ultimate; while in idolatrous faith preliminary, finite realities are elevated to the rank of ultimacy.[4]

Unfortunately, for Tillich, "true religion" or "true faith" turns out to be the Tillichian concern for "Being Itself." Not only do such quasi-religions as Fascism and Communism turn out to be idolatrous because they are addressed to less-than-ultimate objects or concerns,[5] but even the monotheistic religions of Christianity, Judaism, and Islam are tainted with idolatry insofar as they believe in the existence of a personal God who stands against the world as an "object among objects."[6]

Tillich states his case against idolatry so strongly that he sometimes conveys the impression that an ultimate concern about a less-than-ultimate object would not really count as a "religion" at all, and this is where the difficulty lies. Furthermore, since the word *ultimate* suggests "singularity," no polytheistic religions would qualify, because they have *many* objects of concern. *Ultimate* is loaded in favor of some form of monism or monotheism. Now, many of the things we call religions, such as humanism, Communism, Nazism, success, and golf, do not count as true religions, and perhaps not even as religions at all. Although ultimate *concern* may be there, the ultimate *object* of ultimate concern is lacking. With this stroke we have now, unfortunately, lost our common and distinctive essence. Of course, this is the least favorable interpretation of Tillich's account of true religion. Perhaps he does not want to deny that idolatrous religion is religion. Perhaps both have ultimate concern in common, and it is this which makes them religions. Then within this generic framework idolatrous religion could be differentiated from true religion by the fact that in the latter, but not in the former, the concern is addressed to a truly ultimate object. If this is what Tillich intends, then his original definition of *religion* as "being grasped by an ultimate concern" still stands. What he cannot do is define *religion* as "ultimate concern about a truly ultimate object" [7] and still hope to provide us with a common and distinctive essence, since for him the only truly ultimate object is "Being Itself"; and Tillich belongs to a very small minority of religious men who have been ultimately concerned about *that!*

Tillich has not decided what he wishes to accomplish with a definition of *religion,* vacillating between the desire to *inform* us with such a definition and the desire to *convert* us. Later in chapter two we shall see how definitions of *true religion* are used mainly as instruments of conversion. In assessing Tillich's definition, we must make up our minds what kind of definition we are looking for—that is, whether we wish to be informed or converted.

Is Ultimate *the Right Word?*

The word *ultimate,* used in its normal way, applies only to the last member of a series. We may say that death is the ultimate event of life, or that for the moral man the moral point of view is the ultimate value-perspective, or that a certain invention or discovery was its creator's ultimate achievement, or that axioms form the ultimate premises for our deductive reasonings. In all these cases the word *ultimate* suggests the final member of a series. Some of the series of which we might speak as having an ultimate member are temporal, some are axiological, and some are logical. Some also are psychological, as when we speak of an "ultimate concern." But is it really only *ultimate* concerns that we are willing to identify as religious? A man who has an ultimate concern is surely an exceedingly well integrated individual, for he has a single focal point of interest and value to which all his remaining interests and values are related and subordinated and for which he is willing to sacrifice all else if need be. But are *all* religious people this well integrated?

The great difficulty with the word *ultimate* is that it does not itself admit of degrees but is only the final member in a series of degrees. We need a definition of *religion* that will give us an adjective *religious* that will admit of degrees, and no definition of *religion* in terms of "ultimate concern" will do this without distorting the meaning of *ultimate* beyond recognition. Without a conception of degrees of religiosity we are stuck with the conclusion that the not-so-well-integrated "average churchgoer" whose religious concerns are less intense and thoroughgoing than those of the "saints" cannot be called religious at all. Yet we do wish to say that the saints are more religious than most of us and that we are less religious than they—but religious all the same! Can we say this in terms of *ultimate* concern? No, it would appear that only the saints have it. If so, Tillich's definition of *religion* is unacceptable for our purposes; it is too narrow or exclusive.

Ultimate just won't do because it does not admit of degrees. Words such as *deep* or *intense* that do admit of degrees would be good substitutes. There are degrees of depth and intensity in many realms of human interest, including concern. Thus the religious man will be a man of "deep or intense concern," and since we can recognize differences in degree of intensity of concern, we can say that some of us are more religious than others. We can also use this scale to differentiate men whose lives exhibit religious qualities from other men who are not religious at all. If there is a continuum of intensity of concern ranging from the deep to the superficial, religious men will be men of deep concern at one end of the scale, and nonreligious men will be men of superficial concern at the other end of the scale. Since there will be no sharp dividing line between the two ends, we will have difficulty in deciding whether men in the middle are to be called religious or irreligious—just as in practice we do have this difficulty. Further, since it is quite possible for us to have a plurality of intense concerns around which we organize our lives and in which we find life's "meaning," we can allow a place for a kind of religious polytheism, which seems difficult to do if we restrict ourselves to the word *ultimate*. Also, we can identify religious beliefs, objects, practices, and so on as those about which men are intensely concerned and through which they express these concerns. Finally, we can use our concept of religion to formulate a workable definition of *the philosophy of religion*. It is the attempt to formulate and justify theories about the most universal or fundamental features of reality, knowledge, and value about which men, relying exclusively on the use of human intelligence, have been most deeply or intensely concerned. The scope of the philosophy of religion is thus much smaller than that of religion itself. For one thing, we are not required to discuss success and golf in a philosophy of religion course, since by almost any reckoning they are not universal or fundamental features of reality, knowledge, and value, as philosophers have usually regarded these concepts. (Incidentally, the scope of theology is also much smaller than that of religion itself. Theologians are not preoccupied with success, golf, and fishing either, since revelations or interpretations of revelatory events are not integral to these matters.)

Is the Definition Too Inclusive?

Does Tillich's definition of *religion* as "being grasped by an ultimate concern" force us to call some things religions that we do not want to call by this name? Is the definition too inclusive? Is "ultimate concern" not only common to but also *distinctive of* all religions? This is a question about which even the experts themselves might legitimately disagree, and in the final analysis we must simply decide whether or not to make this criterion of "ultimate concern" not only common to but also distinctive of all religions. There is no doubt that while doing justice to the great diversity of world religions the definition also widens considerably the scope of what we would normally call religion. This is almost inevitable in any attempt to find a lowest common denominator for such diverse phenomena.

The strain that results from this widening of the scope of religion comes out most clearly in Tillich's own recognition that his definition commits him to the view that even the dedicated atheist is a deeply religious man because he is ultimately concerned about the Truth or what he takes to be the Truth, namely, that God does not exist. We cannot be successfully irreligious by passionately denying or renouncing God, but only by not caring at all, by cultivating indifference.[8] Here we seem to be caught in an embarrassing trap. We want to say that atheistic Buddhists and humanists are religious, but we do not want to say that the ordinary, run-of-the-mill Western atheist is religious. Furthermore, even though crime, dope addiction, and alcoholism frequently involve an intensity and comprehensiveness of involvement that a minister or priest could well covet for his parishioners, are we willing to call them religions? Moreover, given this conception of religion, it would be impossible to distinguish among religious ideals, moral ideals, prudential ideals, aesthetic ideals, legal ideals, political ideals, and so on. So long as these ideals are taken with ultimate seriousness, we would have to call them all religious. Although "ultimate concern" seems to be common to all religions, it does not seem to be distinctive of them. So we need something more to provide us with the differentia of *religion*.

In providing us with the lowest common denominator for *religion*, Tillich's definition not only overburdens the concept as we ordinarily apply it, but it is so general that it loses sight of much of the concreteness of detail that is usually implicit in our everyday use of the word and that is not conveyed by the vague phrase "intense concern." We usually have many more specifics in mind that we wish to communicate to others when we talk about "religion." Thus the search for a common essence as an approach to defining *religion* needs to be supplemented by another approach that incorporates this richness of detail, and we shall now develop such an approach under the heading "the search for family resemblances." These two approaches have been regarded by some as mutually exclusive, but actually they are mutually complementary. The search for a common essence provides in-depth studies of one, or of a small number, of the family traits of religion, while the search for family resemblances furnishes the desired breadth of perspective.

The Search for Family Resemblances of Religion

WITTGENSTEIN'S CONCEPTION OF FAMILY RESEMBLANCES

The influential twentieth-century philosopher Ludwig Wittgenstein thought that there are many perfectly meaningful, useful words in our language that have no "common essence" of connotation. These words are not used to name some characteristic or set of characteristics common to and distinctive of all the objects to which we normally apply such words. Wittgenstein thought that the common-sense assumption that there has to be a common essence where there is a common name is exceedingly naive, and he recommended that instead of making this assumption uncritically we should "look and see" if it is so.[9] He believed that we would not always find a common essence for many perfectly useful words, such as *game, language, knowledge,* and so on. That he was correct with respect to *all* the words he used to illustrate his point may be questioned,[10] but his general idea that some words have only "family resemblances" instead of "common essences" is a very fruitful one to explore, especially in its application to the word *religion.* Wittgenstein himself did not apply it to *religion,* but others who have been influenced by him have made preliminary studies of its possible application in this area.[11] We shall first discuss briefly what is meant by "the search for family resemblances," and then we shall see if the search throws any light on our understanding of *religion.*

Not all objects called by a common name have a common essence, but they are frequently related to one another by "a complicated network of similarities overlapping and criss-crossing: sometimes overall similarities, sometimes similarities of detail," [12] according to Wittgenstein. He compared this web of resemblances to the complicated way in which members of a human family resemble one another and are recognizable as members of the same family.[13] Suppose that there are five brothers and sisters who are easily recognizable as members of the same family, but among whom there is not a single family trait that each has in common with *all* the others, as illustrated by the following diagram. Their resemblance to one another may depend not on a common essence, but on a complicated web of traits shared with one or more, but not with all, of the other members of the family. (In the diagram, the presence of a family trait is indicated by P and the absence by A.)

FAMILY TRAITS	FAMILY MEMBERS				
	Alex	Bill	Cathy	Dave	Enid
Over 6 feet tall	P	P	P	P	A
Blue eyes	P	P	P	A	P
Blond hair	P	P	A	P	P
Pug nose	P	A	P	P	P
Irritability	A	P	P	P	P

The obvious weakness of the family resemblance comparison is that if we were to add one additional family trait to our diagram, namely "Having the same parents," we would have a characteristic that was both common to and distinctive of each member of the family. But even this trait would not necessarily be common to all; suppose that Enid resembles all her brothers and sisters in all the respects indicated and yet is an adopted child! Nevertheless, there is always the possibility that such an additional family trait has been overlooked and will later turn up in any attempt to explore the meaning of a word in terms of family resemblances. When such a trait is discovered, this would seem to mean that our search for family resemblances has turned up a common essence as well and that the two approaches complement rather than conflict with each other. Perhaps this will turn out to be the case with the concept of "religion."

FAMILY TRAITS OF RELIGION

Many college students in the Western world who register for their first course in World Religions or Comparative Religions have some weird misconceptions about the non-Christian religions. They may think, for example, that in most of the non-Christian religions it is really the supernatural Christian God who is known

SELECTED FAMILY TRAITS OF SOME RELIGIONS

FAMILY TRAITS	Christianity, Judaism, Islam	Vedanta Hindu Pantheism	Early Buddhism and Hinayana Buddhism	Early Greek Olympian Polytheism	Aristotle's Concept of Unmoved Mover
1. Belief in a *supernatural* intelligent being or beings	P	A?	A	A	P
2. Belief in a *superior* intelligent being or beings	P	P	A	P	P
3. Complex world view interpreting the significance of human life	P	P	P	P	P
4. Belief in experience after death	P	P	P	P?	A
5. Moral code	P	P	P	A	P
6. Belief that the moral code is sanctioned by a *superior* intelligent being or beings	P	P	A	A	A
7. An account of the nature of, origin of, and cure for evil	P	P	P	P?	P
8. Theodicy	P	P?	A	A	A
9. Prayer and ritual	P	P	P	P	A
10. Sacred objects and places	P	P	P	P	A
11. Revealed truths or interpretations of revelatory events	P	P	P?	P	A
12. Religious experience—awe, mystical experience, revelations	P	P	P	P	A
13. Deep, intense concern	P	P	P	P	P?
14. Institutionalized social sharing of some of traits 1–13	P	P	P	P	A?
15.					
16.					
17.					

Key: P = Present, A = Absent, ? = Unclear.

Communism	Moral Naturalistic Humanism	Spinozistic Pantheism	Success, Wealth, Golf, Fishing, etc.								
A	A	A	A								
A	A	A?	A								
P	P	P	A								
A	A	A	A								
P	P	A	A								
A	A	A	A								
P	P	P	A								
A	A	A	A								
P?	A	A?	A								
P	A	A	A?								
A	A	A	A								
A	A	A	P								
P	P	P	P								
P	A?	A?	A?								

and worshiped, but he is called by some other name such as the Buddha, the Brahman, or Allah, and that this knowledge is somewhat perversely distorted, since the devotees of these religions have not received all the benefits of the Christian revelation. Many students assume that most of the world religions teach that the individual human "soul" is created by God and is destined to everlasting existence in some place of reward or punishment, and that a program of "salvation" from the latter and for the former is invariably provided. Many students further assume that all world religions include a moral program—again somewhat distorted, of course—which contains the essentials of the Ten Commandments and the Sermon on the Mount and which is derived from and sanctioned by the Supreme Being. In short, it is typical for Westerners to assume at the outset of a study of the concept of "religion" or the phenomena of the world religions that the field of inquiry is considerably less diversified than it in fact turns out to be. Yet it is precisely this diversity that makes it so difficult to discover some common essence for "religion" and that has suggested that the search for family resemblances might be a more fruitful approach to the concept of "religion." Let us see how such a search can be conducted.

We shall now look at a selected list of family traits and family members for the concept of "religion." In the chart on the preceding pages, the family traits listed in the column on the left are all prominent characteristics of at least some of the things that we call religions, and the list of family members is a partial list of some of the things to which we apply the word with some degree of regularity. Neither list is in any way complete, especially the list of family members, and you can add to each list as you see fit. This chart and the discussion that follows are *not* to be construed as a survey of the field of comparative religion. The family members that are included were selected mainly because they permit us to introduce a preliminary discussion of the difficulties involved in discovering a common essence. The exercise as a whole is valuable because it allows us to make a place for the richness and concreteness of meaning that *religion* normally has and that we realized were missing at the end of our discussion of the search for a common essence, and because it may suggest a way of providing for the differentia of "religion" that we lacked earlier. We shall now give a brief explanation of why each family trait is listed as present in some of the family members included in our chart and absent from others.

1. Belief in a Supernatural Intelligent Being or Beings

The emphasis here is on the word *supernatural,* which means "beyond nature." By *nature* we mean the totality of spatiotemporal events and relations with which we must cope in our everyday experience and which is the primary subject of scientific investigation. By contrast, the realm of "supernature" would be that of whatever realities are presumed to have their being "beyond" or "outside of" this realm of spatiotemporal facts and relations. Since "beyond" and "outside" are themselves spatial concepts, perhaps we can speak of the "supernatural" only metaphorically. Be that as it may, it is clear that some of our religions do include belief in such a transcendent being or beings. The God of Christianity, Judaism, and Islam is clearly such a supernatural being who is thought to have existed (again speaking metaphorically) "before" time and "before" the world of nature came into being, and on whom the natural order of things is thought to depend for its very existence and energy. The Brahman of the genuinely pantheistic versions of Hinduism is not a totally supernatural being in the way in which the God of the Western religions is thought to be. He is thought of as the Whole of whom men are the most important parts but who also expresses himself in every event and configuration of nature. For the pantheist, "all is God"; and many versions of Hinduism are pantheistic in this sense. In such pantheisms God may be thought to transcend the world as the whole transcends the part, but not in the way the creator God transcends created nature in the Western supernaturalistic religions. The immanence of the Brahman in the spatiotemporal order of things makes the word *supernatural* seem inappropriate here. It should be noted that in other versions of Hinduism it might be more appropriate to regard the concept of the Brahman as involving supernaturalism. In these versions, the Brahman is thought of as transcending the world, not as creator transcends creation, but rather as reality transcends illusion; for the natural order of things is thought to be that of total illusion and deception (*maya*), and only the Brahman is thought to be real. Here there is no immanence of God in nature, and it might be appropriate to speak of this kind of Hinduism as involving a form of supernaturalism.

Aristotle's Unmoved Mover is beyond the spatial order of everyday events. The great Thinker on Thinking is not described as having such spatial attributes as size and shape, and the order of nature is thought to depend on him for its motion in the way in which an effect depends on a final cause. But he is apparently not "beyond" time, since Aristotle conceives of the world of nature as coexisting with the Unmoved Mover throughout an infinite past. Similarly, Spinoza's God clearly does not transcend the spatio-temporal order of nature because he is identical with the totality of Nature, but even here there may be room for question since he thinks that Nature has an infinity of attributes "beyond" what we human beings are able to know or conceive. The version of Buddhism that was espoused by the Buddha himself and his immediate followers, and the Hinayana Buddhism that prevails today in such southeastern Asian nations as Ceylon, Burma, Thailand, Laos, and Cambodia, have no place for gods of any sort. Though the early versions of Greek Olympian polytheism as developed by Homer and Hesiod had many gods, the chief of whom was Zeus, these gods were not conceived as in any sense "beyond" or "prior to" nature. They were not creators of nature but were rather created out of the original chaos of nature itself through the personification of such natural entities as Darkness, Light, Earth, Heaven, Time, and so on. Finally, belief in supernatural intelligent beings is explicitly rejected in Communism and moral humanism, and it has no integral place in the "religions" of success, wealth, golf, and fishing. Thus we may conclude that although belief in the supernatural is a prominent feature of many religions, it is by no means common to them all.

2. Belief in a Superior Intelligent Being or Beings

Superior divinities are not at all the same thing as *supernatural* divinities. A superior intelligent being must be conceived as a god of immense, superhuman intelligence and power; but it is not necessary that such gods be regarded as existing beyond the spatio-temporal universe. Supernatural gods are of course superior beings, but not all superior beings are supernatural gods. The clearest case of this is found in Greek Olympian polytheism, where the gods are thought of as integral parts of the order of nature, though they are certainly immensely intelligent and powerful parts of this order. Also, there are some versions of pantheism that identify God with the totality of nature (as including man and history). The difficulty here is to find a case where this God is thought of as being superior in both power and intelligence to man. For Spinoza, God and Nature are identical and infinitely more powerful than man, but it is doubtful that Spinoza wanted to attribute intelligence to Nature in a sense that would imply that Nature has a "mind of its own," so to speak, though this is a somewhat controversial matter of interpretation. However, Spinoza thought that Nature is intelligent in the sense that it is partly comprised of the sum total of finite, human intelligences. The question of whether Spinozistic pantheism possesses this trait is thus not a matter of whether Spinoza's God is a being of superior power, but whether he is an *intelligent* being.

Belief in superior intelligent beings is clearly lacking in early Buddhism and Hinayana Buddhism, Communism, humanism, and success, wealth, golf, and fishing. Thus even this belief is by no means common to all religions.

3. Complex World View Interpreting the Significance of Human Life

What is the purpose or meaning or importance of human life, and what is the ultimate destiny of humanity or of the individual human being? What are the powers at work in the cosmos that further or frustrate the individual human being's search for the meaning of life and for his own ultimate destiny? These questions are answered in a great variety of ways by many of the religions of man. Christians find their questions about the meaning and destiny of human life answered in the complex drama of Creation, Fall, Incarnation, Atonement, Kingdom of God, Death, Final Judgment, Heaven, and Hell. Jews find theirs in the story of the Chosen People and the struggle of the nation and individual to discover and live in obedience to the will of God, and in the long-run connection between righteousness and prosperity and unrighteousness and catastrophe here in this world for the Chosen People as a whole, if not for each individual member. The same may be said of Islam, except that the long run is clearly extended beyond the present life to the realm of "experience after death," where the righteous will dwell forever in a hedonistic paradise. However, the hope for a Messiah plays a vital role in Judaism that it does not play in Islam. Buddhism sees human life within the framework of inevitable suffering and the long path to be traversed in gaining final release from it. This includes a doctrine of karma, or destiny, which is in part decided by the behavior of the individual; a doctrine of reincarnation of the individual in many forms of life; and an account of diverse steps to be taken in obtaining ultimate release from the Wheel of Rebirth and the final extinction of suffering through the extinction of individuality itself. Similar views are found in Hinduism, though in Hinduism individuality is extinguished only in the sense that the individual is reunited with or reabsorbed into the Brahman, both in mystical experience and in final liberation from the Wheel of Rebirth. Early Greek Olympian polytheism did not offer a universal answer to the question of the meaning and purpose of human life, but aristocratic individuals were directed to pursue honor and fame in war and athletics. Death, however, permanently ended human life and the purpose it incorporated. Aristotle saw the meaning and purpose of human life in terms of activity and fulfillment of the potentialities of human nature, but for him the purpose of life was the active pursuit in this world of such virtues as wisdom, justice, temperance, and courage and the enjoyment of health, property, friends, good children, long life, and freedom from misfortune. In short, the answers to the question of the meaning of life found in early Greek polytheism and in Aristotle were only remotely connected with belief in the gods and most of the other family traits of the religions. Communism finds the significance of human life in the pursuit and achievement of equality of property, opportunity, happiness, and social responsibility. However, the Russian and Chinese versions of Communism differ today in their assessment of the relative importance of the individual and the state. The post-Stalinist Russians tend to view the communist state as the most efficient means to the end of promoting the welfare of the individual, whereas the Maoists tend to view it as an end in itself, for the sake of which almost any sacrifice of individuals is justified. Naturalistic humanism, such as that espoused by John Dewey and many others of like mind, holds that the world of nature constitutes the sum total of reality, that nature does not have to be explained but provides the context within which all legitimate explanations take place, that it has always existed, and that sometimes it is friendly to man and sometimes not. Man's purpose is to pursue and achieve whatever ideal ends he sets for himself, such as the values of human association, happiness, artistic creativity, and scientific productivity, and any other goals that may arise from his natural drives, interests, and activities. To the naturalistic humanists, supernaturalism is only a source of confusion because it gives men illusory hopes and expectations, and salvation is man's fulfillment in time. Spinoza saw the purpose of life to be the overcoming of the passions and appetites that enslave man and the living of a life of reason that culminates in what he called the "intellectual love of God." But it must be remembered that for Spinoza God cannot return this love, because love is a human attribute that cannot be predicated of God. God has no purposes or plans for man, since he has no purposes and plans at all. Purposes and plans are human traits and products, just as is the distinction between good and evil, which does not exist at all for God. Finally, what shall we say of success, wealth, golf, and fishing? Do we find here a complex world view interpreting the significance of human life? Perhaps the best answer here is a negative one, since whatever world view is involved in these "religions" is an exceedingly simple one involving no great cosmic dramas or heroic struggles, and since few of the devotees of these "religions" would want to claim that *everyone* could find the meaning of life in these activities. Nevertheless, it must be admitted that this family trait is a nearly universal characteristic of all the phenomena we would normally call religions.

4. Belief in Experience After Death

Does the individual continue to have experience and in that sense to "live" after death? Although it is common for us Westerners to assume that one of the main functions of a religion is to guarantee the continuation of individual experience after death, there are some religions that fail to do this; and even those religions that do so are sharply divided in their understanding of what is involved in experience after death. Christianity and Islam attach more significance to experience after death than do the other great world religions, since they consider experience after death in heaven or hell to be a permanent condition of the individual. Indeed, one of the main functions of these religions is to assure their adherents that experience after death is an inevitability and that experience in heaven is highly desirable. By contrast, one of the main functions of Hinduism and Hinayana Buddhism is to assure their adherents that experience after death is *not* a permanent condition of the individual and that it is *not* desirable. The cycle of reincarnation need not endure forever, and one of the main functions of these religions is to provide a means of escape from the Wheel of Rebirth and continuing individuality. The religions of the West and those of the East are irreconcilably at odds with one another over the question of the desirability of the infinite prolongation of finite individuality, though they do agree that there is experience after death while disagreeing on the question of its permanence. We did not mention Judaism along with Christianity and Islam, partly because Judaism is considerably less doctrinaire than the other two and partly because Judaism itself has always been sharply divided on this point of doctrine. There is little or no basis for belief in experience after death in the Old Testament, and the main emphasis of the Old Testament is on God as the God of the Chosen People here and now. The New Testament indicates that the Sadducees and the Pharisees disagreed over the question of resurrection. This division has continued to exist in Judaism ever since, though the majority opinion has been that of the Sadducees, who denied the doctrine of resurrection. Today Orthodox Jews tend to reject belief in experience after death while Reform Jews tend to accept it. At any rate, most Jews would not regard the idea that individual experience ends permanently at death as sufficient grounds for rejecting belief in and devotion to God. Moving along to early Greek Olympian polytheism as expressed in the writings of Homer and Hesiod, we find that there is belief in experience after death, but it is radically different from anything we would find familiar today. Later Greek and Roman polytheism developed an elaborate doctrine of the Underworld and experience after death in which the unfortunate suffered and the fortunate were happy, but this was not the case in Homer and Hesiod. The spirit of the individual did exist in a kind of underworld, but its condition was highly undesirable. Homer says that the souls of the dead are "like bats fluttering and screeching in a cave." Existence was vague, shadowy, powerless, and hardly conscious, though souls could temporarily recover enough power to carry on a conversation by drinking blood. The souls of such great heroes as Achilles and Agamemnon fared no better than those of anyone else, and death was something dreaded by hero and villain alike. As for Aristotle, in his early years under the influence of Plato he did believe in the immortality of the individual soul, but in his mature philosophy he completely rejected this belief. Communists, humanists, and Spinoza explicitly reject belief in experience after death as a dangerous deception and regard human fulfillment in this life as the final end of man. Success, wealth, and similar "religions" have nothing at all to say about the matter of experience after death. Thus this trait is far from being a universal characteristic of all religions.

5. Moral Code

Not every code of conduct or system of values is a *moral* one, and some religions fail to incorporate the moral point of view. If we take a moral code to be one that is designed to promote the welfare of humanity as a whole and that we would will humanity as a whole to act upon, then moral action guides must be distinguished from prudential action guides designed to promote the welfare of the individual or of the specific group, such as the tribe or the nation. Most primitive religions probably sponsor a code of conduct designed to benefit the individual or the group, but in many of the great world religions, such as Christianity, Judaism, Islam, Hinduism, and Buddhism, there are elements of universalism that are more or less explicitly developed into genuinely moral concerns. Communists believe that their way of life would be most advantageous to humanity as a whole, and humanists make moral concerns the very center of their way of life. The code of conduct followed by the heroes of Homer's *Iliad* and *Odyssey* was designed to bring fame and honor to the aristocracy, but the ordinary foot soldier was barely mentioned at all and his behavior hardly seemed to matter. Aristotle did not make a clear distinction between moral and prudential elements, and it was commonly assumed by the later Greeks, particularly by such philosophers as Socrates, Plato, and Aristotle, that the welfare of the individual was so intimately connected with the welfare of the group that prudential and moral concerns could never conflict in the long run. Insofar as Spinoza advocates an action guide, it seems most appropriate to describe it as prudential, since its main concern is with instructing the individual on how to live a life of cool reason. Those who make a religion out of success, wealth, golf, or fishing are also highly individualistic in the sense that they manifest little concern that humanity as a whole share in their ends. Thus not all religions incorporate a moral code, though most of them do sponsor a set of values and a code of conduct that in some instances are moral and in some instances are nonmoral.

6. Belief That the Moral Code Is Sanctioned by a Superior Intelligent Being or Beings

Many Westerners share the attitude expressed by Dostoevsky's Ivan Karamazov, that "If God does not exist, then anything is permitted." That is, we consider it self-evident that there can be no moral code and no incentive to subscribe to a moral code unless we believe that it is divinely sanctioned. But only a brief glance at the world religions should be enough to cure us of this misconception by exposing its cultural relativity. It is true that in the Western religions morality is divinely sanctioned, and doubtless this is also true of some versions of Hinduism. But it is definitely not true of Hinayana Buddhism, for the simple and obvious reason that there are no divinities. It is also not true of Communism and humanism for the same reason. Early Greek religion had divinities, but it is doubtful that it had a moral code. Even the gods constantly engaged in what were immoralities by later standards. One of the tasks assumed by such later Greek writers as Aeschylus and Plato was that of moralizing the gods; but here it was morality that prompted religious reform and not religion that imposed morality. Aristotle and Spinoza both believed in a superior being; and in his complex doctrine of the moral virtues, Aristotle has the beginnings of a moral code; but for both of these philosophers there is little logical connection between human values and divine will. Aristotle's God is far from an omniscient being and apparently has no knowledge of or interest in human behavior, and Spinoza insists that the distinction between good and evil is a purely human one, of which God is entirely ignorant. Thus some religions have no moral code, some religions have no divinities, and even where both moral codes and divinities are present there is often little or no connection between the two.

7. An Account of the Nature of, Origin of, and Cure for Evil

The attempt to deal with the nature of, origin of, and cure for evil is a nearly universal trait of religion, but the theories proposed differ significantly from religion to religion, and even within many of the major world religions there are important differences. The nature of evil is understood more easily in terms of the sorts of things that are regarded as evil than in terms of an abstract formal definition of *evil* as such. The world religions tend to agree more about the nature of evil in this sense than they do about its origin and cure. It is commonplace to distinguish between *natural evil,* those undesirable results of natural happenings such as famine, flood, drought, storms, illness, deformity, accidents, suffering, and death, and *moral evil,* the undesirable conditions and consequences of the choices and actions of moral agents, human and superhuman (such as fallen angels). Most of the major world religions agree that there is evil of both types in the world, and it seems somewhat strained to call wealth and fishing religions in some contexts, because they have nothing to say about major catastrophe and must concern themselves with such trivia as "the deal that fell through" and "the big one that got away." At any rate, for the major religions of the world it is fundamental that there is moral and natural evil in the world, that people are in the grips of pain, frustration, finitude, and death. Those of us who live in the twentieth century have been confronted so vividly with the atrocities of wars, revolutions, and persecutions that we do not need to be convinced further of the existence of moral evil, no matter what our religious background might be.

We begin to get a variety of answers, however, when we ask, How did evil originate? The Western theistic religions heavily emphasize the role of moral disobedience in introducing pain, suffering, frustration, and death into the cosmos. They hold that there was no evil before the Fall, but Satan and his cohorts and then Adam and his descendants chose to disobey God, and all evil in the world somehow originated from this moral disobedience. It is doubtful, however, that the presence of natural evil in the world can be adequately accounted for in terms of moral disobedience alone, for there seems to have been an ample supply of it long before any human moral agents appeared. Eastern religions such as Hinduism and Buddhism fully develop the idea that evil originates in sheer finitude and fragmentariness of perspective and in the desire for fragmentary goals and objects, although Western theologians sometimes introduce such themes. Because man is gripped by ignorance, confusion, and passion, it is inevitable that he will choose evil over good. Such motifs are often combined in these religions with the claim that there is something unreal, illusory, provisional about evil, which has led many to suspect that the persistence of some of India's great social ills, such as those generated by the caste system, is the result of an underlying conviction that such evils are not really there at all. Both Hinduism and Buddhism also see evil as originating to some extent in immorality, for the sufferings of this world are partly if not entirely the working out of one's karma, the harvesting in this life of the fruit of one's choices and deeds in previous incarnations. The ancient Greek polytheists saw evil as originating in part with the gods, who were fickle, mischievous, and at times downright immoral. Zeus had two jars, one containing Good and the other containing Evil, and at times he threw down to man the contents of one jar and at other times the contents of the other. Naturalistic explanations of the nature and origin of evil are possible without the superstructure of God and immortality, and the naturalistic humanists and Spinozists opt for them. Such explanations hold that evil has a number of relatively independent conditions such as finitude, ignorance, moral indifference, and perversity, and that evil occurs in a natural order of things that is sometimes, but not always, inhospitable toward human projects and purposes. Communism tries to give an economic interpretation of the nature and origin of evil, seeing the origins of man's sufferings in economic inequities.

Although the major religions tend to hold out the hope that evil can be cured, they differ drastically in their interpretations of how this is to be effected. In addition to stressing righteous living, Christianity also emphasizes the grace of God and in its full-blown soteriology introduces the elaborate machinery of the Trinity, the Incarnation, the Kingdom of God, the resurrection of the dead, and everlasting life. Judaism and Islam tend to emphasize sacrifice and righteous living as cures for evil, here if not also hereafter. For Hindus and Buddhists alike, salvation lies in the loss of the finite self and ultimate release from the Wheel of Rebirth. According to Hindu beliefs this may be ultimately effected in a variety of mutually complementary ways, such as the disciplines of intellectual knowledge, heartfelt love, elaborate yoga techniques of meditation, and ritual worship. Hinduism is generous enough to believe that all the major religions of the world provide opportunities for salvation and contribute to the cure of evil in the world. For the Buddhists the pure essence of religion lies in the acknowledgment of evil as pain or suffering and in the development and practice of means of release from it. The central message of Buddhism lies in its Fourfold Truths: that there is omnipresent suffering, that this is generated by finite desires, that these desires and their consequent suffering may be suppressed or overcome, and that the Eightfold Path is the effective means to this ultimate end of religion. Involved in the Eightfold Path are right knowledge (of the Fourfold Truths), right aspiration (which involves concentration on the goal of release from desire and the Wheel of Rebirth), right speech, moral compassion and behavior, hard work in an occupation conducive to salvation, heroic effort of will in the suppression of desires for finite objects and ends, right mindfulness and self-knowledge, and the practice of techniques of yoga meditation and mysticism. It is certainly most interesting that even those religions that make no place at all for God and immortality are nevertheless deeply cognizant of the problem of evil in the sense that they acknowledge its presence and espouse a cure. Some religious thinkers are content to live with the notion that there is no such thing as an *ultimate* cure for evil, that it is here and in some sense always will be. Variations of this view can be found in Greek polytheism, implicitly perhaps in the writings of Aristotle and Spinoza, and quite explicitly in the writings of the naturalistic humanists. Such thinkers do insist, however, that the absence of an ultimate cure does not imply that we should not take all measures within human power to mitigate suffering and injustice wherever we find it. Unlike the naturalistic humanists, the Communists do offer an ultimate cure, the classless society. The means to that end are class struggle, revolution, the dictatorship of the proletariat, and the elimination of economic inequities.

We can now see that although the major religions tend to address themselves to the question of the nature of, origin of, and cure for evil, there is nevertheless tremendous diversity, especially in the answers given to the questions of how evil originates, how it is to be cured, or even whether it can be cured at all in some ultimate sense.

8. Theodicy

Theodicy may be treated as another aspect of the problem of evil. Theodicy is the attempt to reconcile belief in the goodness and power of God with the fact of evil in the world; it is peculiar to the monotheistic religions that attribute moral perfection and immense power to God. It is by no means a universal trait of the religions. It is not a central problem for atheistic religions such as Buddhism, though Buddhism centers around the problem of evil in a wider sense. Nor is it directly a problem for Aristotle and Spinoza and those theistic religions that do not attribute moral perfection to God. If there were a religion that conceived of God as totally impotent, it too would not be confronted with the problem of theodicy; but it is doubtful that such a religion exists. All this is by way of saying that the problem of theodicy makes sense only within the framework of its presuppositions: that God exists, that he is immensely powerful, that he is morally good, that evil exists, and that evil has an originative cause that is responsible for its existence. What those who wrestle with the problem of theodicy usually try to show is that despite all this, God is not responsible for the origin of evil. Yet how can this be true? We shall explore this matter in detail in later chapters.

Of course, even in those religions that do not explicitly try to cope with the problem of theodicy as such, views of evil can be related to the problem of theodicy. Various religions use various ways of denying that there is a problem of theodicy—for example, by denying that God (in some metaphysical sense) exists, or by denying that evil exists. The first alternative is taken by the Hinayana Buddhists, at least to the extent that they do not affirm theism, and by such naturalistic humanists as John Dewey and Bertrand Russell. Jean Paul Sartre, too, would deny that there is a problem of theodicy on the grounds that there simply is no God and consequently no problem of reconciling his existence, power, and compassion with the presence of evil in the world. The second alternative, that of denying the existence of evil, is taken by those who regard evil as illusion and by those who regard it as total privation of being, though it is always open to question how seriously such thinkers, both Eastern and Western, take themselves. At any rate, if in some sense there really is no such thing as evil, no authentic examples of it, then there is no problem of theodicy at all. Spinoza seems to hold that from an ultimate point of view the distinctions of good and evil do not apply, and at the same time he suggests that even from a human point of view they might not apply if our vision and understanding are sufficiently comprehensive. Those thinkers who insist that evil is only good in disguise and that it is possible to realize this through deeper understanding and enlightenment came very close to denying that there is a problem of theodicy by denying that there is such a thing as evil at all.

Theistic solutions to the problem of theodicy also vary. They limit God with respect to goodness or power or perhaps even both. Though Zeus was perhaps limited in goodness, he was not limited in power, but all the other Olympian gods were limited in both goodness and power. Such religious reformers as Aeschylus and Plato attempted to clean up the Greek gods morally and make them more worthy of worship in an age of increased moral sensitivity. One of the disputants in David Hume's *Dialogues Concerning Natural Religion* offered the theory that the world had been made by an infant, amateur deity who was incompetent in that he did not know what was good and would not have been able to bring it about even if he had known, though the limitation in goodness here may have been viewed as a consequence of limitation in power. Literary figures such as James Thompson and Thomas Hardy sometimes suggested that God is deficient in goodness, that he is a malicious king of the immortals making sport of innocent mortals. Yet another way of denying the goodness of God is by holding, as Aristotle and Epicurus did, that God is indifferent to what goes on in our world. From the human point of view such indifference is a deficiency of goodness. Epicurus taught that God or the gods lived in a state of perfect and eternal happiness in their own heaven and were both ignorant of and unconcerned about happenings in this world; thus men need not be disturbed by fear of divine caprice, anger, intervention, or punishment.

Various ways of limiting God in power have been devised, for example by the recognition of a powerful counterprinciple of evil such as the principle of Darkness in Zoroastrianism, or the figure of Satan in Judaism, Christianity, and Islam. It is also done in a slightly different way in these same religions through the recognition of the ability of nondivine agents to choose for themselves, even if God does choose to limit himself by creating creatures with free wills. This of course is a controversial claim, and it will not be readily apparent to all the devotees of these religions that a limitation of God's power is involved in the existence of free but finite moral agents. We shall explore this controversial claim in more detail in our discussions of the attributes of God as conceived by supernaturalism and panentheism in Chapters 7 and 8 and in our discussion of the teleological argument in Chapter 11. For now, we need only note that the problem of theodicy is far from being a universally present trait of religion.

9. Prayer and Ritual

Prayer and ritual are to be found in most of the great world religions and in early Greek religion, but here there are immense differences. For example, intercessory prayer and personal address are found only in the theistic religions, but in some religions such as Hinayana Buddhism only prayers of meditation are found. Aristotle thought that it was foolish to pray, since God had no knowledge of or interest in affairs in our world. Spinoza, however, came close to allowing for a kind of prayer of meditation in his notion of "the intellectual love of God," but he allowed no place for prayers of intercession or ritual worship. Needless to say, Communists and humanists do not pray, though there may be something akin to ritual in the formal public celebrations of the communist states. Ritual is more characteristic of some religions than it is of others. For example, ritual is elaborately developed in High-Church Christianity, but it is nearly absent in Quakerism and in the original version of Buddhism.

10. Sacred Objects and Places

Most of the great world religions have objects or places that are regarded as especially sacred: the Cross, the Star of David, the Bo Tree, the scriptures of the various world religions, temples, churches, shrines of worship, sacred cities such as Delphi, Jerusalem, or Mecca, sacred rivers, trees, animals, mountains, heavenly bodies, and so on. Even the Communists seem to regard the shrine of Lenin as a holy place, and the Chinese Communists cherish the little red book of the sayings of Chairman Mao. But it would be difficult to find anything comparable to this in Aristotle and Spinoza, and humanists generally tend to beware of the holy. As for success, wealth, golf, and fishing, would you say that the meaning of the word *sacred* extends to their paraphernalia and places?

11. Revealed Truths or Interpretations of
   Revelatory Events

What is *revelation?* Definitions vary. Cognitive elements are usually involved, and it is agreed that these cognitive elements are derived from or certified by uniquely religious experiences or inspirations, as contrasted with universally available rationality. Most of the great world religions have a tradition of revelation that is usually incorporated in sacred scriptures such as the Old and New Testaments, the Torah, the Koran, the Vedas and the Upanishads, and the Pali Canon. However, within this framework of agreement there are enormous differences of interpretation as to what is further involved in revelation. Not all revelations come from divine sources. Again, early and Hinayana Buddhism prove to be the chief exceptions, though there is room for doubt that the Buddha himself intended his teachings to be regarded as revelations at all, since he thought that every man using his natural faculties could attain to the desired level of enlightenment. However, later followers did regard the Buddha as somehow specially and uniquely inspired and codified his sayings and the traditions about him into the Pali Canon and later scriptures. Even where revelations are thought to come directly from the divine, there are many different interpretations of the precise relation between divine "sender" and human "receiver." Sometimes it is thought that the divinity directly takes possession of the human spokesman, as in the case of the Greek oracles and many of the mystics. Sometimes the divinity is incarnate in human form and speaks for himself, as in Christianity and Hinduism. Sometimes the voice of the divinity is heard coming from a burning bush, or a voice from heaven is heard over the Jordan River, or a still, small voice is heard within. Sometimes there is simply an acute sense of personal presence, of encounter with a "Thou." Sometimes the divinity writes the inspired words on tablets of stone and delivers them to his spokesman. Sometimes angelic intermediaries are sent to give the word. Sometimes special inspiration or guidance is given to prophets, seers, or writers of the canonized books of scripture (though the very notion of *inspiration* stands in desperate need of clarification and analysis). Sometimes fallible men are left to interpret as best they can the unique events in which the divine is believed to have manifested itself.

With the possible exception of Buddhism, revelation is missing both from the atheistic religions, such as Communism and humanism, and from those theistic religions that assume either implicitly or explicitly that all of their cognitive elements can be arrived at and justified by natural "philosophical" intelligence, as in the cases of Aristotle and Spinoza.

12. Religious Experience—Awe, Mystical Experience, Revelations

What exactly is to count as a "religious experience"? As we have just seen, revelatory experiences take many forms. Furthermore, there are many types of experience that we would call religious besides those involving revelations—for example, experiences of deep prayer or contemplation, experiences involving a sense of profound awe and reverence in the presence of the holy, experiences of release from finite selfhood or of the absolute dependence of the finite self upon the Whole of Reality, conversion experiences, varieties of mystical ecstasy, and so on. The list of experiences that we would be willing to call religious could be drawn out almost indefinitely, but as the chart of family traits and family members indicates, it is difficult if not impossible to find anything that we would call a religious experience in such "religions" as those of Aristotle, Communism, humanism, and success, wealth, golf, and fishing. Can you think of any exceptions to this? Would conversion experiences be exceptions?

Religious experience is present in most of the great world religions, however. But it does not follow from this that each sincere devotee of one of these religions receives personal revelations or enters states of mystical ecstasy frequently or even at all. Can a person be a Christian, for example, without being a mystic? There are many Christians who insist on an affirmative answer to this question.

13. Deep, Intense Concern

The criterion of deep, intense concern has already been discussed in detail, and certainly it is a nearly universal trait of religion, common to if not distinctive of almost all the religions. But is even this trait a *necessary* condition for calling something a religion? Suppose that we were to run across a carefully formulated doctrine of God coupled with a metaphysical account of the human soul and with a detailed answer to the question of the purpose or meaning of human life, and yet we knew little or nothing about the depth of personal involvement with this "God" on the part of the person who had worked it all out. Would we say that we were confronted with a "religion," or must we first assure ourselves of the depth and intensity of personal involvement? Is the mere possibility of deep personal involvement enough? This type of problem becomes particularly acute with a philosopher such as Aristotle, who gives us little or no insight into the depth of his personal involvement with and concern about his Unmoved Mover or Thinker on Thinking. It is at best a conjecture that he was "ultimately concerned" about all of this. Are we willing to say that he had a "religion"? If there is any room for doubt here, then this nearly universal trait of religion is not a necessary condition for applying the word.

14. Institutionalized Social Sharing of Some of Traits 1 Through 13

To what extent must a religion involve social sharing of and reinforcement of beliefs, attitudes, practices, values, institutions, and so on? Can there be a purely "private" religion? If so, which and how many of the traits must be present? Alfred North Whitehead defined *religion* as "what a man does with his own solitariness," [14] but many sociologists, such as Durkheim, Wach, and Yinger, insist that religion is essentially a social phenomenon.[15]

Two distinct questions may very well be involved here. First, must there be *social sharing* of some of traits 1 through 13, which involves telling others orally or in writing about the beliefs, practices, values, and so on that are involved and receiving some kind of social agreement, comfort, and support in return? This is probably an almost universal trait of religion. Even Aristotle and Spinoza did this, not to mention humanists and golfers. Second, must this community of shared traits be *institutionalized* into a somewhat elaborate and enduring set of social relationships involving distinctions between leader and follower, prophet, priest, and layman? This question can be answered negatively in some instances. But the line between social sharing and permanent institutions is a difficult one to draw—so difficult, in fact, that perhaps no crystal-clear answer can be given to these two questions.

Certainly, in some religions social sharing is of utmost importance, as for example in Christianity, with St. Paul's insistence that "you are members of one another" and in the doctrine of the communion of the saints. Recent sociological studies indicate that it is extremely difficult if not impossible for a set of religious beliefs, practices, and values to survive for very long under conditions of complete social isolation;[16] thus there is much practical wisdom involved when the religions stress the importance of social sharing.

GENERAL CONCLUSIONS OF "THE SEARCH FOR FAMILY RESEMBLANCES"

1. The only family members in our chart that clearly exhibit all the family traits are Christianity, Judaism, and Islam, though Hinduism comes very close. This suggests that these Western religions have had a definitive influence on our very conception of religion. We do in fact take them as paradigms for the application of the concept, since they exhibit *all* the important traits that we ascribe to a "religion." We might conjecture that if we were making an ordinary-language analysis of religion in Ceylon we would have set up our list of family traits in such a way as to get a P in each case for Hinayana Buddhism, or in India a clear-cut P in each case for Hinduism—and in the languages of these countries it would be the Western religions that would be found wanting! If this is the case, then *religion* in English is only an approximate translation of any corresponding words in these other languages.

2. The family members on the chart are arranged in such a way that fewer and fewer P's appear as we move to the right in the direction of success, wealth, golf, and fishing, and get further and further away from our paradigms of Christianity, Judaism, and Islam. This suggests that as we Westerners become acquainted with other cultures and new developments in our own cultures, we are willing to extend the application of *religion* to those phenomena that bear some significant similarities to our own standard religions. It further suggests that as these similarities become fewer and fewer in particular cases, we come to have more and more reservations about the legitimacy of extending *religion* to cover these cases. This explains why we are uneasy about calling success, wealth, golf, and fishing religions—they are like Christianity *only* in that they involve deep, intense concern. We say that such "religions" are only "borderline cases," or that in speaking of them as religions we are only speaking metaphorically.

3. In deciding whether to call something a religion, it is not merely the *number* of respects in which it resembles our paradigms that guides us, it is also the *importance* of these traits. Other traits besides deep, intense concern, such as a complex world view interpreting the significance of human life or an account of the

nature of, origin of, and cure for evil, are nearly universal in the religions, and this may be one clue that guides us in assessing their importance. What other traits are of crucial importance? To us Westerners belief in God and in experience after death weigh heavily, though even these are not deemed absolutely necessary. A typical Western atheist who passionately denies God and immortality, who never indulges in anything resembling prayer, ritual, or mysticism, and whose principles we regard as less than moral would not be called a religious man; but a dedicated Hinayana Buddhist who fails to affirm God and immortality and yet does engage in something resembling prayer, ritual, mysticism, and morality is called a religious man, mainly because his situation does exhibit a significant number of important resemblances to our paradigmatic religions.

4. The traits provide the differentia of "religion." We are willing to call a religion only a finite set of beliefs and practices through which we express our ultimate concerns, not a limitless set of them as Tillich's definition would require. The list of family traits on our chart represents the hard core of the traits that the "religions" must manifest, and although it is by no means complete, it nevertheless could not be indefinitely extended. Neither could the list of family members be indefinitely extended. There are many sufficient but no necessary conditions for calling something a religion if the Wittgensteinian approach is correct. So long as there are family resemblances, it is not necessary that there be common essences in order for there to be limits on the correct application of a concept and rules to guide us in making those applications. However, is the contention that there are *only* family resemblances completely correct? What shall we say about the several nearly universal traits of religion that we have discovered? Would we call something a religion that completely failed to involve deep concern, answers to questions about the significance of human life, and perhaps even some account of the origin of, nature of, and cure for evil? Is the search for family resemblances completely at odds with the search for common essences? In looking to see, have we not found? In being nearly if not completely universal, these traits come as close to being necessary conditions for calling something a religion as we could expect to find for such a complex ordinary-language concept.

Suggestions for Further Reading

TILLICH'S DISCUSSIONS OF ULTIMATE CONCERN

BROWN, D. MACKENZIE, *Ultimate Concern: Tillich in Dialogue* (New York, Harper & Row, 1965), First and Second Dialogues.

TILLICH, PAUL, *Systematic Theology*, Vol. I (Chicago, University of Chicago Press, 1951), pp. 11–15, 211–18.

————, *Dynamics of Faith* (New York, Harper & Row, 1958), pp. 1–12.

TILLICH'S DISCUSSIONS OF LESS-THAN-ULTIMATE OBJECTS
AND BEING ITSELF

TILLICH, PAUL, *Systematic Theology*, Vol. I (Chicago, University of Chicago Press, 1951), pp. 218–52; Vol. II (1957), Introduction.

————, *The Courage to Be* (New Haven, Conn., Yale University Press, 1952), pp. 182–90.

————, *Christianity and the Encounter of the World Religions* (New York, Columbia University Press, 1963), pp. 3–12.

WITTGENSTEIN ON UNIVERSALS AND FAMILY RESEMBLANCES

AARON, R. I., "Wittgenstein's Theory of Universals," *Mind*, Vol. LXXIV (April 1965), pp. 249–51.

AMBROSE, ALICE, "Wittgenstein on Universals," in K. T. Fann, ed., *Ludwig Wittgenstein: The Man and His Philosophy* (New York, Dell, 1967), pp. 336–52.

BAMBROUGH, J. R., "Universals and Family Resemblances," *Proceedings of the Aristotelian Society*, Vol. LXI (1960–61), pp. 207–22.

RICHMAN, ROBERT J., "Something Common," *The Journal of Philosophy*, Vol. LIX, No. 26 (December 1962), pp. 821–30.

WITTGENSTEIN, LUDWIG, *Philosophical Investigations* (New York, Macmillan, 1965), Part I, Sections 65–77.

SOME MODERN ANALYSES OF RELIGION

ALSTON, WILLIAM P., *Philosophy of Language* (Englewood Cliffs, N.J., Prentice-Hall, 1964), pp. 88–90 (a Wittgensteinian analysis).

BEARDSLEY, MONROE C., and BEARDSLEY, ELIZABETH L., *Philosophical Thinking* (New York, Harcourt Brace Jovanovich, 1965), pp. 23–43.

BLACKSTONE, WILLIAM T., *The Problem of Religious Knowledge* (Englewood Cliffs, N.J., Prentice-Hall, 1963), pp. 36–46.

FERRÉ, FREDERICK, *Basic Modern Philosophy of Religion* (New York, Scribner's, 1967), pp. 30–83.

YINGER, J. MILTON, *Religion, Society and the Individual* (New York, Macmillan, 1957), pp. 6–17.

Notes

1   H. Richard Niebuhr, *The Meaning of Revelation* (New York, Macmillan, 1955), p. 77.

2   Paul Tillich, *Christianity and the Encounter of the World Religions* (New York, Columbia University Press, 1963), p. 4. Tillich also defines *faith* as "the state of being ultimately concerned" in his *Dynamics of Faith* (New York, Harper & Row, 1958), p. 4, so his discussions of faith may also be taken as discussions of religion.

3   See the Suggestions for Further Reading for Tillich's own discussions of ultimate concern and ultimate objects.

4   Tillich, *Dynamics of Faith*, p. 12.

5   Tillich, *Christianity and the Encounter of the World Religions*, pp. 5 ff.

6   Paul Tillich, *The Courage to Be* (New Haven, Conn., Yale University Press, 1954), pp. 182–90.

7   Tillich's insistence that the object be truly ultimate is well expressed in Sermon 20 of his *The New Being* (New York, Scribner's, 1955). That he wants both the concern and the object of religion to be truly ultimate is made clear in his *Dynamics of Faith,* p. 10.

8   Tillich, *Dynamics of Faith*, pp. 45–46.

9   Ludwig Wittgenstein, *Philosophical Investigations* (Oxford, Basil Blackwell & Mott, 1953), Part I, Section 66.

10   This has been done, for example, by A. J. Ayer, *The Problem of Knowledge* (Harmondsworth, Eng., Penguin, 1957), pp. 10–12.

11   See William P. Alston, *Philosophy of Language* (Englewood Cliffs, N.J., Prentice-Hall, 1964), pp. 88–90.

12   Wittgenstein, *Philosophical Investigations,* Part I, Section 66.

13   *Ibid.,* Section 67.

14   Alfred North Whitehead, *Religion in the Making* (New York, Macmillan, 1926), p. 16.

15 See the discussion in J. Milton Yinger, *Religion, Society and the Individual* (New York, Macmillan, 1957), pp. 6–17.

16 This point is made emphatically in Leon Festinger, Henry W. Riecken, and Stanley Schachter, *When Prophecy Fails* (New York, Harper & Row, 1956), especially Chapters 1, 7, and 8.

chapter two

What
Is
Religion? SOME PERSUASIVE
DEFINITIONS

In Chapter 1 we noted that definitions are used for many purposes. Up to this point we have been offering a definition of *religion* that would be representative of the way in which we use the word in our ordinary, everyday discourse; but it is possible to offer definitions with many other ends in view. We shall now examine a selected group of definitions that have been used primarily to influence attitudes and values rather than to communicate factual information.

Stevenson's Concept of "Persuasive Definition"

A definition that has as its primary function the altering, weakening, or reinforcing of attitudes and values is usually called a persuasive definition. Charles Stevenson, who introduced the concept,[1] suggests that when a definition is preceded by such words as *true* or *real,* we can normally expect a persuasive definition to follow.[2] Thus if someone professes to define *true love* or *real courage* or to tell us "the real meaning of freedom" or "the true meaning of religion," we should be prepared for a definition that is intended to influence our attitudes or values. Stevenson distinguishes between two aspects of "meaning" conveyed by many of our words: the "descriptive meaning," by which is meant the relatively fixed, conventional connotations or definitions of a word, and the "emotive meaning," by which is meant the emotional impact that a word can be expected to have. Many of our words are emotively neutral in the sense that they are used primarily for communicating information, but other words—such as *good, bad, culture, justice, Communism, democracy, religion*—can normally be expected to arouse a predictable positive or negative emotional response. Such words make effective tools for the altering of attitudes and values when they are given persuasive definitions that evoke approval or disapproval.

Frequently, many of us—especially propagandists, orators, ministers, politicians, and advertisers—use a word that has a standardized emotional impact and give the word an entirely different descriptive meaning from the one it normally carries. Usually the standardized emotional response is transferred to the new descriptive meaning given to the word; and without realizing the psychological trick that has been played on them, people find themselves approving of something they normally dislike, or vice versa, merely because a word has been used that normally evokes a positive, or negative, emotional response. Emotively loaded words that are vague and have little fixed connotation may be given a fixed meaning that they do not normally have, or words that have a fixed meaning may be given a meaning that is quite different, and the standardized emotional response may be expected to carry over. In the bizarre world of George Orwell's *1984* we have some extreme examples of this in the "doublethink" definitions "War is peace," "Freedom is slavery," and "Ignorance is strength." [3] Since a kind of deception is involved in the use of persuasive definitions, serious moral issues would seem to be involved. Is there not a kind of moral integrity involved in the correct use of language? We should realize, however, that opposition to persuasive definition is not opposition to all linguistic revision and innovation whatsoever. Linguistic innovation is often done quite openly and explicitly, with no intent to deceive or to capitalize on nonrational emotive impact, and good reasons for linguistic reform may be given in many cases. Not all innovative definitions are persuasive definitions.

Although the word *religion* is an extremely flexible word, it nevertheless has a relatively fixed descriptive meaning, which we have previously explored. It is also a word to which we normally respond warmly, like *God, mother,* or *the flag.* Thus it is a word that lends itself to persuasive definition, and it is not surprising to find that such definitions of *religion* have been offered by philosophers, theologians, and plain men—but this is not to say that they were clearly aware that they were doing so. In this chapter we shall discuss the persuasive definitions of *religion* offered by two influential philosophers, Kant and Schleiermacher. We shall not assert that the definers deliberately set out to formulate persuasive definitions, but only that the definitions themselves can be viewed profitably in this way. The definers may very well have been operating with a quite different understanding of what they were doing. They may have assumed that in some other realm of being there is a pure Platonic essence of *religion,* which constitutes the true referent of the word and which they had at last succeeded in isolating and identifying. Do you feel that this is an inflated conception of what the philosopher is supposed to be doing?

Most of the familiar persuasive definitions of *religion* are reductive definitions, in that they focus on one of the familiar traits of religion—such as Tillich's "being grasped by an ultimate concern" —and insist that it alone constitutes the essence of "true religion." Such definitions suggest that this trait alone is important and that other traits are unimportant because they belong only to "pseudo-religion" "idolatrous religion," or to the "superficial trappings" or "spurious conceptions" of religion. In dealing with the traits of religion there are two distinct questions that must be kept clearly separate but are usually collapsed into one another by persuasive definers: First, how important *for purposes of accurate communication* are the traits? Second, how important *for other purposes* are the traits—that is, how much relative importance is attached to them in the various world religions, or how important are they when viewed from inside the standpoints of theism, humanism, morality, nationalism, prudence, and so on? If the two questions are clearly distinguished, the second is one of the most vital questions of the philosophy of religion, but judgments of importance of this second type should be argued for on the basis of whatever kinds of rational evidence one can produce to support them.

Merely producing an arbitrary, unconventional definition in which a single trait is exalted to the status of exclusive significance does not constitute such evidence, and this is basically what is wrong with most persuasive definitions of *religion*. For example, we may wish to argue for a specific version of religion in which prayer and ritual are to be eliminated, and we may be able to give good reasons for doing so. But merely to produce a definition of *religion* that excludes prayer and ritual from "true religion" (as did Kant, for instance) or that excludes "belief in *a* supernatural being" (as did Tillich) is not to give any good reasons at all, but merely to use a persuasive definition as an instrument for nonrational conversion. We cannot prove that our own religion is superior to all others simply by producing an unconventional definition of *religion* that makes everything else inferior by definition.

To illustrate the uses of persuasive definitions of *religion,* we shall look at examples that focus particularly on the *moral* traits and the *feeling* traits of some specific religion and that insist that these traits alone constitute the essence of "true religion."

RELIGION AS MORALITY: KANT

The eighteenth century, in which Immanuel Kant flourished, was one of almost unbounded optimism about what raw human intelligence could achieve in the realm of religious knowledge. With the significant exception of David Hume, it was generally agreed that revelation was no longer needed, since reason could do everything that needed to be done; and even if revelation was recognized as a way of knowing, it was relegated to outmoded past history or to the illiterate masses who were too ill-trained and uninformed to understand the philosophical proofs for such accepted religious truths as the existence of the great "Author of Nature," the immortality of the soul, and the universal truths of morality. Of course, most of the rationalists of the eighteenth century accepted the "theoretical" proofs for the existence of God—that is, the cosmological argument, which attempts to conclude the existence of a First Cause from the existence of certain types of effects in the world, or the teleological argument, which attempts to conclude the existence of an Intelligent Designer of the world from evidences of design and order to be found in the world. For reasons that will be discussed in later chapters (especially Chapter 9), Kant rejected these and other theoretical proofs for the existence of God and other proofs for immortality; but he nevertheless shared with the rationalists of his century the conviction that reason alone is sufficient for all religious knowledge. The title of his principal work in the philosophy of religion, *Religion Within the Limits of Reason Alone,*[4] accurately reflects Kant's own position, but the type of reason that for him was sufficient to comprehend religion was "practical" or "moral" reason rather than "theoretical" or "metaphysical" reason. Kant's very definition of *religion* as "the recognition of all duties as divine commands"[5] reflects his practical orientation; and as we follow his development of this definition we see more and more clearly that we have in Kant the complete reduction of religion to morality. Morality alone constitutes the essence of "true religion," and nothing else really matters. Everything else either derives from this or belongs to "pseudoreligion." This viewpoint can be illustrated by examining Kant's treatment of several of the family traits of religion, beginning with the paramount place he assigned to the presence of a moral code.

The Presence of a Moral Code

We have defined *morality* as a code of conduct that satisfies two criteria, the first material and the second formal: First, it must be designed to promote the welfare of humanity as a whole, and second, it must be one that we would will humanity as a whole to act on.[6] The first criterion demands that the consequences of the code of conduct for humanity as a whole be taken into account if that code of conduct is to be called moral. However, Kant refused to consider consequences and regarded the second, formal criterion of universalizability as alone sufficient and necessary for calling a code of conduct moral. If we will that everyone should always act on such a concrete rule of behavior, or "maxim," as "always keep your promises" or "always tell the truth," then conduct in accordance with and for the sake of the rule is moral conduct. The central principle of morality for Kant was the categorical imperative, which is: "Act only on that maxim whereby thou canst at the same time will that it should become a universal law."[7] Thus our moral duty is to act in accordance with and for the sake of those rules of behavior that pass the test of universalizability;[8] and a morally good man, a man of good will, is a man who always so acts.

How do we arrive at and justify the categorical imperative and the absoluteness of morality? For Kant the categorical imperative was a self-evident, a priori principle of reason by which every rational creature would know himself to be necessarily bound. It did not need to be proved, yet it was firmly grounded in reason. It could not be derived from anything more fundamental than itself and did not need to be, since it was in itself an absolutely certain, rational beginning point for moral knowledge; and given the intimate connection between morality and religion envisioned by Kant, it was also an absolutely certain beginning point for religious knowledge. Because of it religion could be comprehended within the limits of reason alone. Religious knowledge begins as moral certainty. In the philosophical order of knowing we are first acquainted with and certain of the categorical imperative; and from it we derive any knowledge of God and immortality that might be available to us. Kant was one of the first modern philosophers to argue that ethics is epistemologically independent of theology; he rejected the traditional medieval Christian view that we begin with knowledge of God and then derive ethics from his will or his commands. Kant insisted that first we know morality, and from this we derive our very concept of God. Much twentieth-century ethical theory has been very sympathetic with Kant's rejection of the dependence of morality on theology,[9] but it has been uncommon to follow him in reversing the relationship and making a knowledge of God and immortality dependent on rational moral knowledge. But thanks to Kant and like-minded men, we Westerners need no longer assume uncritically that the atheist must renounce morality in the process of renouncing God.

God, Revelation, and Morality

How, in Kant's opinion, is our knowledge of God derived from our knowledge of morality? Kant thought that a kind of practical knowledge of God's existence and nature could be derived from morality. God's existence is required, since there must be a being of sufficient power and knowledge to guarantee the immortality of the human soul and the just distribution of reward and punishment. Immortality in turn is required if all morally good men are to be happy and all morally wicked men are to be unhappy, which morality requires that they be, and which they are not in the present world. Thus another existence after death must be postulated in which this requirement will be satisfied and in which men can make limitless progress toward moral perfection. This is Kant's famous moral argument for the existence of God,[10] since only God could bring about the required immortality. Many have not found this argument convincing. Some of the basic questions to be raised about it are: (1) Is it so self-evident that the virtuous ought to be happy and the wicked unhappy? (2) Even if we assent to this, is it inevitable that what ought to be will be? How could this be demonstrated? (3) Can the notion that the virtuous ought to be and will be happy in the "next life" be combined with the notion that in the next life the individual will be able to make *limitless* progress toward moral perfection? Exactly how much imperfection is compatible with just that degree of virtue that makes one eligible for happiness and immortality? (4) Could the moral perfection of the individual be achieved in a finite span of time, and if so, why is immortality, or endless experience after death, required? Finally, we may wonder how seriously Kant himself took his practical proofs for God and immortality, since he finally tells us that morality does not really require belief in the "objective reality" of God and immortality: "Indeed, the *minimum* of knowledge (it is possible that there may be a God) must suffice, subjectively, for whatever can be made the duty of every man." [11] This would seem to require that Kant modify his definition of *religion* to the recognition of all duties as *possibly* divine commands. We may wonder to what extent Kant effects the complete reduction of the idea of God to the idea of morality.

As for God's nature, we can infer that he is omnipotent and omniscient since only a being with these attributes could guarantee immortality and justice and thus satisfy the demands of morality. Kant thought that our entire conception of God is derived from our knowledge of morality and must be if that conception is to be accurate. Kant dismissed revelation as an unreliable source of information about God. With many of the prominent thinkers of his century he was concerned with the question of by what criteria genuine revelation could be distinguished from spurious revelation. From Locke to Kant it was agreed that reason provides these criteria; and for Kant it was practical reason, that is, our knowledge of morality. Only in the light of morality can we recognize genuine revelations, and in this manner Kant reduced revelation to rational morality. He stated his position as follows:

> Though it does indeed sound dangerous, it is in no way reprehensible to say that every man creates a God for himself, nay, must make himself such a God according to moral concepts (and must add those infinitely great attributes which characterize a Being capable of exhibiting, in the world, an object commensurate with Himself), in order to honor in Him *the One who created him*. For in whatever manner a being has been made known to him by another and described as God, yea, even if such a being had appeared to him (if this is possible), he must first of all compare this representation with his ideal in order to judge whether he is entitled to regard it and to honor it as a divinity. Hence there can be no religion springing from revelation alone, i.e., without *first* positing that concept, in its purity, as a touchstone. Without this all reverence for God would be idolatry.[12]

> Nor could anything be more fatal to morality than that we should wish to derive it from examples. For every example of it that is set before me must be first itself tested by principles of morality, whether it is worthy to serve as an original example, that is, as a pattern, but by no means can it authoritatively furnish the conception of morality. Even the Holy One of the Gospels must first be compared with our ideal of moral perfection before we can recognize Him as such; and so He says of Himself, "Why call ye Me (whom you see) good; none is good (the model of good) but God only (whom ye do not see)?" But whence have we the conception of God as the supreme good? Simply from the *idea* of moral perfection, which reason frames *a priori* and connects inseparably with the notion of a free will. Imitation finds no place at all in morality, and examples serve only for encouragement, that is, they put beyond doubt the feasibility of what the law commands, they make visible that which the practical rule expresses more generally, but they can never authorize us to set aside the true original which lies in reason, and to guide ourselves by examples.[13]

Duties to God, Prayer, and Ritual

We shall look at Kant's treatment of prayer and ritual within the larger framework of his treatment of the question, "Is there such a thing as an absolute duty toward God?" [14] Kant's answer makes it obvious that his definition of *religion* as "the recognition of all duties as divine commands" is a persuasive definition. In the exposition of this definition he makes it clear that nothing except *moral* duty really matters and that, by definition, the other family traits of religion, such as prayers of adoration and ritual worship, are of no importance.

In Christianity, Judaism, and Islam it is commonly assumed that men do have duties to God that transcend their moral duties to their fellow men. Indeed, most of the major world religions seem to make a place for uniquely religious values and obligations that cannot be reduced to moral values and obligations. This thought is expressed in a variety of ways. For example, as will be explained in the next section of this chapter, Abraham's near sacrifice of Isaac at God's behest [15] cannot be fully comprehended by moral categories. The first three of the Ten Commandments require that we have no other gods, that we make no graven images of gods, and that we not take the name of God in vain.[16] Jesus insisted that the first and greatest commandment is to love God with all our heart and soul and mind and strength; and this is clearly distinct from the second commandment, which is a moral one—to love our neighbor as ourself.[17] When the woman brought the jar of costly ointment and anointed Jesus with it, the moral-minded onlookers insisted that the costly nard had been wasted, because it could have been sold for a great price and the money given to the poor. This is probably what morality would have required; but Jesus honored the woman for performing a uniquely beautiful and religious act, the significance of which could not be reduced to the moral requirements of the situation.[18] It has thus been far from obvious within the Judaeo-Christian tradition that man's duty to love, worship, adore, obey, and glorify God can be reduced to his moral duty toward his fellow men; and insofar as these absolute duties toward God find expression in prayer and ritual worship, it has been far from obvious that these religious acts have no place in religion.

Kant must be regarded as a religious reformer who wished to purify religion of certain traits that he believed to be undesirable, and who, to accomplish this end, employed a persuasive definition of *religion* that in effect reduces religion to morality. He tells us that the commandment to love God with all our heart and soul and mind and strength is equivalent in meaning to his own philosophical contention that we ought to do our moral duty for its own sake, that is, "for no motive other than unconditioned esteem for duty itself." [19] (Do you think this interpretation really does justice to this commandment?) In commenting on the place of prayer, ritual, and duties to God in "true religion," Kant tells us that *"Whatever, over and above good life-conduct, man fancies that he can do to become well-pleasing to God is mere religious illusion and pseudo-service of God."* [20] He also makes clear that this conclusion is mainly a consequence of his very definition of *religion* itself:

> This definition of a religion in general obviates the erroneous representation of religion as an aggregate of *special* duties having reference directly to God; thus it prevents our taking on (as men are otherwise very much inclined to do) *courtly obligations* over and above the ethico-civil duties of humanity (of man to man) and our seeking, perchance, even to make good the deficiency of the latter by means of the former. There are no special duties to God in a universal religion, for God can receive nothing from us; we cannot act for Him, nor yet upon Him.[21]

All forms of worship other than man's moral duty to his fellow men are finally dismissed with the pejorative labels *superstition* and *fanaticism:*

> The illusion of being able to accomplish anything in the way of justifying ourselves before God through religious acts of worship is religious *superstition,* just as the illusion of wishing to accomplish this by striving for what is supposed to be communion with God is religious *fanaticism.* It is a superstitious illusion to wish to become well-pleasing to God through actions which anyone can perform without even needing to be a good man (for example, through profession of statutory articles of faith, through conformity to churchly observance and discipline, etc.).[22]

With a mere definition of *religion* Kant believes he has shown that no "true religion" contains a belief that God really exists (the mere possibility is enough), that no "true religion" contains a reliable and self-authenticating revelation, and that no "true religion" makes a place for prayer, ritual, or any other expression of unique duties to God. Quite apart from the question of the desirability or undesirability of these changes, we may justly wonder whether a mere definition can accomplish such sweeping reforms. Even if we agree that such changes would be desirable, it seems that they require more justification than the mere production of an unconventional and persuasive definition.

Kierkegaard's Reaction to Kant

Since the notion of persuasive definition was not available to him, Søren Kierkegaard could not attack Kant on that basis, but in his own way Kierkegaard dramatically emphasized the point that the concept of religion is much richer than Kant would allow and that in the religions there are distinctive *nonmoral* values and obligations. He carried his protest to the extreme of insisting that in the name of religion and religious duty many downright *immoral* deeds have been done—and in his opinion rightly so. In his *Fear and Trembling,* he took Abraham's near sacrifice of his son Isaac (Genesis 22) as a paradigm of an immoral act required by one's absolute duty to God.

If, as we have concluded, a moral act must be designed to promote the welfare of humanity as a whole and must at the same time be universalizable for humanity as a whole, then it is difficult to see how human sacrifice under religious auspices can be called moral. The word *immoral* seems more appropriate. Is not human sacrifice immoral? Is it in the best interest of everyone alike? Would a moral and loving God really require it? Kant did not include human welfare within his conception of the moral, and Kierkegaard followed him in regarding universalizability as the sole condition necessary and sufficient for identifying moral acts and separating them from the immoral. Kierkegaard then insisted that Abraham's situation cannot be universalized. In this instance the act of human sacrifice is a particular act of absolute obedience to God, and in no sense is it intended that every human being should sacrifice some other human being to God. Morality requires that a father love his son, not that he kill him.[23] Kierkegaard said, "For faith is this paradox, that the particular is higher than the universal";[24] and he insisted that such nonmoral religious values and obligations involve a "teleological suspension of the ethical." [25]

Kierkegaard was fully aware of the familiar attempt to reconcile the Abraham story with morality that was based on the fact that Abraham did not actually sacrifice Isaac, that God provided a substitute sacrifice at the last minute. From the outcome of the story it is commonly concluded that God did not really command human sacrifice and that this story does not really show that nonmoral, indeed immoral, acts are sometimes required in the world religions, or even within the Judaeo-Christian tradition. Kierkegaard regarded this as a cheap Sunday-morning edition of the Abraham story that entirely misses the point. It loses sight of the fact that God *did* command Abraham to sacrifice Isaac, that Abraham fully intended to go through with it, and that within the Christian tradition a man is guilty of what he wholeheartedly intends to do whether he actually does it or not. The moralistic interpretation of Abraham suffers from its awareness of the end of the story from the very beginning; we might just as well sleep through a sermon on Abraham; in a moment the "trial" is over and everything falls into moral perspective again.[26] We forget that Abraham himself *did not* know that God would spare his son, that he *did* intend to do the immoral thing in the service of God, and that he suffered agony for days as a consequence. In Kierkegaard's words,

People construe the story of Abraham in another [that is, the moralistic] way. They extol God's grace in bestowing Isaac upon him again—the whole thing was only a trial. A trial—that word may say much or little, and yet the whole thing is over as quickly as it is said. One mounts a winged horse, the same instant one is at Mount Moriah, the same instant one sees the ram; one forgets that Abraham rode only upon an ass, which walks slowly along the road, that he had a journey of three days, that he needed some time to cleave the wood, to bind Isaac, and to sharpen the knife.

.   .   .

If I were to talk about him, I would first depict the pain of his trial. To that end I would like a leech suck all the dread and distress and torture out of a father's sufferings, so that I might describe what Abraham suffered, whereas all the while he nevertheless believed. I would remind the audience that the journey lasted three days and a good part of the fourth, yea, that these three and a half days were infinitely longer than the few thousand years which separate me from Abraham.[27]

Kierkegaard argued that if we view the Abraham story strictly from the moral point of view and remove its theistic background and overtones, all that remains is the crude fact that Abraham wanted to murder Isaac.[28]

In holding that the religious stage along life's way is quite distinct from the ethical stage, Kierkegaard has been accused of ignoring the fact that there is such a thing as "Christian ethics" and that the presence of a moral code is a common family trait of the world religions. Kierkegaard did not intend to deny all of this, though the extremes of his literary style sometimes leave him open to such criticisms. His viewpoint may be summarized as an insistence, against Kant, that religion cannot be reduced to morality because there are many dedicated men of religion who do subordinate moral to theistic values while subscribing to both, and who would sacrifice the former for the latter if their religious situation seemed to demand it. On this point Kierkegaard found himself to be essentially in agreement with another great nineteenth-century religious thinker, Friedrich Schleiermacher, who wrote that "experience teaches that not only the most admirable but also the most abominable, not only the most useful but also the most inane and meaningless things, are done as pious acts and out of piety." [29]

If we "look and see" what is actually there in the religions of man, we will find that in some there is no morality at all; in others moral duties are subordinated to *nonmoral* theistic duties that transcend but do not contradict them; and in others theistic obligations require that the *immoral* thing be done. Although we may believe that one of these forms of religion is best, we cannot prove it to be best merely by offering a persuasive definition of *religion* that makes everything else inferior by definition; we must support our evaluation with more objective reasons than that.

The problem of the relation between religious and moral values has persisted throughout the history of religions, and it is as much alive today as it ever was. For example, in Germany recently a man was indicted for sexually molesting, torturing, and finally murdering three young boys on three separate occasions. It was learned that after each murder the murderer had confessed his crimes to a priest. The priest never informed the authorities of the secrets confessed to him and had no part in the murderer's eventual arrest. How were moral and religious obligations related in the mind of this priest? What would you have done?

RELIGION AS FEELING: SCHLEIERMACHER

Near the turn of the nineteenth century a significant reaction against the rationalistic optimism of the eighteenth century began to develop, and this reaction eventually made itself felt in the understanding of religion. Friedrich Schleiermacher's attempt to reduce religion to feeling is an example of this trend and of the attempt to radically reform religious values by producing an unconventional, persuasive definition of *religion*. By general consent Schleiermacher was the greatest theologian of the nineteenth century, but he was a theologian with strong philosophical interests that dominated his thinking in the early, pantheistic period of his intellectual development. Schleiermacher came from a background of Pietism, a movement that emphasized individual piety and religious experience as the essentials of religion, and during his career he was closely associated with the Romanticist movement in German thought, which attached almost exclusive importance to aesthetic feelings and the aesthetic response to the world. The Pietistic emphasis on pious feelings and the Romanticist emphasis on aesthetics colored his whole conception of religion and gave rise to a form of pantheistic mysticism in his early years that later yielded to a more orthodox form of Christianity.

While he was still a young man Schleiermacher was a chaplain at the University of Berlin, where he was associated with the circle

Romanticists that flourished there at the time. He delivered a series of speeches on religion that were addressed specifically to the broad segment of the university community that had rejected religion—philosophers, scientists, and aesthetes whom Schleiermacher called "cultured despisers of religion." In these speeches, published in book form in 1796 under the title *On Religion: Speeches to Its Cultured Despisers,* he attempted to persuade these "cultured despisers" that they had not really rejected religion at all but only spurious misconceptions of it. Indeed, he felt that if he could bring them to an understanding of "true religion," they would discover that instead of being irreligious, as they thought themselves to be, they were in fact the most truly religious of all. Schleiermacher was particularly anxious to deliver religion from two misconceptions that he called doctrinalism and moralism, both of which had been mistakenly identified with religion and rejected by the "cultured despisers." Schleiermacher thought that if he could show that "ideas and principles are all foreign to religion," [30] then the despisers of religion would see that they had not rejected "true religion" at all.

Doctrinal Traits

Many of the family traits of religion as we ordinarily understand it involve doctrinal, or cognitive, elements. This is obviously so with respect to belief in God or the gods, belief in experience after death, belief that a moral code is sanctioned by a superior being, accounts of the nature of, origin of, and cure for evil, theodicy, revealed truths, interpreted religious experiences, and so on. It is also true that many of the doctrines that have been propagated in the name of religion have fallen into disrepute, such as the belief that the universe was created in literally seven days, that God created all the biological species during this period, and that the earth is the center of the universe. Even by the early part of the nineteenth century many traditional religious doctrines had been discredited by the "cultured despisers of religion" to whom Schleiermacher addressed himself. In rejecting these beliefs as mere superstitions, the despisers felt that they were also rejecting religion itself. Certainly they were right in the sense that there were many people, even within the religious and philosophical establishments, who identified religion with proper doctrine or knowledge.

As a corrective against the extremes of doctrinalism, Schleiermacher proposed that all the cognitive elements be eliminated from our understanding of *religion*. Among the cognitive elements that have no place whatsoever in true religion are belief in divine providence,[31] "theories of the origin and end of the world," and "analyses of the nature of an incomprehensible Being," [32] belief in "miracle, inspiration, revelation, supernatural intimations," [33] philosophical "proofs," [34] and belief in a supernatural God and the immortality of the individual human soul.[35] Against doctrinalism Schleiermacher argued that it is possible to believe in any or all such doctrines without being truly religious,[36] and that it is quite possible to be truly religious without assenting to any of them: "Quantity of knowledge is not quantity of piety." [37] To the cultured despisers of religion Schleiermacher said: "Piety cannot be an instinct craving for a mess of metaphysical and ethical crumbs"; "religion is no slavery, no captivity, least of all for your reasons"; and "it matters not what conceptions a man adheres to, he can still be pious. His piety, the divine in his feeling, may be better than his conception, and his desire to place the essence of piety in conception, only makes him misunderstand himself." [38]

In his eagerness to exclude outmoded and discredited beliefs from religion, Schleiermacher went to the extreme of completely excluding all beliefs on the ground that they are totally unimportant. In order to understand this value judgment, we need to know the point of view from which it is made. If he is suggesting that doctrines play no role in our ordinary understanding of religion, then he is clearly mistaken; we have already seen that they do. But if he is saying only that doctrines are of no importance when viewed *from within* the perspective of his Romanticist pantheistic mysticism, then we are less likely to be trapped into agreement if we do not share that perspective. To say that doctrines are unessential in true religion is deceptive, however, because the proof for this statement is based on a persuasive, unconventional definition of *religion* that is simply a revisionist value judgment disguised as a bit of scientific lexicography. Doubtless there are ways of eliminating discredited beliefs from our religions, whatever we take these to be, without eliminating *all* beliefs. This seems to be, in Martin Luther's phrase, "throwing out the baby with the bath water." Moreover, there is a legitimate distinction to be made between a "religion" and a "good religion." Even if we agree with Schleiermacher's value judgment that doctrine (and morality) have no integral place in a *good* religion, we are not thereby committed to saying that they play no role whatsoever in our ordinary understanding of *religion*. If we do agree with Schleiermacher, however, it will be difficult for us to account for the deep concern of many religious believers with the *truth* of what they believe.

Moral Traits

We have seen that most of the great world religions make a place for morality, even those that do not regard morality as derived from and sanctioned by God or the gods. It is also true that men have done many things in the name of religious morality that we would regard as immoral; consider the case of the Inquisitors who tortured and killed their victims, acting on the universalized maxim that any man ought to be so treated if it will lead to the salvation of his immortal soul. Some of Schleiermacher's "cultured despisers of religion" rejected religion on such moral grounds as these, and doubtless many of the Romanticists rejected it on the grounds of an aesthetic individualism that regarded the universal rules of morality with disdain; to them Schleiermacher said simply that morality has no integral place in true religion, and he specifically intended this to be a repudiation of Kant's reduction of religion to morality. Unfortunately, he merely succeeded in replacing one persuasive, reductive definition of *religion* with another!

Even before Kierkegaard, Schleiermacher had stated that many nonmoral and even immoral acts had been done out of piety. Furthermore, he maintained, the distinction between the subject, the person who has a moral obligation, and the object, the person to whom the duty is directed, while inescapable in morality, is completely lost in the sort of mystic ecstasy that constitutes the essence of "true religion." The mystic feels himself to be one with the All. Piety is essentially passive, whereas morality is essentially active. As for ethics, "the pious man confesses that, as pious, he knows nothing about it." [39] "Religion by itself does not urge men to activity at all. If you could imagine it implanted in man quite alone, it would produce neither these [moral deeds] nor any other deeds. The man, according to what we have said, would not act, he would only feel." [40]

In the way in which we ordinarily use the word *religion* the trait of morality is a widely prevalent, but not universal and necessary, characteristic. But Schleiermacher is arguing for a much stronger claim: that morality is necessarily not a characteristic of any religion if we have the right understanding of religion. Again, however, this right understanding of religion turns out to be identical with those traits that are important when viewed from within the standpoint of pantheistic mysticism. Once again, Schleiermacher is neither doing scientific lexicography nor providing us with good reasons for thinking that morality is "unimportant." He is only making morality unimportant by definition, since it is not mentioned in the definition of *true religion* that he offered. Let us now look at his definition of *true religion*.

Feeling Traits

Several of the family traits of religion that we explored earlier, such as deep concern, awe, and mystical experience, are "feeling" traits or at least involve prominent elements of feeling. We have also seen that religious experience takes many diverse forms. Schleiermacher seized upon one of the many types of religious experience and made it into the very essence of true religion. In his speeches it was the mystical, pantheistic feeling of unity with the Infinite Whole of Reality; but in a later work he called it the "feeling of absolute dependence." [41] In his speeches he urged the "cultured despisers" to "turn from everything usually reckoned religion, and fix your regard on the inward emotions and dispositions, as all utterances and acts of inspired men direct." [42] If this is done, it will be discovered that "true religion is sense and taste for the Infinite." [43] In the type of mystical experience that constitutes the essence of true religion, "the whole soul is dissolved in the immediate feeling of the Infinite and Eternal." [44] He further explained what is involved in all this by saying:

The contemplation of the pious is the immediate consciousness of the universal existence of all finite things, in and through the Infinite, and of all temporal things in and through the Eternal. Religion is to seek this and find it in all that lives and moves, in all growth and change, in all doing and suffering. It is to have life and to know life in immediate feeling, only as such an existence in the Infinite and Eternal. Where this is found religion is satisfied, where it hides itself there is for her unrest and anguish, extremity and death. Wherefore it is a life in the infinite nature of the Whole, in the One and in the All, in God, having and possessing all things in God, and God in all. Yet religion is not knowledge and science, either of the world or of God. Without being knowledge, it recognizes knowledge and science. In itself it is an affection, a revelation of the Infinite in the finite, God being seen in it and it in God.[45]

As a description of one particular type of religious experience, this is all very well; but as a definition of *religion* it is merely persuasive. Our ordinary understanding of religion is far richer than that. Hegel remarked that if Schleiermacher's definition of *religion* was correct, then a dog should be a better Christian than most men, since dogs feel more absolutely dependent than we do. Schleiermacher brought his own understanding of religion back in line with ordinary language when he admitted that religious feeling eventually and inevitably expresses itself in doctrine and moral action. But he found himself logically committed to saying that almost any doctrinal framework and almost any action guide will do, so long as they provide a suitable vehicle for the expression of pious feeling. Do you agree, or are you concerned that your religious beliefs and moral principles also be true?

Members of different religions rationalize their toleration of one another by saying that "it really doesn't matter what you believe so long as your heart is in the right place." Does this indicate that to some extent religion has been reduced to pious feeling in the popular mind, and if so, is this the kind of pious feeling that Schleiermacher had in mind or the kind that Tillich had in mind? Or does this indicate that religion has been reduced to morality, following Kant?

In this chapter we have examined persuasive definitions of *religion* that reduce "true religion" to morality or feeling. Other persuasive definitions of *religion* reduce "true religion" to belief—that is, to some of the doctrinal traits of religion. Two such definitions are: "True religion is belief in a supernatural, personal, intelligent Being" and "True religion is belief in the Lord Jesus Christ." [46] Are you familiar with any others?

It is obvious that before we can go on to deal with substantive problems in the philosophy of religion, we must have some understanding of the meanings of *philosophy* and *religion*. Some of the intricacies of the concept of religion have now been explored, but other relevant concepts remain to be developed. The concept of reason is usually present in attempts to define *philosophy,* and Western thinkers have been intrigued by the problem of relating the reason of philosophy to the revelation or inspiration that is integral to religion. In the next three chapters we shall explore this problem, which we shall call the relation of philosophy and theology, in order to arrive at a sound understanding of the concept of *the philosophy of religion.*

Suggestions for Further Reading

ON PERSUASIVE DEFINITIONS

CHRISTIAN, WILLIAM A., "Some Varieties of Religious Belief," *Review of Metaphysics,* Vol. IV (June 1951), pp. 597–616.

STEVENSON, CHARLES, *Ethics and Language* (New Haven, Conn., Yale University Press, 1960), Chapter 9.

ON THE RELATION OF MORAL AND RELIGIOUS VALUES

BRAITHWAITE, R. B., *An Empiricist's View of the Nature of Religious Belief* (Cambridge, Eng., Cambridge University Press, 1955) (a contemporary reduction of religion to morality).

FLEW, ANTONY, *God and Philosophy* (New York, Dell, 1966), Chapter 5.

GARNETT, A. C., *Religion and the Moral Life* (New York, Ronald Press, 1955).

HEPBURN, RONALD W., *Christianity and Paradox* (New York, Pegasus, 1968), Chapter 8 and pp. 186–204.

KANT, IMMANUEL, *Critique of Practical Reason* (New York, Liberal Arts Press, 1956), Part I, Book II, Chapter 2, pp. 114–53.

———, *Religion Within the Limits of Reason Alone* (New York, Harper & Row, 1960), especially Book IV, pp. 139–90.

KIERKEGAARD, SØREN, *Fear and Trembling* and *The Sickness unto Death* (Princeton, N.J., Princeton University Press, 1968), especially *Fear and Trembling*.

MATSON, WALLACE I., *The Existence of God* (Ithaca, N.Y., Cornell University Press, 1965), Part I.

PERRY, RALPH BARTON, *Realms of Value* (Cambridge, Mass., Harvard University Press, 1954), pp. 470–78.

SCHLEIERMACHER, FRIEDRICH, *On Religion: Speeches to Its Cultured Despisers* (New York, Ungar, 1955), pp. 15–18, 29–31, 47–48.

SPINOZA, BENEDICT, *Theologico-Political Treatise,* Chapter 14 (a position very similar to that of Kant). This is available in R. H. M. Elwes, ed., *The Chief Works of Benedict De Spinoza,* Vol. I (New York, Dover, 1951), pp. 182–89.

SCHLEIERMACHER ON RELIGIOUS FEELING AND EXPERIENCE

BARTH, KARL, *From Rousseau to Ritschl* (London, SCM Press, 1959), Chapter 8.

BRANDT, RICHARD, *The Philosophy of Schleiermacher* (New York, Harper & Row, 1941), pp. 105–44, 258–79.

BURTT, E. A., *Types of Religious Philosophy* (New York, Harper & Row, 1951), pp. 289–96.

CARNELL, E. J., *An Introduction to Christian Apologetics* (Grand Rapids, Mich., Eerdmans, 1959), pp. 74–82.

NIEBUHR, RICHARD R., *Schleiermacher on Christ and Religion* (New York, Scribner's, 1964), Chapter 4.

SCHLEIERMACHER, FRIEDRICH, *On Religion: Speeches to Its Cultured Despisers* (New York, Ungar, 1955).

———, *The Christian Faith* (Edinburgh, T. & T. Clark, 1956).

Notes

1 Charles Stevenson, "Persuasive Definitions," *Mind,* Vol. XLVII (July 1938). Most of this article is incorporated in Chapter 9 of Charles Stevenson, *Ethics and Language* (New Haven, Conn., Yale University Press, 1944). See p. 210 for his definition of *persuasive definition.*

2   Stevenson, *Ethics and Language,* pp. 213–14.

3   From *1984* by George Orwell. Copyright 1949 by Harcourt Brace Jovanovich, Inc. Reprinted by permission of Brandt & Brandt.

4   Immanuel Kant, *Religion Within the Limits of Reason Alone* (La Salle, Ill., Open Court, 1934).

5   *Ibid.,* p. 142.

6   These material and formal elements in morality and their interrelations are discussed by William K. Frankena in "Recent Conceptions of Morality," which appears in Hector-Neri Castaneda and George Nakhnikian, eds., *Morality and the Language of Conduct* (Detroit, Wayne State University Press, 1965), pp. 1–21.

7   Immanuel Kant, *Fundamental Principles of the Metaphysics of Morals,* trans. by Thomas K. Abbott (New York, Liberal Arts Press, 1949), p. 38.

8   We will leave to courses in ethics the knotty problems of what exactly is involved in being able to will the universalization of a rule of behavior.

9   The pioneer work in this movement is G. E. Moore, *Principia Ethica* (Cambridge, Eng., Cambridge University Press, 1959), Chapter 4.

10   This discussion is paraphrased from pp. 126–36 of Immanuel Kant, *Critique of Practical Reason,* trans. by Lewis White Beck. Copyright © 1956 by the Liberal Arts Press, Inc. Reprinted by permission of the Liberal Arts Press, a division of the Bobbs-Merrill Company, Inc.

11   Kant, *Religion Within the Limits of Reason Alone,* p. 142 n.

12   *Ibid.,* p. 157 n.

13   Kant, *Fundamental Principles of the Metaphysics of Morals,* p. 26.

14   This question was posed by Kierkegaard. See *Fear and Trembling* and *The Sickness unto Death* by Søren Kierkegaard, trans. by Walter Lowrie (Princeton, N.J., Princeton University Press, 1941), Princeton Paperback #129, p. 78.

15   See Genesis 22.

16   See Exodus 20:3–7. Should the fourth commandment, to keep the Sabbath holy, be classified as a duty to God or to man or somehow to both?

17   Mark 12:30–31.

18   Mark 14:3–9.

19   Kant, *Religion Within the Limits of Reason Alone,* p. 148.

20   *Ibid.,* p. 158.

21   *Ibid.,* p. 143.

22 *Ibid.,* p. 162.
23 Kierkegaard, *Fear and Trembling,* p. 70.
24 *Ibid.,* p. 65.
25 *Ibid.,* pp. 67, 77.
26 *Ibid.,* p. 64.
27 *Ibid.,* pp. 62–64.
28 *Ibid.,* p. 41.
29 Friedrich Schleiermacher, *The Christian Faith* (Edinburgh, T. & T. Clark, 1956), p. 10.
30 Friedrich Schleiermacher, *On Religion: Speeches to Its Cultural Despisers* (New York, Ungar, 1955), p. 38.
31 *Ibid.,* p. 10.
32 *Ibid.,* p. 12.
33 *Ibid.,* p. 72.
34 *Ibid.,* p. 15.
35 *Ibid.,* pp. 76, 81, 82.
36 *Ibid.,* p. 76.
37 *Ibid.,* p. 27.
38 *Ibid.,* pp. 25, 75, 79.
39 *Ibid.,* p. 29.
40 *Ibid.,* p. 27.
41 Schleiermacher, *The Christian Faith,* pp. 16 ff.
42 Schleiermacher, *On Religion,* p. 15.
43 *Ibid.,* p. 32.
44 *Ibid.,* pp. 12, 13.
45 *Ibid.,* p. 28.
46 For an excellent review of many persuasive definitions of *religion* that are built around doctrinal, or cognitive, traits, see William A. Christian, "Some Varieties of Religious Belief," *Review of Metaphysics,* Vol. IV (June 1951), pp. 597–616.

chapter three

The Relation of Philosophy and Theology SOME MODERATE POSITIONS

In our brief discussion of revelation in Chapter 1 we noted that theologians are not agreed on exactly what revelation involves or how it works. Perhaps this uncertainty did not come as any great surprise; but it is rather surprising to discover that philosophers who are committed to reason instead of revelation as a source of knowledge have the same difficulty. Before we discuss the relation of philosophy and theology, it will be helpful to review briefly the ways in which the concept of rationality has been regarded in the Western world. Various philosophers have defended as "legitimate" a number of different functions of reason, such as those discussed below.

Functions of Reason

1. THE CREATION AND INTERPRETATION OF FORMAL SYSTEMS

Such formal conceptual schemes as deductive logic and mathematics lie at the very heart of rationality, and philosophers have recently realized that it is possible to devise a number of alternative logics and mathematics. It may be that some of these systems are more useful to us in dealing with the world than others, and it is certainly true that such natural sciences as physics, chemistry, and astronomy have been remarkably successful in modern times, largely as a result of the fact that such pioneers as Galileo, Kepler, and Newton learned how to apply formal mathematical schemes to the natural world. Philosophers do not agree as to why the application of formal systems to the world of nature has been so successful, because they have not yet resolved to their own satisfaction the question of the relation of logic and ontology—that is, the question of the relation of reason and being.

Deductive arguments that have the formal structure of logically valid arguments have often appeared in the writings of metaphysicians, philosophers of religion, and even theologians. Logic informs us that some formal patterns of reason are correct and others incorrect, but the mere fact that we conduct our reasoning in a formally correct manner does not guarantee that our conclusions are true. It is only when we have both a formally correct pattern of reasoning and true premises that the truth of our conclusion is assured. Philosophers and theologians disagree on the question of how we know that the logically fundamental premises from which we deduce our conclusion are true, theologians claiming that they are revealed and philosophers insisting that even here we must rely on reason alone.

2. THE DISCOVERY AND PREDICTION
OF CAUSAL CONNECTIONS

Reason discovers patterns of causal connection in the world through the use of observation and those successful procedures of testing empirical hypotheses that constitute inductive logic, and it applies the discoveries thus made to an understanding of connections between events. From known patterns of cause and effect we may infer the presence of a certain kind of unknown cause if the effect is given, or a certain kind of effect if the cause is given. Assumptions about the regularity of nature that cannot be proved except by assuming the very things we are attempting to prove seem to be inevitably involved in such reasoning, but making inferences in accord with the correct patterns of inductive logic seems to be the function of reason in dealing with causal connections between events.

Causal arguments often appear in the writings of metaphysicians and theologians as well as in those of scientists, and one of the main disputes to be resolved in our discussion of some of the proofs for the existence of God in Chapters 10 and 11 is whether the use of causal reasoning made by metaphysicians is legitimate. Theologians are vitally interested in causal connections, for these lie at the root of inferences about historical events in biblical times; and the concept of *miracle,* in which many theologians are also interested, is often defined in terms of *exceptions* to normal patterns of causal connection.

3. THE FORMATION OF CONCEPTS

Reason formulates those universal concepts that function as the terms of our propositions. Various accounts of how this is done are set forth, and different accounts of how it is done for different types of concepts are often given. Many of our concepts are abstracted from sense experience, we are told; and some philosophers have insisted that all meaningful concepts must have their origin in sense experience. Other philosophers insist that only such concepts as *red, color, hard, sweet, loud,* and *pungent* are dependent on sense experience, and that there are other meaningful concepts, such as *time, space, substance, cause, effect, relation,* and *number,* that are not derived from experience but are produced independently by reason and then applied to the interpretation of experience in something like the way a mathematical system is, in their opinion, constructed a priori and then applied to experience. Except for the nominalists, who deny that there are any universal concepts at all and claim that there are only words, it is generally agreed that one of the functions of reason is the formation of concepts, even when there is disagreement about exactly how this is done; and even the nominalists concede that the giving of names is one of the functions of reason.

If theologians and metaphysicians are to say anything at all they must make use of concepts, and often they make use of the same concepts, so that the vocabulary of theologians and metaphysicians is often largely—though not completely—interchangeable. A theology may differ from a metaphysic in vocabulary, just as two metaphysics may differ from each other in this respect.

4. THE CLARIFICATION OF MEANING

Metaphysicians, theologians, scientists, and plain men often say things that are puzzling and require clarification. Rational analysis of concepts and statements provides this clarification when it is provided at all. Some modern philosophers insist that aside from logic this is the principal if not the only rational activity in which the philosopher may legitimately engage. But those who are committed to the analysis of unclear language are not agreed as to what is involved. Some suggest that the clarification of concepts consists in breaking them up into simpler and clearer concepts that originate in sense experience or are ostensibly definable, and that the clarification of propositions consists in breaking them down into a series of simpler propositions that can be verified in sense experience. Others want to add that the simpler concepts and propositions must have the advantage of being easily translatable into the notation of some system of symbolic logic. Others hold that it is adequate to produce a series of simpler, ordinary-language concepts or sentences that are equivalent in meaning to the puzzle being analyzed. Others contend that it is enough to show how the perplexing bit of language originated or how it is used in typical cases of everyday discourse. Still others believe that a concept can be clarified simply by looking it up in a dictionary, a suggestion that has more to commend it than might appear on the surface.

Given one or more of the above conceptions, metaphysicians and even theologians are constantly engaged in the clarification of meaning, though not always to their own satisfaction or to that of many of their colleagues.

5. THE INTUITION OF SELF-EVIDENT TRUTHS

Some philosophers have believed that one of the functions of reason is the intuition of certain fundamental propositions that are self-evident in the sense that they do not stand in need of proof and may serve as the basis of proof for all that follows from them, and in the sense that all that is required to know that they are true is to understand what they say. From the time of Plato, many different propositions have been regarded as self-evident truths. For example, such metaphysical assertions as "a thing cannot both be and not be itself," "out of nothing, nothing comes," "every event has a cause," and "it is impossible to regress to infinity in the order of causes" have been regarded as self-evident, as have such normative assertions as "we ought to keep our promises," "it is intrinsically good that the righteous should be rewarded and the wicked punished," and "we ought to act on that concrete rule of behavior which we would willingly universalize." Until the discovery of alternative logics and mathematics, it was common to regard the fundamental axioms and principles of logic, arithmetic, geometry, and so on as self-evident truths. In our era this function of reason has become highly suspect; for we now realize that different and even contradictory axioms have appeared self-evident to different people at different times, that alternatives to them may be constructed, and that sometimes the alternatives work better than the original axioms. Moreover, philosophical analysis has been highly successful in showing that some of these "self-evident" axioms are false, some are formal truths or tautologies, some are high-order empirical generalizations, and some are nonsense. Most theologians, unlike some philosophers, have never been guilty of making the arrogant claim that their truths are rationally self-evident.

6. INSIGHT

Reason gives insight; it is creative as well as inferential. It provides us with fresh perspectives in which old problems either dissolve or find their proper resolution in a comprehensive conceptual scheme. This is true of the reason of creative scientists as much as of the reason of creative philosophers. What teacher of philosophy has not berated Sir Francis Bacon for overlooking this function of reason? Reason is largely a matter of creative genius that knows no "method" and is not limited by already available conceptual schemes, whether of logic, science, or metaphysics (should we also include theology?). The creative thinker often regards himself as inspired by a power that takes possession of him, and insight often comes in a sudden flash, like a revelation. Without insight there would be no progress, no creative advance in science or philosophy or art. None of the other functions of reason we have discussed can take its place. Indeed, insight is involved in the very act of constructing formal systems (though not necessarily in applying them; this can be done by any "thinking" machine that is properly programed). Insight is the famous "method of speculation" that in fact knows no method but generates methodology itself. It lies at the basis of every creative advance in science and every new metaphysic, and from it metaphysical systems derive their basic premises. Crucial questions, which we shall discuss later, are whether there are any fundamental differences between the insights and inspirations of scientists and metaphysicians on the one hand and of theologians on the other, and whether there are tests for showing that one of these insights is more valid than another. Although many contemporary philosophers see the clarification of language as the primary function of the philosopher, traditional philosophers have flourished mainly by virtue of their insight. It has not been their deductive rigor and acumen, scientific brilliance in discovering causal relations, nor expertise in analyzing language that has made philosophers the great men of reason they have been, but rather the scope and freshness of their creative insight into the nature of things. To what extent may the same be said of religious prophets and theologians? There are obvious analogies that many philosophers have preferred to ignore, and in tracing them perhaps we can arrive at an answer to the question of how philosophy and theology are to be related. Perhaps in the final analysis the difference between reason and revelation is not so sharp as many thinkers in the Western intellectual tradition have tried to make it.

The several functions of reason that have been sketched here do not exhaust the concept of rationality by any means, but enough has been said to enable us to begin our exploration of the relationship between philosophy and theology.

If, as we have said, philosophy is the attempt to formulate and justify beliefs about the most universal or fundamental features of reality and values using only human intelligence, and theology is the systematic conceptual elaboration of the faith response to revelation or revelatory events, the question arises as to how these disciplines are to be related to each other. Both philosophy and theology try to inform us about the most universal or fundamental features of reality, knowledge, and value, but one approaches this through reason and the other approaches it through revelation. Theologians believe in order to understand, whereas philosophers understand in order to believe. *Philosophy* and *theology* have other meanings, some of which will be discussed later; but it is the traditional way of conceiving them that generates the problem to which this and the next two chapters are addressed: How can these two seemingly contradictory disciplines be related to each other? This problem has often been called that of the relationship between faith and reason, but it may be better not to use that label, since the usual notion of *faith* is far too rich for our purposes. Faith involves many emotional and dispositional elements, such as trust, loyalty, and passionate assent, with which we shall not concern ourselves. We are interested in the relation of the cognitive or doctrinal elements of philosophy and theology and in the question of why they claim our trust, loyalty, and passionate assent. At present we need not be concerned so much with what philosophy and theology say about values as with what they claim about the fundamental features of reality. The same considerations that apply here will also normally apply to the relation between theological and philosophical value theory.

One function of the philosophy of religion is to survey and critically assess the possibilities for resolving a religious problem, and we shall see in this chapter and in Chapters 4 and 5 that Western philosophers and theologians alike have been concerned with the problem of relating their disciplines and that they have explored a number of interesting possibilities. We shall examine six important ways of relating theology and metaphysics, some of which have been offered by theologians and some of which have been offered by philosophers: (1) the subordination of philosophy to theology, (2) the subordination of theology to philosophy, (3) the elimination of theology in favor of philosophy, (4) the elimination of philosophy in favor of theology, (5) the elimination of "subject matter" from both philosophy and theology, and (6) the equating of philosophy and theology as competing historical, rational belief systems.

The Subordination of Philosophy to Theology: St. Thomas Aquinas

WHEN we say that one thing is subordinated to another, we normally intend to suggest that it is inferior to that other in doing what they both try to do. Some theologians have regarded philosophy as inferior to theology as a source of accurate information about God, experience after death, the ultimate destiny of man, and other fundamental features of reality in which religious men are especially interested. We shall notice that a number of reasons may be given for regarding one of these disciplines as inferior or superior to the other. One may be inferior because it is a less reliable way of knowing, or because the truths known in it are of less importance in the living of a particular kind of religious life, or because its truths are more certain or expressed more clearly than the truths of the other, or because one is more widely available to the masses of men, and so on. The first position we shall explore, the subordination of philosophy to theology, has been widely accepted in the Catholic Church and even among Protestants who have seriously considered the matter.

St. Thomas Aquinas (c. 1226–74) was personally committed to the theological approach to fundamental religious truths; but he conceded that for those who are capable of doing it, philosophy could be an important preparation or preamble for faith and that philosophy is important as an instrument for refuting infidels. In his opinion, adequate philosophical proofs based only on the natural light of reason could be constructed for such religious truths as the existence of God, the unity of God, and the like.[1] Of course all genuine religious truths that reason can know are also known in the faith response to revelation, so philosophy and theology overlap in their content. Nevertheless, philosophy can accomplish a great deal. It is quite correct as far as it goes, but the difficulty is that it does not go far enough. Since truth is one, true philosophical knowledge can never contradict the truths of faith, but it is incomplete in that it does not contain those truths that are vital to man's salvation and the distinctively Christian orientation toward the universe. Revelation is required to compensate for the deficiencies of philosophy. All philosophical knowledge is thus subordinated to and limited by a superior theological knowledge of those important truths that only revelation discloses, such as the doctrine of the creation of the world *ex nihilo* (out of nothing), the doctrine of the Trinity, the doctrines of the Incarnation and the Atonement, the doctrines of the resurrection of the body and the Last Judgment, and so on. Reason can take us only part of the way up the ladder of religious knowledge, but it is the same ladder no matter how we proceed. At the end of his discussion of rational knowledge and the beginning of his discussion of theological knowledge, St. Thomas wrote:

> Since natural reason ascends to a knowledge of God through creatures and, conversely, the knowledge of faith descends from God to us by a divine revelation—since the way of ascent and descent is still the same—we must proceed in the same way in the things above reason which are believed as we proceeded in the foregoing with the investigation of God by reason. First, to be specific, we must treat of things about God Himself which surpass reason and are proposed for belief: such is the confession of the Trinity; second, of course, the things which surpass reason that have been done by God, such as the work of the Incarnation and what follows thereon; third, however, the things surpassing reason which are looked for in the ultimate end of man, such as the resurrection and glorification of bodies, the everlasting beatitude of souls, and matters related to these.[2]

For St. Thomas, theology is the "queen of the sciences" and superior to philosophy as a source of religious truth for a variety of reasons. The salvation of man's soul depends on some of the truths of theology, such as the Incarnation and the Atonement. The truths of theology are thus more vital than those of philosophy, since philosophical knowledge of God is not a saving knowledge of God.[3] Furthermore, revelation is a better way of knowing the highest spiritual truths than is reason, because revelation is from God, who cannot be in error about himself, and because reason is inextricably tied to the origin of all natural knowledge in the senses, a fact that makes reason unsuitable for knowing the highest non-sensory or spiritual truths. Reason seems condemned to think of eternal, nonspatial, immaterial objects by making use of temporalized, spatialized, corporealized images or "phantasms" drawn from the senses, except where a purely negative knowledge of spiritual objects is concerned. We are told that "the investigation of the human reason for the most part has falsity present within it, and this is due partly to the weakness of our intellect in judgment, and partly to the admixture of images." [4] Rational knowledge of incorporeal things is thus inescapably distorted:

> Incorporeal beings, of which there are no phantasms, are known to us by comparison with sensible bodies of which there are phantasms. Thus we understand truth by considering a thing in which we see truth; and God, as Dionysius says, we know as cause, by way of excess and by way of remotion. Other incorporeal substances we know, in the state of the present life, only by way of remotion or by some comparison to corporeal things. Hence, when we understand something about these beings, we need to turn to the phantasms of bodies, although there are no phantasms of these beings themselves. [5]

Thus within the framework of reason alone we must think of angels as oversized men with wings, of God as the great white-bearded male giant in the sky, and the like. Just how serious and how consistent St. Thomas was about this matter of the corruption of rational knowledge by phantasms is difficult to say, but he repeatedly makes use of this consideration in explaining his subordination of philosophy to theology. [6] Somewhat inconsistently, he admits that revealed truth as put forward in Holy Scripture also makes use of sensory images, though not so much in some places as in others. [7] But the very thing that is a weakness for philosophy is a strength for theology:

> As Dionysius says, it is more fitting that divine truths should be expounded under the figure of less noble than of nobler bodies; and this for three reasons. First, because thereby men's minds are the better freed from error. For then it is clear that these

things are not literal descriptions of divine truths, which might have been open to doubt had they been expressed under the figure of nobler bodies, especially in the case of those who could think of nothing nobler than bodies. Second, because this is more befitting the knowledge of God that we have in this life. For what He is not is clearer to us than what He is. Therefore similitudes drawn from things farthest away from God form within us a truer estimate that God is above whatsoever we may say or think of Him. Third, because thereby divine truths are better hidden from the unworthy.[8]

Actually, our knowledge of divine things elicited in this world by both philosophy and theology still leaves a great deal to be desired, though theology is considerably less defective in this respect than philosophy. St. Thomas hopes that both kinds of defective knowledge will be supplanted in the next life by a more adequate way of knowing, the direct vision of divine things.[9]

St. Thomas's final reason for regarding philosophy as inferior to theology is that the latter is more generally available than metaphysics to the masses of men. Were it not for the faith response to revelation, few men would have any knowledge of God at all, since few men have the mental capacity, the time, or the energy for studying natural theology.[10] A world in which few men know God would be repugnant to a God of mercy and moral integrity;

> beneficially, therefore, did the divine Mercy provide that it should instruct us to hold by faith even those truths that the human reason is able to investigate. In this way, all men would easily be able to have a share in the knowledge of God, and this without uncertainty and error.[11]

Doubtless this summary of the Thomistic position raises many questions. After we explore some of the other ways of relating philosophy and theology, we should try to imagine how one systematic answer to the problem could be criticized from the vantage point of other systematic answers. For now, we shall consider two questions about the Thomistic position that must perplex us no matter which systematic resolution finally attracts us most: First, how does St. Thomas know that philosophy never contradicts theology, and second, what are the criteria for distinguishing genuine from spurious revelation?

DOES PHILOSOPHY EVER CONTRADICT THEOLOGY?

St. Thomas assures us that philosophy never contradicts theology. Truth is one, no matter how we arrive at it. The way up and the way down are the same. Only the *sources* of truth are twofold.

> Now, although the truth of the Christian faith which we have discussed surpasses the capacity of the reason, nevertheless that truth that the human reason is naturally endowed to know cannot be opposed to the truth of the Christian faith. For that with which the human reason is naturally endowed is clearly most true; so much so, that it is impossible for us to think of such truths as false. Nor is it permissible to believe as false that which we hold by faith, since this is confirmed in a way that is so clearly divine. Since, therefore, only the false is opposed to the true, as is clearly evident from an examination of their definitions, it is impossible that the truth of faith should be opposed to those principles that the human reason knows naturally.[12]

Given our vantage point in history, it is certainly surprising to be told that philosophy and theology never contradict each other. Many modern philosophers, such as Sartre and Dewey, insist that there is no supernatural God, and this clearly contradicts Christian supernaturalism. These and many others deny that there is experience after death or that morality and human values have any supernatural origin and sanction. Even from the perspective of St. Thomas's own day such a claim seems inexcusable if it is represented as descriptive of what philosophers and theologians actually say. Even Aristotle, whom St. Thomas regarded as "the Philosopher," implicitly denied the Christian doctrine of creation of the world *ex nihilo* by insisting that God and the world had coexisted with one another from eternity and by denying that the individual soul is immortal. Was St. Thomas simply ignorant of the fact that Aristotle and many other pre-Christian Greek philosophers, such as the Skeptics, often opposed, at least implicitly, some of the revealed truths of Christianity; or did he find some other way out of the difficulty?

Much Greek philosophy was not available to the Latin-speaking world in the thirteenth century, though many of the important works were available to the Moslem intellectual community in Arabic translations. Most of Aristotle had been rediscovered and translated into Latin, but the majority of the works of Plato and other Greek and Roman thinkers were unknown. Still, St. Thomas knew enough about Greek, Roman, and Arabic philosophy to realize that a simple description of what philosophers believe often results in an apparent conflict between philosophy and theology. He resolves the difficulty by insisting that where philosophers contradict theologians, the arguments with which they support their positions are always weak and inconclusive. For example, it is true that reason cannot prove the truth of creation *ex nihilo,* that this is a doctrine of faith alone, but it is also true that philosophy cannot produce an adequate proof of any contradictory theses.[13] Thus St. Thomas is not saying that philosophers never contradict theologians, but that *true* philosophy never contradicts theology. He informs us that:

> If in what the philosophers have said we come upon something that is contrary to faith, this does not belong to philosophy but is rather an abuse of philosophy arising from a defect in reason. It is therefore possible for the principles of philosophy to refute such an error by showing either that it is absolutely impossible or that it is not necessary, for just as what belongs to faith cannot be proved demonstratively, so certain notions contrary to these cannot be shown demonstratively to be wrong but can be shown not to be necessary.[14]

There is room for genuine suspicion that the claim that "true philosophy never contradicts revelation" is not an informative descriptive one. If *true philosophy* is understood to mean "philosophy that never contradicts revelation," then St. Thomas is telling us nothing more substantive than that "a philosophy that never contradicts revelation is a philosophy that never contradicts revelation."

WHAT CRITERIA DISTINGUISH GENUINE FROM SPURIOUS REVELATION?

The question of what constitutes genuine revelation is an important one, no matter which of the several positions that attach positive significance to revelation as a way of knowing religious truth one may hold. Again, from our modern vantage point, this problem may appear to be more serious than it did in the thirteenth century. This is an age of greatly increased communication between the devotees of the great world religions, an age of the confrontation of cultures. We can no longer be ignorant of or blind to the fact that the world religions differ drastically in doctrinal content, and we must wonder who is right and whether there is any way to distinguish genuine from spurious revelation. Even within our own Western culture, new sects are constantly springing up, based on new revelations. Why do we not join them? Revelations, like wonders, never seem to cease. On what grounds are they rejected? [15]

Of course, on a smaller scale there was also a confrontation of cultures in the thirteenth century. St. Thomas wrestled with the problem of the relation between Christianity and Mohammedanism. He rejected the Koran as spurious revelation because for him the crucial advantage of Christian truth over both Islam and all philosophical wisdom was that only Christian revelation is from God, who cannot be in error about himself. The superior position of theology over philosophy rests on the fact that theology "derives its certitude from the light of the divine science, which cannot err." [16] Theology "accepts its principles, not from the other sciences, but immediately from God, by revelation." [17] Sacred doctrine treats God "not only so far as He can be known through creatures just as philosophers knew Him . . . but also so far as He is known to Himself alone and revealed to others." [18] "For these 'secrets of divine Wisdom' . . . the divine Wisdom itself, which knows all things to the full, has deigned to reveal to men." [19] To insist that one's own doctrine is true because it comes from God is to beg the question, for one's opponents can say exactly the same thing about their own beliefs. Mohammed did precisely that, claiming that the Koran was from Allah. *If we are not already committed to one side or the other, how can we tell who is right?* To say that

Christianity alone is right because it alone is from God simply begs the question, for this is precisely the question in dispute!

St. Thomas marshaled other arguments against the authenticity of Mohammedan revelation as embodied in the Koran.[20] The main argument was that Christian revelation is always accompanied—and thus confirmed—by the working of miracles, whereas Mohammed "did not bring forth any signs produced in a supernatural way, which alone fittingly gives witness to divine inspiration; for a visible action that can be only divine reveals an invisibly inspired teacher of truth." [21] By contrast, Christian revelation is repeatedly confirmed by the working of miracles.[22]

This is not the proper place to subject the concept of *miracle* to philosophical analysis nor to produce any a priori arguments for or against the occurrence of miracles. It is enough to point out that the superiority of one world religion over all others cannot be justified on the grounds that it alone has miracle workers. It is true that Mohammed himself did not work miracles, as a matter of principle: Miracle working was so rampant in the Middle East in his day that he was convinced that it would prove nothing; but he did claim one miracle—the giving of the Koran. Moreover, miracle workers abound in other religions, such as Hinduism, Buddhism, and Greek Olympian polytheism; thus the working of miracles does not provide a valid criterion for separating genuine from spurious revelation. And even the Bible acknowledges that false prophets can work miracles.[23]

The Subordination of Theology to Philosophy: Hegel

GEORG Wilhelm Friedrich Hegel (1770–1831) was a philosopher who had a deep, lifelong interest in philosophy and theology and in the problem of how they are related. His solution to the problem was just the reverse of St. Thomas's. For Hegel philosophy was clearly superior to theology[24] as a source of knowledge about ultimate reality. The superiority of philosophy rested on the superiority of reasoned proof to unreasoned faith and on the preeminent clarity and purity of philosophical thinking. As we shall

preeminent

see, he would have found St. Thomas's reasons for subordinating philosophy to theology quite unconvincing. Indeed, in Hegel's eyes, theology was defective in some of the same ways in which St. Thomas believed philosophy to be defective.

Hegel distinguished between the form and the content of philosophy and theology. The content of both is the same, since the subject matter of both is reality as a whole in its ultimate and universal characteristics. In this respect both of them differ from the special sciences, such as biology, physics, and chemistry, which have selected fragments of reality as their subject matter. In Hegelian terms both philosophy and theology provide us with knowledge of the Absolute, which Hegel also calls God. It is not true that one discipline has exclusive access to special truths which only it can investigate and with which the other is incompetent to deal. The theologian knows just as much as and no more than the philosopher—though the philosopher knows it better. Theology suggests everything that philosophy knows. Philosophy simply makes explicit the truths that are implicit in theology, and historically philosophy emerges from theology as clarity emerges from confusion. Theology is regarded as a necessary preamble to and preparation for philosophy.

In form, however, philosophy and theology are quite different. In the first place, philosophy approaches God through reason, whereas theology approaches God through feeling and faith. What is known about ultimate reality in intuitive feeling by the theologian is *proved* to be true by the philosopher. Hegel agreed with his contemporary Schleiermacher that theology is generated out of a mystical feeling of unity with the object of religious knowledge. But what the theologian accepts on faith without adequate evidence is accepted by the philosopher on the basis of completely adequate evidence, and reason is perfectly competent to give us adequate knowledge of whatever there is to know about ultimate reality. Hegel would agree with St. Thomas that theology comes first to the masses of men and that only a few philosophical minds are capable of *knowing* the truth as opposed to merely *believing* it. Hegel did not regard this limitation as an indication that philosophy is defective, but rather that the masses of men are defective.

In the second place, the language in which theology speaks about

God is different from and inferior to that of philosophy. Theology employs the language of myth, whereas philosophy speaks the literal truth. When we understand what Hegel meant by mythical language, we see that in his opinion theology suffers from the same defect that St. Thomas attributed to philosophy—its thinking is corrupted by the admixture of sensory images. Hegel called this pictoral or representative or figurative thinking, and he contrasted it with the pure conceptual thinking of philosophy. Thus on the one hand mythical language is very close to art in the sense that it makes use of particular sensory images, but on the other hand it is also very close to philosophy since universal truths are implicitly contained within this welter of imagery. Mythology is sensory imagery used to conceive of nonsensory reality.

In contending that philosophical reasoning about divine things is inescapably corrupted by the admixture of sensory images, St. Thomas may or may not have been denying that philosophy has access to concepts not involving sensory images. If he was denying this, Hegel would have thought him clearly mistaken and would have produced examples of many pure philosophical concepts that reason itself generates and that do not involve sensory images. Among such concepts he would have mentioned those of *concept, being, nonbeing, becoming, subject, object, substance, part, whole, quantity, quality,* and *relation.* On this point he seems to have the better side of the argument. What would you say about the concepts of mathematics and formal logic?

We may wonder what is so defective about thought expressed through sensory imagery. Hegel's answer is that such thought can generate confusion by focusing our attention on the wrong aspect of the image and thus can seriously mislead us. If the gods are represented in human form, we are likely to take them as actually having human form. If God, man, and the world are seen as only accidentally related, we are likely to believe it. In Thomistic terms, if the incorporeal and eternal substances are represented in corporeal and temporal forms, we are all too likely to take them as actually possessing those forms. For Hegel, only the pure conceptual thought of philosophy can present us with knowledge of ultimate religious truth in a form that is not misleading and tainted with error. He tells us that theology sees through the form of mythical representations by virtue of which the life of the Absolute is pictured in seemingly discrete stories, quasi-temporal myths, and cultic symbols.

Philosophy uses such language without being taken captive by it. The revelation of the Absolute is not confined to religion, but can and must also be thought in the logical form of truth. This comprehensive truth corresponds to the comprehensive and eternal actuality of the Absolute in *all* its opposite manifestations.[25]

But is it so inevitable that we be misled by the images of theology? Is it not possible to clarify the meaning of our myths in such a way that their exact point is clearly stated? Hegel would reply that this is exactly what philosophy does: Philosophy is essentially the demythologizing of theology. To demythologize theological language is nothing more than to translate the "true meaning" of the figurative and confusing myths into a language that one regards as literal and clear. In Hegel's case this superior language was that of his own philosophical system, but many modern demythologizers, such as Rudolf Bultmann, prefer the language of Heidegger's existentialism. Theologians in high places are not the only ones who engage in demythologizing, however. Hardly a sermon is preached in Christendom in which the minister fails to tell his congregation the "true meaning" of a biblical story by using nonbiblical concepts and categories of interpretation. Who has not been informed at one time or another that "day" in the Genesis creation story really means "geological eon," that "angels" are actually only "unseen powers that work for righteousness," that "heaven" and "hell" are not real places but only "states of mind," and so on?

What is the literal truth about divine things, the actual content of philosophy, as Hegel understands it? To get a complete answer there is no substitute for reading Hegel. But, in brief, Hegel's view of the absolute truth boils down to this: God is the whole of reality, and all the parts of reality are necessary to that whole. Reality is rich in detail and content. As in Stoicism, reality and reason are regarded as identical. Reason develops itself through time, which is to say that reality and God develop through time; and there is a point to this development. In the beginning God does not know himself. It is through all the laws and processes of nature, human culture, human history, the state, law, morality, and human thought and creativity—including art, religion, and philosophy—that God comes to understand himself. These constitute the rich details of the parts of the whole, and the whole would not be what it is without them. Indeed, reason would not understand itself without them; for it is in human self-understanding that God comes to know himself. From unconscious reason in nature and natural law through fully self-conscious reason in philosophy, God gradually comes to understand himself through time. But he has no mind of his own. His mind is human mind, and he understands himself only insofar as we understand him. As Hegel says, this understanding is the end toward which everything aims:

> This being-at-home-with-self, or coming-to-self of Mind may be described as its complete and highest end: it is this alone that it desires and nothing else. Everything that from eternity has happened in heaven and earth, the life of God and all the deeds of time simply are the struggles for Mind to know itself, to make itself objective to itself, to find itself, be for itself, and finally unite itself to itself; it is alienated and divided, but only so as to be able thus to find itself and return to itself.[26]

For Hegel, it is only in speculative philosophy that this process of God's coming to know himself reaches its climax. "God is attainable in pure speculative knowledge alone, and only *is* in that knowledge, and is merely that knowledge itself." [27] What is the method of speculative philosophy? How can we translate the myths of theology into the literal truths of speculative philosophy?

WHAT IS THE METHOD OF SPECULATIVE PHILOSOPHY?

Hegel clearly states that the distinctive method of inquiry used by the speculative philosopher is not the empirical method of the natural sciences nor the deductive method of mathematics and formal logic, though these rational methods have their proper place in the scheme of human (and divine) knowledge. The philosopher's method is that of *dialectic,* which consists in subjecting all historical views about the ultimate nature of things to relentless critical examination; acknowledging their incompleteness and incoherence; observing that they give rise to other views that attempt to compensate for their confusion, incompleteness, and incoherence and that these views are themselves confused, incomplete, and incoherent; formulating a more complete and coherent account; and repeating the whole process over and over again until at last a genuinely clear, comprehensive, and coherent view of the nature of ultimate reality is attained.[28] Hegel subjected the whole history of philosophy to this type of dialectical analysis, and he was confident that in his own philosophical system all the one-sided truths of his philosophical predecessors were contained in a genuinely rational whole of human-divine self-understanding. Philosophy cannot exist apart from its history. Hegel tells us that "the history of Philosophy is a revelation of what has been the aim of spirit throughout its history; it is therefore the world's history in its innermost signification." [29] The common charge that Hegel thought that philosophizing should have ceased with Hegel, since at last in the Hegelian system the Absolute had come to understand itself fully, is not completely justified; for Hegel says that his own philosophical view "is the standpoint of the present day, and the series of spiritual forms is with it for the present concluded." [30] He does not say that philosophy is *forever* concluded. We may want to quarrel with the results of this method as Hegel applied it—that is, with the contents of philosophy as Hegel presented them to us. But what of the method itself? Would not that insight into ultimate reality that is subjected to relentless criticism and is perfectly clear, coherent, and comprehensive be the truth? What more could we want? For one thing, we might also want consistency, which Hegel himself at times did not seem to regard as a virtue. What else might we require of such a method?

HOW CAN WE TRANSLATE THE MYTHS OF THEOLOGY INTO THE LITERAL TRUTHS OF SPECULATIVE PHILOSOPHY?

There are many assumptions underlying this question. It assumes that we have a clear and viable distinction between myth and literal language. We have seen that Hegel offered a distinction; try subjecting it to critical analysis to determine whether it is valid. The question also assumes that a literal language is available into which we can translate the myths of theology. Are we satisfied that the Hegelian vocabulary is adequate? Where could we find an adequate literal vocabulary—in Heidegger's existentialism, in Aristotle's ontology, in natural science, or where?

For dialectical purposes, let us grant Hegel his assumptions. He certainly assures us that philosophy *can* make clear and explicit what is confused and implicit in theological language. He also generously provides us with the outcome of the process. As we have seen, St. Thomas Aquinas insisted that there are certain truths of revelation that reason cannot investigate, but Hegel thought that reason can discover the "real truth" implicit in the myths that St. Thomas perhaps took a bit too literally. To the Thomistic claim that these revealed truths are necessary for man's salvation, Hegel would reply that the theological doctrine of salvation is itself only a myth, the real truth of which only philosophy can discover. In summary form, here are some of the results of Hegel's demythologization:

MYTH	LITERAL TRUTH
God is Father.	Reality may be thought of as an abstract whole without at the same time thinking of the rich details of its parts.
God is Son.	Reality is rich in parts and may be thought of as objectifying itself in its parts.
God is Holy Spirit.	The whole and the parts are united and come to know this in developing self-consciousness.
God created the world.	The whole objectifies and actualizes itself in its parts.
God is incarnate in a man.	Humanity is one with the whole of reality.

MYTH	LITERAL TRUTH
Christ atones.	Finitude and suffering are necessary parts of the whole.
Men are sinners.	Men declare their independence of the whole.
Men are saved or reconciled.	Men come to realize and accept their unity with the whole.
Life is eternal.	Men love God and are loved by him here and now.

Unfortunately, Hegel gives only the results of his translations from the mythical, figurative language of theology into the literally true language of philosophy; he does not provide us with the rules of procedure by which he moves from the one to the other. He does not tell us *how* to do it correctly or why his translations are correct and other translations incorrect. In all likelihood, this problem is resolved no better by modern demythologizers, such as Rudolf Bultmann, who prefer to translate the myths of the Bible into the language of existentialism, than it was by Hegel. If it should turn out finally that there are no rules for making such translations, then we shall be left with only a radical form of Protestantism in which the myths of theology mean whatever the individual wants them to mean. In that case interpretation would be more of an art than a science, and demythologizing might be only remythologizing.

Suggestions for Further Reading

THE THOMISTIC SUBORDINATION OF PHILOSOPHY AND THEOLOGY

AQUINAS, ST. THOMAS, *On the Truth of the Catholic Faith,* trans. by Anton C. Pegis (Garden City, N.Y., Doubleday, 1957), esp. Book I, General Introduction by Anton C. Pegis, pp. 15–44, and pp. 59–76; Book IV, pp. 35–40.

COPLESTON, FREDERICK, *A History of Philosophy,* Vol. II (London, Burns Oates & Washbourne, 1950), Chapter 32.

GILSON, ETIENNE, *Elements of Christian Philosophy* (New York, Doubleday Mentor-Omega Books, 1960), pp. 11–45.

PEGIS, ANTON C., ed., *Basic Writings of Saint Thomas Aquinas,* Vol. I (New York, Random House, 1945), pp. 5–24.

HEGEL'S OWN DISCUSSIONS OF THE PROBLEM

HEGEL, GEORG WILHELM FRIEDRICH, *Encyclopedia of Philosophy* (New York, Philosophical Library, 1959), pp. 276–87.

————, *Lectures on the History of Philosophy,* Vol. I (New York, Humanities Press, 1955), pp. 61–81.

————, *Lectures on the Philosophy of Religion,* Vol. I (New York, Humanities Press, 1968), pp. 18–23.

————, *The Phenomenology of Mind* (New York, Humanities Press, 1955), pp. 750–808.

SOME CONTEMPORARY DISCUSSIONS OF DEMYTHOLOGIZING

BARTSCH, H. W., ed., *Kerygma and Myth* (London, S.P.C.K., 1957). This is a theological debate on demythologizing with a lead essay by Rudolf Bultmann.

BULTMANN, RUDOLF, *Jesus Christ and Mythology* (New York, Scribner's, 1958).

HEPBURN, RONALD W., "Demythologizing and the Problem of Validity," in Antony Flew and Alasdair MacIntyre, eds., *New Essays in Philosophical Theology* (New York, Macmillan, 1955), pp. 227–42.

KNOX, JOHN, *Myth and Truth* (Charlottesville, Va., University Press of Virginia, 1964).

MACQUARRIE, JOHN, *God-Talk* (New York, Harper & Row, 1967), Chapter 8.

————, *The Scope of Demythologizing* (New York, Harper & Row, 1968), especially Chapters 6 and 7.

Notes

1   St. Thomas Aquinas, *On the Truth of the Catholic Faith,* trans. by Anton C. Pegis (Garden City, N.Y., Doubleday, 1957), Book I, p. 63. The first three of the four books deal with those truths of faith that reason can investigate: Book I with God, Book II with Creation, and Book III with Providence and man. In Book IV we come to those truths of faith that reason is not competent to investigate.

2   *Ibid.,* Book IV, pp. 39–40.
3   Anton C. Pegis, ed., *Basic Writings of Saint Thomas Aquinas,* Vol. I (New York, Random House, 1945), p. 6.
4   Aquinas, *On the Truth of the Catholic Faith,* Book I, p. 68.
5   Pegis, *Basic Writings of Saint Thomas Aquinas,* Vol. I, p. 80.
6   St. Thomas Aquinas makes many passing references to this claim that rational knowledge of religious truth is corrupted by the admixture of sensory images. For examples see *On the Truth of the Catholic Faith,* Book I, pp. 64, 65, 68.
7   Pegis, *Basic Writings of Saint Thomas Aquinas,* Vol. I, p. 15.
8   *Ibid.,* p. 16.
9   Aquinas, *On the Truth of the Catholic Faith,* Book IV, pp. 37, 38.
10 *Ibid.,* Book I, pp. 66, 67.
11 *Ibid.,* p. 68.
12 *Ibid.,* p. 74.
13 *Ibid.,* Book II, Chapters 35–38; and Pegis, *Basic Writings of Saint Thomas Aquinas,* Vol. I, pp. 449–53.
14 Aquinas, *On the Truth of the Catholic Faith,* Book I, p. 25.
15 *The Book of Mormon* is one example of a modern revelation. See also Leon Festinger, Henry W. Riecken, and Stanley Schachter, *When Prophecy Fails* (New York, Harper & Row, 1956); and Charles S. Braden, *These Also Believe* (New York, Macmillan, 1949).
16 Pegis, *Basic Writings of Saint Thomas Aquinas,* Vol. I, p. 9.
17 *Ibid.,* p. 10.
18 *Ibid.,* p. 11.
19 Aquinas, *On the Truth of the Catholic Faith,* Book I, p. 71.
20 *Ibid.,* pp. 73, 74.
21 *Ibid.,* p. 73.
22 *Ibid.,* pp. 72, 73, 77.
23 See Deuteronomy 13:1–3; and compare Revelation 13:13–14.
24 Hegel actually uses the term *religion* where we shall use the word *theology.* Hegel gives his own persuasive definition of *religion,* which reduces it to the knowledge of some of the doctrinal or cognitive traits of religion. What he calls religion is roughly what we have earlier identified as theology, and theology is only a small part of *religion* as we ordinarily understand the term today.
25 Georg Wilhelm Friedrich Hegel, *Encyclopedia of Philosophy* (New York, Philosophical Library, 1959), pp. 283–84.
26 Georg Wilhelm Friedrich Hegel, *Lectures on the History of Philosophy,* Vol. I (New York, Humanities Press, 1955), p. 23.

27 Georg Wilhelm Friedrich Hegel, *The Phenomenology of Mind* (New York, Humanities Press, 1955), p. 761.
28 For Hegel's own discussion of dialectical method, see the *Encyclopedia of Philosophy,* pp. 67–77.
29 Hegel, *Lectures on the History of Philosophy,* Vol. III, p. 547.
30 *Ibid.,* p. 552.

chapter four

The Relation of Philosophy and Theology SOME EXTREME POSITIONS

The Elimination of Theology in Favor of Philosophy: Rationalism

S⊤. Thomas Aquinas clearly regarded philosophy as inferior to theology, and Hegel regarded philosophy as superior, at least in form, to theology, but neither proposed that the other discipline had no useful or essential contribution to make to the human attempt to know ultimate religious truth. However, other philosophers have taken more extreme positions. Some have suggested that theology is at least in principle dispensable, that it ought to be and ultimately will be eliminated as a source of religious truth as men become more rational. Some of those who hold this view maintain that theology has always done more harm than good and that the human race would have fared far better without theology, faith, priesthood, and all the elements of irrationalism that tend to accompany them. All who would eliminate theology in favor of philosophy agree that reason alone is the sole reliable and authentic source of truth and that the total elimination of theology would be no great loss.

Rationalism has several distinct but perfectly legitimate meanings. In a broad sense, a rationalist is one who is committed to the view that reason alone (as opposed to faith or revelation) is the only reliable source of truth. A rationalist in this sense is not necessarily a rationalist in the narrower sense of one who holds that the intuition of self-evident axioms and logical deductions from them constitute the basic methodology of philosophy and even of science. Within the broad sense of *rationalism,* with which we are presently concerned, we can identify and distinguish both theistic and atheistic rationalism. In our discussions, theistic rationalism will be represented primarily by the eighteenth-century Deists; atheistic rationalism will be represented mainly by John Dewey of our own century, though someone like Bertrand Russell might have served our present purposes just as well.

THEISTIC RATIONALISM: EIGHTEENTH-CENTURY ENLIGHTENMENT

During the eighteenth century, the prevailing philosophical climate in both Europe and America was one of total confidence in the ability of human reason to know all truths and to solve all social problems. With respect to items of religious belief, it was generally agreed that adequate philosophical proofs could be produced for the existence of God, the creation of the world, the immortality of the soul, and the absoluteness and universality of morality. (The traditional metaphysical proofs for the existence of God were especially popular, particularly the teleological argument, or the argument from design, which attempts to prove that the universe was designed and created by an intelligent and powerful "Author of Nature.") Although they differed from one another in many details, the Deists of the eighteenth century and the later Transcendentalists and Unitarians tended to agree that such items of religious belief were within the reach of reason alone, and that other religious doctrines, such as the Trinity, the Incarnation, and transubstantiation, were dispensable if not dangerous. These doctrines were relegated to the realm of irrational superstitions. It was believed that faith in God, the Creation, immortality, and morality constituted the heart of that true religion that was natural to all men everywhere, and that except for priestly corruptions these doctrines were taught in all the religions of the world. We saw how mistaken they were about that in our discussion of the search for family resemblances in Chapter 1. The true task of reason, they believed, was to strip away all the superficial trappings and theological corruptions that the priesthood had introduced into the historical religions for its own ends and to allow these simple, common-sense, natural, intuitively self-evident truths to prevail.

The confidence of the Age of Enlightenment in the ability of reason to solve all religious problems was reflected in the titles of many of the books that were written in this era: John Locke, *The Reasonableness of Christianity* (1695); John Toland, *Christianity Not Mysterious* (1696); Matthew Tindal, *Christianity as Old as Creation* (1730); Thomas Chubb, *The Sufficiency of Reason in Matters of Religion* (1732); Ethan Allen, *Reason the Only Oracle of Man* (1784); Immanuel Kant, *Religion Within the Limits of Reason Alone* (1793); Thomas Paine, *The Age of Reason* (1793–95).

We shall consider whether these Enlightenment writers were correct or incorrect in thinking that reason could prove the existence of God and other such matters when we examine in detail the philosophical proofs for the existence of God in Chapters 9, 10, and 11; but it is clear that the tenability of the position of theistic rationalism depends heavily on favorable results of these proofs. We should also note that one of the most devastating criticisms of rationalistic optimism in religion ever produced also appeared during the great Age of Reason: David Hume's *Dialogues Concerning Natural Religion,* published posthumously in 1779. After Hume's withering attack on "natural religion," general philosophical confidence in the ability of man's reason to deal with divine things was never the same.

As for revelation, the theistic rationalists had little confidence in it. Some of them were willing to admit the abstract possibility that revelations might be given to selected individuals, but they insisted that if such a thing did happen it was stale, secondhand information when passed along to anyone else. Others believed that revelations were given as a temporary expedient to a primitive humanity that had not yet reached the age of mature rationality, but the theology based on these revelations had been corrupted through the ages, and reason was required to separate the pure truth of religion from its perversions. All those who attached any significance to the notion of revelation agreed that genuine revelations could be distinguished from spurious revelations only by the use of rational criteria and that ultimately reason could eliminate reliance on revelation.

Other theistic rationalists were even more skeptical. They were convinced that all claims to revelation were spurious, that they were inventions of the priesthood designed to deceive the populace and to further the advantage of the priestly and ruling classes. Thomas Paine (1737–1809) wrote that "the Christian theory is little else than the idolatry of the ancient mythologists, accommodated to the purposes of power and revenue; and it yet remains to reason and philosophy to abolish the amphibious fraud." [1] Paine summarized his objections to the notion of revelation as follows:

> The idea or belief of a word of God existing in print, or in writing, or in speech, is inconsistent in itself for the reasons already assigned. These reasons, among many others, are the want of a universal language; the mutability of language; the errors to which translations are subject; the possibility of totally suppressing such a word; the probability of altering it, or of fabricating the whole, and imposing it upon the world. [2]

The most popular argument against the notion of revelation, however, was a moral one: The scriptures present us with so many immoralities supposedly sanctioned by God that there can be no truth in them. Paine wrote,

> Whenever we read the obscene stories, the voluptuous debaucheries, the cruel and torturous executions, the unrelenting vindictiveness, with which more than half the Bible [that is, the Old Testament] is filled, it would be more consistent that we called it the word of a demon, than the Word of God. It is a history of wickedness, that has served to corrupt and brutalize mankind; and, for my own part, I sincerely detest it, as I detest everything that is cruel. [3]

Although Jesus was generally admired as a great moral teacher, the overall theology of the New Testament also came under attack on moral grounds. The doctrine of the Incarnation presupposed that God had illicit intercourse with a human virgin betrothed to another man, and the doctrine of the blood atonement involved a divine murder and vindictiveness unworthy even of a scoundrel.

Paine expressed his opinion of a sermon he had heard as a child on the doctrine of redemption by the death of the Son of God as follows:

> I revolted at the recollection of what I had heard, and thought to myself that it was making God Almighty act like a passionate man, that killed his son, when he could not revenge himself in any other way; and as I was sure a man would be hanged that did such a thing, I could not see for what purpose they preached such sermons. This was not one of those kind of thoughts that had any thing in it of childish levity; it was to me a serious reflection, arising from the idea I had that God was too good to do such an action, and also too almighty to be under any necessity of doing it. I believe in the same manner to this moment; and I moreover believe, that any system of religion that has anything in it that shocks the mind of a child, cannot be a true system.
>
> . . . But the Christian story of God the Father putting his son to death, or employing people to do it, (for that is the plain language of the story), cannot be told by a parent to a child; and to tell him that it was done to make mankind happier and better, is making the story still worse; as if mankind could be improved by the example of murder; and to tell him that all this is a mystery, is only making an excuse for the incredibility of it.[4]

The theistic rationalists always seemed to take the myths of theology quite literally, and consequently they had little difficulty in ridiculing supposed revelations.

The theistic rationalists of the eighteenth century also launched their own attack on the claim that authentic revelation may be recognized as such because it is accompanied by miracles. They followed Newton in their confidence in the absolute lawfulness and orderliness of nature. They argued that when God created the world, he did either a perfect job or an imperfect job. If he did a perfect job, there was no need for him to interfere with the orderly workings of events within the world, since any deviation from perfection would be for the worse. If there was a need for him to suspend the laws of nature, this implied that he had bungled the job in the beginning. For theists, this was hardly an admissible hypothesis. Besides, it was much more credible that those who had reported the occurrence of miracles were liars than that the order of nature had been temporarily suspended. Who do you think has the better side of this argument?

ATHEISTIC RATIONALISM: JOHN DEWEY

Innumerable philosophers who are committed to reason as the only reliable source of truth are convinced that reason cannot prove that God exists, that the soul is immortal, that morality is absolute, and so on. So much the worse for theistic religion, they tell us. The case for atheistic rationalism has never been better stated than by John Dewey (1859–1952) in *A Common Faith.* In one sense Dewey is not an atheist, for he does sponsor a concept of *God,* which we shall examine in Chapter 6; but in relation to traditional metaphysical and supernaturalist concepts of *God* he is an atheist. Also, in the narrow sense of *rationalism* Dewey is not a rationalist; but in the broad sense, in which reliance on reason alone instead of faith and revelation is emphasized, he is a rationalist. Dewey, as a naturalist for whom the world of nature as a whole constitutes the sum total of reality, held that the operations of scientific method take place within nature and will not carry us beyond nature to the supernatural. Consequently, in his opinion there are no supernatural entities. If scientific methodology cannot lead us to a supernatural God and immortality, then we must learn to do without them and find viable substitutes for them, such as human ideals and human fulfillment here and now.

Dewey wrote during an era in which most theologians, with the exception of the fundamentalists, were facing up to the gradual encroachment of modern scientific ideas on traditional religious doctrines. The liberal theologians were willing to admit that the theory of evolution had made untenable the doctrine of specific creation, that developments in astronomy and geology had made the Genesis story of the seven days of creation seem like a fairy tale, that modern views of the spatiotemporal universe had made the doctrines of "heaven above and hell below" and Christ's ascension into heaven unacceptable to the modern mind, and so on. Dewey points out that every time a traditional religious doctrine is surrendered to the onslaught of modern science, the liberal theologians counter with the claim that "the particular doctrine or supposed historic or literary tenet surrendered was never, after all, an intrinsic part of religious belief, and that without it the true nature of religion stands out more clearly than before." [5] Modern liberals think that they can surrender such doctrines to science and still retain the "essence of Christianity," which consists of belief in the existence of a benevolent and powerful God who eternally rewards the righteous and punishes the wicked, and a belief in the brotherhood of man. This hard core of religious belief is all that really matters, say the liberals. All else can be surrendered to science without significant loss.

Dewey finds great difficulties with the position of the liberals who take pride in being more "rational" than their fundamentalist opponents who are unwilling thus to compromise with science. In one sense the liberals are worse off than the fundamentalists because of the poverty of their doctrinal framework. They have little to believe in and hope for, whereas the fundamentalists have much. However, as Dewey points out, both liberals and fundamentalists are in the same predicament in the sense that even the liberals insist on preserving for themselves "a certain indispensable minimum of intellectual content" [6] that has not been obtained by, and is not obtainable by, the use of the scientific method. What the liberals do not realize is that no item of belief is justified unless it can be supported by the use of the scientific method. Reason is the only source of truth, and the method of reason is simply the method of science. Dewey tells us that

> what is not realized—although perhaps it is more definitely seen by fundamentalists than by liberals—is that the issue does not concern this and that piecemeal *item* of belief, but centers in the question of the method by which any and every item of intellectual belief is to be arrived at and justified. . . . The fundamental question, I repeat, is not of this and that article of intellectual belief but of intellectual habit, method and criterion. . . . The mind of man is being habituated to a new method and ideal: There is but one sure road to access to truth—the road of patient, cooperative inquiry operating by means of observation, experiment, record and controlled reflection. . . . The scientific-religious conflict ultimately is a conflict between allegiance to this

method and allegiance to even an irreducible minimum of belief
so fixed in advance that it can never be modified.[7]

Dewey correctly points out that modern science is not itself
to be identified with any particular set of beliefs but rather with
a methodology for obtaining rationally justified beliefs.[8] Theology,
by contrast, consists of items of belief that are held by "faith" and
that have not been and in Dewey's opinion cannot be justified by
the use of the scientific method. He certainly focuses attention on
the crucial question: What rational method, if any, may we use
in justifying our religious beliefs? Unless we have an adequate
answer, we can never claim that our religion has a rational foundation; and it would seem that our most cherished religious beliefs
are no more valid than the rankest of superstitions. But we may
also want to know: Is the scientific method the only legitimate
method of reason? If so, then what exactly are the limits of the
scientific method? We shall return to these questions in later discussions, though the first question has already been answered
negatively in our discussion of the Hegelian dialectic.

In trying to discover a rational foundation for religious beliefs,
we must ask ourselves the question: Why is it that there are so
many denominations and such a proliferation of diverse doctrines
even within Christendom, to say nothing of the world religions
generally? Aside from historical explanations of the origin and
promulgation of differing theological opinions, there is perhaps
one crucial epistemological explanation, which is suggested by
Dewey's attack on the theologians. Perhaps the main difficulty
with theology is that it simply has no method for justifying its
beliefs and resolving its disputes. Perhaps theologians are destined to disagree endlessly about the content of religious truth,
with no method for, and thus no hope of, resolving their disagreements, except by the irrational methods of indoctrinating children
and converting adults through excessive emotional appeals. Protestants tenaciously adhere to their cherished beliefs, and Catholics
tenaciously adhere to theirs; but there is simply no way to *know*
who is right, since by their own admission it is all merely a matter
of faith. Theology endures because of the obstinacy of the theologians, but theologians who disagree with one another on truly

fundamental issues can never hope to resolve their differences. In the final analysis one man's faith is as correct as another's; or perhaps there is no such thing as correctness in such matters, because there are no epistemological criteria of correctness and incorrectness.

In a sense, the ordinary religious believer might easily find himself in agreement with this type of attack on theology. Although in practice he will "argue his religion" any time, anywhere, he often professes that he does not like to do so, that there is no point in it. Why does he say this? He may intuitively sense that there is no way to resolve theological disagreement, that in the final analysis there are no methods available for doing so. Certainly philosophers of religion would generally subscribe to this sort of attack on theology. Of course, the atheistic rationalists believe that theistic rationalists as well as theologians are without method and that their search for a rationally justified theism is futile. Whether or not any attempt to do constructive philosophizing about religious issues is futile is a question to be resolved at the end of the study of the philosophy of religion rather than near the beginning.

The Elimination of Philosophy in Favor of Theology: The Crisis Theologians

T HE solution to the problem of the relation of philosophical metaphysics and theology that is most widely accepted at the present time in continental European theological circles is that which has been worked out by such "crisis theologians" as Karl Barth and Emil Brunner, who believe that God intervenes at certain critical points in human history to make himself and his will known to men. For the crisis theologians, as for the atheistic rationalists, the enterprise of rational or natural theology is a colossal failure. Yet they insist that revealed theology is a spectacular success. The former should be eliminated, but God will preserve the latter. The crisis theologians are more than willing to admit that philosophical attempts to prove the existence of a personal God, immortality, and even absolute morality are a fraud; and they are delighted by philosophical skeptics, such as Hume, who arrive at the conclusion on philosophical grounds that reason is impotent to deal constructively with divine things. Yet, rather than give up divine things, they give up reason. As Martin Luther put it, "Reason is a whore."

This is not to say that the crisis theologians reject the authority of reason in its own "proper" spheres, such as in scientific and historical investigation. God gave us reason to use in these spheres. What the crisis theologians reject is the use of reason in matters of religion and ethics. The theistic rationalists of the eighteenth century believed that we could simply read the "book of nature" or the "book of creation" and find religious truths engraved therein; but the crisis theologians are convinced that those who claim to arrive thus at constructive results are either simply reading the revealed truth about the existence of a personal God *into* nature rather than *off of* nature, or else they are finding there merely a false god. The whole enterprise of natural theology is a subterfuge, and as such it must be eliminated. This is not to say that all the crisis theologians deny that God left an imprint of himself on the world of nature and the spirit of man that is there to be read by anyone capable of seeing it. On biblical grounds they generally affirm that there is a "revelation in Creation," and Brunner believes that the futile human attempts to know divine things made by philosophers of religion and by all the non-Christian religions of the world are pale reflections of this revelation. The difficulty with the rational attempt to know God is that human reason itself has been corrupted by original sin and is in no position to interpret correctly the evidence that would otherwise be open to all. It is because of original sin that philosophical metaphysics and value theory must be eliminated and that the non-Christian religions of the world are mere idolatrous confusions. Brunner tells us that

> the fact that sinful human beings cannot help having thoughts about God is due to the revelation in Creation. The other fact, that human beings are not able rightly to understand the nature and meaning of this revelation in Creation is due to the fact that their vision has been distorted by sin.[9]

He goes on to note that

> between the revelation in Creation and the natural man there
> stands the fact of Sin. . . . Sin not only perverts the will, it also
> "obscures" the power of perceiving truth where the knowledge
> of God is concerned. So where a man supports the view of the
> reality of a *"theologia naturalis"* in the sense of correct, valid
> knowledge, he is actually denying the reality of sin, or at least
> its effect in the sphere of man's knowledge of God. . . .
>
> The history of religions shows that mankind cannot help pro-
> ducing religious ideas and carrying on religious activities. It also
> shows the confusion caused by sin. . . .
>
> From the beginning of Greek philosophy men have continu-
> ally tried to reach a clear and certain knowledge of God, not
> along the path of religion, but by the way of philosophy, by the
> speculative thought, and thus to overcome the irrationalism of
> the purely religious formation of ideas. These philosophical doc-
> trines of God now confront one another in irreconcilable oppo-
> sition. Above all, none of them can possibly be combined with
> the Christian Idea of God. The relation of the "God" of Plato
> or of Aristotle with the God of the Biblical revelation is that of
> the Either-Or. The same may be said of every other idea of God
> which has been attained purely by philosophical speculation . . .
> the God of thought *must* differ from the God of revelation. The
> God who is "conceived" by thought is not the one who discloses
> Himself; from this point of view He is an intellectual idol.[10]

The crisis theologians produce *ad hominem* arguments against
anyone who disagrees with their position. Everyone who refuses
to see things their way is simply a hell-bound sinner, because doubt
about the validity of their position is itself a manifestation of sin.
Brunner defines doubt as "the intellectual form of sin." [11] He explains that

> doubt is not a function of the reason as such, but it is the fruit
> of the falsely autonomous human reason, which sets itself up as
> an absolute authority. It does not spring from the erroneous and
> sinful fundamental axiom that human reason is the measure of
> all things, that everything that lays any claim to truth must prove
> itself before the court of rational argument. This declaration of

sovereignty and autonomy by the human reason is simply the desire to be like God, or self-deification.[12]

What the crisis theologians do not explain is why it is not equally arrogant for the theologian to presume that he gets his beliefs "straight from the horse's mouth," so to speak, rather than from human reason. If theologians are also sinners, then whom should we believe?

One difficulty with the position that original sin spells the doom of philosophical metaphysics and ethics is that even the theologians who accept the doctrine of original sin are not agreed as to its effect on the mind of man. Just how errant is the intelligence of man because of Adam's sin? Even from the theologians we get a wide spectrum of answers. The extreme position of the crisis theologians is only one possibility. Another point of view is represented by the Thomistic tradition, which holds that human intelligence is weakened but not made impotent by original sin. Natural theology was a genuine path to the knowledge of some religious truth for St. Thomas, in spite of his commitment to the revealed doctrine of original sin. In discussing the penalties that humanity suffers as a consequence of original sin, St. Thomas wrote that

> greatest, of course, among the spiritual penalties is the frailty of reason: from this it happens that man with difficulty arrives at knowledge of the truth; that with ease he falls into error; and that he cannot entirely overcome his beastly appetites, but is over and over again beclouded by them.[13]

Until theologians decide among themselves whether original sin makes reason frail or impotent in metaphysics, it would appear that philosophers have little cause for alarm.

A more serious philosophical difficulty with the position of the crisis theologians is the vicious logical circularity of their argument. The doctrine of original sin is a revealed doctrine that is used to prove that only revealed doctrines are true. Anyone who questions the authenticity of all claims to revelation will hardly be persuaded by such an argument. If one does not accept the revealed doctrine of original sin in the first place, then there is no problem. The argument convinces only those who are already convinced; but it has no logical force, however psychologically persuasive it might be to those who already believe. Is there any significant difference between using reason to prove that only reasoned doctrines are true and using revelation to prove that only revealed doctrines are true?

Another difficulty with the position of the crisis theologians is their insistence that there are revealed truths that lie entirely beyond all attempts to rationally justify our beliefs, which simply makes more pointed Dewey's insistence that theologians have no method for justifying their beliefs and resolving their disagreements, and that as a consequence "anything goes" in theology. Brunner himself says that not every claim to revelation is authentic, that "not all that comes in the name of revelation *is* revelation." [14] But the criteria that the crisis theologians offer to distinguish between genuine and spurious revelations simply will not do. It is not sufficient to say that genuine revelations are from God himself and carry with them the witness of the Spirit, whereas spurious revelations are merely human constructions. This simply fails to discern which ones are indeed from God, and that is precisely the question at issue. In all sincerity Mohammed claimed that the Koran was from God. Anyone who feels deeply about his beliefs and is able to work up a sustained enthusiasm for them can claim that God attests to their authenticity, and innumerable heretics have made just that claim. But no methods seem to be available for determining which revelations are from God and which ones are not. Every heresy is God-authenticated to its adherents, and that which can be used to prove everything actually proves nothing.

Suggestions for Further Reading

SELECTED WRITINGS OF THEISTIC RATIONALISTS

ALLEN, ETHAN, *Reason the Only Oracle of Man* (New York, Scholar's Facsimiles & Reprints, 1940), especially Chapter 1, Section 2, which presents the teleological argument; Chapter 6, which attacks revelation; and Chapter 7, which attacks miracles.

CONWAY, M. D., ed., *The Writings of Thomas Paine,* Vol. IV (New

York, Putnam's, 1896), especially pp. 45–46 and 236–46, on the teleological argument; pp. 23–25 ff., on revelation; and pp. 77–81, on miracles.

VOLTAIRE, *The Sermon of the Fifty* (New York, Ross Paxton, 1934).

DEWEY ON SCIENTIFIC METHOD AND RELIGION

DEWEY, JOHN, *A Common Faith* (New Haven, Conn., Yale University Press, 1934), especially Chapter 2.

———, "Antinaturalism in Extremis," in Y. H. Krikorian, ed., *Naturalism and the Human Spirit* (New York, Columbia University Press, 1944), pp. 1–16.

HARTSHORNE, CHARLES, *Reality as Social Process* (New York, Free Press, 1953), Chapters 11 and 12.

LAMONT, CORLISS, "New Light on Dewey's Common Faith," *Journal of Philosophy,* Vol. LVIII (January 1961), pp. 21–28.

RANDALL, JOHN H., JR., "The Religion of Shared Experience," in Sidney Ratner, ed., *The Philosophy of the Common Man* (New York, Putnam's, 1940).

SCHAUB, EDWARD L., "Dewey's Interpretation of Religion," in Paul A. Schilpp, ed., *The Philosophy of John Dewey* (New York, Tudor, 1951), pp. 393–416.

THOMPSON, SAMUEL M., *A Modern Philosophy of Religion* (Chicago, Henry Regnery, 1955), pp. 219–26.

RELEVANT DISCUSSIONS BY THE CRISIS THEOLOGIANS

BARTH, KARL, *Church Dogmatics,* Vol. II (Edinburgh, T. & T. Clark, 1957), Part I, pp. 79–85, Barth's attack on the Thomistic synthesis of theology and metaphysics.

———, *The Knowledge of God and the Service of God According to the Reformation* (London, Hodder and Stoughton, 1938), especially Lecture I.

BRUNNER, EMIL, *Revelation and Reason,* trans. by Olive Wyon (Philadelphia, Westminster Press, 1946), especially Chapters 14, 21, and 22.

———, *The Christian Doctrine of God,* trans. by Olive Wyon (Philadelphia, Westminster Press, 1950), especially pp. 132–36 and Chapter 3.

———, *The Philosophy of Religion* (London, James Clarke, 1958), especially Chapter 5.

Notes

1   M. D. Conway, ed., *The Writings of Thomas Paine,* Vol. IV (New York, Putnam's, 1896), p. 25.
2   *Ibid.,* p. 83.
3   *Ibid.,* p. 34.
4   *Ibid.,* p. 65.
5   John Dewey, *A Common Faith* (New Haven, Conn., Yale University Press, 1934), p. 32.
6   *Ibid.,* p. 30.
7   *Ibid.,* pp. 32, 34, 39.
8   *Ibid.,* pp. 38–39.
9   From *The Christian Doctrine of God* by Emil Brunner, trans. by Olive Wyon, p. 134. Copyright MCML by W. L. Jenkins, the Westminster Press. Used by permission. Permission also granted by Lutterworth Press.
10 *Ibid.,* pp. 133, 135–36.
11 From *Revelation and Reason* by Emil Brunner, trans. by Olive Wyon, p. 208. Copyright MCMXLVI by W. L. Jenkins, the Westminster Press. Used by permission.
12 *Idem.*
13 St. Thomas Aquinas, *On the Truth of the Catholic Faith* (Garden City, N.Y., Doubleday, 1957), Book IV, p. 218.
14 Brunner, *Revelation and Reason,* p. 204.

The Elimination of "Subject Matter" from Both Philosophy and Theology: Logical Positivism

Dᴜʀɪɴɢ the 1920's and 1930's, a philosophical movement developed and flourished that was convinced that it had finally found a panacea for all man's metaphysical and theological ills. Many different labels have been applied to this movement; we shall call it logical positivism, since that label is probably as accurate and suggestive as any. Although the logical positivists had many differences of opinion with respect to the issues that concerned them, we shall begin with a sort of generalized summary of positivistic thought at its best. Then we shall attempt to decide whether or not positivism was in fact the cure-all that it optimistically believed itself to be in its heyday.

To begin with, the positivists correctly pointed out that there is a significant logical difference between the notions of the *truth* or *falsity* of a proposition and the notion of the *meaning* of a proposition. If someone said to you, "Blue is more identical than music," [1] your initial reaction in all likelihood would not be "Is that true?" but "What does that mean?" Or if someone posed to you the question asked in a Zen Buddhist *koan,* "What is the sound of one hand clapping?" you would try to get some clarification of the meaning of the question before you tried to answer it. Thus there is indeed a fundamental logical difference between the *meaning* of an assertion and its *truth;* and as the logical positivists were quick to point out, the question of meaning is logically even more fundamental than the question of truth. We cannot begin to determine whether an assertion is true or false until we know what it means, and the question of the truth or falsity of a claim simply does not arise until we have satisfied ourselves that the claim is meaningful and not a bit of sheer nonsense. It is difficult to quarrel with this much of the positivistic position.

The positivists went on to provide criteria for distinguishing between meaningful and meaningless assertions. Some meaningless assertions could be identified as such because they violate the basic rules of grammar and syntax that govern the correct use of and combinations of the concepts and phrases involved. "God is three in one" would have been regarded by most positivists as syntactically defective in the sense that it does violence to the most elementary rules for combining mathematical concepts into intelligible assertions, and as syntactically defective it would have been regarded as neither true nor false, since it is only with respect to meaningful assertions that the question of truth or falsity arises.

The main thrust of the positivistic attack on metaphysics, however, came from another direction. The statements "God is love" and "The Absolute is perfect" do not appear to be syntactically defective in any way; yet the positivists were convinced that such assertions are so nonsensical that anyone who wonders if they are true or false is seriously misguided. The general criterion of meaning that the positivists wanted to apply to such syntactically well-formed but logically contingent assertions about the world came to be known as "the principle of verification," or "the empiricist's criterion of meaning." Many versions of this principle were produced within the positivistic movement; rather than review all the variations, we shall attempt to state the strongest possible generalized version. An assertion is *meaningful* if and only if some sense observation would be directly or indirectly relevant to its confirmation or refutation; an assertion is *meaningless* if and only if no sense observation would be directly or indirectly relevant to its confirmation or refutation. To put the matter another way, we might say that, for the positivists, a meaningful statement is one for which we might collect evidence either for or against using the scientific method; and a meaningless statement is one for which no evidence either pro or con could be obtained using the scientific method. Which of the following assertions are meaningful and which are meaningless by the positivists' criterion?

1. Jesus was born in Bethlehem.
2. Jesus worked miracles by the power of God.
3. There is life on Mars.
4. God is a living God.
5. Adam did not have a navel.
6. Adam walked with God in the cool of the evening.
7. Yesterday I met a perfect stranger.
8. Yesterday I communed with a perfect being.

Most positivists would say that the even-numbered assertions in this list are meaningless and the odd-numbered assertions meaningful by their criterion. Do you agree that no sense experience would be relevant to confirm or refute the even-numbered assertions? The answer depends on how we conceive the notion of *relevance*. The positivists discovered that if the notion is very strictly conceived, the most general and theoretical aspects of the natural sciences are ruled out, and if relevance is more loosely conceived to allow for theoretical physics, scientific cosmology, and so on, the door is also opened for traditional metaphysics. Unfortunately, they never succeeded in finding a way out of this dilemma.

Nevertheless, it is clear that for a time the positivists were convinced that at last they had found the solution to all man's religious and metaphysical yearnings and puzzles. The solution was that such concerns are all nonsense. Traditional philosophers of religion had debated the question of the truth and falsity of religious and metaphysical doctrines, but they had been debating pseudo-problems. With respect to such nonsense, the question of truth and falsity simply does not arise. It is neither true nor false that "God exists"; it is simply sheer nonsense to say so. The positivists were eager to point out that they are not atheists, who believe that the assertion "God exists" is *false*. Neither are they agnostics, for whom there is *insufficient* evidence for determining the truth or falsity of the claim that "God exists." Since, in their opinion, *no* evidence for or against this assertion could be collected using the methods of scientific inquiry, the assertion is simply meaningless. A. J. Ayer explained that

> It is important not to confuse this view with the view that is adopted by atheists, or agnostics. For it is characteristic of an agnostic to hold that the existence of a god is a possibility in which there is no good reason either to believe or disbelieve; and it is characteristic of an atheist to hold that it is at least probable that no god exists. And our view that all utterances about the nature of God are nonsensical, so far from being identical with, or even lending any support to, either of these familiar contentions, is actually incompatible with them. For if the assertion that there is a god is nonsensical, then the atheist's assertion that there is no god is equally nonsensical, since it is only a significant proposition that can be significantly contradicted. As for the agnostic,

although he refrains from saying either that there is or that there is not a god, he does not deny that the question whether a transcendent god exists is a genuine question. He does not deny that the two sentences "There is a transcendent god" and "There is no transcendent god" express propositions one of which is actually true and the other false. All he says is that we have no means of telling which of them is true, and therefore ought not to commit ourselves to either. But we have seen that the sentences in question do not express propositions at all. And this means that agnosticism also is ruled out.

Thus we offer the theist the same comfort as we give to the moralist. His assertions cannot possibly be valid, but they cannot be invalid either. As he says nothing at all about the world, he cannot justly be accused of saying anything false, or anything for which he has insufficient grounds. It is only when the theist claims that in asserting the existence of a transcendent god he is expressing a genuine proposition that we are entitled to disagree with him.[2]

The positivists felt that to realize that all metaphysics, whether religious or nonreligious, is only so much nonsense is to be cured of a monstrous malignancy; and they were satisfied that at last they had effected such a cure. Once their view had made its full impact, man would no longer be disturbed by metaphysical and theological perplexities and disputes. It must be understood that the positivists explicitly intended their position to apply to the utterances of both philosophical metaphysics and revealed theology. Both are equally nonsensical, because scientific method can neither confirm nor refute them. The theologian cannot hide behind the positivists and exult in the thought that philosophical metaphysics is indeed just so much nonsense. Theology is doomed by the same blow that strikes down philosophical metaphysics, if indeed the blow is fatal —and the logical positivists fully intended it to be. The theologian cannot claim that he still has faith in the doctrines of theology, for theology *says nothing*. There is nothing there to have faith in; nothing is being said. Both traditional philosophy and traditional theology are eliminated by the principle of verification in one fell swoop. Neither has any genuine subject matter.

The positivists were convinced that since only science possesses a method that can be used to determine whether declarative assertions about the world are true or false, it follows that only science possesses any genuine subject matter. *All* questions of truth and falsity fall into the province of the empirical sciences, and there are *no* such questions left over for the metaphysicians and theologians. If metaphysicians and theologians do make use of observations and techniques for testing empirical hypotheses in the course of their work, then they are simply doing natural science or historical science or something of the sort in an amateurish manner. But if they do not make use of the scientific method in justifying their truth-claims, then they have no method at all at their disposal and consequently no truth-claims to justify. The positivists assumed that theology and metaphysics can be genuinely different from the empirical sciences only if they have a unique nonscientific method for discovering the truth; but since there are no nonscientific rational methods available, theology and metaphysics are bereft of subject matter. The traditional conception of philosophy is entirely rejected. For the positivists, "true philosophy" is not the pursuit of truth, however general or fundamental that truth might be. Rather it is the pursuit of meaning, and its method is that of analysis. Moritz Schlick wrote that "Science should be defined as the 'pursuit of truth' and Philosophy as the 'pursuit of meaning'." [3] Questions of truth and falsity belong exclusively to science; all such subject matter is eliminated from both theology and metaphysics. However, if we recognize the positivistic proposal about the true meaning of philosophy as a persuasive definition of *philosophy,* we shall be in a better position to focus attention on the crucial question of methodology and less likely to get bogged down in a dispute over the real nature of philosophy.

DIFFICULTIES WITH LOGICAL POSITIVISM

Since the heyday of logical positivism in the 1920's and 1930's, the philosophical community has learned a great deal about the issues that the positivists discussed. The principle of verification has not proved to be the panacea that it was originally expected to be, and apparently the consensus now is that perhaps the traditional problems of theology and metaphysics are the right ones after all—though fresh approaches to them are being taken, thanks largely to the renewed attention focused on the nature of language, its multiple functions, and its relation to reality by the positivists and their descendants.

One major difficulty with the positivists' principle of verification is that it is simply impossible to draw a sharp line between assertions that directly or indirectly relevant observations would tend to confirm or refute, and other assertions for which no such evidence could possibly be produced. Brand Blanshard has pointed out very clearly how difficult it is to completely separate metaphysics and experience.

> The trouble that now arose was not with what the criterion excluded but with what it included. If every statement were to be called meaningful about which some item of empirical evidence could be found, was there any statement, however wild, that could not put in a legitimate claim? Dr. Ewing pointed out, for example, that this criterion would open the door wide to the metaphysics it had been designed to exclude. (See: A. C. Ewing, "Meaninglessness," *Mind,* Vol. 46 [1937].) Professor Ayer had taken as a peculiarly clear example of metaphysical pseudo-proposition that the world of sense experience is unreal, but our sense experience is at least relevant to this issue, since without it there would be no issue at all; hence the pseudo-proposition is restored to its former place. He had also instanced as an example of metaphysical futility Bradley's question whether the Absolute transcended the process of evolution; but since scientific observations were clearly relevant to whether there was such a process as evolution, Bradley's question must be called significant after all. Theologians could discuss God's omnipotence, at least in terms of the schoolboy's query whether he could make a stone so big that he could not lift it; they could discuss his goodness, since the distribution of pain supplied evidence that was both clearly empirical and clearly relevant; they could discuss immortality, for if God's goodness was now meaningful, it had an obvious bearing on whether his creatures would be blotted out; they could even discuss such distinctively theological dogmas as the incarnation, since the evidence for this lay partly in historical fact. But if such matters as these could be significantly canvassed, what speculative issue could be ruled out? The gate-keeper assigned to

guard the precincts was suddenly found dispensing tickets right and left to deplorably seedy specimens of the metaphysical and theological underworld.[4]

What then are the limits of the scientific method? At present no one seems to know, since it is not possible to determine in any neat and definitive way whether or not experience has any bearing on our theoretical ruminations. The most speculative parts of theoretical science seem to shade off almost imperceptibly into metaphysics, and no one can say for sure where one ends and the other begins. The difference may be one of degree only. If we learn through experience that a spatiotemporal universe exists, then this observation is obviously relevant even to the claims of the supernaturalist who maintains that this natural order of things was created or ordered by a supernatural intelligence. If there were no such universe, there could be no such claims. Just *how* relevant the observation is is another matter, but the positivists learned that they could not insist on conclusive verifiability without losing virtually the whole of modern theoretical science. Of course the evidence must be strong if we are to assert confidently that any such belief is *true,* but the question here is one of meaningfulness and not of truth.

Another crucial difficulty with the claim that a meaningful assertion is one that can be verified and a meaningless assertion is one on which no experience has any bearing is that the whole burden of separating sense from nonsense is placed on the human imagination. Positivists cannot insist that a meaningful assertion is one that in fact has been verified or falsified. "There is life on Mars" has not been verified or falsified as yet, but the statement is regarded as meaningful because we are able to *imagine* a set of experiences that would verify or falsify it. The problem is that our powers of imagination vary significantly from one individual to another and from one era to another. A moron might not be able to think of a set of circumstances that would verify or falsify statements about life on Mars, but any person of average intelligence would find it easy to do so. However, the untrained person of average intelligence would be hard pressed to imagine a set of experiences that would confirm or refute some of the more abstract hypotheses of the natural sciences. Furthermore, even scientific imagination varies from age to age and from individual to individual. If the theory of the curvature of space had been proposed before Einstein's time, it would have been universally regarded as a meaningless hypothesis, given the verification theory of meaning, since no one would have been able to imagine a set of circumstances that would either verify or falsify it. Surely it would be absurd to insist that the imaginative powers of twentieth-century men, even of our most brilliant scientists, exhaust the possibilities for all time to come. The verification theory of meaning cannot be accepted, if for no other reason than that we simply cannot truthfully claim that today's imagination exhausts the possibilities for all the future. We must keep the path of inquiry open. Although it would be a great advantage to have an easily applicable criterion for separating sense from nonsense, we must decide whether the positivistic criterion is really worth the price that we would have to pay for it.

Since the heyday of positivism philosophers have realized that the question of what constitutes a meaningful assertion is an exceedingly complicated one that no simple formula could ever answer adequately. Although it fails to do so, the verification criterion was deliberately designed to make nonsense of metaphysics and theology and to allow only scientific discourse to be meaningful, but what if we do not want to do this? Certainly the verification principle represented a drastic departure from the "ordinary" meaning of the word *meaning;* for if there is anything that most people regard as meaningful it is the discourse of metaphysics, theology, and ethics. Alternative conceptions of meaningfulness are indeed available, and when we finally arrive at an adequate set of criteria for separating sense from nonsense, it is likely that they will be so complicated that they will be useless as weapons against those who would inform us about the most fundamental and universal features of reality.

The positivistic insistence that if philosophy is to be different from science it must have a method of its own, because any correct use of the scientific method makes a man a scientist, may not hold up under examination either. There may actually be other rational methods besides the scientific method. Furthermore, from Aristotle to Hegel and beyond, philosophy has been differentiated from science not so much by its method as by its subject matter. Traditionally, philosophy is said to have "reality as a whole" as its subject matter, whereas the sciences focus on selected parts of reality, such as bodies in motion, living things, the events of history, the makeup of the human psyche, and so on. If this is indeed the case, then *any* legitimate rational method of inquiry might be used by the philosopher without rendering him a nonphilosopher, and philosophy can return to its original task of seeking both meaning and truth with respect to the ultimate nature of things. William James was probably right when he wrote that "since philosophers are only men thinking about things in the most comprehensive possible way, they can use any method whatsoever freely. Philosophy must, in any case, complete the sciences, and must incorporate their methods." [5] We have seen that we cannot draw any a priori limits on the possible connections between experience and theory, and if there are such connections then philosophers as well as scientists might make significant contributions to their discovery.

The Equating of Philosophy and Theology as Competing Historical, Rational Belief Systems: Berdyaev, Niebuhr, and Others

THE other view of the relation between philosophy and theology to be developed in this chapter is one that is frequently suggested but not brought to fruition in the writings of many modern religious thinkers, including Josiah Royce, Ernst Troeltsch, H. Richard Niebuhr, and Nicolas Berdyaev. In their discussions, this position is usually deeply intertwined with commitments to metaphysical idealism, existentialism, specific theological doctrines, and even other solutions to the problem of the relation of philosophy and theology, from all of which it must be separated if it is to speak clearly for itself. We shall now attempt to develop and defend this position, which holds that philosophies and theologies are competing historical, rational belief systems, each of which must be accepted or rejected on its own merits or demerits. No sweeping assumptions are made to the effect that all theological (or philosophical) belief systems as a whole are either superior or inferior to, entirely preferable or not at all preferable to, or more or less intelligible than all philosophical (or theological) belief systems as a whole. This position rests on two contentions: first, that with respect to the *general* characteristics of both theological and philosophical belief systems, there are far fewer differences and far more similarities than either philosophers or theologians have been willing to admit and, second, that these common general characteristics include criteria in accordance with which the merits or demerits of *particular* belief systems of both types may be assessed. Let us now discuss some of these general characteristics.

CHARACTERISTICS COMMON TO PHILOSOPHY AND THEOLOGY

Insight

In our discussion of the functions of reason at the beginning of this chapter, we noted that the great philosophers, metaphysicians, scientists, and perhaps even theologians have flourished mainly by virtue of the breadth and depth of their insight into the nature of things. Insight is the creative function of reason, producing both theory and the methods for testing it. Without it reason simply has nothing whatsoever to say that even remotely resembles theory, whether it be scientific theory or philosophical theory. Without it there are no formal systems or rational methodologies, for insight alone constructs them. Many philosophers have acknowledged that insight is fundamental to the philosophical enterprise, even more basic than logical argument or analysis. For example, consider this comment written during his postpositivistic period by Friedrich Waismann, who was a member of the original "Vienna Circle" of logical positivists in the 1920's.

> To ask, "What is your aim in philosophy?" and to reply, "To show the fly the way out of the fly-bottle" is . . . well, honor where it is due, I suppress what I was going to say; except perhaps this. There is something deeply exciting about philosophy, a fact not intelligible on such a negative account. It is not a matter of "clarifying thoughts" nor of "the correct use of language" nor of any other of these damned things. What is it?

Philosophy is many things and there is no formula to cover them all. But if I were asked to express in one single word what is its most essential feature I would unhesitatingly say: vision. At the heart of any philosophy worth the name is vision and it is from there it springs and takes its visible shape. When I say "vision" I mean it: I do not want to romanticize. What is characteristic of philosophy is the piercing of that dead crust of tradition and convention, the breaking of those fetters which bind us to inherited preconceptions, so as to attain a new and broader way of looking at things. It has always been felt that philosophy should reveal to us what is hidden. (I am not quite insensitive to the dangers of such a view.) Yet from Plato to Moore and Wittgenstein every great philosopher was led by a sense of vision: without it no one could have given a new direction to human thought or opened windows into the not-yet-seen. Though he may be a good technician, he will not leave his marks on the history of ideas. What is decisive is a new way of seeing and, what goes with it, the will to transform the whole intellectual scene. This is the real thing and everything else is subservient to it.[6]

The sort of insight that produces theory does not normally come at the end of a long series of arguments, though philosophers have known since the time of Plato that argument may lead to insight. Usually it comes suddenly, at the beginning, and from it all else emerges. Often hours of wonder and puzzlement precede the ecstasy of insight, but not hours of testing "proofs." Philosophy may begin in wonder, but it advances as insight unexpectedly takes possession of the wonderer. Again, in writing of the creative advances made by Descartes, Einstein, and Hilbert, Waismann notes that we often mistakenly assume that their discoveries

> were the result of a "method" or "procedure," as if the great men arrived at their solutions by drawing logical inferences. This leaves out the most essential thing—the flashing of a new aspect which is *non*-inferential. The moments of seeing cannot be foreseen, any more than they can be planned, forced, controlled, or summoned by will-power. . . . Whoever has pondered some time over some dark problem in philosophy will have noticed that the solution, when it comes, comes with a suddenness. It is not through working very hard towards it that it is found. What

happens is rather that he suddenly sees things in a new light—as if a veil had been lifted that screened his view, or as if the scales had fallen from his eyes, leaving him surprised at his own stupidity not to have seen what was there quite plain before him all the time. It is less like finding out something and more like maturing, outgrowing preconceived notions.[7]

Doubtless there have been many second-rate theologians just as there have been many second-rate philosophers, mere technicians who have contributed little to their field. However, the great prophets, preachers, religious reformers, and theologians have been men of tremendous creative insight. They too have made moral and theological discoveries and have been so overwhelmed by them that they have regarded them as God-given. Creative thinkers in any area of human concern commonly feel themselves to be passive recipients, suddenly and unexpectedly possessed by insight; they generally attach so much significance to this experience of creativity that it is small wonder that insight is often regarded as God-given. Indeed, it may very well be in all such cases—a possibility that is worth exploring. Men may be closer to God in their moments of creative insight than at any other time. Insight begins to look like the "receiving end" of revelation, and revelatory experiences begin to take on their proper status as the beginning points of rationality. Revelation is special inspiration, and insight is just as special and just as much a matter of inspiration. Perhaps the dichotomy between revelation and reason has been a false one all along. The viable distinction may be that between disciplined and undisciplined rationality, and philosophers and theologians alike are capable of either.

Although insight is the first and foremost function of reason, it is by no means the final and definitive function. It does not follow that "one belief system is as good as another" simply because all belief systems rest initially on insight. Insights vary from philosopher to philosopher and from prophet to prophet, and somehow they must be put to the test. Insight produces fable and fiction as well as truth, and it must be integrated with all else that we know. When insight stands alone it is on precarious ground; to make it secure, further elements of rationality must come into play. When it stands alone it is "mere speculation," but it is not yet "truth." Alfred North Whitehead noted that initially "speculative Reason is in its essence untrammelled by method," [8] but he added that one of the great achievements of the Greeks was that they subjected speculative insight to the need for further discipline.

> The real importance of the Greeks for the progress of the world is that they discovered the almost incredible secret that the speculative Reason was itself subject to orderly method. They robbed it of its anarchic character without destroying its function of reaching beyond set bounds. That is why we now speak of the speculative Reason in the place of Inspiration. Reason appeals to the orderliness of what is reasonable while "speculation" expresses the transcendence of any particular method.

> .   .   .

> We have to seek for a discipline of the speculative Reason. It is of the essence of such speculation that it transcends immediate fact. Its business is to make thought creative of the future. It effects this by its vision of systems of ideas, including observation but generalized beyond it. The need of discipline arises because the history of speculation is analogous to the history of practice. If we survey mankind, their speculations have been foolish, brutish, and nasty. The true use of history is that we extract from it general principles as to the discipline of practice and the discipline of speculation.[9]

What further discipline is required?

Argument

One additional discipline that is required is that of argumentation. To argue is to present evidence designed to support some conclusion. Philosophers argue. They try to undergird their insights with supporting evidence, but inspiration is almost always temporally prior to argumentation. Waismann correctly points out that for a philosopher, "what is decisive is that he has seen things from a new angle of vision. Compared to that everything else is secondary. Arguments come only afterwards to lend support to what he has seen." [10] In discussing the historicity of metaphysics and theology, we shall note that there are limits to what we might expect from philosophical argumentation. Nevertheless, evidence is presented; and when such a presentation is done correctly, it is an act of rationality.

Is not this the crucial difference between philosophy and theology? Are not philosophical belief systems supported by evidence, whereas theological belief systems are entirely unsupported? Certainly this is the traditional distinction between philosophy and theology: Philosophies rest on rational justification, whereas theologies rest on faith. The most overwhelming bit of evidence for this is that there is little or no argumentation in the Bible; it is almost pure insight. This is true enough for the most part, although St. Paul certainly argued against innumerable deviations from and corruptions of the faith, and biblical writers did interpret miracle-working and the fulfillment of prophecy as strong evidence for their views. Moreover, argumentative proof for many influential philosophical theses is also difficult to come by. Much philosophizing is proclamation rather than proof. For example, it is a matter of pure conjecture why Thales thought that water was the first principle of all things; Hegel's "proof" that the whole course of events in the world represents the process by which the Absolute comes to consciousness of itself is virtually nonexistent; and Whitehead's "proof" that in God there are both temporal and nontemporal aspects is extremely difficult to discover.

Though there is little or no argumentation in the Bible (and considerably less in the writings of metaphysicians than we might expect), nevertheless theologians as well as philosophers do argue. Athanasius argued against Arius and the world; St. Augustine argued against Pelagius; Luther argued against Catholicism; Barth argues against Brunner. They support their conclusions with appeals to scriptural, traditional, and mystical insights; and they argue that their opponents are untrue to the Scriptures or the Fathers or the Church or religious experience. Even the most antirationalistic of theologians, such as Barth and Brunner, are willing to admit that a kind of redeemed rationality has a legitimate role to play in theology. Anyone who has read the writings of the theologians must be aware that arguments appear on page after page and that often theologians too in their own way are concerned with presenting evidence to support their beliefs. A systematically developed theology can be and often is a rationally ordered system in which some beliefs entail other beliefs and are acknowledged to be logically incompatible with still others. Certainly theologians are sufficiently committed to logical consistency to be constantly on the defensive against all those forms of heresy and infidelity that are logically incompatible with their convictions. For example, the naturalistic doctrine of the eternal existence of the natural order of things is rejected by Christian theologians because it is logically incompatible with the Christian doctrine of the creation of the world *ex nihilo*. At any rate, philosophy cannot be differentiated from theology on the grounds that the former is supported by arguments and the latter is not.

Other attempts might be made, however, to save something of the traditional distinction between philosophy and theology. It might be maintained that theologians simply use bad arguments, whereas philosophers argue correctly; or it might be argued that all parts of a philosophical system are rationally supported, whereas this is true only of the derivative theses of theology. As for the first contention, that theologians use bad arguments whereas philosophers do not, there is overwhelming evidence against this. Many philosophers are careless thinkers. Often the theologian who is untrained in logic has intuitions about what constitutes a good argument that are as reliable as those of the metaphysician who is weak in logic, and it cannot be a defining characteristic that a theologian is untrained in logic, however many of them may have been so untrained. Philosophical systems themselves differ significantly with respect to the degree to which they are logically ordered, and the same may be said of theological systems. It might be maintained that all theological arguments are appeals to authority and that this is what renders them fallacious, but many appeals to authority are perfectly legitimate when the authority is indeed an expert in his field. The problem then becomes one of listing the criteria for expertise in theology, and although it is difficult, it is probably no more so than listing the criteria for expertise in philosophical metaphysics.

The second contention, that all philosophical theses, at least ideally, are supported by rational evidence whereas only derivative theological theses can be so supported, is based on the idea that the theologian believes in order to understand. This means that he makes certain axiomatic faith assumptions that can then be used to illuminate a whole host of perplexities, in the sense that innumerable derivative theses can be drawn from these axiomatic assumptions which the theologian and the members of his community of believers find congenial. However, the axioms themselves must be simply accepted without supporting evidence. By contrast, it may be claimed, *all* philosophical theses are at least ideally based on proof or evidence. There is one crucial difficulty with this position: It may be suspected that, in practice, metaphysicians also believe in order to understand in just the same sense. A metaphysical thesis is accepted not because it has itself been explained but rather because of its explanatory power. That which is used to prove everything else cannot itself be proved, as Jeremy Bentham pointed out. Somewhere even philosophers simply must reach a "rock-bottom" starting point. It is not even ideally possible for all philosophical theses to be proved, since every argument, whether it be deductive, inductive, vertical, or horizontal, must have premises as well as a conclusion. If the premises of *all* arguments must themselves be proved (without circularity), the result will be an infinite regress of proofs of proofs of proofs, and this is an impossibility. Attempts have been made to discover indubitable certainties that would block this infinite regress of proofs, either in self-evident truths or in primitive experiental facts as reported in "protocol sentences." The intuitionism that relies on self-evident truths certainly resembles all too closely theology declaring its axioms of faith, and not a single viable example of a protocol sentence has been produced. All conceptualizations about the "facts" seem to be inextricably intertwined with theory and even with value. Philosophers sometimes introduce metaphysical "postulates" to block the required infinite regress of proofs, but such a step is only a subterfuge if it is intended to differentiate philosophy and theology. Philosophical systems built on such postulates are classic examples of believing in order to understand. Talk about "postulates" presents only a thin disguise for the fact that the entire belief system is built on faith commitments.

Criteria

In practice, both philosophers and systematic theologians tend to appeal to the same basic set of criteria in assessing the adequacy or inadequacy of a system of religious belief. They appeal to logicality, simplicity, coherence, comprehensiveness, consistency, clarity, and conformity with experience; and any philosophical or theological position may be rejected on the grounds that it fails to meet any one of these criteria. They are not at all easy to apply, and only a continual public exchange of ideas can ensure even a modicum of success. If these criteria are to do their work, philosophers must constantly engage in dialectical exchanges with other philosophers and even with theologians, and theologians must constantly engage in dialectical exchanges with other theologians and even with philosophers. No purely private world-views can be adequate, for no individual can hope to apply successfully all these criteria to a private world-view. The methodological skeptic may reply that the difficulty is that all too many belief systems do compete in the arena of public discussion and succeed equally in satisfying our criteria. Unfortunately, this widely accepted dogma has never once been demonstrated; and no demonstration of it could possibly be produced that did not appeal to precisely the same criteria that the skeptic wants to reject. Language is such that only a limited amount of skepticism can be expressed within it. If skepticism is carried too far, language breaks down altogether and it becomes linguistically impossible to express that skepticism meaningfully without self-contradiction.

By what right do we insist that theological belief systems conform to the same criteria of adequacy that we apply to philosophies? Are we not laying theology on a Procrustean bed? Are we not treating it as "just another philosophy"? Is this not simply another version of the elimination of theology in favor of philosophy? Theologians are likely to react with such questions as these to the position now being developed, but they simply need to review their own practices to realize that these criteria belong as much to them as to philosophers. Which of these criteria would the theologians want to eliminate? The most likely candidate is consistency, which is explicitly rejected by such theologians as Tertullian, Kierkegaard, and Brunner; but actually they are in the minority among theologians. A rejection of consistency is usually only a lame excuse for undisciplined thinking, and interpretations of what is involved in "paradox" may be given that do not make use of the notion of logical inconsistency.

It becomes apparent that theologians subscribe to our criteria of adequacy more when they are attacking their opponents than when they are making explicit their own conception of methodology. Theologians often reject what other theologians have to say on the grounds of illogicality, incoherence, lack of simplicity or comprehensiveness, inconsistency, lack of clarity, and unfaithfulness to experience. It might be maintained that one difference between philosophers and theologians is that the latter are more demanding of their adversaries than they are of themselves, but it is doubtful that even this difference will bear up under examination. A double standard often operates in *both* philosophy and theology, with philosophers as guilty as theologians of demanding more of their opponents than they demand of themselves. For example, Kant rejected traditional metaphysics on the ground that it applied the categories of cause, effect, and the like to the real world and did not restrict their application to the world of appearance; but he saw nothing wrong with talking about real things in themselves as the causes of sense experience and the real, free self as the cause of moral knowledge and activity. Kant seemed to think that it was all right for *Kant* to do this, but he rejected the whole of traditional metaphysics for doing the same thing. The elimination of this type of double standard would bring philosophy and theology to the same level as rational belief systems, each individual instance of which must be accepted or rejected on its own merits. If the dichotomy between reason and revelation is a false one from the outset, this is just what we might expect.

We shall make use of these criteria when we turn to some of the substantive problems of the philosophy of religion in later chapters. These are criteria for the adequacy not only of philosophical and theological systems but of all intelligible discourse. The only completely clear-cut alternative to them is a blank mind and total silence—not theology.

Commitment

Both philosophy and theology demand commitment. Both can be "religious" in Tillich's sense, involving ultimate seriousness and existential concern and involvement. Theologians often talk as if they have some kind of monopoly on seriousness and commitment, but history betrays the claim. Both Socrates and Jesus were serious enough about their commitments to die for them. Again, each individual must be considered as such. Many theologians are doubtless only superficially committed, and many philosophers are deeply involved in what they believe. The sweeping generalization that theologians alone are men of existential seriousness whereas all philosophers are men of superficial commitment will not bear up under examination. Depth of commitment or the lack thereof cannot be made into a defining characteristic of either theology or philosophy. Existential seriousness is properly a characteristic of men, not of disciplines.

It is true that there are often certain psychological differences between philosophers and theologians. Philosophers attempt to attain some degree of calm detachment from and cool reflection on the issues that concern them, and they are often only tentatively committed rather than inflexibly committed to their positions, regarding them as subject to revision and review in the light of further developments. Once more, however, it may be better to take individuals as they come. St. Thomas was probably a man of cooler detachment than St. Augustine, and there are doubtless vast temperamental differences of this sort between Brand Blanshard and Jean Paul Sartre. Furthermore, theologians are coming to emphasize more and more the historicity of theology and the role of fallible human responsiveness in the interpretation of revelatory events (insight-giving events). Even theologians often relinquish or revise their most cherished beliefs. Many philosophers have been dogmatists, and many theologians have insisted that revelation is given only to fallible human interpreters. Both philosophers and theologians need to find some balance between seriousness of commitment and purpose on the one hand and the acknowledgment that all of us are only human on the other.

Historicity

Philosophies and theologies flourish in time, suffer from limitations of time and place, and owe a historical debt to some community of thinkers and believers. At their best they represent the wisdom of their age, but none of them endures forever without revision and reinterpretation. This is not to say that either enterprise is futile. It is to say only that there is always uncertainty and that there always seems to be room for improvement. We must attempt to find the most adequate understanding of ultimate reality that is available to us. For some of us metaphysics is a psychological necessity; and when we are confronted with the difficulties that the most antimetaphysical philosophers have had in avoiding metaphysics, we may begin to suspect that it is also somehow a logical necessity. It may be that epistemology and metaphysics are inseparable and that the problems of each are resolved only within the framework of the other. However, many philosophers, such as Hegel and Whitehead, warn us not to expect finality from the enterprise of philosophy; and many theologians also present their convictions with great modesty. Theologians such as Niebuhr and Berdyaev are becoming increasingly aware of the historicity of the enterprise of theology and warn us that the interpretation of revelatory events is carried out by fallible men who are limited by their own place in history and who are themselves sinners.

Metaphysics is an inspired, poetic view of ultimate reality into which reason has introduced some semblance of order, but exactly the same thing is true of systematic theology. Arguments in metaphysics turn largely on insight and are as close in function to art as they are to science. Yet they do not cease to be rational. Waismann argues that philosophical arguments were at one time

quite mistakenly . . . supposed to be proofs and refutations in a strict sense. But what the philosopher does is something else. *He builds up a case.* First, he makes you see all the weaknesses, disadvantages, shortcomings of a position; he brings to light inconsistencies in it or points out how unnatural some of the ideas underlying the whole theory are by pushing them to their farthest consequences; and this he does with the strongest weapons in his arsenal, reduction to absurdity and infinite regress. On the other hand, he offers you a new way of looking at things not exposed to those objections. In other words, he submits to you, like a barrister, all the facts of his case, and you are in the position of the judge. You look at them carefully, go into the details, weigh the pros and cons and arrive at a verdict. But in arriving at a verdict you are not following a deductive highway, any more than a judge in the High Court does. Coming to a decision, though a rational process, is very unlike doing sums. A judge has to judge, we say, implying that he has to use discernment in contrast to applying, machine-like, a set of mechanical rules. There are no computing machines for doing the judge's work nor could there be any—a trivial yet significant fact. When the judge reaches a decision this may be, and in fact often is, a rational result, yet not one obtained by deduction; it does not simply follow from such-and-such: what is required is insight, judgment. Now in arriving at a verdict, you are like a judge in this that you are not carrying out a number of formal logical steps: you have to use discernment, e.g. to descry the pivotal point. Considerations such as these make us see what is already apparent in the use of "rational," that this term has a wider range of application than what can be established deductively. To say that an argument can be rational and yet not deductive is not a sort of contradiction as it would inevitably be in the opposite case, namely, of saying that a deductive argument need not be rational.

This alters the whole picture. The point to be emphasized is that a philosopher may see an important truth and yet be unable to demonstrate it by formal proof. But the fact that his arguments are not logical (i.e. deductive) does nothing to detract from their rationality.[11]

Just as theologians must modify their authoritarian interpretations of revelation, so philosophers must modify their authoritarian interpretations of rationality. The concept of reason is a historical concept, which time itself modifies. In the seventeenth and eighteenth centuries deduction, often taken together with intuitionism, provided the basic model for the understanding of the terms *rationality* and *proof*. In the second part of the nineteenth and first half of the twentieth centuries, induction and "scientific method" molded the prevailing understanding of these terms. Today's multifunctional logics give us an extremely broad and diffuse understanding of these concepts. "Reason" is no fixed mold into which our belief systems either neatly fit or fail to fit, and we do not possess a final interpretation of what constitutes rationally justified belief. Not only does rational insight create methodology, it is ever creating new methodologies, new logics, new techniques of analysis, new criteria of adequacy. Thus we cannot assume the finality of reason's understanding of itself, for we do not know today what new tests for truth reason will bring forth tomorrow. We can only apply as best we can those tests which are now available to us.

It is entirely possible to recognize the limitations of reason and yet keep the faith that has been at the heart of our human confidence in reason through the centuries, the faith that when all is said and done there is only one belief system that perfectly satisfies our rational criteria of adequacy. Yet we must not be blind to the fact that this is a faith, for at present no belief system is universally acknowledged to satisfy all the criteria. Faith and reason seem to be more unequivocally opposed than are philosophy and theology.

Suggestions for Further Reading

THE POSITIVISTIC ASSAULT ON METAPHYSICS
AND TRADITIONAL PHILOSOPHY

AYER, A. J., *Language, Truth and Logic* (New York, Dover, 1936), especially the Introduction to the second edition and Chapters 1, 2, and 6.

CARNAP, RUDOLF, "The Elimination of Metaphysics Through Logical Analysis of Language," in A. J. Ayer, ed., *Logical Positivism* (New York, Free Press, 1959), pp. 60–81.

SCHLICK, MORITZ, "Meaning and Verification," *Philosophical Review,* Vol. XLV (July 1936).

———, "The Future of Philosophy," *Publications in Philosophy* (Stockton, Cal., The College of the Pacific, 1932). Reprinted in all three editions of D. J. Bronstein, Y. H. Krikorian, and P. P. Wiener, eds., *Basic Problems of Philosophy* (Englewood Cliffs, N.J., Prentice-Hall, 1964).

STANDARD DISCUSSIONS AND CRITICISMS OF THE
VERIFICATION PRINCIPLE

ALSTON, WILLIAM P., *Philosophy of Language* (Englewood Cliffs, N.J., Prentice-Hall, 1964), Chapter 4.

BLANSHARD, BRAND, *Reason and Analysis* (London, George Allen & Unwin, 1962), Chapter 5.

HEMPEL, CARL G., "Problems and Changes in the Empiricist Criterion of Meaning," *Revue Internationale de Philosophie,* Vol. IV (January 1950). Reprinted in A. J. Ayer, ed., *Logical Positivism* (New York, Free Press, 1959), pp. 108–29.

MASCAL, E. L., *Words and Images* (New York, Ronald Press, 1957), Chapter 1.

RYLE, GILBERT, "The Theory of Meaning," in Charles E. Caton, ed., *Philosophy and Ordinary Language* (Urbana, Ill., University of Illinois Press, 1963), pp. 128–53.

URMSON, J. O., *Philosophical Analysis* (Oxford, Clarendon Press, 1956), Chapter 7.

WISDOM, J. O., "Metamorphoses of the Verifiability Theory of Meaning," *Mind,* Vol. LXXII (July 1963), pp. 335–47.

RELEVANT DISCUSSIONS OF REVELATION AND THEOLOGY

BERDYAEV, NICOLAS, *Truth and Revelation* (London, Geoffrey Bles, 1953), especially Chapter 3.

BURROWS, MILLAR, *An Outline of Biblical Theology* (Philadelphia, Westminster Press, 1946), Chapter 2.

CAMPBELL, C. A., *On Selfhood and Godhood* (London, George Allen & Unwin, 1957), especially Lectures I and II.

COBB, JOHN B., JR., *A Christian Natural Theology* (Philadelphia, Westminster Press, 1965), Chapter 7.

NIEBUHR, H. RICHARD, *Radical Monotheism and Western Culture* (New York, Harper & Row, 1960), especially Chapter 1 and Supplementary Essays I and III.

————, *The Meaning of Revelation* (New York, Macmillan, 1955), especially Chapter 1.

————, *The Purpose of the Church and Its Ministry* (New York, Harper & Row, 1956), especially Part III.

ROYCE, JOSIAH, *The Sources of Religious Insight* (Edinburgh, T. & T. Clark, 1912), especially Chapters 1, 2, and 3.

SMITH, JOHN E., *Reason and God* (New Haven, Conn., Yale University Press, 1961), Chapter 13.

TROELTSCH, ERNST, *Christian Thought* (New York, Meridian Books, 1957), Part I.

DISCUSSIONS OF INSIGHT, SPECULATIVE REASON,
AND METAPHYSICAL METHOD

BROAD, C. D., "Critical and Speculative Philosophy," in John H. Muirhead, ed., *Contemporary British Philosophy* (New York, Humanities Press, 1924), pp. 96–100.

Hanson, Norwood Russell, *Patterns of Discovery* (Cambridge, Eng., Cambridge University Press, 1969), especially Chapter 4 on theories in science.

Hartshorne, Charles, *Creative Synthesis and Philosophic Method* (La Salle, Ill., Open Court, 1970).

———, *Man's Vision of God* (Hamden, Conn., Archon Books, 1964), Chapter 2.

———, *Reality as Social Process* (New York, Free Press, 1953), Chapter 10.

Lee, Donald S., "Ultimacy and the Philosophical Field of Metaphysics," *Tulane Studies in Philosophy,* Vol. XV (1966), pp. 71–102.

Royce, Josiah, *The Sources of Religious Insight* (Edinburgh, T. & T. Clark, 1912), pp. 3–9 and Chapter 3.

Thompson, Manley, "Metaphysics," in Roderick M. Chisholm, Herbert Feigl, William K. Frankena, John Passmore, Manley Thompson, *Philosophy* (Englewood Cliffs, N.J., Prentice-Hall, 1964), pp. 125–232.

Waismann, Friedrich, "How I See Philosophy," in H. D. Lewis, ed., *Contemporary British Philosophy* (London, George Allen & Unwin, 1956), pp. 445–90. Reprinted in A. J. Ayer, ed., *Logical Positivism,* (New York, Free Press, 1959), pp. 345–80.

Whitehead, Alfred North, *The Function of Reason* (Princeton, N.J., Princeton University Press, 1957), Chapter 3.

SOME CONTEMPORARY DISCUSSIONS OF PHILOSOPHICAL METHOD

Collingwood, R. G., *An Essay on Philosophical Method* (Oxford, Eng., Clarendon Press, 1950).

Johnstone, Henry W., Jr., *Philosophy and Argument* (University Park, Pa., Pennsylvania State University Press, 1959).

Passmore, John, *Philosophical Reasoning* (London, Gerald Duckworth, 1961).

The Monist, Vol. XLVIII, No. 4 (October 1964) (entire issue devoted to philosophical arguments and methodology).

Toulmin, Stephen E., *The Uses of Argument* (Cambridge, Eng., Cambridge University Press, 1958).

Notes

1   This example is suggested by Moritz Schlick in his "The Future of Philosophy," *Publications in Philosophy* (Stockton, Calif., The College of the Pacific, 1932), p. 59.

2   A. J. Ayer, *Language, Truth and Logic* (New York, Dover, 1936), pp. 115–16, by permission of Dover. Permission to quote also granted by Victor Gollancz.

3   Schlick, "The Future of Philosophy," p. 54.

4   Brand Blanshard, *Reason and Analysis* (London, George Allen & Unwin, 1962), p. 230. Distributed in the United States by Open Court Publishing Company.

5   William James, *Some Problems of Philosophy* (London, Longmans Green & Company, 1948), pp. 25–26.

6   Friedrich Waismann, "How I See Philosophy," in H. D. Lewis, ed., *Contemporary British Philosophy* (London, George Allen & Unwin, 1956), pp. 482–83.

7   *Ibid.,* pp. 488–89.

8   Alfred North Whitehead, *The Function of Reason* (Copyright © 1957 by Princeton University Press), p. 51.

9   *Ibid.,* pp. 52, 65–66.

10 Waismann, "How I See Philosophy," pp. 483–84.

11 *Ibid.,* pp. 480–81.

chapter six

The World
Without
God NATURALISM
AND HUMANISM

In this chapter we shall be doing theology in a sense in which we did not do it in Chapters 3, 4, and 5. In our ordinary religious discourse, the term *theology* has more than one perfectly legitimate meaning. One of these senses involves the opposition of "philosophy" and "theology"; this opposition we have now explored and discovered to be much weaker than many have supposed. In another sense, however, philosophy and theology are even less obviously opposed. Many philosophers and theologians have been doing "theology" in this second sense—that is, they have been engaging in "God-talk." Religious philosophizing has often been called natural theology, and this is not a self-contradictory notion like "round square," or "hot vacuum." *Theology* is "the *logos* or rationale of the concept of God," and a *theologian* is "one who explores the logic or rationale of the concept of God." Many philosophers have been theologians in this sense. It is impossible to find any *necessary* opposition between philosophy and theology if *theology* is taken to mean "God-talk" instead of "revelation-dependent-talk." God-talk is certainly a permissible condition of philosophy; however, it is not a necessary one, especially if God is construed as a supernatural entity. Many philosophers have not believed in a supernatural God or even found it necessary to talk about such a God, not even bothering to explicitly deny his existence. They have simply devoted themselves to other problems of philosophical interest and concern in such areas as the philosophy of science, of mind, of knowledge, of value, of language, and so on. Even more interestingly, however, such God-talk is not even a necessary condition of theology (as revelation-dependent-talk). Many theologians who have been revelation-dependent-talkers have not been theologians in the sense of God-talkers. For example, many of the Zen and Hinayana Buddhists, who take their inspiration from their Enlightened One, decline to engage in metaphysics altogether and neither affirm nor deny that God exists, or that he has or lacks certain attributes. Belief in the existence of a supernatural God is certainly not universal even among those Western theologians who are willing to participate in metaphysical discussion, just as it is not universal among philosophers who are willing to participate in metaphysical discussion. Paul Tillich and many of the "new theologians" who have been influenced by him deny that a supernatural God exists, yet they still consider themselves to be theologians. The present-day "death of God" theologians, such as Thomas J. J. Altizer, deny that there is *now* a supernatural God, though they are convinced that there was *once* such a God who died on the Cross, never to be raised from the dead.

The concept of *God* takes its meaning from the framework of conception and commitment within which it functions. *God* has many quite distinct meanings for religious thinkers. The supernaturalist concept of *God,* which we shall soon explore, is the basic ordinary-language understanding of the term—but by no means the only one. A case could perhaps be made for saying that other current understandings of *God* in our Western languages are logical derivatives of, departures from, simplifications of, or revisions of this basic supernaturalist sense. Nevertheless, this logical priority does not automatically confer on supernaturalism any ontological priority. The substantive problems of the philosophy of religion, to which we now turn, cannot be settled finally by ordinary-language analysis. The philosophically provocative question is whether a concept of *God* and of *ultimate reality* can be developed that satisfies the criteria of adequacy that both philosophers and theologians will accept.

Do we have available to us any views of ultimate reality that are sufficiently logical, coherent, comprehensive, consistent, clear, and grounded in experience to be worthy of our respect and commitment, and that deserve to be called meaningful and true? If so, what are they? Do they or do they not make a place for God? What does the word *God* mean in these contexts? How is God related to the world? Many philosophers and theologians have attempted to provide us with affirmative, constructive answers to these questions. The sheer variety of answers that have been offered is itself overwhelming, and we cannot review them all. They all make a place for *God* in some sense of the term, but most of them require a radical revision of the supernaturalist concept of *God,* which has usually dominated our Western God-talk. All of them attempt to relate God and the world. In this and the next two chapters, we shall examine three concepts of ultimate reality that claim to approximate closely the ideal, and that are especially alive for modern men. First we shall look at humanistic naturalism, then at traditional supernaturalism, and finally at modern panentheism, or process theology. Are the revisionary definitions of *God* offered by humanism and panentheism to be regarded as persuasive definitions? Are all revisionary definitions persuasive? No. Persuasive definition always involves deception, deliberate or otherwise; but no deception is present when a revisionist openly and explicitly calls attention to the novelty of what he is doing with words.

In looking at these three world views, the individual must finally judge for himself which of them, if any, is true. As we saw in Chapter 5, reason does not relieve anyone of the necessity for making responsible judgments in matters of ultimate concern. Yet, no verdict can be considered "responsible" that is not worked out in dialectical exchanges with others.

Family Traits of Naturalism

THE view of ultimate reality presented by the naturalist is one of the most clear-cut, reasonable, and natural alternatives to traditional supernaturalism for the disenchanted Westerner. We shall consider six basic assumptions of the naturalistic world view, but we should be aware that *naturalism* is a somewhat flexible concept. Not all of the thinkers who are commonly called naturalists will explicitly subscribe to all of these assumptions or attach the same importance to them, and borderline cases will arise under *any* definition of *naturalism* where it is difficult to decide if a given thinker is a naturalist. The most we can claim for our definition of *naturalism* is that the *majority* of naturalists seem to subscribe to these theses, either explicitly or implicitly. The naturalists themselves admit that it is difficult to discover the common and distinctive characteristics of *naturalism*.[1] Like *religion,* the word *naturalism* could profitably be analyzed in terms of family resemblances, and the six characteristics that we shall discuss do seem to be the most prominent family traits. As for the members of this family, it is in the present century that naturalism has had its heyday; and prominent among recent naturalists are such thinkers as George Santayana (despite his occasional excursions into Platonism), John Dewey, Morris Cohen, Sterling Lamprecht, Roy W. Sellars, John H. Randall, Jr., Sidney Hook, Ernest Nagel, and Bertrand Russell. They represent a return to the general metaphysical outlook of the ancient pre-Socratic philosophers, particularly the Greek Atomists, though they give this outlook a distinctly modern flavor. They hold such predecessors as Aristotle, Lucretius, and Spinoza in high regard and are willing to concede that these thinkers almost discovered the truth. They do not identify quite so closely with the atheistic materialists of the seventeenth and eighteenth centuries, such as Hobbes, Diderot, de La Mettrie, and d'Holbach, because of the reductionism of the earlier periods, though these materialists were the naturalists of their own day. Like Dewey, they can all find much to agree with in Hegel, as he was interpreted in Chapter 3. The emergent evolutionists of the post-Darwinian era were important percursors of our contemporary naturalists, though those few emergent evolutionists like Samuel Alexander who predicted the eventual emergence of God out of cosmic processes were at best only borderline naturalists; their classification as such depended, of course, on what they meant by *God.* Other marginal naturalists were such figures as J. B. Pratt and William P. Montague, who believed in cosmic teleology.

What are some of the basic, defining traits of naturalism? In the first place, *atheism* and *naturalism* are closely associated but by no means interchangeable concepts for us, since the naturalist is one who affirms that *only nature exists* and by implication that the supernatural does not exist.[2] By *nature* is meant "the spatio-temporal universe as a whole existing independently of knowing mind." It is often called the world or the cosmos, and for the naturalist the cosmos is ultimate reality. The world is all of reality; it is all there is; there is no "other world." Of course, this is a metaphysical claim, one that seems absolutely essential to naturalism. The naturalist must have at least this much metaphysics in him, although twentieth-century naturalists are often very reluctant, insecure metaphysicians who are inclined to retreat into metaphysical agnosticism or even into positivism at the slightest pressure or provocation.[3] When this retreat is made, the point of calling them naturalists seems to be lost, and the familiar labels of "agnostic" or "positivist" are more fitting. Only by making the metaphysical claim that "only the spatiotemporal cosmos exists" can the naturalist offer a position that is *contrary* to that of the supernaturalist, which is what he clearly wants to do. To assert that "I do not know whether nature alone exists" or that "metaphysical statements and their contradictories are equally meaningless" is not quite sufficient.

The claim that only nature as a whole exists is not enough to make one a naturalist, however. The further claim is required that *nature as a whole is nonpersonal,* that whatever order there is within nature is inherent and was not introduced by any sort of intelligence of cosmic proportions.[4] This rules out the view of the immanentist, that a "divine" world designer like Homer's Zeus who is somehow an immanent and integral part of the natural world has ordered the processes of nature for purposes of his own. It also rules out the view of the panentheist, that a God who includes the whole of the natural world as an integral and immanent part of himself has ordered the processes of nature for purposes of his own. The typical naturalist wishes to dispense with not only the supernatural but also cosmic teleology: There is neither a transcendent nor an immanent God nor a God who is somehow both at once. The naturalist does not wish to deny that men and animals have their own values and their own respective measures of purposive intelligence, but only that nature as a whole evaluates and is purposively intelligent, that there is anything like a "world soul." He rejects anthropomorphism in metaphysics. Intelligence, purpose, the capacity for love, hate, moral concern, existential anguish, guilt, fear, satisfaction, and frustration are all vitally important functions of high-grade organisms such as man; but they are distinctive of such organisms all the same. Nature as a whole cannot be understood by analogy with high-grade organisms. Human values, purposes, and personality traits have a place in nature and arise out of natural human needs and capacities, but nature as a whole has no values, purposes, or personality traits.

Further, the naturalist holds at least implicitly that *nature as a whole, including the basic stuff within it, is eternal and necessary* in the sense of being uncreated, indestructible, and self-sufficient.[5] He has no supernatural being to create the world of nature, and he is averse to admitting that anything can come into being without a cause. Although they may regard it as a trivial tautology or cliché, naturalists and supernaturalists alike generally admit that "out of nothing, nothing comes."

Closely related to the view that nature as a whole is self-sufficient is the view that *all natural events have causes that are themselves natural events.*[6] The occurrence of every spatiotemporal event is caused by some other spatiotemporal event or events. Continuity reigns throughout nature; there are no radical gaps or dualisms. Although both naturalists and supernaturalists agree that every event has a cause, the naturalist is unwilling to admit supernatural causes. For him every cause is a natural cause. There are no miracles or acts of God. Neither are there any uncaused happenings. The universe as a whole did not suddenly spring into being out of nothing and without a cause; neither was it created by a supernatural being; so it must have always been here. The Greeks, Spinoza, and many of the precursors of twentieth-century naturalism committed themselves explicitly to this metaphysical view, and today's naturalists seem to be committed to it implicitly even when they would prefer to ignore the question of origins. Many devotees of the major Western religions argue that "the world couldn't have just happened, so it must have been created by God," and they take this to be a refutation of naturalism. However, the naturalist is not claiming that nature as a whole "just happened." His position is that "the world couldn't have just happened, so it must be eternal, necessary, self-sufficient, uncreated, indestructible, and all the rest." It is true that nature as a whole is uncaused, but it is not an uncaused *happening* or *event*. Rather, it is the self-sufficient *context* within which all happenings are located. Many Christians, especially, seem unaware of the fact that this is a viable metaphysical option.

In addition, the naturalist is committed to the view that *scientific method is the only legitimate rational method for discovering truth.*[7] Analysis gives us meaning, to be sure, but only scientific method gives us knowledge of truth. Some naturalists tend to conceive of scientific method in much the same way as the logical positivists did—as involving the empirical verification or falsification of descriptions and explanatory hypotheses. Much recent thought about scientific method goes beyond this narrow empiricism to stress the role played in the actual day-to-day work of theoretical scientists by formal systems like those of mathematics and logic and by imaginative constructions and rational criteria of coherence, simplicity, consistency, and so on. The often tenuous combination of abstract theory and sense observation that the more theoretical and speculative sciences actually manifest is recognized. If the notion of *scientific method* is expanded in this way, the claim that "only scientific method yields knowledge" begins to resemble more and more the older philosophical claim that "only rational method yields knowledge." If this is what is meant, no philosopher who wishes to avoid self-contradiction could seriously object to it. Unfortunately, naturalists tend to shift back and forth between the narrower and wider senses of *scientific method* as happens to be convenient for purposes at hand. Any adverse remarks about scientific method in the following discussion should be understood to apply only to the narrower claim that only the empirical verification and falsification of hypotheses yields knowledge.

Finally, naturalism is intimately associated with humanism, which is both a philosophy of man and the view that human welfare is of ultimate importance and ought to be furthered at every opportunity.[8] Man is a thoroughly natural entity and is to be understood through the use of only natural categories of explanation. Human values arise out of perfectly natural human needs and are to be harmonized and furthered by the use of man's natural intelligence. There is no cosmic basis or sanction for this humanistic axiology, but none is needed. Human values are indeed *human* values, and this is all that needs to be said for them. If the notions of *God* and *religion* are to have any continuing significance at all, they must be given that significance within the framework of humanism. Later we shall explore this connection in more detail.

Naturalism is thus the view that (1) only nature exists, (2) nature as a whole is nonpersonal, (3) the basic stuff of nature is eternal and necessary, (4) all natural events have natural causes, (5) only scientific method yields knowledge, and (6) ethics and the humanistic philosophy of man are adequate. At least, these are the basic family traits of naturalism. Within the framework of these six assumptions, there is room for much squabbling among the naturalists with respect to the basic contents of the world and the arrangement of these contents in relation to one another. These squabbles are themselves of great philosophical interest, but we shall only note some of them here without attempting to resolve them. Try to decide for yourself whether there is enough agreement on one side or the other of any of these issues to warrant treating it as a family trait and how important these disagreements are for the philosophy of religion.

No naturalist wishes to hold that the universe *as presently constituted* is eternal and necessary. The present arrangement of the galaxies, or of our solar system, or of the chemical elements, or of plant, animal, and human life now inhabiting the earth is not a permanent feature of the universe. It is only space-time itself and its most primitive contents that are eternal, uncaused, self-sufficient, and indestructible. But what are these most primitive contents? Naturalists have usually been predisposed to some form of materialism, that is, to the view that matter in lawful motion is the most primitive ingredient in space-time. But what is matter? For the Greek Atomists, matter consisted of exceedingly minute particles of stuff (the atoms) having definite size, shape, weight, and solidity and capable of adhering to one another to form larger composite bodies as they moved about in space (the void) in accord with the laws of mechanics. The atoms themselves were eternal, uncaused, self-sufficient, and indestructible. "Necessity" in this sense is attributed only to God by the supernaturalist, but the naturalist attributes it to the most primitive features of nature. The basic Atomistic view of matter was adopted by many of the founding fathers of modern experimental science and refined into the sciences of chemistry and physics, but in very recent decades these sciences have abandoned the view that atoms are indestructible particles of stuff having definite size and shape in favor of the view that all matter can be reduced to pure energy. In the most recent versions of naturalism, it would have to be physical energy that is eternal, uncaused, self-sufficient, and indestructible rather than matter in any of the traditional senses of the term. Even the suggestion made by panpsychists that all physical energy must be understood as *psychophysical* energy could be incorporated into a naturalistic world view if the implication that nature *as a whole* has "a mind of its own" was avoided.

There is also much disagreement among the naturalists concerning the contents of nature and the laws that describe the orderly patterns of change that are found within the spatiotemporal universe. Some naturalists have been reductive materialists, who hold that only matter in its most primitive form *really* exists and that the laws that describe and predict the behavior of the most primitive world stuff are perfectly adequate for describing and predicting the behavior of more complex but somehow less real natural entities. The reductionist maintains that all the laws now used for explanation and prediction in the sciences of biology, psychology, and sociology could in principle be converted into the laws of physics and chemistry. During the period of his preoccupation with behavioristic psychology, John Dewey himself seems to have passed through a reductionistic phase. If we have reservations about reductionism, however, we cannot employ them to write off naturalism altogether. Not all naturalists have been reductive materialists; the position is very much out of vogue with most contemporary naturalists. Naturalism is perfectly compatible with a much richer view of the contents of nature and of the complexity of natural law, a view that holds that in relation to matter, life is a new kind of thing; that in relation to life, personality is a new kind of thing; that in relation to personality, society is a new kind of thing; and that all these new levels of complexity within the world must be understood in accordance with new and unique categories of explanation and prediction. Many naturalists have been emergent evolutionists, who hold that when the basic energy of nature reaches certain grades of concentration and complexity, radically new forms of natural being are generated that cannot be reduced to their primitive origins without loss. Although the naturalist opposes radical gaps in nature, he apparently finds nothing wrong with the introduction of diversity into the natural order of things as long as it takes place in small steps over an extended period. Even if the notion of "emergence" is more a disguise for our ignorance than a genuine explanation of the evolution from pure energy of primary and secondary qualities, life, consciousness, self-consciousness, and society, nevertheless a naturalist may consistently reject reductionism. Such a rejection would depend finally on what thorough scientific investigation reveals the actual content of the spatiotemporal universe to be.

A third disagreement arises between the deterministic naturalist, who makes no place for genuine novelty and self-initiative within the universe, and the libertarian naturalist, who does allow for genuine novelty and self-initiative. At first glance it seems that all naturalists are determinists, since they all seem to hold that every event has a cause. However, this causal formula is subject to stronger and weaker interpretations. The stronger naturalistic interpretation is that every event has both necessary *and* sufficient conditions in the antecedent world, in the absence of which the event cannot occur and in the presence of which precisely it and it alone must occur. The weaker interpretation is that every event has necessary but *not* sufficient conditions in the antecedent world, in the absence of which the event cannot occur but in the presence of which it would not be the case that precisely it and it alone must occur. The stronger interpretation holds that each cause has only one possible effect, but the weaker interpretation allows for a limited range of effects. The libertarian accepts the weaker and the determinist the stronger version of the "every event has a cause" principle. A naturalist may be either a libertarian or a determinist.

It is important to understand that there is so much room for disagreement within the naturalistic camp, particularly since so many critics of naturalism have ignored this fact. Critics often identify naturalism with reductive materialism or determinism, and in claiming to refute these positions they also claim to have refuted naturalism. Naturalism does not die so easily, however. To slay the dragon, one must direct his attention to more fundamental aspects of the naturalistic position. The essential points on which the naturalist disagrees with other religious world views are of more interest to the philosophy of religion than are the points on which naturalists disagree with one another. Of the six basic theses of naturalism, the first four are metaphysical, the fifth is methodological, and the sixth is mainly anthropological and axiological. Let us now turn first to the basic naturalistic metaphysics and then to the naturalistic anthropology and axiology. Methodological considerations will be introduced throughout our discussion.

The Naturalistic Metaphysics

NATURALISM is often presented as if it were simply a generalized outcome of the findings of the special natural sciences. An attempt is often made to disguise the fact that *naturalism is a metaphysics,* but it is a metaphysics all the same, insofar as it succeeds in distinguishing itself from agnosticism and positivism. The first four of the general theses of naturalism—that only nature exists, that nature as a whole is nonpersonal, that nature as a whole is eternal and necessary, and that all natural events have causes that are themselves natural events—are not well-established conclusions arrived at within the framework of any of the special natural sciences such as physics, chemistry, biology, or astronomy; nor are they expressions of the necessary presuppositions held by all the sciences; nor is it at all obvious that they are a consequence of using scientific method within the realm of metaphysics. Although the naturalist usually wishes to convey the impression that "science is on my side," none of the special natural sciences presupposes any of these four assertions (though the last—that all causes are natural causes—seems at first to have a better claim to being a general presupposition of the sciences than any of the others). Actually, in order to do his work effectively the scientist needs only the imperative "look for natural causes," rather than the metaphysical assertion "all events have natural causes," which would amount to an a priori metaphysical guarantee that he will always find what he is looking for. Any of the sciences can be pursued just as successfully under the metaphysics of supernaturalism as under the metaphysics of naturalism. The sciences no more "prove the truth" of naturalism than they do of any other metaphysical theory, and the link between natural science and naturalism is more of a psychological association than a logical integration. This psychological association with the natural sciences does nothing whatsoever to substantiate logically the truth of the naturalistic metaphysics. William Ernest Hocking correctly interpreted the relation of naturalism to natural science when he wrote that

> the special sciences, such as physics, chemistry, biology, have nothing to say for or against naturalism; inasmuch as they have nothing to say about the world as a whole. Each of them deals with a partial province. Neither singly nor all together do they constitute a philosophy. And none of them makes any statement about the non-existence of objects outside its domain; nor do they make any collective statement to the effect that all of reality is included in what they survey. It is not science which adopts naturalism: it is naturalism which adopts science as the metaphysical guide. Science cannot be brought forward as a witness in favor of naturalism,—not directly.[9]

The naturalistic philosophy is not a *scientific* alternative to supernaturalism. Rather it is an a priori *metaphysical* alternative having to do with the most fundamental and universal characteristics of reality as a whole, one that is specifically designed to contradict the supernaturalistic metaphysics. It is only natural to expect that the contradictory of a metaphysical system should itself be a metaphysical system. But what is a metaphysical system? How are beliefs that fall within the province of the natural sciences to be distinguished from metaphysical beliefs? There may be no absolute distinction, but some fruitful possibilities may be followed as far as they will take us.

WHAT IS A METAPHYSICAL ASSERTION?

Because it is never possible to be sure that our assertions actually have the characteristics we think them to have, there seems to be no defensible way to differentiate the properties of metaphysical and scientific assertions. Not every assertion that is offered as a metaphysical assertion actually satisfies the criteria by which metaphysical assertions are to be identified. For example, it is sometimes popularly claimed that "science is proving the Bible to be true," a statement that entails a curious mixture of archeology, history, astronomy, metaphysics, and ignorance. Just as some metaphysical assertions are offered as scientific assertions, so some scientific assertions are offered as though they were metaphysical. However, it is possible to roughly identify the properties that one must believe an assertion to have if he is to classify it as either metaphysical or scientific. Let us consider the five criteria for making such a classification.

1. A metaphysical assertion is one believed to say something about either *all* of reality as a whole or *each* of the parts of reality, whereas a scientific assertion is believed to say something about *some* of the parts of reality. This is one of the oldest and most traditional criteria for demarcating metaphysical and scientific beliefs, dating back to Aristotle. To express it more loosely, a metaphysical assertion is believed to be a "universal truth," to "say something about everything," whereas a scientific assertion is believed to be a "limited truth," to "say something about only some things." Metaphysics has being as such or reality as a whole for its subject matter, whereas the natural sciences have selected parts of reality for their subject matter. Although scientific theories may not say something about everything, they may be very general nevertheless. Of course, scientific assertions may be logically universal propositions, but many logically universal scientific propositions have subjects that are believed to constitute only part of reality, such as "all men are mortal" or "all arsenic is poisonous." By contrast, a logically universal proposition that is believed to have all of reality as its subject is metaphysical. We must recognize the limitations of this traditional criterion of demarcation, however. The fact that an assertion seems to have all of reality as its subject matter is at best a sufficient but not a necessary condition for classifying it as metaphysical, as philosophers tend to use the term. There are many metaphysical beliefs that have only part of reality as their subject matter, such as "all men have free will," "all men have immortal souls," "some men have free will," "some men have immortal souls," and "some events (miracles) have supernatural causes." Furthermore, these metaphysical beliefs about parts of reality show that the fact that an assertion seems to have part of reality as its subject matter is only a necessary but not a sufficient condition for identifying it as scientific.

2. A metaphysical assertion is one that at a given time is not believed to be testable in experience, whereas a scientific assertion is one that is believed to be testable in experience. Metaphysical assertions are a priori; scientific assertions are a posteriori. Metaphysical entities are "invisible"; scientific objects are "visible." A metaphysical assertion is one that we cannot imagine to be verifiable or falsifiable by sense observation, whereas a scientific assertion is one that we can imagine to be verifiable or falsifiable by sense observation. This all sounds good in theory, but in practice it is at this very point that it becomes difficult if not impossible to distinguish between science and metaphysics, difficult to be sure that no observation could count for or against a given claim. We cannot insist on *conclusive* verifiability or falsifiability without relegating practically the whole of present-day natural science to the realm of metaphysics. We can at most claim that some observation should be relevant, but so weak an interpretation of testability blurs the line between science and metaphysics. One gradually shades off into the other, and the difference between metaphysical and scientific assertions is reduced to one of extremely weak testability as opposed to relatively weak testability. Like our first criterion, that of extremely weak testability is at best a sufficient but not a necessary condition for classifying an assertion as metaphysical. As our third criterion will indicate, there are some metaphysical theories that suffer from an excess of support from experience rather than an insufficiency of it. Criteria 2 and 3 can never be used simultaneously to identify a belief as metaphysical.

In our discussion of logical positivism, we suggested that no a priori limitations on the possible connections between theory and experience could be set. We never know for sure whether a purely speculative insight will at some point be found to have empirically testable consequences. Any attempt to differentiate between the assertions of science and those of metaphysics will have to reckon with the possibility that the line between the two can never be sharply drawn. Borderline assertions are bound to arise that seem to satisfy some of our criteria but not others, or that seem to be empirically testable to the more creative and imaginative among us but not to the less imaginative, or that are discovered to be testable in one age after having been regarded as not testable earlier.

3. A metaphysical assertion is one that is believed to be supported by or exemplified in *every* experience of *everything,* whereas a scientific assertion is believed to be supported only by *some* experiences of *some things.* This criterion is closely related to the first and is at best a sufficient but not a necessary condition of metaphysics. *If* there are any metaphysical assertions that satisfy this criterion, the difficulty is that they are verified or at least exemplified in every experience of everything and are not falsifiable by any experience of anything. As in science, experience is clearly relevant here, but in metaphysics every experience of everything has a bearing. Here it is not the case that metaphysics is totally out of touch with experience, that it refers to no identifiable state of affairs. Here metaphysics suffers from a superabundance of evidence. If the naturalist is correct in claiming that every natural event has a cause, this claim is exemplified in every experience of everything and refers to every identifiable state of affairs. It is clear that both naturalists and supernaturalists want to allow everything to support their views. For the naturalist, everything experienced testifies to the ultimate self-sufficiency of nature as a whole, and for the supernaturalist, everything experienced testifies to its ultimate contingency. But are they both correct in making these claims? We shall examine some relevant arguments in Chapters 10 and 11.

4. Scientific generalizations are believed to be useful in the process of imaginatively reconstructing the contingent details of the past and of predicting and controlling future events, whereas those metaphysical assertions that express "universal truths" cannot be so used, since it is believed that they will be exemplified no matter what happens or when it happens. Since everything that happens conforms to them, they have no direct bearing on the practical scientific problem of making things happen one way rather than another or of predicting one outcome rather than another. Even if we could in some sense predict that future events would conform to or exemplify our metaphysical theories, this would not be like scientific prediction at all, since scientific predictions could conceivably go wrong, whereas metaphysical predictions could not. Although the naturalist is willing to predict that future natural events will have natural causes from his principle that all natural events have natural causes, in his opinion

this is not a prediction that could conceivably go wrong. This criterion is also as old as Aristotle, for whom metaphysical knowledge was the best knowledge of all, despite its utter uselessness. Considered by itself, this uselessness appears to be neither a necessary nor a sufficient condition for identifying an assertion as metaphysical. Some useless statements are not useless because they are universally exemplified, but for some other reason. A nonsense assertion such as "Monkeys multiplied by moonshine equals masculinity" is quite useless, but it is not universally exemplified.

5. Metaphysical generalizations do not express statistical probabilities, whereas scientific generalizations do express such probabilities. Scientific laws describe repeatable patterns of contingent events within the natural order of things, but metaphysical statements describe either necessary patterns of events or the general characteristics of nature or reality as a whole. Some philosophers have said that metaphysical generalizations express necessities that would be true in any possible world, that they describe the abstract common features of all possible worlds, that they would be universally compatible with, and nonfalsifiable in, any world whatsoever. Even if examples of such assertions can be found, this is again only a sufficient but not a necessary condition for calling a belief metaphysical. "All men have immortal souls" and "some events have supernatural causes" are clearly metaphysical, but by no means obviously or necessarily true in all possible worlds.

There are thus several relatively independent and sufficient criteria for identifying a belief or an assertion as metaphysical, as philosophers commonly employ the term; and when it is said that a belief is metaphysical it is always a contribution to clarity if the criterion or criteria being used are specified. To summarize, we may say that an assertion is metaphysical if we believe that *one or more* of the following conditions is satisfied: (1) It is about reality as a whole or each of the parts of reality; (2) we can imagine either no relevant verifying or falsifying experiences for it, or only extremely inconclusive verifying or falsifying experiences for it; (3) it is supported by or exemplified in every experience of everything; (4) it is useless in the attempt to reconstruct imaginatively the contingent details of the past or to predict and control the contingent details of the future; (5) it does not express statistical probabilities—that is, it does not describe contingent but repeatable patterns of events within the natural order of things. It must be remembered that criteria 2 and 3 can never be used together, though as sufficient conditions they may be used separately; and criterion 4 must always be used in conjunction with at least one other criterion.

Science cannot prove metaphysical beliefs to be true, but this is not to dismiss them as false, meaningless, arbitrary, irrational, uninteresting, or worthless. It is simply to say that metaphysics is not science. (Incidentally, for the most part, supernaturalists have been aware of this all along, whereas naturalists have tended to confuse the two.) If metaphysical theories are not accepted because science can prove them to be true, then why are they accepted? It is not because they answer our scientific questions, but rather because they answer our metaphysical perplexities, because they provide satisfying answers to such metaphysical questions as: Why is there something rather than nothing? Did the world have an origin? If not, what must we say about it? If so, how did it originate? Are there any characteristics that all realities must have in common? If so, what are they? Are there any assertions that would have to be true in all possible worlds? If so, what are they? Instead of answering our scientific questions about particular things or kinds of things, metaphysical systems try to answer the questions we have about everything. A metaphysical system is a rationally unified vision of ultimate reality, of reality as a whole. Metaphysical theories are accepted because of their explanatory power, not because they have themselves been explained. It is because of their usefulness in explaining the structure of ultimate reality and in explaining away alternative views and insights that we are attracted to them. Metaphysical insights are those that are used to prove all else but that cannot themselves be proved. They are to be tested in terms of their consistency, coherence, intelligibility, closeness to experience, and power to illuminate; and they are not all equally successful in these respects. There is certainly a sense in which metaphysics is a priori speculation, but not all a priori speculation works equally well. Some a priori insights have much greater explanatory power than others.

Of course, many naturalists are unwilling to acknowledge openly that their metaphysical theses fall within the realm of a priori speculation. They wish to give the impression that metaphysics is perfectly continuous with natural science and is simply the realm of high-order scientific generalization. They offer their metaphysical truths as abstract generalizations from experience and scientific observation and are probably quite sincere in regarding metaphysical knowledge as a superior level of factual knowledge. But how do the first four theses of naturalism actually measure up to the normal criteria for distinguishing metaphysics and science, especially the criterion of verifiability, which is so crucial to the naturalist's commitment to "scientific method" as the sole source of knowledge? Certainly the claims that only nature exists, that nature as a whole is nonpersonal, that it is eternal and sufficient, and that all events have natural causes are offered as saying something accurate about reality as a whole or each of its parts. These naturalistic theses are not high-order empirical generalizations, with the possible exception of the claim that all events have natural causes; and even this causal doctrine is not regarded as falsifiable, since the naturalist is unwilling to allow anything such as alleged miracles, acts of God, or uncaused events to count against it. What observations could be made that are compatible *only* with the naturalistic view of the exhaustiveness, impersonality, and self-sufficiency of nature and not equally compatible with the supernaturalistic views of creation and providence? Even if some observations are relevant, none furnish conclusive empirical evidence for these aspects of naturalism. At best the empirical evidence for naturalism is extremely weak, as we shall see in later chapters, though this is not a conclusive argument against the view. If the naturalist rejects supernaturalism on the grounds that its truth cannot be proved by the use of scientific method, he must in all fairness reject his own metaphysics on the same grounds. Again, we might raise the question of the usefulness of the theses of naturalism in imaginatively reconstructing the contingent details of the past or in predicting the future. Do we seem to be confronted here with science or metaphysics? Finally, do the theses of naturalism express statistical probabilities? Let us examine this last aspect of the problem in more detail, since it has a special relevance to the question of whether the naturalist arrives at his own metaphysics through the use of scientific method.

It is usually maintained that scientific method operates only within the framework of nature but cannot operate on nature as a whole—that it can give us an estimation of the probability of an event occurring as it does within nature, but not the probability of nature as a whole occurring as it does. In view of the fact that there seems to be only *one* nature as a whole, what would probability and predictability be as applied to it? And if there are more than one of them, then how would anyone gather statistics about natures as wholes? What the naturalist attempts to tell us about nature as a whole is certainly not a matter of statistical probability. He has not examined many universes and discovered a favorable comparison between our own world and other worlds known to be eternal, self-sufficient, and nonpersonal. This sort of difficulty is often presented as a crucial objection to the claim of some supernaturalists that nature as a whole was *probably* created by a supernatural God, but it is *equally* a difficulty for the naturalist who might try to claim that nature as a whole is *probably* eternal, impersonal, exhaustive of reality, and so on. The naturalist cannot legitimately claim that scientific method yields his metaphysical theories, as the function of this method is narrowly understood to involve the verification and falsification of contingent probabilities. If scientific method investigates only natural occurrences, then it cannot investigate nature as a whole, since the whole of space-time is not an occurrence within space-time.

Our principal examination of the arguments for and against naturalism, supernaturalism, and panentheism will take place in Chapters 9, 10, and 11; but we might at this point take a brief look at some points of contention. How does the naturalist try to support his position with argument? Frequently he contends that supernaturalism is false because its truth cannot be established by the use of scientific method, the method of empirical verification of hypotheses. Such a move is deceptive, for it is an attempt to place the entire burden of proof on the shoulders of his metaphysical opponents, to show (along lines to be explored in the Chapters 9, 10, and 11) that supernaturalism cannot be defended by the traditional proofs for the existence of God, and to conclude that his position thereby wins by default. However, no philosophical position really wins over *all* its opponents by such default. Naturalism may try to win over supernaturalism this way, but it obviously cannot win over positivism or agnosticism this way, because the positivist and the agnostic place the burden of proof squarely on the shoulders of anyone who has anything to say. In the case of the naturalist, they might argue that there is little or no empirical support for the claims that the world as a whole exhausts reality, that it is eternal and impersonal, and so on; and as a consequence they might insist either that such claims are meaningless or that at least no one knows them to be true. In all fairness, anyone, even the supernaturalist, would seem to have the right to shift the burden of proof to the shoulders of his opponent, since the burden of proof should fall to anyone who makes philosophical claims.

The naturalist sometimes argues that the assumptions of the completeness, self-sufficiency, and impersonality of nature are *simpler* assumptions than are those of the supernaturalist or panentheist and are to be preferred because of that simplicity. LaPlace is reported to have told Napoleon, who asked his opinion of supernaturalism, that "I have no need of that hypothesis." Presumably this meant that everything that needs to be accounted for by an adequate explanatory system can be accounted for by naturalism, without multiplying principles of explanation after the fashion of the theistic opponents of naturalism. This is quite a question-begging argument, however, as a bit of analysis will show. No scientific or metaphysical hypothesis is preferable to a competitive hypothesis merely because it is simpler. It is not the simplest hypothesis *per se,* but rather the hypothesis that is simplest and at the same time does full justice to its subject matter, that men of reason must prefer. Simplicity *and* comprehensiveness must coincide in a rationally adequate world view. A description of an apple that makes no mention of its color and taste would be simpler than a description that does mention its color and taste, but it would be lacking in comprehensiveness. Likewise, an adequate metaphysical description of ultimate reality must be the one that is simplest and at the same time does full justice to its subject matter. At this point, the question-begging of the naturalist becomes apparent: He is assuming not only that his position is simpler than that of the theist but also that his position completely accounts for everything that there is; it is precisely on the point of comprehensiveness that the theist disagrees with him, but the naturalist makes it one of the premises of his argument. Once the argument is made explicit, its circularity becomes obvious: A simple hypothesis that does full justice to its subject matter (ultimate reality) is preferable to a more complex hypothesis; naturalism is a simple hypothesis that does full justice to the subject matter of ultimate reality; therefore, naturalism is preferable to the more complex hypothesis of the theist. The second premise begs the question, and this is not a situation in which a lack of evidence for a hypothesis such as theism warrants its rejection. If the naturalist maintains that at least everything remotely capable of being given in experience can be accounted for under his assumptions, this is true; but it is also true of the assumptions of supernaturalism. The natural sciences can flourish whether or not nature is eternal, self-sufficient, and so on. The trouble with adding the "everything that can be given in experience" qualification is that the naturalist thus loses the very justification he wants for his basic metaphysical theses. Nature as a whole is not given in experience; certainly its completeness, eternity, and impersonality are not so given; and, as has been shown, there are no probabilities to guide us in these matters.

The naturalist may argue that there is at least one important difference between the theses of naturalism and those of super-naturalism. He may insist that at least the world of nature as he conceives it is known by everyone to exist, which is certainly more than can be said about God. However, the hypothesis that nature exists independently of mind is highly controversial and is by no means as obvious as common sense is likely to assume. Many idealistic philosophers would not be willing to grant the naturalist his starting point of space-time. For such idealists as Leibnitz and Kant, space and time are not primitive features of the "real world" in and of itself, out of which minds may eventually emerge. Rather, space and time are necessary forms of experience that the active knowing mind imposes on the real world as it is encountered in experience. If this is so, then space-time cannot be used as a starting point for the eventual emergence of minds; rather, minds must be presupposed before there can be space-time. To the ideal-ist, the naturalist has the cart before the horse; and the common-sense assumption that we exist in space-time, which itself existed long before we did, is by no means obvious to everyone. For the idealist, space-time exists in us. We shall not attempt to decide whether the naturalist is right in his dispute with the idealist over the subjectivity or objectivity of space-time. We shall simply assume that he is, but we should be aware that this assumption is by no means self-evident to everyone and that it stands in need of philosophical proof. Furthermore, it is probably safe to say that whatever proof is given will not involve simply another application of scientific method. Actually, the bare claim that "the world exists independently of mind" is quite irrelevant, even if idealism is rejected. It is compatible with either naturalism or supernaturalism and does not support either view in any obvious way. The naturalist makes a much stronger claim, that only the world exists; and the supernaturalist also makes a much stronger claim, that the world is not the only thing that exists. They thus differ as to *why* and not as to *whether* the world exists, the former insisting that it is eternal and necessary, the latter insisting that it is created and contingent.

For now, let us note that one of the most fruitful arguments that the naturalist may use against the supernaturalist is the argument from conceptual clarity and intelligibility. He may hold that the position of supernaturalism or any form of theism is unclear and unintelligible by comparison with his own.[10] Of course it is doubtful that the naturalist can argue this way with equal success against every form of theism, especially panentheism, which we shall examine in Chapter 8. Supernaturalism is another story, however. Interestingly enough, supernaturalists have been suicidal enough to begin to develop this argument against themselves, and contemporary Christian antisupernaturalists have carried it far toward its conclusion; in later discussions we shall allow these unwitting allies of naturalism to develop these considerations for us. This matter of intelligibility seems to give rise to an element of subjectivity in metaphysics; both naturalism and supernaturalism seem to be infected with it. Metaphysical theories must satisfy our metaphysical curiosity, but different people find different metaphysical insights to be satisfying, and if all metaphysical positions were equally intelligible there might be no way around this subjectivity. The metaphysical views that some of us find satisfying are really not satisfactory because they are riddled with confusion and lack of clarity. Although naturalism is in a sense an a priori insight into ultimate reality, as are supernaturalism and other metaphysical views, it does not follow from this alone that such alternative metaphysical insights are equally justified. In the final analysis, the strongest argument for any systematic metaphysical insight might be that it is less confused than any of its competitors. Can naturalism make this claim for itself? We shall see.

Humanism, Religion, and God

THE HUMANISTIC PHILOSOPHY OF MAN

Since a naturalist could very well be an egoist or a nationalist or a racist or what have you, there is no necessary logical connection between the metaphysics of naturalism and the humanistic theory of moral value, but as a matter of contingent historical fact naturalists have tended to be humanists. Humanism is both a philosophy of man and a theory of moral value. It sees man as an integral part of the natural order of things and as explicable only in natural categories of explanation. Man is exactly what the sciences of man—biology, psychology, sociology, anthropology, and so on—discover him to be. He is a complex organism, biochemically continuous with the rest of nature. He is a social animal with socially produced and transmitted habits and patterns of response. He is an intelligent animal capable of understanding and manipulating himself and his environment. He is a purposive animal whose aims arise naturally from his basic biological and social constitution and environment. His purposes often conflict with one another and with the purposes of other men, and intelligence has a crucial role in resolving conflicts of interest and maximizing satisfaction within the human community. Human life has exactly the significance that an intelligent, rational, scientific investigation of man and his potentialities discloses—no more and no less. Man sets ideal ends for himself: the values of human association, happiness, artistic creativity, scientific productivity, moral harmony, human growth and fulfillment, and any other goals that may arise from his natural drives, interests, and activities. These ideal ends are not mere abstractions; man finds that he has the means to achieve many of them, and he is continually involved in such achievement. However, bitter experience teaches that nature, society, and human ingenuity do not provide the necessary means to some of these ends. Frustration is inevitable, but so is satisfaction. One of the ideal ends is to maximize the latter and minimize the former, and various individuals can achieve this in varying degrees and in various situations. Although some humanistic naturalists may have been overly optimistic, the present-day humanistic naturalist is likely to hold that progress is possible but not inevitable. Ultimately every individual is destined to die, and that will be the end of him and of all his projects that are not carried on by others. The human race itself may one day perish, either by its own doing or through irresistible hostile natural processes. However, none of this is cause for undue alarm, pessimism, or despair. Men do not live forever, but it does not follow that they do not live at all; men cannot realistically hope for infinite satisfaction and achievement, but it does not follow that there is never any sort of satisfaction and achievement. Although there may be no final achievement, there is worthwhile achievement nonetheless. While life lasts it is good, for most men at any rate, and intelligent planning can make it better. Although there may be no final *cosmic* meaning or purpose for human existence, there are *human* meanings and purposes that no one can afford to ignore or dismiss. The question "Does life have meaning?" definitely has an affirmative answer for the humanist, but it is no thanks to God or the cosmos that this is so.

The humanistic naturalist insists that the ideal ends that men have are those which they set for themselves, and the best justified of these ideal ends are those which are sanctioned by intelligence. No appeal to the supernatural is desirable or necessary in order to understand man and his values. Man is a product of nature, not of divinity. His values neither have nor require a supernatural basis, origin, or sanction. His values do not require any sort of cosmic grounding in the ultimate nature of things. As the naturalist Roy W. Sellars expressed it, naturalism "excludes cosmic purpose, a meaningful totality, and any variation of the Platonic form of the good." [11] Insofar as human ideals are justified, it is reason and not God that sanctions them. Valuation is a human function, not a function of the cosmos as a whole. Nature as a whole is nonpersonal, so it takes no stand either for or against the fulfillment or frustration of human projects. The humanistic claim that human values are distinctively human is closely related both to the naturalistic denial of the supernatural as a source and sanction for human morality and to the rejection of immanentistic or panentheistic claims that nature as a whole contains or is somehow a personal center of purposive intelligence and value. There is absolutely nothing about nature as a whole that would in any way provide a cosmic ground for human ideals. To the claim of the supernaturalist that men would lack the motivation for being moral if there were no cosmic or supercosmic underpinnings for it, the naturalist replies that we must take human motivation as it comes. In doing so, we discover that many humanists are adequately motivated to be moral and that many theists are dismally undermotivated. There is no necessary connection between either the naturalistic or the supernaturalistic metaphysics and human motivation, and the facts do not justify even the more modest claim that the theist will probably be better motivated than the humanist. Many critics of theism have rejected it on the grounds that the vast majority of its devotees are moral hypocrites.

If naturalism, supernaturalism, immanentism, and panentheism are all metaphysical theories, we might wonder what practical difference the adoption of any one of these world views might make. As metaphysical theories, they are all compatible with any sense experience whatsoever. Somehow the world will always *look* the same whether we are naturalists, supernaturalists, or what have you. In some way these views have little or no "cash value" in terms of sense experience. (Whether they have any "cash value" in terms of some distinctively religious type of experience is a question that we shall explore later.) A supernaturalist will never be able to make any sense observations that could not be made by a naturalist; the world will always look the same from either viewpoint. Why then should we adopt one view rather than another if they make no experiential difference? Of course, some supernaturalists believe that there is no need to answer this question, since they mistakenly believe that supernaturalism does at some points make a specific difference in what we see, taste, hear, smell, and touch. When miracles are worked the world is experienced differently. If there were no supernatural God, the waters of the Red Sea would not have rolled back before Moses, Elijah's pyre (rather than that of the prophets of Baal) would not have ignited, Jesus could not have given sight to the blind, and so on. The problem here is one of thinking clearly about the meaning of the claim that the world would be experienced differently if supernaturalism were true. It does not mean that a naturalist or unbeliever could not see what the believers saw. Pharaoh as well as Moses saw; the prophets of Baal as well as Elijah saw; unbelievers as well as disciples saw—and insisted that Jesus worked miracles by the power of the Devil rather than by the power of God. The world *looked* the same to believers and unbelievers alike, and this is all that is meant by the statement that the world would not be experienced differently if supernaturalism or naturalism were true. It is not so much a matter of making observations as it is a matter of giving a metaphysical interpretation to the observations that everyone is able to make. The naturalist sees everything that the supernaturalist sees, but he interprets the observations differently. He can always deny that such alleged miracles happened at all, but there is always something phony about such sweeping repudiations of the spectacular. Sometimes he has to admit that he sees all that the supernaturalist sees, and when he does he must fall back on his fundamental metaphysical thesis: All natural events have natural causes. He holds that some of these spectacular events happened, but if we were able to investigate them thoroughly, we would find them to be completely explicable in terms of natural causes. The difference between the naturalist and the supernaturalist is metaphysical, not observational. Even some supernaturalists have been fully aware of the fact that the unbeliever sees all that the believer sees. Kierkegaard, for example, insisted that there would have been no advantage whatsoever to being a literal "contemporary with Christ." There were many who saw it all yet did not believe; and there are many who are "contemporaries with Christ" only in spirit who do believe. Observation alone would not have removed one's doubts. Seeing any event as a miracle or act of God (or *not* as such) is a matter of metaphysical interpretation, not a matter of scientific observation. However, from the fact that both interpretations are equally metaphysical it should not be inferred that both interpretations are equally valid. This is a matter for much further argumentation, and we shall turn to it again in Chapters 9, 10, and 11.

If naturalism, supernaturalism, immanentism, and panentheism have little "cash value" in terms of sense experience, let us ask again what practical difference it might make if we adopt any one of these world views. The answer to this seems to come into sharpest focus in the dispute over whether there is a cosmic or supercosmic ground for human values. It would make a tremendous difference in the *attitude* we take toward nature or reality as a whole if naturalism were true instead of another world view. If things are ultimately as naturalism envisions them to be, then it would be entirely out of place to take any sort of religious attitude toward nature as a whole, despite the fact that naturalists have often recommended that we take an attitude of "natural piety" toward it.[12] If naturalism is true, then nature as a whole is not something about which we could or should be ultimately concerned. It is not an appropriate object of religious affection or involvement or worship or devotion. Nature as a whole is not to be admired for its intelligence or wisdom, since these are only human attributes. Since it is incapable of responding in kind, it is inappropriate to love it with all one's heart and soul and mind and strength. Since it is oblivious of all our responses, gratitude toward it for its generosity seems entirely out of place, as does animosity toward it for its niggardliness. It has no moral or aesthetic aims or attributes; we cannot see in nature as a whole any paradigms of moral integrity or decadence, since they are simply not there to be seen. It is totally insensitive to human happiness and unhappiness alike. Naturalism has no problem of evil or theodicy to solve; nature as a whole is neither good nor evil, neither friend nor foe. When a naturalist asks if nature is "friendly to man," [13] the metaphor is misleading, even if the answer is "partly yes, partly no."

If the naturalistic picture of nature is correct, what is there about nature to revere except mute power and self-sufficiency? What is there about nature as a whole that would evoke "natural piety"? What does "natural piety" involve? If it involves merely relying on nature to provide for our human needs, we must always balance such reliance against the knowledge that nature does not always "come through." If it is merely a matter of knowing when to stop asking questions of nature, we come dangerously close to blocking the path of inquiry. If it involves seeing man as part of a larger whole, we must constantly remind ourselves that this whole of nature is very much unlike man because it has no values or personal traits. If it involves a deep appreciation of the limitless richness and productivity of a natural order in which man eventually appeared, this appreciation cannot include a conviction that nature somehow planned, intended, purposed, or tried to do what it has done. All anthropomorphic thinking about nature must be ruthlessly excluded. However, there is room for suspicion that when a naturalist takes the attitude of "natural piety" toward the cosmos, he packs a great deal more of traditional theism into it than his avowed metaphysics will consistently permit!

We have said that the normal religious attitudinal response to nature as a whole would be inappropriate if naturalism were true. Does its being true therefore mean nothing more than that these attitudinal responses are inappropriate, or is this merely a test of a naturalist's sincerity? How would a naturalist determine whether he and his fellow naturalists were misusing the naturalistic metaphysics? Suppose that a naturalist either secretly or openly loved nature with all his heart and soul and mind and strength and expected to be loved by nature in return.

DEWEY'S ACCOUNT OF RELIGION AND GOD

Let us not be misled into thinking that humanistic naturalists are completely opposed to the cultivation of religious attitudes. They are all for the cultivation of the religious response to something—but what is this something? They give de facto recognition to the claim that nature itself is not a suitable object of religious attitudes and devotion by proposing that we direct our religiosity toward humanity, human ideals, and the attempt to actualize these ideals. It is a fact of some significance that most of them have not followed Spinoza in identifying God with nature. Although they pay lip service to piety toward nature, it is mainly piety toward humanity that deeply interests them. Though he warned against the worship of humanity viewed in isolation from nature, John Dewey wanted to naturalize and humanize the religious response to life. He believed that religious attitudes are those that "lend deep and enduring support to the processes of living." [14] Religious experiences are any experiences "having the force of bringing about a better, deeper and enduring adjustment in life." [15] If the word *God* is to be used at all, it must be explicitly redefined to make it clear that, for the humanistic naturalist, God and religious devotion have nothing to do with the supernatural or with cosmic teleology. For Dewey, the word *God*

> denotes the unity of all ideal ends arousing us to desire and actions. Does the unification have a claim upon our attitude and conduct because it is already, apart from us, in realized existence, or because of its own inherent meaning and value? Suppose for the moment that the word "God" means the ideal ends that at a given time and place one acknowledges as having authority over his volition and emotion, the values to which one is supremely devoted, as far as these ends, through imagination, take on unity. If we make this supposition, the issue will stand out clearly in contrast with the doctrine of religions that "God" designates some kind of Being having prior and therefore non-ideal existence.
>
> .   .   .
>
> We are in the presence neither of ideals completely embodied in existence nor yet of ideals that are mere rootless ideals, fantasies, utopias. For there are forces in nature and society that generate and support the ideals. They are further unified by the action that gives them coherence and solidity. It is this *active* relation between ideal and actual to which I would give the name "God." [16]

Although the working unity of human ideals and activities that Dewey mentions may itself fall somewhat short of being an ideal object of ultimate religious devotion, adoration, worship, and concern, the naturalist must rest content with the insight that this is all we have. Is it enough?

Along with most other humanistic naturalists, Dewey emphatically insists that "God" in the traditional supernaturalistic sense does not exist. In relation to traditional supernaturalism Dewey is clearly an atheist, and this fact should not be obscured by his proposal that we continue to use the word *God* in the manner suggested. For Dewey, *God* in the traditional supernaturalistic sense has no actual referent, and supernaturalism has been a source of constant mischief. It has frustrated man's attempts to come to a rational, scientific understanding of himself and his world. It has siphoned off human energies that might have been profitably channeled into the solution of this-worldly ills and poured them into the empty and illusory pit of otherworldliness. It has offered false hopes and vain promises of better things to come by the grace of God alone, dwarfed the significance of human experience here and now, and frustrated man's attempts to improve his situation. Human power and responsibility have been diminished, if not completely negated, by supernaturalistic views of the omnipotence of God. The supernaturalistic sense of *God* has been a curse rather than a blessing to humanity, but a radically redefined sense of *God* might change that, engendering in man a confidence in his own ability to understand himself and his world, a due regard for the day-to-day values of human existence, a new openness toward this-worldly responsibilities, and a new willingness to meet the moral and intellectual challenges of the times and to cope responsibly with the task of building a better future for himself and his fellow men. The qualities of human life and experience that contribute to such a successful adjustment to the enduring problems of human existence are those that Dewey proposes to call religious. Dewey and the other humanistic naturalists of this century were advocating a "Godless or atheistic religion" long before the death-of-God theology and the notion of "Christian atheism" became popular with the most avant-garde of today's theologians.

Dewey is very generous in his redefinition of *God,* allowing almost *any* ideals to qualify; but most other humanistic naturalists who wish to use the word at all reserve the label for distinctively *moral* ideals and the factors that contribute to their actualization. Humanistic naturalists are ultimately concerned about moral involvement with the welfare of mankind. Dewey often indicates a preference for the ideals of moral humanism, assuming perhaps that the ideals of, say, egoism or nationalism or racism could never be fully "unified." Does the rejection of a position on the grounds that it is lacking in unity represent an application of "scientific method"?

We have seen that for the humanistic naturalist, the best-justified ideal ends are those that are sanctioned by human intelligence rather than by God or the cosmos. What does this sanction by human intelligence involve? The humanist is clearly not an egoist who believes that he ought to promote only his own personal welfare, nor a nationalist who believes that he ought to promote only the welfare of his country, nor a racist who believes that he ought to promote only the welfare of the members of a certain race. He is a moralist who believes the welfare of all men to be of ultimate importance and who believes that it is his duty to further that welfare by every means at his disposal. How is this commitment to the humanistic moral outlook to be reconciled with the naturalist's methodological commitment to scientific method as the sole source of truth? How does scientific method help him to select among the alternatives? Assuming that the humanist is not a subjectivist who believes that value judgments are incapable of truth or falsity or rational justification, how can the humanistic naturalist reconcile his commitment to both morality and scientific method as the sole source of truth? It is doubtful that the two can be reconciled if scientific method is narrowly conceived as the empirical verification and falsification of hypotheses. So understood, scientific method yields a knowledge of "the facts" but not a knowledge of "the good." Since the time of David Hume, most philosophers have recognized the impossibility of passing logically from the *is* to the *ought,* from judgments of fact to judgments of value. This is not to say that there can be no rational justification of values, norms, and ideals; it is only to say that such rational justification must be different from empirical scientific proof, that any rational methods involved must be different from scientific method. It might be possible, for example, to deduce one's ideals from more abstract ideals, or it might be possible to claim that ultimate ideals are rationally chosen under conditions of freedom, enlightenment, and impartiality.[17] However, such justifications are quite different from simple observations of the facts. The humanistic naturalist moves too easily from the *is* to the *ought,* from the desired to the desirable. In matters of value, John Dewey asked, "why not rest the case with what is verifiable and concentrate thought and energy upon its full realization?"[18] The answer is that if we rest the case simply with what is verifiable, we shall never arrive at the good. Scientific method can certainly show us how to implement our ideals effectively once the ideals

WILLIAMS, DONALD, "Naturalism and the Nature of Things," *Philosophical Review*, Vol. LIII (September 1944), pp. 417–43.

ON HUMANISM AND RELIGION

BURTT, E. A., *Types of Religious Philosophy* (New York, Harper & Row, 1951), pp. 332–49.

HUXLEY, JULIAN, *Religion Without Revelation* (New York, Harper & Row, 1957).

KURTZ, PAUL, ed., *Moral Problems in Contemporary Society: Essays in Humanistic Ethics* (Englewood Cliffs, N.J., Prentice-Hall, 1969).

LAMONT, CORLISS, *Humanism as a Philosophy* (New York, Philosophical Library, 1957).

LAMPRECHT, STERLING, *The Metaphysics of Naturalism* (New York, Appleton-Century-Crofts, 1967), pp. 179–83 and Chapter 13.

NAGEL, ERNEST, "Naturalism Reconsidered," *Proceedings and Addresses of the American Philosophical Association*, Vol. XXVIII (1954–55), pp. 10–12.

POTTER, CHARLES F., *Humanism, A New Religion* (New York, Simon & Schuster, 1930).

————, *Humanizing Religion* (New York, Harper & Row, 1933).

RANDALL, JOHN H., JR., "Naturalism and Humanism," in F. E. Johnson, ed., *Patterns of Faith in America Today* (New York, Harper & Row, 1957), pp. 155–84.

REESE, CURTIS W., *Humanistic Religion* (New York, Macmillan, 1931).

————, *The Meaning of Humanism* (Boston, Beacon Press, 1945).

SANTAYANA, GEORGE, *Reason in Religion* (New York, Scribner's, 1905).

SELLARS, ROY W., *Religion Coming of Age* (New York, Macmillan, 1928), Chapters 14, 15, and 16.

Notes

1   Discussions of the meaning of *naturalism* may be found in Ernest Nagel, "Naturalism Reconsidered," *Proceedings and Addresses of the American Philosophical Association*, Vol. XXVIII (1954–55), pp. 5, 7–13; Sterling Lamprecht, *The Metaphysics of Naturalism* (New York, Appleton-Century-Crofts, 1967), Chapter

14; Y. H. Krikorian, ed., *Naturalism and the Human Spirit* (New York, Columbia University Press, 1944), Chapter 15; John H. Randall, Jr., "Naturalism and Humanism," in F. E. Johnson, ed., *Patterns of Faith in America Today* (New York, Harper & Row, 1957), pp. 155–56; and J. B. Pratt, *Naturalism* (New Haven, Conn., Yale University Press, 1930), Chapter 1.

2 The thesis that only nature exists is discussed in Krikorian, *Naturalism and the Human Spirit,* pp. 288, 357–58; Lamprecht, *The Metaphysics of Naturalism,* pp. 173–83, 202; Sidney Hook, *The Quest for Being* (New York, St. Martin's Press, 1961), pp. 192–93; Roy W. Sellars, *The Philosophy of Physical Realism* (New York, Russell & Russell, 1966), p. 15; Roy W. Sellars, *Religion Coming of Age* (New York, Macmillan, 1928), p. 141; and George Santayana, *The Works of George Santayana,* Vol. XIV (New York, Scribner's, 1937), pp. 196–97.

3 Naturalists often talk like positivists or metaphysical skeptics. See, for example, Krikorian, *Naturalism and the Human Spirit,* pp. 288–89; Hook, *The Quest for Being,* pp. 159–71; and John H. Randall, Jr., *Nature and Historical Experience* (New York, Columbia University Press, 1958), pp. 126–27.

4 For naturalistic arguments against cosmic teleology, see Nagel, "Naturalism Reconsidered," pp. 10–11; Hook, *The Quest for Being,* pp. 236–37; Lamprecht, *The Metaphysics of Naturalism,* pp. 172–73; Santayana, *The Works of George Santayana,* Vol. XIV, p. 328; Sellars, *Religion Coming of Age,* pp. 147–48, 155–58, and Chapters 12 and 13; Sellars, "Does Naturalism Need Ontology?" *Journal of Philosophy,* Vol. XLI, No. 25 (December 1944), p. 686; and John Dewey, *A Common Faith* (New Haven, Conn., Yale University Press, 1934), pp. 19–20, 41–42.

5 Many naturalists prefer to avoid the question of origins, but those who discuss it prefer the thesis of the eternity and self-sufficiency of nature. It seems that all naturalists are implicitly committed to such a thesis. Roy W. Sellars is quite explicit about it. See Sellars, *The Philosophy of Physical Realism,* pp. 12, 15, and *Religion Coming of Age,* pp. 146, 162–73, 212. See also Hook, *The Quest for Being,* pp. 235–36, and Pratt, *Naturalism,* p. 56. It is interesting that major proponents of both the "big bang" and the "steady state" cosmologies in contemporary speculative cosmology are committed to the eternity and self-sufficiency of nature. See, for example, George Gamow, *The Creation of the Universe* (New York, New American Library, 1952), pp. 36–37, 134, and Fred Hoyle, *The Nature of the Universe* (New

York, New American Library, 1950), Chapter 6, especially pp. 111–15.

6   The thesis that all events have natural causes is discussed by Nagel, "Naturalism Reconsidered," pp. 8–9, 14; Krikorian, *Naturalism and the Human Spirit*, p. 288; Hook, *The Quest for Being*, pp. 185–86; Lamprecht, *The Metaphysics of Naturalism*, Chapters 9 and 10 and pp. 163, 202–03; Pratt, *Naturalism*, pp. 47–58; and Sellars, *Religion Coming of Age*, pp. 147–52.

7   That only scientific method is legitimate is defended and discussed in Nagel, "Naturalism Reconsidered," pp. 12–17; Krikorian, *Naturalism and the Human Spirit*, Chapter 10 and pp. 358–59, 374–76; Hook, *The Quest for Being*, pp. 75–79, 175–78, 183–88, 191–95, 213–28; and Donald Williams, "Naturalism and the Nature of Things," *Philosophical Review*, Vol. LIII (September 1944), p. 417. Dewey's commitment to scientific methodology is discussed in Chapter 2 of this book.

8   For readings on the naturalist's commitment to humanism, see the second section of the Suggestions for Further Reading at the end of this Chapter.

9   William Ernest Hocking, *Types of Philosophy* (New York, Scribner's, 1929), p. 49.

10   Several naturalists have developed the conceptual argument against supernaturalism. For examples, see Hook, *The Quest for Being*, pp. 115–25, and Sellars, *Religion Coming of Age*, pp. 168–73.

11   Sellars, "Does Naturalism Need Ontology?" p. 686.

12   Discussions of "natural piety" may be found in Dewey, *A Common Faith*, pp. 25–26; Hook, *The Quest for Being*, p. 208; Lamprecht, *The Metaphysics of Naturalism*, pp. 213–14; and Santayana, *The Works of George Santayana*, Vol. IV, pp. 131–42.

13   Dewey, *A Common Faith*, pp. 55, 56.

14   *Ibid.*, p. 15.

15   *Ibid.*, p. 16.

16   *Ibid.*, pp. 42, 50–51.

17   Such a concept of "rational choice" is developed in Paul W. Taylor, *Normative Discourse* (Englewood Cliffs, N.J., Prentice-Hall, 1961), Chapter 6. See my discussion of it in Rem B. Edwards, "On Being 'Rational' About Norms," *Southern Journal of Philosophy*, Vol. V, no. 3 (Fall 1967), pp. 180–86.

18   Dewey, *A Common Faith*, p. 72.

chapter seven

God
and the
World SUPERNATURALISM

Most of the theology that the Western world has produced has been supernaturalistic. Supernaturalism is the classical view of traditional Western theism as this has been developed since Philo in the first century and the early church fathers in the second century A.D. It is not the view of biblical religion, as is so often assumed, for biblical religion was neither clearly supernaturalistic nor panentheistic but contained a profusion of religious insights out of which either view might have developed. When Greek prejudices against the pluralistic, dynamic aspects of reality were wedded to the Hebraic concept of God by the early church fathers, the result was supernaturalism. Since the second century A.D. the early church fathers, Augustine, Anselm, Aquinas, Luther, Calvin, Kierkegaard, Barth (hesitatingly), Brunner, and the overwhelming majority of Judaeo-Christian theologians have been supernaturalists. Many philosophical thinkers, such as Descartes, Locke, and the deists, have also been supernaturalists. Of course, there is ample room for quarrels within the family of supernaturalism. There is also room for close relatives like Plato, Plotinus, Kant, and metaphysical idealists through the ages who would have been supernaturalists were it not for the fact that they have only an apparent but not a real nature for God to be "beyond." Nevertheless, the main family traits of supernaturalism are identifiable, and practically all the theists of the Western world are committed to its basic theses

166

either explicitly or implicitly and with varying degrees of emphasis. Even those theologians whose main emphasis is on Christology, soteriology, eschatology, or morals typically presuppose a supernaturalistic metaphysics. But what is supernaturalism?

Family Traits of Supernaturalism

I F supernaturalism is thought of as the contrary of naturalism, then its main traits can easily be summarized. (1) First of all, it is the view that nature is *not* the only thing that exists. The supernaturalist believes that God and possibly even heaven and hell exist in a realm of reality that somehow lies beyond nature. This is the realm of supernature, the "other world." (2) Since the supernaturalist is not an immanentist, he agrees with the naturalist that nature as a whole is nonpersonal; but he offers the claim that at least nature expresses the will and purposes of a being greater than nature, God. (3) Nature as a whole and even the most basic stuff within it is contingent and created. (4) Some natural events, such as acts of God, miracles, and the creation of nature itself, have supernatural causes. (5) There are other avenues of truth besides scientific method, either "reason" more broadly conceived, or faith or revelation. (6) The humanistic philosophy of man and ethics are inadequate, since man was created by God in his own image and is not a mere product of natural causes, and since morality has some sort of grounding in the ultimate nature of things.

In this discussion we shall be concerned mainly with the supernaturalistic concept of God, but we should realize that all the metaphysical traits of supernaturalism go hand in hand. In affirming that there is a realm of reality that lies beyond nature, it denies that nature alone exists. In affirming that nature owes its existence to a transcendent God, it denies the metaphysical necessity and self-sufficiency of the world and also denies that all causes are natural causes. Supernaturalism is "other-worldly," and it insists that the existence of that other world is somehow an ontological presupposition of the existence of this world. It was God who created the heavens and the earth in the beginning, the firmament shows his handiwork, and the heavens declare his glory.

The supernaturalist offers a concept of God and of his relation to the world that is the contrary of that of the naturalist, and at first it might appear that the two views have equal explanatory power. In some sense this might be true, but it does not follow that both views are equally justified. There is one respect in which naturalism seems to have a distinct advantage over traditional supernaturalism—that of superior clarity or intelligibility. Can we really "make sense" out of the notions of a transcendent God and heaven? Although supernaturalists have offered us a view of the supernatural, they have at the same time always insisted that they are attempting to say the unsayable, think the unthinkable, understand the mysterious, comprehend the incomprehensible. They constantly warn us that they do not mean what they say and that they cannot say what they mean. They concede that we are driven to think temporally of the eternal, spatially of the nonspatial, corporeally of the incorporeal, nonspiritually of the spiritual, finitely of the infinite, complexly of the utterly simple, and so on. Our concepts apply only analogically, metaphorically, symbolically, paradoxically to divine things. Some supernaturalists have gone so far as to insist that we can speak only negatively of supernatural things, that we have no positive concepts that apply at all, that God is completely hidden, incomprehensible, ineffable. The line between such a thoroughgoing "negative theology" and utter, total skepticism or agonisticism is an exceedingly fine one, if it can be drawn at all. Others claim that God is so "wholly other" that it is only by the grace of God that our thoughts about him have any meaning at all. Still others insist that we can know only *that* God exists but not *what* he is like; yet they write many volumes telling us what he is like. Those who most vehemently insist that there are infinite qualitative differences between God and man do not hesitate to explicate God's qualities. All of this indicates that the supernaturalist is at least vaguely aware of the unintelligibility of his position, though he is confident that such unintelligibility is all for the glory of God. We never know how seriously to take him or even how seriously he takes himself. Despite all his disclaimers, however, the typical supernaturalist speaks with great confidence of God and his relation to the world. Realizing that we do not know quite how to take it, we must now look at what he has to say.

The Attributes of God

GOD and possibly even heaven and hell exist in a realm of reality that lies beyond nature, the supernaturalist maintains. But who is God? What is God like? How shall we conceive of him? What is the meaning of *God?* A lengthy list of attributes can be drawn up after a reading of the basic literature of supernaturalism. Just how many attributes there are no one seems to know for sure. Supernaturalists tend to play favorites with those attributes of God that are of special interest to them, so it would not be entirely amiss if we did the same. Few supernaturalists would quarrel with the contents of our list, though they might wish to extend it indefinitely or quibble about the order of importance in which the attributes are listed. We shall attempt to list them in an order in which the explication of one leads naturally into the discussion of another, for in the unity and simplicity of God all the attributes are thought to be thoroughly integrated and logically interconnected. We shall begin with the attribute of transcendence, for it is here that the problem of the intelligibility of supernaturalism is generated and comes into sharpest focus. From a discussion of transcendence we shall proceed to a discussion of creativity, omnipresence, eternity, omnipotence, infinity, moral goodness, and holiness.

TRANSCENDENCE

God is a transcendent being. The other-worldliness of supernaturalism rests on this divine attribute. God exists "beyond space" and "before time," since the entire spatiotemporal universe owes its existence to him. The difficulty is that *beyond* is itself a spatial concept, and *before* is a temporal concept. No wonder we must speak metaphorically of divine things. Can supernaturalism even be expressed without self-contradiction? Even if there is no self-contradiction here, there is at least paradox (and the distinction between the two is sometimes very difficult to make). The supernaturalist cannot speak of his spatiotemporally transcendent God without making use of spatiotemporal concepts. In the three-level universe of the biblical period God and heaven were "over" or "above" the earth, and hell was "under" or "beneath" it. In the Lord's Prayer God is addressed as the Father who is "in heaven." In the doctrine of the Incarnation God is said to have "emptied himself" out of heaven and "descended" into our earthly realm. In one version of the Apostles' Creed the crucified Christ is said to have "descended" into hell. The resurrected Christ is said to have "ascended" into heaven and to "sit" at the "right hand" of God. Spatiotemporal relations seem to exist as much in the other world as in this world —yet this world alone is spatiotemporal. In heaven the saints will walk and talk with one another and with God, even if they do not spend eternity strumming harps. Also, more modern versions of supernaturalism, which have felt the impact of modern astronomy and abandoned the notion of the three-level cosmos, must make use of spatial and temporal metaphors. For the supernaturalist, God is still transcendent. Bishop John A. T. Robinson, one of the most influential and outspoken members of the contemporary movement of Christian antisupernaturalism, has pointed out that *"in place of a God who is literally or physically 'up there' we have accepted, as part of our mental furniture, a God who is spiritually or metaphysically 'out there.' "* [1] Even this modernized supernaturalism with which Bishop Robinson and others have so eloquently expressed their discontent must think of God as being somehow "beyond space" and "before time," even if it is only in some spiritual or metaphysical sense. Can such thoughts even be thought? If the notions of *beyond* and *outside* are thoroughly "spiritualized," what do we have left? There may be ways of conceiving *transcendence* that do not involve spatiotemporal otherness, and we shall return to this theme in our discussion of panentheism. However, it is in the creation myth that the spatiotemporality of God's transcendence is most obvious and the paradoxes of transcendence become most acute.

Of course, supernaturalists tend to resist any attempt to probe too deeply into the paradoxes of transcendence. St. Augustine expressed a reverent skepticism when confronted with the question of what God was doing before he made heaven and earth: "He was preparing hell for pryers into mysteries." [2] Actually, Augustine himself preferred the answer that God was not doing anything at all, since any "doing" on God's part would have been creating. Still there is the genuine puzzle of what happened "before creation." The supernaturalist cannot avoid such questions, since for him the universe has only a finite past; but neither can he answer them, since any answer would involve the thought of a "time before time began." The most he can say is that "before time there was eternity," yet he cannot tell us what this "before" means. Even insisting that God himself reveals this to be true does not explain to us what it means. Similar difficulties arise about the claim that God exists "outside space." Yet this type of metaphor is also unavoidable for the supernaturalist, since space is what God created (among other things). Before the heavens were framed, God was; but where was he? "Outside space"? Does this mean that he was *nowhere?* If so, how would this be different from saying that he did not exist at all? The common retort is that he was "in heaven," but this does not solve the problem, since heaven is popularly conceived as being "a space outside all space and a time outside all time." Here the paradox becomes most obviously a contradiction, and a serious problem remains even for those more sophisticated theologians who explicitly recognize such expressions as metaphorical or mythological. What is the nonmetaphorical truth about heaven and creation? If *all* spatiotemporal relations are ruthlessly excluded from our conception of heaven, is anything left? Dare to describe it! If *all* spatiotemporal categories are completely abandoned, can the creation story even be stated? Try to state it! If God is creator, can he be transcendent?

CREATIVITY

It is not at all clear in the light of much recent biblical scholarship that the Genesis creation story conceives of God as creating the world out of nothing, although it has been traditional for supernaturalists to interpret Genesis 1 in this way since the time of Philo in the first century and Irenaeus in the second century A.D. There is no clear formulation of the doctrine in the Bible, although it is commonplace to read the doctrine back into biblical discussions of origins. The God of Genesis 1 is a world designer who resembles Plato's demiurge in many ways. The primordial world-stuff seems to coexist with God and is not created by him at the beginning. "When God began to create the heavens and the earth, the earth was without form and void . . ." is now recognized as a perfectly legitimate translation of Genesis 1:1–2. God begins the process of creation only at verse 3, when he says, "Let there be light." [3] The Jewish and Christian thinkers of the first and second centuries A.D. who first clearly formulated the doctrine of creation *ex nihilo* did develop the orthodox supernaturalistic interpretation, but the insights of the writer of Genesis were not so clearly supernaturalistic.

The ambiguity of the Genesis creation story on the question of creation *ex nihilo* may mean only that biblical religion was neither clearly supernaturalistic nor clearly panentheistic but contained a profusion of insights from which either view might have developed. However, it is clear that most classical supernaturalists have subscribed to the view that the entire natural order of things was brought into being out of nothing by divine fiat at some point in the finite past. The creation story requires the supernaturalist to deny many of the things the naturalist wishes to say about nature and to insist that these things can be said of God alone. It is not nature that is eternal and necessary; it is God. Even the most basic stuff of nature, the primordial chaos without form and void, owes its existence to God. It is not nature that is uncaused, uncreated, self-sufficient, and indestructible; it is God. By contrast with the Creator, the creation is contingent, caused, created, destructible. Only God has been around forever; nature has a finite past and possibly a finite future.

Supernaturalists have disagreed about the source or sources of their belief that the universe has a finite past. Some have believed this is a truth of revelation, others that it is a truth of reason. During the medieval period, for example, St. Thomas Aquinas insisted that revelation alone could supply us with this information, that reason could not disprove the Aristotelian doctrine of the *abeternity* of the world (the coexistence of the world with God from eternity), and that in the philosophical proofs for the existence of God it is possible to show that God is the "first cause" in the "great chain of being," but not that he is the "first cause" in time. Nevertheless, St. Thomas believed on the basis of revelation that there *was* a first moment of time at some point in the finite past. By contrast, St. Bonaventure, among others, thought that reason could prove that the universe has a finite past and thus could substantiate the Christian revelation. For him, the impossibility of an infinite regress applied to the temporal as well as to the ontological series of causes. We shall examine these arguments in more detail in Chapter 10.

For now, let us note simply that no matter what the source of the view that the universe has a finite past might be, it does generate paradoxes for the supernaturalist. It is this view that raises the inescapable problem of "a time before time began." It is this view that requires the supernaturalist to treat the "first moment" of time as an event in a much more extended temporal series, since before the world was, God was, and God acted and spoke. It is this view that forces him to treat the origin of nature as itself an event in time while still maintaining that time and space exclusively belong within, and originated with, the created order of nature. The theory requires him to treat nature as a whole as the supreme effect of a supreme cause, rather than as the locus of all causes and effects. Naturalism succeeds in avoiding such paradoxes, holding that it just does not make sense to think of "a time before time began" or of a "first moment" of time. For the naturalist the past is infinite; every natural event is preceded by another natural event ad infinitum; every natural effect has a natural cause. But for the supernaturalist there is at least one natural effect that has a supernatural cause: the universe as a whole, which is the effect of God's creative activity. In saying that every natural effect has a natural cause, the naturalist is not committed to saying that the universe as a whole has a natural cause. The universe as a whole is not the effect of anything for the naturalist; rather, it is the context within which all causes and effects have their locus. Neither the naturalist nor the supernaturalist believes that everything has a cause; nature for the former and God for the latter are uncaused. The naturalist is not required to treat the whole of space and time as an event, or effect, within space and time; the supernaturalist wants to have it both ways at once. However, if the universe as a whole is an effect, it is so drastically different from all other effects with which we are acquainted that many have seriously questioned the validity of calling it an effect at all. All other effects are events *within* time and space, have natural antecedents, and are manifestations of predictable regularities *within* the natural order of things, and this could not be true of the sudden appearance of nature from nowhere "in the beginning." How much is left of the notion of "an effect" when these characteristics are excluded?

The supernaturalist insists that God's creativity is radically unlike any finite analogue in human nature and experience. All human "making" is not really "creating," since it presupposes a preexistent material and is nothing more than giving new form to old stuff. God's creating is a matter of bringing into being both the stuff and the form of it. Even human artistic and intellectual creativity takes place within a continuum of spatiotemporal events and presupposes necessary (though perhaps not sufficient) antecedent spatiotemporal conditions. None of this is true of God's creative activity in producing the world *ex nihilo*. Nothing is presupposed, not even time; but then must we not say that the creative act by which God produced the world occurred in "a time before time began"?

OMNIPRESENCE

We have seen that the notion of God as transcendent creator is intimately connected with the notion of space. Another traditional attribute of God also involves spatial metaphors, the notion of his omnipresence. It is true that supernaturalists wish to think of God as being in heaven, outside created nature; but it is also true that they wish to think of him as being everywhere, inside created nature. In itself there is no paradox or contradiction, for the typical supernaturalist has never claimed that God exists *only* in heaven or *only* as transcendent creator. In biblical religion God is also the immanent lord of all creation, who constantly directs, controls, and sustains the realm of nature and human history and who constantly interacts in special ways with selected individuals and nations. Gradually the concept of God came to be universalized in such a way that he was thought of as active in the affairs of all men and nations. For the Psalmist, God is an inescapable presence, who cannot be evaded in heaven or hell or in the uttermost parts of the sea. For St. Paul, God is the one in whom we live and move and have our being. In the Koran God is said to be closer to us than our own neck vein. The literature of mysticism is filled with a deep awareness of the universal presence of the divine, and popular religion usually makes a place for the constancy of personal intercourse and communion with God.

Despite the constant affirmation of the omnipresence of God, the attribute of omnipresence has always been something of an embarrassment to classical supernaturalism as this position was developed during and after the first century A.D. Notwithstanding the use of the spatial metaphor of "presence," supernaturalists have insisted that this attribute be interpreted spiritually rather than spatially. The presence of God is indeed something unique. He is not simply present here or there in the way in which all other things are present. He is the only entity who can be said to be everywhere; but what does this mean? In the hands of supernaturalist theologians the attribute of omnipresence really does seem to die "the death by a thousand qualifications." [4] Indeed, this phrase is a fitting epitaph for the entire conceptual framework of supernaturalism. In what sense can the supernaturalist conceive of God as even "spiritually" present? God and the world are so radically different that it is seemingly impossible for God to be present in the world or for the world to be present in God in any intelligible sense. God is being itself, pure actuality, utter unity and simplicity; by contrast, the world is becoming, passivity and potentiality, complexity. God is permanent, eternal, unchanging; the world is transient, temporal, changing. God is incorporeal, spiritual, nonspatial; the world is corporeal, material, spatial. God is necessary, self-sufficient; the world is contingent, dependent. God is creator, absolute cause; the world is created, absolute effect. God is infinite, the world finite. He is perfect, the world imperfect (but good all the same). How could God be present in the world in *any* sense for the supernaturalist? God and the world have absolutely nothing in common. How could an eternal God act in time or ever be incarnate in time? Kierkegaard and most supernaturalists have believed that affirmations of the presence of the eternal in time, of the infinite in the finite, and so on, exemplify the quintessence of paradox (or self-contradiction?) and that the essence of being a Christian is to believe such paradoxes with an infinite passion anyway. Do you think that Christianity stands or falls with supernaturalism, for which the presence of God in the world is such a logical quandary?

ETERNITY

God is eternal. In him there is no change, becoming, temporality, or shadow of turning. He is from everlasting to everlasting, without beginning and without end. Negatively, the eternity of God simply means that God has no beginning and no end. Classical supernaturalism has given a more positive meaning to the concept of *eternity,* however. Eternity is the presence of past, present, and future all at once in a single *totum simul* ("simultaneous totality"). God's eternity involves his knowledge of and containment of the world's past, present, and future in a single "now." Eternity is all time all at once; but there is another paradox: We can conceive of eternity only by making use of temporal metaphors. Eternity is the assimilation of the concepts of past and future *to the concept of the present.* Such a view of eternity does not really take us "beyond time"; it merely attempts to reduce our concepts of the temporal past and future to our concept of the temporal present. From his superior vantage point "outside the world," God views all the events of the world from beginning to end in a single, supertemporal "now." This traditional interpretation of God's eternity is in some ways quite different from the biblical interpretation, in which the eternity of God is more a matter of imperishable moral faithfulness and constancy than of the metaphysical simultaneity of past, present, and future in God. Supernaturalism has wanted to have both the metaphysics and the morality, but it is not at all clear that it can. What is the difference between saying that God perceives the future as present and saying that God perceives the square as round?

Other characteristics of God as the traditional supernaturalist conceives of him are closely related to the attribute of eternity. God's providence, predestining, foreknowledge, omnipotence, creativity, and so on, must be viewed in the light of God's eternity. God knows the future in the minutest detail. For him the future possibilities of the universe are already present and actual, already exhausted. The story is already completely told. The seemingly open future is closed. Everything is settled "from eternity." Nothing really gets settled in time. God predestines all. Even creation is from eternity in God. Creation is contingent, but it is also necessary since there is no contingency in God. For God there really is nothing new under the sun. From God's point of view even the world does not *really* change; it only *appears* to change to ignorant creatures who lack the capacity for grasping it all at once. From eternity God views the whole of history, including the entire drama of the Fall and the story of redemption, in a single magic moment. Is it possible for God to foresee it all at once without predetermining it all? Supernaturalists have given mixed answers to this question; but given their interpretation of the eternity and the omnipotence of God the logic of their position is unequivocally clear. They cannot answer negatively, yet they hesitate to answer affirmatively because of the insuperable problems of theodicy that would follow. How can God be both all-powerful and all-knowing without being responsible for all the evil that is in the world as well as for all the good? We shall examine this problem in more detail in the following discussion of God's omnipotence.

The supernaturalist has resisted attempts to attribute temporality and change to God because he has felt himself to be caught on the horns of a terrible dilemma. Either God is perfect from eternity or he is not. If he is, then any change would be a change for the worse; if he is not, then he is capable of improvement and consequently is not a worthy object of religious devotion. Once again paradox confronts us, for the traditional supernaturalist has conceived of God's perfection in such a way that this perfection makes him imperfect—that is, it makes him the cause of evil as well as good in the world. In our discussion of panentheism we shall explore a possible avenue of escape from this dilemma. It is clear, however, that for the classical supernaturalist the perfection of God involves his eternal all-at-once-ness, his immutability, his pure actuality, and his omnicausality. Only a being with such attributes would be supreme, unsurpassable, and worthy of absolute devotion; yet there is something in all these attributes that makes such a being unworthy of absolute devotion.

OMNIPOTENCE

All power and the exercise of all power belong to God alone. He is the sole originative cause of everything, the world and all its events. Events in the world are causes only in "a secondary and derivative sense"; that is, they are in no sense creative or origina-tive. They simply carry out the agenda that God programed into them from eternity. God's power is infinite. By contrast, the world's power to originate is not merely finite, but nonexistent. The world is totally passive in the hands of God. The causal rela-tion between God and the world is completely one-sided; God acts on and within the world, but in no sense does the world act on and within God. God is almighty; the world has no might. Not only does God foresee all the events of the world, but he also fore-ordains them.

This classical supernaturalistic interpretation of omnipotence has always been a source of perplexity, for it has forced the supernat-uralist to say things about God, man, and the world that he does not really want to say. He wants to say that God is not responsible for evil in the world and that the world is somehow responsible for its own evil, but his lavish interpretation of God's omnipotence has never permitted him to say such things without lapsing into incon-sistency. Many clever maneuvers have been executed to disguise this inconsistency, but it is ineradicably present in classical theol-ogy. Let us briefly examine some of these difficulties.

In the sense of *responsible* that is relevant here, to be responsible for something is simply to be the originative cause of that some-thing and consequently to be subject to praise if that thing is good and subject to blame if it is bad. Since God is pure causality, pure actuality in relation to the world, and since the world is pure effect, pure potentiality in relation to him, God is the originative, initiating cause of, and is thus responsible for, everything that happens in the world. This makes God the instigating cause of all the evil as well as all the good in the world and casts serious doubts on God's moral perfection and integrity. The supernaturalist is thus con-fronted with a dilemma. If he is to be perfectly consistent, he must either give up his belief in the omnipotence of God or his belief in the moral perfection of God. Usually he has simply chosen to be inconsistent, thinking that he could thereby have it both ways at once. Unfortunately, there is no difference between asserting two logically incompatible propositions and not asserting anything at all.

The supernaturalist has made logical mistakes in his attempts to resolve the problem of theodicy, the problem of how belief in the moral perfection of God and the omnipotence of God can be reconciled with the existence of evil in the world. To avoid an obvious contradiction, some supernaturalists have suggested that there really is no evil in the world after all, that evil is somehow illusory, that evil is a privation of reality, or that we see things as evil only because of the limitations of our perspective. If we only had a "God's-eye view" of things we would realize that evil is really good in disguise or at least a necessary aspect of a more inclusive good. It is highly unlikely that a soldier who has just had both his legs blown off or a mother who has just given birth to a monster would agree with this evasion. The crucial difficulty with it is that by the same line of argument all the apparent good in the world can be "proved" to be an illusion, a necessary part of a more inclusive evil, evil itself in disguise. By this same line of argument God can be proved to be an omnipotent demon. Actually, it is doubtful that the notions of *good* or *evil* have any clear meaning in either of these "proofs." What could we say intelligibly once we conceded that all legitimate distinctions are dissolved in a more inclusive point of view? What about the distinction between the "more inclusive" and the "less inclusive"? Assuming that we are not *constantly* dreaming or hallucinating (and most of us are not), what intelligible difference is there between a real excruciating pain and an illusory one, between real torture, murder, or rape and illusory torture, murder, or rape, between real and illusory famine, disease, guilt, and death? Even if there is an intelligible difference, God as the cause of everything would have to be the cause of the illusion! Would not such universal illusion (deception) be a *real* evil?

Most supernaturalists, however, have taken sin and evil too seriously to regard it as an illusion or even as a necessary part of the perfection of the created order of things. As privation, evil is the absence of the *proper* goodness and being of a thing, not the absence of the *total* goodness and being of a thing. For most supernaturalists, evil is evil and that is that. But this only makes it more difficult for them to reconcile their belief in the omnipotence of God with their confidence in his moral perfection. Virtually all of them have wanted to say that moral evil is real and that man rather than God is responsible for its introduction into the created order of things. Even St. Augustine had to allow the existence of at least (and at most) one genuinely originative event within the world: Adam's decision to disobey God; but he was not willing to face up to the full implications of this. If Adam's decision to disobey God originated with Adam, then God was not the cause of it. Thus God is not the sole originative cause of absolutely everything—that is, he is not omnipotent in the required sense. In creating men who have the freedom either to obey or to disobey him, God may have freely chosen to limit his own power, as many supernaturalists have conceded, but there is no getting around the fact that *it was a limitation of his own power.* For Augustine only Adam had this freedom, but for other supernaturalists every man has the freedom to obey or disobey God, even when the odds are heavily against obedience. Men originate their own decisions to sin; only if this is so are they responsible and blamable for the moral evil that they (not God) introduce into the world. Furthermore, if God knows that this evil has been introduced into the world and if he suffers as the world suffers, then God is patient and effect as well as agent and cause—even if only in the one case of Adam's sin. Without taking the Adam myth literally, panentheists have followed out the logic of human responsibility to its fullest, but traditional supernaturalists have resisted.

The supernaturalist's concession that Adam's decision to disobey God originated with Adam and not with God is clouded by the claim that God foreknew from eternity that just that decision would be made. The ruse here is the insistence that God *foreknew* from eternity that Adam would *freely* choose to disobey God. But the very notion of freedom as originative causality loses its meaning in such an interpretation. If God knew from eternity that just that decision would be made, then from eternity the decision could not have been otherwise. There were no genuine options open. There was nothing to originate. Adam could not have decided to obey God, but if this is the case we can no longer say that the choice originated with him at the moment that he made it. *Not even God can be said to know something that is not there to be known,* and if Adam's choice of disobedience is *known* from eternity it must *be* from eternity. The supernaturalist is committed to defending the paradoxical claim that all the facts of the world, including evil, are contingent yet at the same time necessary since there is no contingency in God.

Many of the antisupernaturalists of our day insist that the God of supernaturalism must die so that man may come of age and assume responsibility for himself and his own decisions. The omnipotent God of the supernaturalists can be nothing but a tyrant who allows men no real voice in their own destiny and no genuine responsibility for their own choices of good and evil. Without consciously intending to do so, supernaturalism has engendered a spirit of helplessness, complacency, indifference. It has made men too childlike, too much like clay in the hands of the potter, too ill-equipped emotionally and intellectually to cope in an adult manner with the brutal facts of this-worldly existence. God must die in order that the gods might live, Nietzsche proclaimed; and many of our contemporaries have taken up that cry. The death-of-God theology and atheistic existentialism are primarily protests against the classical supernaturalistic conception of the omnipotence of God.

In the hands of the supernaturalists the meaning of *omnipotence* has fluctuated between the notion of "a logically and religiously adequate form of power" and the notion of "omnicausality." Supernaturalists have usually simply identified the two, but they have seldom if ever suggested that God's omnipotence consists in the chaotic power to do absolutely anything. Whether God can do the logically impossible or the morally repugnant, whether he can make a stone so large that he cannot lift it or another God equal to himself has never really troubled them; and those who raise such questions always miss the point that the omnipotence of God must be at least a logically and religiously adequate form of power, even if it is not omnicausality. In the following discussion of the attribute of infinity we shall see that the limitlessness of God's power has usually been interpreted as falling within the limits of the logically possible and morally permissible.

INFINITY

In its most original and literal sense the attribute of infinity is essentially negative in meaning. *Infinity* means "not finite." To say that God is infinite is to say that he is not limited, but has this meant for the supernaturalist that he is not limited in *any* way or that he is not limited in certain *selected* ways? Clearly it has meant for most supernaturalists that he is limitless only in certain *selected* ways. For most of them God is at least limited by his own essence or nature, by his own goodness, and by logic, though goodness and reason are both understood as integral aspects of the very essence of God. God is limitless only in ways that are consistent with his being a religiously adequate object of supreme worship, adoration, and devotion, though there is considerable popular confusion about this. Infinity is an attribute of God's other attributes. Thus, God is limitless in his power, knowledge, presence, love, creativity, actuality, and so on. But what is involved in his being limitless in power? Does this mean that he can do absolutely anything? No, it has never meant quite this, for there are some things that might possibly be done, in some very abstruse sense of possibility, but that God cannot do. The typical supernaturalist has had to concede this much. For example, St. Thomas Aquinas clearly and emphatically denied that God could do the logically impossible. He could not create a thing that both was and was not itself; he could not not be God; he could not create a nondependent, noncreated creature; he could not exceed his own intellect; he could not destroy the past; he could not create another God equal to himself in all respects. St. Anselm argued that God could not do anything immoral or illogical—that, for example, God could not lie or make that which is true to be false. But all God's limitations are self-limitations. It is significant that in admitting that God is in some sense limited, the supernaturalists have unanimously denied that he is limited by anything outside of or other than himself. He is not limited by some external realm of Platonic ideas, for all forms exist in the mind of God and are integral to his very essence. Limitations by logical possibility and moral perfection are not externally imposed limitations, for consistency and goodness are grounded in the very essence of God and not in some external realm of ideas. Neither is God limited in any way by the world for the typical supernaturalist, and it is at this point that supernaturalism and panentheism part company. For the supernaturalist the world is completely passive in the hands of God. In no way does it benefit God, act on him, or limit him. The relationship of dependence is totally one-sided: The world is completely limited by God, and God is completely free from any conceivable limitation by the world.

The infinity or limitlessness of God's power has thus not involved a violation of the basic principles of *logic* and *morality*. What has it involved? Usually it has involved limitless *causality* and *actuality*. As we have noted, omnipotence and omnicausality are usually equated; but is omnicausality consistent with supreme moral perfection? Can a morally perfect God be the originative cause of all the evil in the world? If he is not, then he is as much limited by the world's originative causality as he is by his own essence. Panentheists have not hesitated to accept the full implications of this alternative, but supernaturalists have been prevented from adopting it by their insistence on the infinite actuality of God. They see God as pure, limitless actuality. His possibilities are exhausted by his actuality from eternity. He cannot change, since he already is everything that he could be. But what is so perfect about the absolutely static?

MORAL GOODNESS

The notion of God's moral goodness is an integral aspect of the broader notion of God's perfection, which will be considered in our discussion of the ontological argument in Chapter 9. For the moment, we can say that the typical supernaturalist has believed God to be supremely good in the sense that he possesses completely all those moral qualities that are involved in his creating a good world and willing the best for his creatures in that world. Such moral qualities as wisdom, truthfulness, justice, loyalty, righteousness, love, benevolence, mercy, fatherhood, and all-around goodness are exemplified to an absolute degree in the divine essence. God is that being than whom none better (morally) could be conceived.

The supernaturalist is clearly at odds with the naturalist, who contends that human moral ideals have no basis or counterpart in the realm of ultimate reality. God is the quintessence of moral goodness, and the devotion to human welfare that the moral ideals of humanism require is exemplified in God's infinite concern for his creatures, particularly those human creatures that are made "in his image." But humanity is not the ultimate object of devotion for the supernaturalist. The supernaturalist can be and often has been as deeply devoted to promoting human welfare as any humanist, without at the same time lapsing into what he believes to be an idolatrous deification of humanity or nature. For the supernaturalist, humanity is not coextensive with ultimate reality or ultimate value; yet God as ultimate reality loves individual human beings as a father loves his children, and wants the best for his creatures.

Since the time of Kant it has been fashionable in philosophical circles to assume (with the humanistic naturalist) that ethics and theology or metaphysics are logically independent disciplines, but it is doubtful that the supernaturalist can consistently accept this view. It is true that a man may be a good man and may understand what is involved in the ideals of moral duty and human welfare without believing in God, but the supernaturalist holds that any man who does not believe in God as a supercosmic paradigm of moral goodness has at best an incomplete understanding of moral goodness. It is only because God exists that our moral decisions have an unconditional significance. The humanist often argues that if there is a God, he wills that we be moral either because it is good or for no reason at all. If it is for no reason at all, then God is an arbitrary tyrant; but if it is because it is good, then it is logically possible to bypass God altogether and simply be moral because it is good. Thus ethics is independent of theology. Doubtless some supernaturalists have been caught in this dilemma, but there is a way to escape it: What is meant by the expression "because it is good"? To say that God wills or approves something because it is good is not to postulate a platonic form of goodness existing independently of God and to which he himself must appeal in justifying his own moral involvement and concern. Rather, it is to say nothing more than that this is the sort of thing about which a divine, ideal observer, a being of limitless freedom, compassion, enlightenment, and impartiality, is involved and concerned. Thus to state that God wills or approves something because it is good is merely to state that this is the sort of thing that a being of infinite freedom, compassion, enlightenment, and impartiality wills or approves, and there is nothing arbitrary about that. Many supernaturalists have always had something like this in mind in claiming that goodness is an integral aspect of the very essence of God. The humanist may counter by offering some other meaning for *good*, or he may insist that in calling something good we may mean that it is the sort of thing that such an ideal observer would will or approve *if* he existed, without at the same time assuming the existence of such a being. The supernaturalist need not insist that this is what everyone means by *good,* only that this is what the word means within the framework of supernaturalism. Perhaps there are no universal, systematically neutral value concepts, since a purely "secular" meta-ethics implicitly presupposes a nontheistic metaphysics. Does not the ideal of coherence require the ultimate integration of axiology and metaphysics?

HOLINESS

God is holy; he is a being of tremendous and fascinating mystery. All the attributes of God discussed thus far are involved in the holiness of God, yet something more must be said. God is radically different in kind from any of the familiar things of this world. His power, knowledge, compassion, and goodness are radically superior to human power, knowledge, compassion, and goodness. God is both infinitely attractive and infinitely awe-inspiring, so completely worthy of reverence that he is fearsome. In the presence of God's holiness men are keenly aware of their own finitude, creatureliness, uncleanness, inadequacy, and sinfulness. God is sacred, sublime, glorious, inexhaustible, majestic, numinous, overwhelming, wonderful. In the love of God with all one's heart and soul and mind and strength there is both attraction and avoidance. The love of God and the fear of the Lord always go hand in hand, for God is holy.

Doubtless it is the sense of the holiness of God that has contributed heavily to the supernaturalist's reluctance to speak of God at all, which we noted at the beginning of our discussion of supernaturalism. It is because he is holy that God is in some sense unthinkable, mysterious, incomprehensible, ineffable. It is because God is holy that religious language is at best symbolic, metaphorical, and analogical and that religious affirmations are so often paradoxical or contradictory. Supernaturalists have tended to explain holiness in terms of transcendence. God is holy because he is utterly beyond the spatiotemporal universe and because this universe is absolutely dependent on him. Is there no other way to account for the mysterious, tremendous fascination of God? Must an absolutely supreme being, an absolutely worthy object of ultimate concern be wholly other? Is there no other way to account for the radical superiority of God's power, knowledge, compassion, and goodness except in terms of nonspatiotemporality? Must mystery involve contradiction? What alternative is there?

In the following chapter we shall explore the panentheistic alternative to supernaturalism, which attempts to avoid the paradoxes we have found to be inherent in the supernaturalistic conception of God and his relation to the world, and which gives a different account of the "unthinkability" of God. The basic philosophical issue treated in this chapter has been the problem of the intelligibility of the supernaturalistic concept of God. At this point, the possibilities are at least open that God exceeds human conception in some respects but not in others, that creative theological thinking might be able to overcome many of the difficulties inherent in supernaturalism by developing a more adequate conception of God, that we have pronounced God to be "unthinkable" prematurely, and that the inadequacy of our thoughts about God is to a significant degree more a consequence of the surpassable inferiority of our thoughts than it is a consequence of the insurpassable excellence of the divinity thought about.

Suggestions for Further Reading

SUPERNATURALISTS ON GOD AND THE WORLD

ANSELM, ST., *Basic Writings* (*Proslogium, Monologium,* Gaunilon's *On Behalf of the Fool, Cur Deus Homo*), 2nd ed., trans. by S. W. Deane, with an introduction by Charles Hartshorne (LaSalle, Ill., Open Court, 1962).

AQUINAS, ST. THOMAS, *On the Truth of the Catholic Faith* (Garden City, N.Y., Doubleday, 1957), Book I on God and Book II on Creation.

AUGUSTINE, ST., *The Confessions of St. Augustine,* trans. by Rex Warner (New York, New American Library, n.d.), especially Books XI, XII, and XIII.

———, *The City of God* (New York, Modern Library, 1950), Book XI, Chapters 1–6.

BRUNNER, EMIL, *Dogmatics,* Vol. I, *The Christian Doctrine of God* (Philadelphia, Westminster Press, 1950), pp. 117–302.

———, *Dogmatics,* Vol. II, *The Christian Doctrine of Creation and Redemption* (Philadelphia, Westminster Press, 1952), pp. 3–45.

HARTSHORNE, CHARLES, and REESE, WILLIAM L., eds., *Philosophers Speak of God* (Chicago, University of Chicago Press, 1953), Chapter 3. Contains relevant selections from Philo, Augustine, Anselm, Al-Ghazzali, Maimonides, Aquinas, Descartes, Leibniz, Kant, Channing, and von Hugel, with commentary and criticism from a panentheistic perspective.

SCHLEIERMACHER, FRIEDRICH, *The Christian Faith* (Edinburgh, T. & T. Clark, 1956), Part I, Sections 1, 2, and 3. A discussion of Christianity in which Schleiermacher reveals himself to be a supernaturalist with a tendency toward pantheism.

Notes

1 From *Honest to God* by John A. T. Robinson. Published in the U.S.A., 1963, by Westminster Press, Philadelphia. Copyright © by SCM Press, London, 1963. Used by permission.

2 *The Confessions of St. Augustine,* Book XI (New York, Pocket Books, 1952), p. 223.

3 For a fuller exploration of this problem see Rem B. Edwards, "Is There a Metaphysic of Genesis?" *Continuum,* Vol. I, No. 3 (Autumn 1963), pp. 368–72.

4 This now-famous expression was first used by Antony Flew. See Antony Flew and Alasdair MacIntyre, *New Essays in Philosophical Theology* (New York, Macmillan, 1955), p. 97.

chapter eight

God and the World PANENTHEISM

Panentheism, or process theology as it is often called, has historical roots that extend far back into the history of Western religious thought, at least as far as Socinus in the sixteenth century. A good case can be made for insisting that the dynamic God of the process theologians is much closer metaphysically to the God of biblical religion than is the static God of the supernaturalists, despite the fact that it is commonplace to identify biblical religion with supernaturalism. Doubtless there have been many anticipations of panentheism in the history of religious thought, though such anticipations have not always been sorted out from supernaturalistic or naturalistic assumptions, with which they are inconsistent. Schelling, Hegel, Fechner, Peirce, James, Hocking, Bergson, Brightman, and many others helped create a climate of opinion within which contemporary process theology could develop, but it is in the second and third quarters of the twentieth century that the attempt to develop systematically a concept of God that "takes time (and space) seriously" has come to fruition. Alfred North Whitehead and Charles Hartshorne have been the central philosophical figures in the movement, though other contemporary religious thinkers, such as Nicholas Berdyaev, F. R. Tennant, and Teilhard de Chardin, have developed their own dynamic conceptions of God more or less independently of their influence. More directly influenced by Whitehead and Hartshorne have been a number of religious thinkers who fall more clearly into the camp of the "theologians" rather than the "philosophers," as the lines between the two are traditionally drawn. Among those who have attempted to work out the implications of panentheism for Christian theology have been such prominent American theologians as Robert L. Calhoun, Nels F. S. Ferré, John B. Cobb, Daniel Day Williams, and Schubert Ogden. Recently, Bishop John A. T. Robinson has added himself to the list.

Whitehead's thought about God is in some ways more difficult and inaccessible than is that of Hartshorne. Like the rest of his philosophy, it is often expressed in a highly specialized technical jargon; often it is not fully worked out; and it is all too easy to become so immersed in difficulties of textual interpretation that one loses sight of the metaphysics itself. For such reasons, we shall concern ourselves primarily with Hartshorne's version of process theology.

God and the World: A New Conception

We have seen that for the classical supernaturalist, God and the world are extremely unlike. The universal characteristics of the world are in no sense universal characteristics of God. The most general interpretative categories that apply to God are in no sense applicable to the world, and those applicable to the world are in no sense applicable to God. We have also seen that this way of radically opposing God and the world has led to ineradicable confusions, if not contradictions, in the supernaturalistic world view. If we list the metaphysical categories applicable to God in supernaturalism, we will see that they are static, monistic categories that pay any price for the concept of an unchanging, utterly unitary, and simple God. In traditional supernaturalism, only the categories applicable to the world are dynamic and pluralistic. Consider the following lists of categorical opposites used in traditional supernaturalism to distinguish God and the world:

GOD	THE WORLD
One	Many
Being	Becoming
Permanent	Changing
Eternal	Temporal
Pure Actuality	Passivity, Potentiality
Incorporeal	Spatial
Simple	Compound
Necessary	Contingent
Self-sufficient	Dependent
Creator	Created
Cause	Effect
Infinite	Finite
Nonrelational	Relational
Perfect	Imperfect

The categories in these two lists are polar opposites, and super-naturalism has traditionally attributed to God only the categories in the one list but not in the other. This has resulted in what Hart-shorne calls a monopolar conception of deity.[1] Furthermore, this monopolar conception of deity is based on a certain value judg-ment, a normative bias that the first- and second-century de-velopers of supernaturalism adopted uncritically from Greek phi-losophy (not from biblical religion). Within the framework of Greek values, there was something intrinsically superior about the static and monistic and something intrinsically inferior about the dynamic and pluralistic. Notice that the category of the "perfect" falls within the list of static categories, and it involves a positive valuation of *all* the static and monistic categories. The category of the "imperfect" similarly involves a negative valuation of *all* the dynamic and pluralistic categories. It is because the dynamic and the pluralistic are inferior that such categories are not applicable to God in traditional supernaturalism. What the panentheist wishes to do is to call into question the basic value judgment on which the traditional concept of God is based, to eliminate the monopolar prejudice against the dynamic and pluralistic, while at the same time accounting fully for the radical uniqueness and holiness of God. If we assume that there is nothing intrinsically inferior about plurality, time, and space, and if we develop an understand-ing of God and his relation to the world that is free from the classical bias against the dynamic, perhaps we can develop a religious philosophy that is genuinely consistent, comprehensive, coherent, and philosophically adequate.

In conceiving of God's perfection in terms of the static, monistic categories, traditional supernaturalists have actually failed to conceive of that perfection in one legitimate and ancient sense of the term. *Perfection* originally was equivalent to *completeness,* and the God of the supernaturalists is a very *incomplete* being. A whole realm of reality, a whole set of metaphysical categories, is excluded from his plenitude. He is complete in a static sort of way, but not in a dynamic sort of way. He is incomplete with respect to all the categories believed to be applicable only to the world. Paul Tillich hints at the incompleteness and hence the imperfection of the God of supernaturalism, though in his own equating of God with "being itself" he is not far from the monopolar prejudice against becoming. On the subject of supernaturalism, or what he called theological theism, Tillich wrote:

> The God of theological theism is a being beside others and as such a part of the whole of reality. He certainly is considered its most important part, but as a part and therefore as subjected to the structure of the whole. He is supposed to be beyond the ontological elements and categories which constitute reality. But every statement subjects him to them. He is seen as a self which has a world, as an ego which is related to a thou, as a cause which is separated from its effect, as having a definite space and endless time. He is a being, not being-itself. As such he is bound to the subject-object structure of reality, he is an object for us subjects. At the same time we are objects for him as a subject. And this is decisive for the necessity of transcending theological theism. For God as a subject makes me into an object which is nothing more than an object. He deprives me of my subjectivity because he is all-powerful and all-knowing. I revolt and try to make *him* into an object, but the revolt fails and becomes desperate. God appears as the invincible tyrant, the being in contrast with whom all other beings are without freedom and subjectivity. He is equated with the recent tyrants who with the help of terror try to transform everything into a mere object, a thing among things, a cog in the machine they control. He becomes the model of everything against which Existentialism revolted. This is the God Nietzsche said had to be killed because nobody can tolerate being made into

a mere object of absolute knowledge and absolute control. This is the deepest root of atheism. It is an atheism which is justified as the reaction against theological theism and its disturbing implications. It is also the deepest root of the Existentialist despair and the widespread anxiety of meaninglessness in our period.[2]

Tillich thus accuses the supernaturalist of conceiving of God as at the same time a cosmic tyrant and yet only a being among other beings, a *part* of the whole of reality. He does not develop the contrast in terms of the static versus the dynamic, as does the panentheist, but he does propose that we think of God as *being itself* rather than as *a being* among others, that we think of God as ultimate or total reality rather than as a part of the whole of things, and that we think of God in such a way that we do not lose our own freedom and individuality in the process. All these motifs would be congenial to the process theologian if he were permitted to interpret the whole of things in *both* dynamic and static terms, though it is doubtful that Tillich would find this acceptable. Tillich also is prejudiced against space and time, but his position is subtle (if not downright ambiguous), and there are passages in which even he talks like a process theologian. The process theologian wants to conceive of God as genuinely complete, but he recognizes that this inevitably involves applying both the static, monistic categories and the dynamic, pluralistic categories to God; and he points out that there is no contradiction whatsoever involved in doing this so long as these categories apply to *different* aspects of God. We cannot conceive of God as both permanent and changing, both infinite and finite, and so on, in precisely the same respect without self-contradiction, but in saying that in *different* respects God is both being and becoming, limited and limitless, and so on, there is no contradiction whatsoever. A thoroughly comprehensive concept of God cannot be developed given the monopolar bias against the dynamic and pluralistic. Hartshorne views "the history of theistic speculations as primarily a long experiment in omissions."[3] Whitehead insisted that "God is not to be treated as an exception to all metaphysical principles, invoked to save their collapse. He is their chief exemplification."[4] For the process theologian, God is as much the chief exemplification of the dynamic, pluralistic categories as he is of the static, monistic ones.

Although a lengthy list of categorical opposites contrasting God and the world may be derived from the thought of the supernaturalists, it is interesting that one pair of categorical opposites usually is conspicuously absent, the whole–part contrast. Seldom, if ever, does the supernaturalist speak of God as the whole of reality and of the world as part of that whole, and it is precisely this deficiency that has prompted Tillich and other critics to say that the God of supernaturalism is not genuinely ultimate. Historically, it has been the pantheists who have held that "all is God" and the mystics, who tend to be pantheists (or panentheists), who have employed the whole–part contrast; and supernaturalists have doubtless avoided it for fear of lapsing into some form of pantheism. For the supernaturalist, God and the world are too radically different to say that "all is God"; yet unless this is somehow the case, God will be deficient in reality. Panentheists tend to side with the pantheists in this regard. Both want to say that "all is God" and that God is the whole of reality of which we and our world are parts, but there are also significant differences between pantheism and panentheism. In the first place, the pantheist, like the supernaturalist, also depreciates the significance of dynamic and pluralistic categories and tends to relegate them to the realm of the "illusory." For him God is all reality, but this simply means that change and multiplicity are unreal and consequently not ingredient in God after all. In the second place, the typical pantheist is also a thoroughgoing determinist who believes that all the parts of the whole are completely determined to be what they are by the whole itself. By contrast, the panentheist maintains that change and multiplicity are real and as such are ingredient in God, and that although God is the whole of reality, he is a whole with self-determining parts. The creatures participate in the originality and creativity of God. God is conceived in such a way that we do not lose our freedom and individuality. Where the pantheist says "God is all things," the panentheist prefers to say "God includes all things." [5] Hartshorne compares supernaturalism, which he calls classical theism, with pantheism in the following way:

> The method here is this: taking each pair of ultimate contraries, such as one and many, permanence and change, being and be-

coming, necessity and contingency, the self-sufficient or nonrelative versus the dependent or relative, the actual versus the potential, one decides in each case which member of the pair is good or admirable and then attributes it (in some supremely excellent or transcendent form) to deity, while wholly denying the contrasting term. What we propose to call "classical theism" is, in the West, the chief product of this method; in the Orient, its chief product is pantheism. The difference between the two is that theism admits the reality of plurality, potentiality, becoming —as a secondary form of existence "outside" God, in no way constitutive of his reality; whereas pantheism, properly so called, supposes that, although God includes all within himself, still, since he cannot be really complex, or mutable, such categories can only express human ignorance or illusion. Thus, common to theism and pantheism is the doctrine of the invidious nature of categorical contrasts. One pole of each contrary is regarded as more excellent than the other, so that the supremely excellent being cannot be described by the other and inferior pole. At once the dilemma results: either there is something outside of deity, so that the total real is deity-and-something-else, a whole of which deity is merely one constituent; or else the allegedly inferior pole of each categorical contrast is an illusory conception. Theism takes one horn of the dilemma; pantheism, the other. The dilemma, however, is artificial; for it is produced by the assumption that the highest form of reality is to be indicated by separating or purifying one pole of the ultimate contrasts from the other pole.[6]

If the ancient bias against change and multiplicity is rejected, the way is open to develop a new concept of God, a God who is both changing and unchanging, both temporal and everlasting, both many and one, both becoming and being, both potential and actual, both contingent and necessary, both created and creator, both effect and cause, both finite and infinite, yet perfect and holy all the same. It is essential that these categorical opposites apply to different aspects of God if contradiction is to be avoided. But it must be recognized that contradiction *can* be avoided in this way. As Hartshorne points out, "There is no law of logic against attributing contrasting predicates to the same individual, provided they apply to diverse aspects of this individual."[7]

Not only do the process theologians want their new concept of God to be free from the one-sidedness of traditional supernaturalism, but they also want it to be as free as possible from the logical paradoxes with which supernaturalism has been plagued. Although he readily admits that not all theological paradoxes can be dismissed as contradictions, Hartshorne does insist that the possibility of contradiction be openly explored and that inconsistency be honestly called inconsistency, and therefore nonsense, when it cannot be eradicated by the patient and persistent attempt to think clearly. He writes that "A theological paradox, it appears, is what a contradiction becomes when it is about God rather than something else, or indulged in by a theologian or a church rather than an unbeliever or heretic." [8] Where the traditional theologian often writes volumes describing the essence of God and making affirmations about him while at the same time he denies that anything can be known of the essence of God and that any affirmations can be made, Hartshorne wishes to avoid such duplicity. He openly admits that he is talking about God and making affirmations about him. He wishes to avoid what he calls "the metaphysical false modesty of seeking to honor deity by refusing to apply any of our positive conceptions to him." [9] And he asks, "What is the difference between refraining from applying any concept to a thing and just not thinking about it?" [10] Where the traditionalist declares the inadequacy of human language and thinks that only the static language of monopolarity does justice to the ineffability of God, Hartshorne points out that monopolar concepts are human concepts too.[11] And when the proponent of the *via negativa* insists that God must be beyond even our monopolar categories, Hartshorne makes the same point, asking, "Does it really alter this to urge that God is superior to and beyond all our concepts—as though 'superior' or 'beyond' were not also our concept? To say that God is better than good is to say that he is more good than good, and this is a doubtfully helpful play of words." [12]

Let us now examine in some detail the dipolar concept of deity developed by the process philosophers. Throughout our discussion, let us remember that the dipolar categories are not external powers to which God is subject or subordinate. Just as the supernaturalist regards the monopolar categories as integral to God's nature, so does the panentheist regard the dipolar categories. As Hartshorne puts it, "God is not 'subject' to the categories, as though they were something antecedent to his own individuality. As we have suggested, in the form in which they apply to him, the categories are that individuality." [13] How can opposing characteristics be attributed to God without contradiction?

PERMANENCE AND CHANGE

In his attempt to develop a new concept of God free from the logical defects and axiological biases of supernaturalism, Whitehead distinguished between the "primordial" and the "consequent" natures of God. The primordial nature of God is the abstract permanent essence of God, God considered "in himself" in abstraction from his relation to "the world." It is a *permanent* aspect of God's abstract nature that he is *both* one and many, being and becoming, unchanging and changing, everlasting and temporal, actual and potential, spiritual and spatial, simple and compound, necessary and contingent, self-sufficient and dependent, creator and created, cause and effect, infinite and finite, related to some world, and perfect. The particular, concrete ways in which God incorporates multiplicity, change, potentiality, complexity, and so on, belong to his consequent nature. By the consequent nature of God is meant God as enriched by his creation of and experience of the world. In his primordial nature, God conceptually envisages the possibilities that might be actualized in all possible worlds. In his consequent nature, God experiences, enjoys, and preserves forever in his faultless memory the achieved structure and value of actualized worlds. The one is God as potential, the other is God as actual; and the actual includes the potential as a permanent aspect of itself. It is a primordial feature of God's essence that he is love and that he has *some* world to love, and his concrete love for the events and individuals of *this* world belongs to his consequent nature. It is an abstract feature of his essence that he knows whatever actualities there are to be known, and it is a concrete feature of his essence that he knows the actualities of this particular universe. The consequent nature of God is constantly being enriched by the world's "creative advance into novelty," [14] and in this sense it is changing; thus God is both permanent and changing. The distinction between the primordial and consequent natures of God should not be interpreted as a distinction between two different Gods, for the two natures of the one God are thoroughly integrated and interconnected. It is only in thought that the two can be distinguished; they cannot be separated ontologically. They never exist independently of each other. The primordial nature of God does not exist "before" he has a consequent nature. God is the whole—both primordial and consequent. It is a permanent feature of his nature that he has *a* consequent nature, but not that he has *this* consequent nature. It is a permanent feature of God that he is changing in some respects, that is, in his perception of and encounter with *some* world. The primodial and consequent aspects of God eternally coexist, though the detailed contents of the consequent nature are temporal achievements. It is necessary that God have both a primordial nature and a consequent nature, but it is contingent that he has just *this* consequent nature. The primordial nature is simply the imperishable common features of God that persist through and are contained within all stages of his expanding actuality. God exists necessarily, but his concrete actuality is contingent.

In rejecting the application of the category of change to God in any sense, the supernaturalist has been driven to the assertion that in God everything is permanent, necessary, unchanging. Yet the supernaturalist has also wanted to say that there is an aspect of contingency about the will of God, that for example there were many possible worlds that God could have chosen to create, and even that God could have chosen not to create any world at all. In other words, that God chose to create *some* world and that he chose to create *this* world are regarded as contingent, impermanent facts about the God in whom there is no contingency and impermanence. The supernaturalist has wanted to attribute contingency not only to God's creativity but also to his providential care for and involvement with the nations and individuals of this contingent world, but he has never really been able to say this sort of thing without contradicting himself. There is no way to assign contingent, free acts of will to a being totally lacking in contingency without lapsing into inconsistency; and the history of supernaturalistic speculation may be seen as a persistent refusal to face up to this cold, hard piece of logic. In the distinction between the primordial and consequent natures of God, the process theologian finds a way of avoiding the contradictions of supernaturalism. The free, willful, contingent, concrete decisions and acts of God all fall within his temporal, changing, contingent consequent nature. God's concern for and intercourse with *this* contingent world must be a contingent fact about both God and the world, though it is a necessary truth about God that he is related in love and creative intercourse with *some* world.

Although the panentheist agrees with the supernaturalist that God could have chosen to create some other world than this, he does not agree that God could have chosen not to create a world at all. He insists that love and creativity are themselves permanent features of God's nature, that love *must* express itself toward some object, and that creativity is as much a necessary and inescapable attribute of God as are moral constancy and perfection. Some supernaturalists have also wanted to regard God as necessarily creative but have nevertheless insisted that God might not have created anything at all. This is nonsense. Others are in a less embarrassingly self-contradictory position, holding that although God necessarily has the *capacity* to create, he is not necessarily creative in actuality. From the fact that God might have not created just this particular world it does not follow that he might have not created any world at all. It is God who is not free from freedom itself. He can no more fail to be freely creative than he can fail to be God, the process theologian maintains. This does not mean that freedom and creativity are external forces that hold power over God; it means that freedom and creativity are integral parts of what is meant by *God*. Exactly what he freely creates is what is meant by *the world,* and though he must have created some world, he need not have created just this world.

CREATOR AND CREATED

Closely related to the creator–created categories are the categories of actual–potential and cause–effect. How can all these categories be applied to God at the same time without self-contradiction? How can they be applied without jeopardizing the supremacy, religious adequacy, and worthiness of God? How can we think of God as both creator and created? Let us first ask what creativity itself is or involves. When God is said to be creator, what is being said about him? For the supernaturalist, being creator involves producing the entire spatiotemporal universe out of nothing by a sheer act of divine will. The production of the world out of nothing is traditionally conceived as an instance of *the actualization of novelty:* Where there once was no world, a new world suddenly appeared by divine fiat. The panentheist regards creativity as a more generally applicable metaphysical category, for there are many instances of the actualization of novelty to be found under the sun. For him, both God and the world are creative, are producers of novel actualities; and a part of man's being created "in the image of God" involves his being a cocreator, a coworker with God. This simply makes a place for the view that creative artists, thinkers, social innovators, and others have long taken of themselves. Of course, there must be differences between divine and human creativity, but there are also significant similarities. There is something divine about creativity in all its instances, and in this respect the most creative artists, thinkers, and social innovators are the most God-like among us. In this respect, men of great insight are closest to God, for insight is the creative function of reason, as we noted earlier. For the panentheist, God is the "chief exemplification" of creativity, but by no means the only one. God is the supreme but not the sole introducer of novel actualities, the supremely creative but not the only creative entity.

In what respect are there significant differences between divine and human creativity? The supernaturalist has attempted to differentiate between the two in at least two ways. In the first place, divine creativity is a pretemporal act, since time is one of its effects and not one of its preconditions. By contrast, the panentheist insists that all creativity takes place in time, that all acts of creativity are in some sense datable, and that all acts of creativity fall somewhere within an infinite time series and none at its beginning. This permits him to avoid the enigma of a time before time began and a first moment of time. In the second place, the supernaturalist insists that divine creativity presupposes no world or world stuff, whereas human creativity does presuppose a world and world stuff. God created the world out of nothing, which is not to say that *nothing* is a kind of *something* out of which he created the world. The word *nothing* should be taken at face value. Human creativity is only the transformation of one kind of something into another kind of something, the imposition of a new form on an already formed world stuff. Again the panentheist disagrees. Since a loving God must always have a world to love, even divine creativity is the transformation of one state of the world into another. *Some* world coexists everlastingly with God, but *this* world is in part the result of God's creative transformation of the past. Of course, for the panentheist, asserting that some world coexists everlastingly with God does not make God just a being alongside the world; rather, it is a way of saying that God always has a body that is an integral aspect of himself as the whole of reality. We shall explore this point further in our discussion of the categories of spatiality–spirituality.

Supernaturalism and panentheism are alike in attributing creativity to God; but in insisting that God is also in some sense created, panentheism makes a radical departure from traditional theology. Not only is God the supreme cause of all creation, he is also the supreme effect of all creation. How can this be? If the world also exemplifies creativity and God is sensitive to the world's creative advance into novelty, then God is in some sense the effect of the world. It is in the consequent and not in the primordial nature of God that he is created, that he is the effect of his encounter with and enjoyment of the world. His primordial nature is uncreated, eternal; but the actuality of his consequent nature is created, temporal. This involves the application to God not only of the category of effect but also of potentiality, passivity, temporality, and many other categories that the supernaturalist reserves for the world alone.

The supernaturalist has never been able to give a satisfactory answer to the child's simple question, "Why did God make the world?" He has conceived of God's perfection in such a way that no answer can be given, and in attempting to conceive of a religiously adequate object of our ultimate concern he has in fact produced a concept of a God who in no sense needs, benefits from, or responds to the world of his creating. God has everything "from eternity," so he could not have made the world because he needed it or expected to benefit from it in any way. A God who is pure actuality and who is so self-sufficient in every way that any change would be a change for the worse has no need of the world, and we are thus confronted with a loving God who needs no object to love, a God who demands our total love, obedience, service, worship, adoration, and glorification but who neither needs nor benefits in any conceivable way from our religious response to him. If the end of man is to obey God and glorify him forever, what is the point of doing so when God cannot benefit from it, when he cannot respond in sensitive passivity to it, when he is in no sense the effect of the world? Only a God whose experience is enriched by his encounter with and enjoyment of the world could have a good reason for creating the world. Something in God must be created by the world, or there is no point in our love, service, and glorification of him. The traditional supernaturalist holds that if God is creative, the world must be created by him. The panentheist agrees with this but adds that if the world is creative, God must be in part created by it. Hartshorne develops his differences with supernaturalism in the following way:

> The aim of creation, it has often been said, is to glorify God. Yes, but after all, does God need to be glorified? No, it was generally replied, he needs nothing. Does it in any way enhance the divine good to glorify it? In no way, for that good is in all respects incapable of enhancement. Why then is it important that God be glorified? Either there has been no answer, or the answer implied has been that it is important to man, and other creatures, for their own sakes, that God should be glorified—that is, in plain English, that God should be praised and made to seem as great as he could in any case be, even without glorification.
>
> All the time that men were being told that their "end" was God, they were also being told, in effect, that it was of no importance to God that they attain this end, but only important to *them*. Thus essentially the end was humanly self-regarding—and in my opinion blasphemous. It made man, what he can never be, something ultimate. "Ultimate beneficiary" is no less an ultimate than ultimate benefactor, and man is not ultimate at all.
>
> It may be replied that the Thomistic doctrine is that the ultimate achieved good is neither man nor God, but the whole creation as end. Very well, let us argue it on that basis. Why or how is the created universe the ultimate beneficiary? This universe is either conscious or not conscious. We are not told it is conscious. If it is not, then the doctrine is that the ultimate recipient of intrinsic good is something unconscious. This defies the very mean-

ing of good, which is satisfaction, fruition of purpose enjoyed by the purposer. On the other hand, if the universe is conscious, then it is either God or a God additional to God. If you say that the intrinsic value of the universe is in the divine consciousness for which it is object, then I reply that either you are saying, unclearly, what I am contending for, or you are indulging in equivocation. God either acquires value, and contingent value, from the contingent fact of creation, or he acquires no value. There is nothing between. Either God, or something other than God, is the ultimate or inclusive beneficiary of achievement. If God is the beneficiary, then it is wrong that God is cause but not effect of creativity. If the ultimate beneficiary is not God, then there are two ultimates, and really two Gods, since ultimacy is the privilege and meaning of deity.[15]

For the panentheist, God is the whole of reality; and as such he must be both creator and created. Creativity is the introduction of novel actualities into this whole, and time is the progression of creativity. Any novelty in a total situation, no matter how minute, makes a new totality, with all previous factors having a new relationship to the novelty. Viewing the world as itself exemplifying creativity allows for freedom, opportunity, self-initiative, and worth for that which is contingent. Hartshorne speaks of "the doctrine of contributionism," the doctrine that the world contributes its created, achieved value to God as the ultimate beneficiary of process. Change and novelty in the world contribute to the novelty, enjoyment, adventure, appreciation, and love of God, in whom we live and move and have our being. God can be loved, served, and glorified after all. As ultimate beneficiary of the achieved value of the world, God is the unifier of the world's multiplicity, the preserver of the world's goodness, the supreme evaluator of the world's value. As Whitehead put it, in the world's creative advance into novelty "the many become one, and are increased by one." [16] There is a positive increment of value in this cumulative increase. God beholds the world and finds it good.

ETERNAL AND TEMPORAL

We have seen that in traditional theology *eternity* has both a negative and a positive meaning. Negatively it means "beginningless and endless in time"; positively it means "past, present, and future all at once." We have already explored the paradoxes of the positive meaning of *eternity.* The process theologian is anxious to avoid them, but he accepts the negative meaning of the word. Thus, he regards God as eternal in the sense that he is beginningless and endless in time. To avoid the paradoxes usually associated with *eternity,* the process theologian often uses the word *everlasting,* which conveys the sense of *eternity* that he accepts and which does not so readily suggest the concept of a simultaneous past, present, and future. God is an everlasting God, beginningless and endless in time, infinite in his love and compassion for and enjoyment of the individuals of the past and in his potentiality for creativity in the future. Where the supernaturalist regards the future as already closed and completely settled "from eternity," the panentheist regards it as open and pregnant with possibilities. Only the past has the settled character that the traditionalist has assigned to the whole of time. The achieved value of the past is preserved forever in the imperishable memory of God, but the realm of the future is the realm of value-yet-to-be-achieved. Even from a divine point of view, the notion of the simultaneity of past, present, and future is nonsense.

The primordial nature of God is eternal, but this means that it is the common and necessary nature of God that persists through all time. It does not mean that all time is present in God all at once. God's primordial nature is beginningless and endless, which is to say that the past and future are infinite, that God's encounter with *some* world is a permanent feature of his essence, and that nothing has the power to frustrate or terminate his being and becoming. If time is a part of what we mean by *the world,* then the world coexists everlastingly with God—that is, God always has *some* consequent nature, and time is also a part of what we mean by *God.* There is no first moment of time, no time before all time began, no space outside of all space. As Whitehead put it, God in his primordial nature "is not *before* all creation, but *with* all creation." [17] Again, this does not mean that the eternal aspects of God are with all time all at once, but rather that they are with all creation as it is created. Attributing temporality as well as eternity to God involves thinking of him as becoming as well as being, as both potential and actual, and it involves a persistent refusal to equate becoming and potentiality with inferiority. God is the necessary, enduring supercase of becoming and potentiality. All potentialities for change are ultimately his, for he finally includes all achieved value within his own enjoyment of actuality. The increment of value through time is cumulative, and time itself is simply the cumulative increment of achieved value. It is in the decisions we make in our present "moment of sheer individuality" [18] that we make our contributions to God—for better or for worse. God "saves" the world once it is created by preserving it forever in his consequent nature. This is our immortality, an "objective immortality" in the faultless, imperishable memory of God.

We noted earlier that the panentheist wishes to develop a concept of God as genuinely complete, as exemplifying all the dipolar categories and not merely the monopolar ones. Have we not failed to account totally for the completeness of God, since he is not complete with respect to time—that is, since the future is not already present to him? No; it is no genuine deficiency if God cannot perceive some square as round, and neither is it a genuine deficiency if he cannot perceive the future as present. If an attribute is in itself unintelligible, then in lacking that attribute God is not lacking in completeness. Time is just not the sort of thing of which there can be a totality all at once.

If time is the progression of creativity, if the world is to some extent creative, if the future is genuinely open even from an ultimate point of view, then the concept of the *omniscience* of God cannot have quite the same meaning in process theology that it has in traditional theology. Traditionally it means that God knows everything—past, present, and future—all at once. But what if the details of the future are simply not there to be known? In knowing the general possibilities for all conceivable worlds, God knows the general possibilities for the future of this particular world, much as a scientist who knows the laws of nature has a general knowledge of the range of possibilities for the future. But a knowledge of abstract generalities is not a knowledge of concrete actualities. What if the concrete actualities are simply not there to be known? What if our future decisions simply have not yet been made? How could God know them, and if he does, then what is the point of saying that they have not yet been made? The panentheist defines omniscience as a total knowledge of everything that is there to be known. God totally knows the past, the perishing present, and the possibilities for the future of this and of all possible cosmic epochs. God is still the one from whom no secrets are hid. He still knows everything that there is to know. He is still omniscient, but in this view his omniscience is consistent with his and with the world's creativity. The ultimate truth about the world is simply the world as known to a perfectly adequate, omniscient knower, but there is no truth about decisions that have not yet been made. God suffers these decisions as they are made, not in advance and not all at once. He discovers the concrete truth about the world as it is created by decisions made within the world at certain moments in time. Time has a bearing on omniscience, just as does eternity.

Although it appears on the surface that the panentheist and the supernaturalist are in disagreement about the omniscience of God, this appearance may be highly deceptive. Actually, they seem to agree that "God is omniscient" means "God knows everything that is there to be known." What they disagree about is an entirely independent metaphysical thesis about time that has nothing directly to do with God and that can be meaningfully debated whether one believes in God or not. This thesis is that "the future is already there in complete detail to be known."

ACTIVITY AND PASSIVITY

The acts and volitions of God are contingent facts about him. If God creates a contingent world and interacts with it, then there must be contingency in God. The particular ways in which God interacts with the world, specifically with human societies and individuals, cannot be known a priori. Some sort of "religious experience" is required for us to be acquainted with the contingent acts of God (the notion of "religious experience" will be examined in Chapters 12, 13, and 14). All the great world religions have some account of God's historical intercourse with men and nations, but the individual and cultural limitations and predilections of human interpreters inevitably color every account. Hartshorne writes that:

With Crisis Theology, which in a fashion is existential, our theory can agree that God is personal and self-related to the creatures, and that his acts of self-relationship are not rationally deducible, but require to be "encountered." However, as Barth and Brunner seem not to see, this is compatible with there being an essence of God which is philosophically explicable and knowable. The concrete volitions of God may be contingent or "arbitrary" (not that they do not express goodness, but that goodness has more than one possible expression in a given case); nevertheless, contingency or arbitrariness, as such, is not itself arbitrary but a necessary, or a priori, and intelligible category. For each man, indeed, religion is a matter of the actions of God as self-related to him, that is, to a wholly contingent being, or to humanity, likewise contingent. Relations whose terms are contingent can only be contingent. Philosophy seeks that general principle or essence of the divine being of which such concrete actions of God are mere contingent illustrations. But from a religious point of view, it is the illustrations that count. Thus the religious and the philosophical attitudes are complementary, not conflicting. Our doctrine appears, then, to effect a peculiarly comprehensive synthesis of past and present thought concerning theism.[19]

Panentheism differs significantly from traditional supernaturalism in attributing passivity to God. God is not such pure activity that he is totally lacking in passivity. God does not simply act; he interacts. To know the world is to be affected and acted on by the world. To love the world is to be emotionally responsive to events within the world. To have compassion toward the world involves suffering as the world suffers. The classical supernaturalist has maintained that love, sympathy, compassion, and even knowledge imply no passivity and responsiveness in God himself. The world is *as if* God were responsive in these ways to it, but God is not a passive and responsive being. St. Anselm's denial in *Proslogium,* Chapter 8, that there is any real compassion, sympathy, or feeling in God is the only position that supernaturalists can consistently take. Here it is most obvious that classical supernaturalism and biblical religion are worlds apart; and, by contrast, panentheism attempts to take seriously the notion of a loving and suffering God. Whitehead spoke of God as "the great companion —the fellow-sufferer who understands." [20] Hartshorne says that "I have no Christology to offer, beyond the simple suggestion that

Jesus appears to be the supreme symbol furnished to us by history of the notion of a God genuinely and literally 'sympathetic' (incomparably *more* literally than any man ever is), receiving into his own experience the sufferings as well as the joys of the world." [21] Hartshorne argues that the supernaturalist has indeed attempted to conceive of the perfection of God in such a way that he is imperfect.

A deity who cannot in any sense change or have contingent properties is a being for whom whatever happens in the contingent world is literally a matter of indifference. Such a being is totally "impassible" toward all things, utterly insensitive and unresponsive. This is the exact denial that "God is love." It means that nothing we can possibly do, enjoy, or suffer can in any way whatever contribute a satisfaction or value to the divine life greater [than] or different from what this life would have possessed had we never existed or had our fortunes been radically other than they are. Strange that for so many centuries it was held legitimate to call such a deity a God of love, or purpose, or knowledge! What we really have is the idea of sheer power, sheer causation, by something wholly neutral as to what, if anything, may be its effects. The naked worship of power is with wonderful exactitude, although unwittingly, enshrined in this doctrine.[22]

Attributing passivity to God has profound repercussions with respect to the attribute of *omnipotence*. God is no longer understood as a supreme tyrant, one who must be killed to make room for human freedom, initiative, responsibility, self-reliance, and maturity. We can account for these values without making the rash suggestion that God is dead or that men will one day outgrow their finitude and contingency altogether by recognizing that we finite and contingent human beings have an appropriate measure of creative power and initiative. Since God is no longer regarded as the sole originative cause operating in the universe, the omnipotence of God can no longer be equated with omnicausality. Omnipotence must now be understood as the supremely admirable, religiously adequate form of power and control over events within the world. Persuasion replaces coercion as a manifestation of God's power over us. Hartshorne writes that:

Religious faith imputes to God at least the kind and degree of power that the world needs as its supreme ordering influence. Or, more briefly, it imputes power adequate to cosmic need. It comes to the same thing to say that divine power must suffice to enable God to maintain for himself a suitable field of social relations, and thus to maintain himself as a social being. His power is absolute, if that means absolute in adequacy, or such that greater power would be no more adequate, and therefore would not really be "greater"—since adequacy is the measure of greatness, on our theory. What then is adequacy of cosmic power? It is power to do for the cosmos (the field of divine social relationships) all desirable things that could be done and need be done by one universal or cosmic agent. Adequacy is *not* power to do for the cosmos things that could only be done by nonuniversal agents. There are such things, and they are the free acts of localized beings, such as man.[23]

Attributing passivity to God also makes the problem of theodicy easier to solve for the panentheist. Since omnipotence is not omni-causality, there is no logical commitment to God's being the active cause of all the moral evil that exists in the universe. In creating creatures who exemplify creativity themselves in their own small way, God permits moral evil, but he does not actively instigate it. He allows us to choose immorality, but he does not coerce us to do so, as an omnicausal agent would have to do. When moral evil is introduced into the world, it is through human and not through divine initiative. Thus we are responsible and culpable, not God; and since God suffers as the world suffers, the pain that we inflict on our fellow creatures is ultimately inflicted on God. Man's inhumanity to man is ultimately man's inhumanity to God, our fellow sufferer who understands. The problem of theodicy is not completely solved, however, by making a place for human freedom and responsibility. God suffers with us not only in our sinfulness but also in our finitude and tragedy. Much of the pain and suffering of the world is *not* a consequence of human moral perversity. For example, the animals were suffering and dying on the earth eons before men evolved from more primitive forms of life. Much of the suffering and frustration and lack of fulfillment that we inflict on others is a result of the finitude of our knowledge and the fragmentariness of our sympathy, not the consequence of a deliberate choice of evil qua evil. Indeed, the great tragedy of existence lies more in the conflict of good with good than in the conflict of good with evil. Nothing immoral is involved when twenty men apply for one job opening or when ten boys fall in love with the same girl, but most of the applicants and lovers are doomed to frustration. The frustration and suffering that result from the conflict of good with good is a metaphysical inevitability in any world consisting of a multiplicity of individuals with a variety of interests and purposes. In a pluralistic universe, the fulfillment of all conflicting interests at the same time is simply incompossible—that is, possible separately but not possible together; and tragedy is the price that must be paid for richness and variety of interests, purposes, experiences, and individuals. Not even an omnipotent being has the power to actualize simultaneously those values that can only be actualized separately and successively; but in the succession of events, opportunities are inevitably lost. God suffers with us in the tragedy of our finitude just as he suffers with us in the consequences of our wickedness. Panentheism makes a place for both the moral and the tragic sense of life.

The other side of the coin of passivity is that the love that we have and express toward our fellow creatures is ultimately expressed toward God, for he is the final beneficiary of our love as well as the final victim of our hatred. How can we love God with *all* our hearts and still love our neighbors as ourselves? How can there be anything left over for our neighbor if God demands our *total* devotion? There is no answer to these questions unless in the process of loving our fellow creatures we *are* loving God in some sense, unless God *is* all, *in* all. We cannot love another fully without loving what he loves, without being loyal to his loyalties. God not only loves the world but is the ultimate recipient of whatever love we express toward the world. Hartshorne interprets the command to love God with all our heart and soul and mind and strength as follows:

> One hundred percent of our interest (mind), devotion (heart), energy (strength), and whatever else is in us (soul) is to have God as its object. It follows that if there be anything additional to God, it must receive zero attention! Yet we are to love ourselves and our fellows. A contradiction? Yes, save upon one assumption, that there cannot be anything "additional to God."

Rather, all actuality must be included in His actuality, and all possibility in His potential actuality. (For we must be interested in possibilities, if we are to love and help our neighbor, or ourselves.)[24]

SPIRITUAL AND SPATIAL

If God is genuinely complete, if he is that being than whom none richer in properties can be conceived, then both spirituality and spatiality must be attributed to him in some preeminent sense. The word *spiritual* has many meanings, but when contrasted with *spatial* it suggests the contrast between personality and body. God is a "Thou" and not a mere "It." The spiritual is the personal or mental pole as contrasted with the bodily or physical pole of both human and divine existence. No radical Platonic or Cartesian dualism is intended by this contrast. The spiritual and the spatial can never be ontologically separated. They can never exist apart from each other, even in the case of divinity. There is always something spatial about the spiritual and something spiritual about the spatial. Neither man nor God is or ever could be a disembodied mind, a ghost within or without a machine. The body is no mere machine but a living organism, a locus of integrated feeling and activity. The spirit is no mere ghost but a unification of the multiplicity of bodily feeling and activity. Each man is a thoroughly unified and integrated living organism, not a spaceless prisoner in a spatial prison. The spiritual and the spatial are two distinguishable poles in a single integrated whole, yet there is something about spirit that transcends the immediacy of both space and time. This does not mean that spirit is in a space beyond space or a time beyond time, but only that personal existence here and now has the ability to include the actualities of the past within itself in memory, the possibilities for the future within itself in anticipation, the universal within the individual in conceptualization, and the other within itself in sympathy and fellow-feeling. There is something transcendent even about human personality, but it is a nonmysterious, familiar sort of transcendence that is thoroughly compatible with immanence. If transcendence is to be attributed to God in panentheism, it must be of an analogous sort but without the fragmentariness of human memory, foresight, understanding, and sympathy. It really makes no sense to think of God as existing "outside space" and "before time," as the supernaturalist would have it. God is transcendent as present personality transcends the immediate here and now in memory, anticipation, conceptualization, and sympathy, as the Whole transcends the parts, as the primordial transcends the consequent, but not as the nonspatiotemporal lies "beyond" the spatiotemporal.

In rejecting the radical dualisms of bygone eras, Whitehead and Hartshorne insist that all personality is embodied personality, even in the supercase of divinity. The idea that the world is the body of God did not originate with Hartshorne, but he does take the analogy with utmost seriousness. All space is God's space, and he is indeed an *omnipresent* God. Hartshorne conjectures that we human beings are related to God in something like the way the cells of our bodies are related to us. Our cells are themselves localized units of feeling with some measure of autonomy. We cannot willfully control their actions in most cases, and they cannot willfully control our actions. But the whole and the parts do interact and influence one another. As the localized cells of my body are injured and suffer, I suffer. I suffer their suffering, and I enjoy their well-being. On the other hand, I also exercise some control over my cells. I place them in situations at which they cannot arrive on their own and subject them to adventures and perils not entirely of their own choosing. My successes and failures are ultimately inflicted on them, and their successes and failures are ultimately enjoyed or suffered by me. So it is with God and the world. We are all members of the body of God, autonomous parts of that divine whole in whom we live and move and have our being (and our becoming). Reality is thus a social process.[25]

INFINITE AND FINITE

Do not the panentheists confront us with "just another finite God"? Definitely not. It is much too simple to say that God is merely finite, just as it is much too simple to say that he is merely infinite. Only those with a "black or white" mentality demand that it be entirely one way or the other, but those who attempt to do full justice to the *logos* of God cannot tolerate simple-minded solutions to complicated problems. Even the supernaturalist usually admits that God is limited by his own moral perfection and by his own reason or logic. But he regards all of God's limitations as self-limitations, and he refuses to concede that God is in any sense limited by the world. The panentheist also insists that God is infinite in some respects and finite in others; but he adds that God is limited by, and is passive and responsive toward, the world. In some respects the power of God is limited: God allows us to be coworkers, cocreators with him, though he always has sufficient control over the world to prevent it from going too far astray. The knowledge of God is in one respect limited: Not even an omniscient being can know future decisions that have not yet been made, that are simply not there to be known. And the presence of God is limited, for the world enjoys a "moment of sheer individuality" before perishing into his consequent nature.

In what respects is God infinite for the process theologian? His primordial possibilities are limitless. Nothing outside God conditions or causes him to exist everlastingly as an omniscient, omnipotent, omnipresent, morally and religiously supreme being. Since "the general potentiality of the universe must be somewhere," specifically in "the primordial mind of God," [26] and since this potentiality is infinite, it is tempting to say that God is infinite with respect to his potentiality and finite with respect to his actuality. But even this is too simple. If some world is coeverlasting with God, if he always has some consequent nature, then the actualities of the past are infinite as well as the possibilities for the future. God's consequent enjoyment of and participation in the world's creative advance into novelty is limitless but constantly increasing. The finite actuality of present creativity is constantly being added to the infinite actuality of past creativity. There is no paradox in this; the finite can be added to the infinite, but the sum is always an infinite sum. It is simply not the case that *all* possibilities will be actualized in an infinite amount of time. It is true that in an infinite amount of time, an infinite number of possibilities will be actualized; but it is also true that an infinite number of possibilities will remain to be actualized. Such is the nature of infinity.

If there are imperfections in God, they are all perfectly compatible with his perfection. The polarity of perfect–imperfect thus does not stand on the same footing with the other polarities we have discussed, but is largely a matter of semantics. If God is imperfect, it is only in a sense in which the corresponding sense of *perfect* has no clear meaning. Hartshorne does speak of God as being imperfect in one respect, that of God's happiness, his enjoyment of achieved value; but he argues that the notion of a completed sum of all possible happiness, all possible achieved value, does not make sense, just as the notion of all time all at once does not make sense. He writes:

> Absolute happiness must then be the logical monstrosity: complete satisfaction of all possible desires—so to speak, infinite success of the advertisers in awakening desires and infinite success of the producers in meeting them. But there are incompatible desires and values. Until one has made this truism central to one's thought about life, one has not the beginnings of practical wisdom. "You must renounce," said Goethe; and this is true not merely because man is a limited, imperfect creature but because values are in principle subject to incompatibilities. A sonnet and a ballad exclude each other's merits. Try to put them together in a superpoem, and here too you will meet alternatives, mutually exclusive possibilities for the superpoem. Even if the whole universe is in question, it cannot be every possible kind of harmonious whole but must be one kind, excluding others that might have been. Since beauty and richness of experience vary not only as to harmony or unification of the factors but also as to variety and depth of the contrasts among them, absolute richness must be absolute unification of absolute variety. But absolute variety could only mean all possible variety. Here again we run into a contradiction: there are mutually exclusive forms of variety.[27]

Furthermore, moral and religious perfection is incompatible with completeness in *all* respects, for example, with omnicausality. A completely good God simply cannot be the initiating, necessary, *and sufficient* cause of all the evil in the world. The perfection of

God must be understood in such a way as to be compatible with his being supremely worshipful. "God is perfect" has traditionally meant that "God cannot be surpassed by anything"; but Hartshorne understands it to mean that "God cannot be surpassed by anything *other than himself*." If perfection involves completeness, God is still complete in all intelligible and desirable respects, but not complete in those respects that are nonsensical or demoniacal in the first place. What is imperfect about that? To say that God is either perfect and incapable of improvement or imperfect and unworthy of worship is to present a false dilemma. The perfection of God is perfectly compatible with his continuing creativity and his continuing enjoyment of the achieved value of the world, and a God who is unsurpassable by any individual other than himself is certainly worthy of worship. Hartshorne says of the superiority of God's unsurpassability that "by categorically superior we mean such that no other individual can rival it, thus leaving open the door to self-excelling." [28] He further explains that

> to say God is perfect might be defined to mean that he is better than any individual other than himself. This would leave open the possibility that, though no individual who is not God can be better than he, still he might himself improve. Unsurpassable by others, he might yet surpass himself, might grow in value. To conceive God as capable of improvement in *goodness* shocks the religious sense, which feels that God could not possibly be more just or merciful than he is. In ethical quality and in wisdom and power, religion conceives God as already as perfect as anything could be. But does religion assure us that God is equally incapable of improvement in happiness? How can this be if God loves us, and through love shares in our sorrows, and is grieved by our misfortunes and errors? But even here we may call God perfect, if we mean by this that he is not to be surpassed in happiness by any being other than himself. To say God can increase in happiness (and if he cannot, then there is no service we can render him) is not to say that any other individual is or could be happier than he, but only to say that he himself could be happier. In other words, if perfect means supreme among individuals, then God is in all respects perfect; but if perfect means incapable of growth or improvement, then only in goodness, wisdom and power is God perfect.[29]

Classical supernaturalism has held that God is just as incapable of improvement in achieved value as he is in moral goodness, but it is doubtful that the notion of "all possible value actualized all at once" makes sense. Our understanding of the perfection of God must take this into account.

> The perfect, one often hears, is what lacks no possible value, so that all possibility of increase in value is cut off. But we must be cautious here. For "all the value possible," or "the sum of all perfections," may not itself be a possible value, since there seem to be "incompossibles" (Leibniz) among possible values. Hence "that whose value leaves no possibility of value unrealized" may be a self-contradictory definition.[30]

HOLINESS

God as understood by the process theologians is still a being of tremendous and fascinating mystery, not lacking in the least in "religious availability." Yet no attempt has been made to account for the holiness of God in terms of contradiction, utter inconceivability, or nonspatiotemporality. The utter uniqueness of God is still intact. The power, creativity, knowledge, compassion, and goodness of God are still radically superior to their fragmentary counterparts in humanity and the world. These attributes are exemplified in God in a totally nondeficient form. The metaphysical completeness of God is better expressed in process theology than in classical supernaturalism; for God is the categorically superior form of both the static, monistic and the dynamic, pluralistic metaphysical categories. God is the ultimate whole, the final unity of all things. The self-sufficiency of God is preserved in the doctrine of the primordial nature of God, while at the same time the concrete love and creativity of God are accounted for in the doctrine of his consequent nature. God's love and creativity do not here die the death of a thousand qualifications. The infinite richness of the actuality of God is preserved in the doctrine that God always has *some* consequent nature, and an intelligible account of the mystery and human unknowability of God may be given in relation to this. It is not the abstract essence of God that is humanly unknowable; but rather it is in God's concrete, consequent richness and contingency that his unknowability is to be located. *If,* for example, the "big bang" cosmology is correct in suggesting that the present cosmic epoch of our universe began about three billion years ago and that some universe preceded even that, how many such cosmic epochs have there been, and what has God suffered and enjoyed within them? In process theology, the moral goodness and absoluteness of God are seen to be still perfect in their adequacy, and an intelligible account is given of how love, compassion, and sympathy really can be attributes of God. There is no room for improvement in love, but there is room for an increase in objects of love. What more could be required in developing a concept of a being completely worthy of our admiration, respect, and ultimate concern, completely worthy of being loved by us with all our heart and soul and mind and strength?

Suggestions for Further Reading

WHITEHEAD AND HARTSHORNE ON GOD AND THE WORLD

HARTSHORNE, CHARLES, *Creative Synthesis and Philosophic Method* (LaSalle, Ill., Open Court, 1970).

————, *The Divine Relativity* (New Haven, Conn., Yale University Press, 1948).

————, *Man's Vision of God* (Hamden, Conn., Archon Books, 1964).

————, *A Natural Theology for Our Time* (LaSalle, Ill., Open Court, 1967).

———— and REESE, WILLIAM L., *Philosophers Speak of God* (Chicago, University of Chicago Press, 1953). The Introduction to this book is one of the best short introductions to process theology available.

————, *Reality as Social Process* (New York, Free Press, 1953).

WHITEHEAD, ALFRED NORTH, *Process and Reality* (New York, Humanities Press, 1929), especially Part V.

————, *Religion in the Making* (New York, Macmillan, 1926).

OTHER PROCESS THEOLOGIANS ON GOD AND THE WORLD

BERDYAEV, NICHOLAS, *The Divine and the Human* (London, Geoffrey Bles, 1949).

BROWN, DELWIN, JAMES, RALPH E., JR., and REEVES, GENE, *Process Philosophy and Christian Thought* (Indianapolis, Ind., Bobbs-Merrill, 1971). An excellent anthology with many valuable critical discussions.

CALHOUN, ROBERT L., *God and the Common Life* (Hamden, Conn., Shoe String Press, 1954), Chapter 4.

COBB, JOHN B., *A Christian Natural Theology* (Philadelphia, Westminster Press, 1965).

————, *God and the World* (Philadelphia, Westminster Press, 1969).

FERRÉ, NELS F. S., *The Christian Understanding of God* (New York, Harper & Row, 1951).

OGDEN, SCHUBERT, *The Reality of God* (New York, Harper & Row, 1963).

ROBINSON, JOHN A. T., *Exploration into God* (Stanford, Calif., Stanford University Press, 1967).

TENNANT, F. R., *Philosophical Theology,* Vol. II (Cambridge, Eng., Cambridge University Press, 1956).

WILLIAMS, DANIEL DAY, *The Spirit and the Forms of Love* (New York, Harper & Row, 1968).

Notes

1 Charles Hartshorne and William L. Reese, *Philosophers Speak of God* (Chicago, University of Chicago Press, 1953), p. 3.

2 Paul Tillich, *The Courage to Be* (New Haven, Conn., Yale University Press, 1952), pp. 184–85. Reprinted by permission.

3 Hartshorne and Reese, *Philosophers Speak of God,* p. 17.

4 Alfred North Whitehead, *Process and Reality* (New York, Macmillan, 1929). Copyright 1929 by the Macmillan Company, renewed 1957 by Evelyn Whitehead. Permission to quote also granted by Cambridge University Press.

5 Charles Hartshorne, *Reality as Social Process* (New York, Free Press, 1953), p. 120.

6 Hartshorne and Reese, *Philosophers Speak of God,* pp. 2–3. Reprinted by permission.

7 *Ibid.,* pp. 14–15.

8 Charles Hartshorne, *The Divine Relativity* (New Haven, Conn., Yale University Press, 1948), p. 1.

9 *Ibid.,* p. 35.

10 *Ibid.*

11 *Ibid.,* p. 26.

12 Hartshorne and Reese, *Philosophers Speak of God,* p. 7.

13 Hartshorne, *The Divine Relativity,* p. 41.

14 Whitehead, *Process and Reality,* p. 42.

15 Hartshorne, *The Divine Relativity,* pp. 130–31. Reprinted by permission.

16 Whitehead, *Process and Reality,* p. 32.

17 *Ibid.,* p. 521.

18 Alfred North Whitehead, *Adventures of Ideas* (New York, New American Library of World Literature, 1955), p. 179. Quoted by permission of the Macmillan Company and Cambridge University Press.

19 Hartshorne, *The Divine Relativity,* pp. xi–xii.

20 Whitehead, *Process and Reality,* p. 532.

21 Hartshorne, *Reality as Social Process,* p. 24.

22 Hartshorne and Reese, *Philosophers Speak of God,* p. 20.

23 Hartshorne, *The Divine Relativity,* p. 134.

24 Charles Hartshorne, *The Logic of Perfection* (LaSalle, Ill., Open Court, 1962), pp. 40–41.

25 This social conception of reality is developed in Hartshorne's book entitled *Reality as Social Process,* especially in Chapters 1–7.

26 Whitehead, *Process and Reality,* p. 73.

27 Hartshorne and Reese, *Philosophers Speak of God,* p. 10.

28 *Ibid.*

29 Hartshorne, *Reality as Social Process,* p. 157.

30 Hartshorne and Reese, *Philosophers Speak of God,* p. 506.

chapter nine

The Existence
of God THE ONTOLOGICAL
ARGUMENT

Does God exist? The answer to this question depends in part on what we mean by *God* and in part on what we mean by *exists*. We saw in Chapters 6, 7, and 8 that *God* has many different meanings within the context of different world views. For the naturalist, God is the working unity of those human ideals that give meaning and direction to life. Within the framework of naturalism the question of God's existence is simply the question of whether there are any such ideals, and it is obvious that an affirmative answer to this question must be given: Men do have such ideals. Paul Tillich has suggested that any object of ultimate concern may be called God [1] and that the only "true atheist" is the man who is uninvolved, indifferent, not deeply interested in anything. Within this context the question of the existence of God is the question of whether men are deeply concerned, and again the necessity of an affirmative answer is obvious, in the case of many men at any rate: Many of us are deeply concerned about *something*. Often, however, the question of God is understood as a *metaphysical* question and not simply as a question about human ideals and concerns. Within the framework of both supernaturalism and panentheism this is the case, and here the question of the existence of God cannot be resolved quite so easily. It is not as obvious that there is a supreme, intelligent, creative being as it is that men do have ideals and deep concerns, and the present chapter is devoted to *the metaphysical problem of the existence of such a supreme, intelligent, creative being*. After having completed Chapters 7 and 8, we may feel that it is very nice to know that there are alternative ways of conceiving of such a being and his relation to the world, such as those offered by supernaturalism and panentheism; but so what? Are there any reasons for believing that God in either of these metaphysical senses is really there? Are these theistic world views mere fancy? Can we prove that God exists? In what sense of "proof"? We shall now consider questions such as these.

Existence and Proof

When we ask about the existence of God, we must be as clear as we can not only about the meaning of *God* but also about the meaning of *existence*. The word *existence* has a number of meanings, not all of which do full justice to the problem of the existence of God. In one sense, to exist is to be an item located within and as a part of the spatiotemporal universe and capable of being encountered through sense experience. To exist in this sense is to be a natural object, a creature. Paul Tillich has insisted that "It is as atheistic to affirm the existence of God as it is to deny it. God is being-itself, not *a* being." [2] For him, God is "above existence." It is clear that "to exist" in this context means to be a natural, perceptible object; and neither the supernaturalist nor the panentheist nor the Tillichian ontologist wishes to affirm that God exists in this sense. Have we thereby dismissed the problem of the existence of God on purely linguistic grounds? What exactly are we asking when we ask about the existence of God? Surely something is at stake here. Suppose we asked the question: Does the universe, or the whole of nature, exist? Is this a mere pseudoquestion? Presumably the naturalists would not think so. Would we not be disturbed if someone told us that there was no universe, no nature at all? Yet the universe is not an item within the universe, and nature as a whole is not an object within the whole of nature, and it is perfectly sensible to deny that such things exist, given the present sense of *exist*. But given some other sense of *exist*, it is perfectly sensible and correct to affirm that they exist. In a second sense, "to exist" is to be a legitimate object of reference. Something is there, we are talking about something, when we speak of the universe, the whole of nature, the totality of space, the whole of reality. To exist in this sense is to have denotation as well as connotation. To affirm that nature as a whole exists is to say that "nature" is a non-empty class, not that nature as a whole is an item within nature. Similarly, to affirm that God exists is to say that the word *God* has denotation as well as connotation, that the concept is not empty, that it refers to something that is really there. This is the problem of the existence of God. We explored some conceptual connotations of *God* in Chapters 7 and 8. Now we want to know if the word refers to anything. Only if we answer this question can we choose between some form of theism and naturalism.

Are there any reasons for believing in God? Certainly. There are plenty of them, and some of the most fundamental of these are encapsulated within the traditional rationalistic "proofs" for the existence of God, to which we shall soon turn. Of course, we must realize that to say that there are plenty of reasons for believing in God is not to say that there are plenty of *good* reasons for believing in God. The traditional proofs are highly controversial. There are many who insist that all the traditional reasons for believing in God are unacceptable. Who is right about all this? In the end you must judge for yourself. No one can answer this question for you. But we can explore the pros and cons of the matter for whatever they might be worth.

What are philosophical proofs, and who is required to give them? A proof is an argument that has a bearing on a conclusion. To give a proof is to give evidence for a conclusion, to try to rationally justify a belief. To state a proof is to state an argument, and the statements that count as evidence for the conclusion are the premises of the argument. Not all arguments show that their conclusions are true, however. There are bad arguments and good arguments. A bad argument is one that fails to show that its conclusion is true, either because one or more of its premises are false or because the general pattern of reasoning involved is incorrect. A good argument, an argument that proves the truth of its conclusion, is one that has all true premises and a correct pattern of reasoning. A proof can be attacked either by attacking its pattern of reasoning or by attacking one or more of its premises. Who must give philosophical proofs? Anyone who has anything philosophical to say. It is common to try to place the burden of proof on the other fellow, but this is unfair. Both the proofs for the existence of God and the criticisms of those proofs have premises. *Each* side must support its case as best it can; it is most unfair to insist, as is so often done, that the burden of proof lies with the theist.

In philosophy, as in other disciplines, conclusions are usually supported by a number of related arguments. Seldom is a philosopher content to advance only *one* proof for his beliefs. His convictions never stand or fall with a single argument but with a complex set of lines of converging evidence and independent arguments that have a bearing on a common conclusion. It is sometimes maintained that unless a very strict proof or set of related proofs is offered, nothing is proved at all. For example, it is sometimes held that unless all the premises of an argument are absolutely certain and the pattern of reasoning indubitably valid, the proof is utterly worthless. If one adheres strictly to this rigid deductive ideal, however, one is forced to conclude that there are *no* worthwhile proofs anywhere except possibly in mathematics, and even here the tendency is to regard axioms as system-relative and not absolutely indubitable in all possible contexts. Certainly there are no such proofs to be found either in natural science or in philosophy. Of course, some philosophers have mistakenly believed that they were offering such proofs, but in the final analysis we must settle for a more modest understanding of what constitutes a rationally justified philosophical belief. Occasionally, perhaps, even some of the traditional proofs for the existence of God have been interpreted as providing conclusive evidence for their theistic conclusions. From the outset, however, we must recognize that it is a mistake so to regard them, not because we know before we even begin that they do not prove anything, but rather because we know that there are *no* philosophical beliefs anywhere that are supported by conclusive evidence. To expect indubitable premises and rigorous deductive validity from the traditional proofs is to expect too much. No philosophical proofs of anything rest on indubitable premises. Philosophical proof simply cannot meet such exacting requirements, but this is not to make lame excuses for sloppy thinking. We must be as exact as we can be, but at the same time we must recognize that all philosophical knowledge "swims in a continuum of uncertainty," as Charles Sanders Peirce once put it.

Often the theistic proofs are criticized on the grounds that one is not required to accept the conclusion unless one first accepts the premises. This is true, but the theistic proofs are not peculiar in this respect. All arguments for everything everywhere are like this. If this is a weakness, it is a weakness of the entire enterprise of rationality and not simply a weakness of the philosophy of religion. What, then, is it like to give a philosophical proof? As we saw in Chapter 5, Friedrich Waismann suggested that giving philosophical proof is very similar to what a lawyer does in a courtroom. The philosopher "builds up a case." He explains as best he can why he believes what he does and why he rejects the chief alternatives to his position, and he is always willing to examine and re-examine the elements out of which his case is built. Many lines of converging evidence must be put together into a coherent case, and assessing the strength of that case, like giving a judgment in a courtroom, is not like running a mathematical proof through a computer. Many complex elements enter into the case for belief in God. Often the diverse "proofs" are compared, quite correctly, to strands or fibers in a rope, no one of which does the work of the whole rope, yet some of which must do some work if the rope is to have any strength at all. As in a courtroom verdict, the verdict for or against the existence of God cannot be rendered in some purely automatic fashion. Finally, when all is said and done, someone must simply pass judgment. If the final appeal is to intuition, we can only hope not to make this appeal prematurely so as to block the path of inquiry. All important philosophical beliefs stand or fall this way, and the case for or against God is not unique in this respect. As with all important philosophical beliefs, someone must finally pass judgment; and you are the judge. But what is the case?

Usually a division is made between the a priori proofs for God, which attempt to show that the existence of God follows from the very idea or concept of God, and the a posteriori proofs, which involve at least one empirical premise. The first argument we shall examine, the ontological argument, is an a priori proof. Other arguments we shall examine, such as the cosmological and teleological arguments, are a posteriori proofs. So is the argument from religious experience (which we shall examine in Chapters 12, 13, and 14), given a very generous interpretation of the concept of the *empirical*.

The Ontological Argument: St. Anselm

O<small>NE</small> of the most captivating "proofs" for the existence of God was offered by St. Anselm, Archbishop of Canterbury, in the eleventh century A.D. in his *Proslogium*. Versions of his argument have been defended by such religious thinkers as St. Bonaventure, Duns Scotus, Descartes, Leibniz, Spinoza, and Hegel, and in our own century its ablest defenders have been Karl Barth, Charles Hartshorne, and Norman Malcolm.[3] There have been many critics of St. Anselm's argument as well as many defenders. The earliest criticism was offered by a monk named Gaunilon, and St. Anselm's brilliant reply to Gaunilon is a classic contribution to the great religious and philosophical literature of the world. St. Thomas Aquinas attacked the proof, though he accepted versions of the cosmological argument as sound. David Hume attacked the proof as he understood it, along with other classical proofs. Immanuel Kant developed some of the most severe criticisms of the proof. It is widely assumed today that he dealt the death blow to the ontological argument, though this assumption may not be warranted. In our century, renewed attention has been given to the argument, and there are many significant contemporary critics.

St. Anselm offered his own versions of the cosmological argument and other evidences for the existence of God in an earlier work titled the *Monologium,* but he wrote in the Preface to the *Proslogium* that he had long desired "a single argument which would require no other for its proof than itself alone; and alone would suffice to demonstrate that God truly exists . . . ."[4] His discussion of how he finally made his discovery is a superb illustration of creative rational insight at work:

> Although I often and earnestly directed my thought to this end, and at some times that which I sought seemed to be just within my reach, while again it wholly evaded my mental vision, at last in despair I was about to cease, as if from the search for a thing which could not be found. But when I wished to exclude this thought altogether, lest, by busying my mind to no purpose, it should keep me from other thoughts, in which I might be successful; then more and more, though I was unwilling and shunned it, it began to force itself upon me, with a kind of importunity. So,

one day, when I was exceedingly wearied with resisting its importunity, in the very conflict of my thoughts, the proof of which I had despaired offered itself, so that I eagerly embraced the thoughts which I was strenuously repelling.

Thinking, therefore, that what I rejoiced to have found, would, if put in writing, be welcomed to some readers, of this very matter, and of some others, I have written the following treatise, in the person of one who strives to lift his mind to the contemplation of God and seeks to understand what he believes.[5]

St. Anselm did not believe that reason and faith were mutually exclusive alternatives; rather, he regarded them as mutually complementary, prefacing his ontological proofs with the remark that "I do not seek to understand that I may believe but I believe in order to understand. For this also I believe—that unless I believed, I should not understand." [6] In speaking of "proofs" we are acknowledging that St. Anselm actually offered *two* quite distinct ontological arguments, though he may not have realized clearly that he was doing so, and few if any of the classical critics realized it. The first form of the ontological argument appears in Chapter II of the *Proslogium,* and the second form appears in Chapter III. These two short chapters are here reprinted in full.

CHAPTER II

Truly there is a God, although the fool hath said in his heart, There is no God. And so, Lord, do thou, who dost give understanding to faith, give me, so far as thou knowest it to be profitable, to understand that thou art as we believe; and that thou art that which we believe. And indeed, we believe that thou art a being than which nothing greater can be conceived. Or is there no such nature, since the fool hath said in his heart, there is no God? (Psalms xiv.1). But, at any rate, this very fool, when he hears of this being of which I speak—a being than which nothing greater can be conceived—understands what he hears, and what he understands is in his understanding; although he does not understand it to exist.

For, it is one thing for an object to be in the understanding, and another to understand that the object exists. When a painter first conceives of what he will afterwards perform, he has it in his understanding, but he does not yet understand it to be, because he has not yet performed it. But after he has made the painting, he both has it in his understanding, and he understands that it exists, because he has made it.

Hence, even the fool is convinced that something exists in the understanding, at least, than which nothing greater can be conceived. For, when he hears of this, he understands it. And whatever is understood, exists in the understanding. And assuredly that, than which nothing greater can be conceived, cannot exist in the understanding alone. For, suppose it exists in the understanding alone: then it can be conceived to exist in reality, which is greater.

Therefore, if that, than which nothing greater can be conceived, exists in the understanding alone, the very being, than which nothing greater can be conceived, is one, than which a greater can be conceived. But obviously this is impossible. Hence, there is no doubt that there exists a being, than which nothing greater can be conceived, and it exists both in the understanding and in reality.

CHAPTER III

God cannot be conceived not to exist.—God is that, than which nothing greater can be conceived.—That which can be conceived not to exist is not God. And it assuredly exists so truly, that it cannot be conceived not to exist. For, it is possible to conceive of a being which cannot be conceived not to exist; and this is greater than one which can be conceived not to exist. Hence, if that, than which nothing greater can be conceived, can be conceived not to exist, it is not that, than which nothing greater can be conceived. But this is an irreconcilable contradiction. There is, then, so truly a being than which nothing greater can be conceived to exist, that it cannot even be conceived not to exist; and this being thou art, O Lord, our God.

So truly, therefore, dost thou exist, O Lord my God, that thou canst not be conceived not to exist; and rightly. For if a mind could conceive of a being better than thee, the creature would rise above the Creator, and this is most absurd. And, indeed, whatever else there is, except thee alone, can be conceived not to exist. To thee alone, therefore, it belongs to exist more truly than all other beings, and hence in a higher degree than all others. For, whatever else exists does not exist so truly, and hence in a less degree it belongs to it to exist. Why, then, has the fool said in his heart, There is no God (Psalms xiv.1), since it is so evident, to a rational mind, that thou dost exist in the highest degree of all? Why, except that he is dull and a fool? [7]

If the differences between the first and second forms of the ontological argument are not immediately apparent to you, do not be dismayed. They have not been immediately apparent to most of the argument's critics through the centuries. We shall see that most critics have not read or at least not understood the second form of the argument and that prior to Barth, Hartshorne, and Malcolm this second form of the ontological proof went both unnoticed and virtually untouched by criticism for centuries. To explain and make clear the differences between the two forms of the argument, let us reword each as follows:

Form 1

(1) All perfections are attributes of God.
(2) (Mere, contingent) existence is a perfection.
Therefore, (mere, contingent) existence is an attribute of God.

Form 2

(1) All perfections belong to God.
(2) (Necessary) existence is a perfection.
Therefore, (necessary) existence belongs to God.

The first form of the argument is an attempt to show that God has the same kind of existence that other things such as paintings have: contingent existence, which involves conceivable nonexistence. As Hartshorne repeatedly points out, most of the standard criticisms of the argument are addressed to this first form, and as such they are fully justified. However, the second form of the argument is an attempt to show that God has a radically unique kind of existence, that the concept of God is non-empty in a radically unique way. It is not mere contingent existence but necessary existence which is here predicated of God. Not only can God not fail to exist, but we cannot fail to think of him as existing. His nonexistence is inconceivable. Given the first form of the proof, nonexistence would be an imperfection. Gives the second form of the proof, *both* nonexistence and merely contingent existence (that is, possible nonexistence) would be imperfections. If it is possible even to conceive of God's nonexistence, then only the imperfection of merely contingent existence is being attributed to him by the conceiver. Of course such a contingent God does not exist. But the proof is not an attempt to show that such a contingent God does exist. If one even conceives of God as one who might or might not be there, then one has not really conceived of God; and if one denies that such a God exists, it is not the God whose existence is proved by the second form of the ontological proof. *This* God is one whose possible nonexistence is unthinkable, inconceivable. And what is the criterion of conceivability? It is that of self-contradiction. The fool who says in his heart, "There is no God," either does not understand what is meant by God and thus does not deny God's existence at all, or else he is contradicting himself. He is saying that a necessary being might not exist, which is merely the self-contradictory claim that a necessary being is a contingent being. The fool entertains the thought of a necessary being that is not a necessary being.

Ten Objections to the Ontological Argument

Now that we understand both forms of the ontological argument, we are in a better position than most critics have been to examine some standard criticisms and see how well the critics have done. Although we cannot cover everything, we shall examine some of the most basic objections to the argument, more or less in historical order, and we shall develop possible lines of reply to each of these objections.

OBJECTION 1

Objection 1 states that the ontological argument attempts to pass from the thought of the existence of a thing to the actual existence of that thing, and it is never legitimate to move thus from the realm of concepts to the realm of existents. Gaunilon offered this criticism of the ontological argument in his *On Behalf of the Fool,* and it has been echoed by numerous critics, including St. Thomas Aquinas and Kant. As Gaunilon stated it, "If it should be said that a being which cannot be even conceived in terms of any fact, is in the understanding, I do not deny that this being is, accordingly, in my understanding. But since through this fact it can in no wise attain to real existence also, I do not yet concede to it that existence at all, until some certain proof of it shall be given." [8] St. Thomas Aquinas argued along similar lines:

Now, from the fact that that which is indicated by the name God is conceived by the mind, it does not follow that God exists save only in the intellect. Hence, that than which a greater cannot be thought will likewise not have to exist save only in the intellect. From this it does not follow that there exists in reality something than which a greater cannot be thought. No difficulty, consequently, befalls anyone who posits that God does not exist. For that something greater can be thought than anything given in reality or in the intellect is a difficulty only to him who admits that there is something than which a greater cannot be thought in reality. [9]

This objection to the ontological argument is widely accepted, but that is no proof of its truth. What can be said by way of reply? In the first place, as a criticism of the first form of the argument it is certainly valid. With respect to contingent things, it is indeed illegitimate to move from the realm of thought to the realm of existence. The existence of a merely contingent thing never follows from its conception, and if God is a merely contingent being, then his existence cannot be proved this way at all. On the other hand, the criticism does not apply at all to the second form of the proof. This objection does nothing to refute St. Anselm's contention that in the unique case of God we cannot fail to pass from the realm of conception to the realm of necessary existence without contradicting ourselves. The critic is in effect saying that although God does exist in the understanding, it does not follow from this that he *really* exists. In other words, although God exists in the mind, *he might not* exist in reality at all. But this is why the fool is indeed a fool if he understands by *God* what St. Anselm understands by *God*. To say that God might not exist in reality is to assert once more that God, who has a necessary form of existence, has a merely contingent form of existence or, worse yet, that he has no existence at all. Again the fool falls into self-contradiction. It is logically impossible to hold that something exists both necessarily and contingently in exactly the same respect, as it is logically impossible to hold that something both necessarily exists and does not exist at all. As St. Anselm put it in his reply to Gaunilon, "He, then, who conceives of this being conceives of a being which cannot be even conceived not to exist; but he who conceives of this being does not conceive that it does not exist; else he conceives what is inconceivable. The non-existence, then, of that than which a greater cannot be conceived is inconceivable." [10] In one sense, of course, it is possible to think that "God might not exist"—that is, the words can be so combined and spoken. But not every combination of words is consistently meaningful; and if St. Anselm is correct, this combination of words is self-contradictory.

OBJECTION 2

Objection 2 holds that if the existence of God can be proved this way, the existence of *anything* (such as a perfect island, a perfect devil, money in my empty pockets, or imaginary men) can be proved this way. Again it was Gaunilon who first developed this line of criticism, and it is closely related to the alleged impossibility of moving from the order of thought to the order of existence. It is a *reductio ad absurdum* argument that attempts to show that if we follow St. Anselm's pattern of reasoning, we will arrive at consequences that we know to be false or ridiculous.

Two lines of reply may be given to this criticism. In the first place, if other things have the same kind of existence that God has, then the existence of these other things *can* be proved this way. The fact that a perfect island, a perfect devil, nonexistent money, or imaginary men cannot be proved to exist this way shows only that the kind of existence attributed to God is radically different from the kind of existence attributed to all such contingencies. God exists in a totally unique way. He does not exist contingently at all. He is not the sort of being that might or might not be there. He is not even in the same series with contingent beings; he is not the greatest of all contingent beings but the greatest of all conceivable beings, that is, a being who is necessary and self-sufficient. He is the being who could not not exist, the one being who could not die. In his reply to Gaunilon, St. Anselm admits that *if* his pattern of argumentation did apply to anything other than God, the existence of these other things *could* be proved this way. The trouble is that islands, devils, money, and men do not exist in this way at all. We know from experience that they all might or might not exist, and there is no contradiction involved in conceiving of them as nonexistent. In Chapter III of the *Proslogium,* St. Anselm pointed out that "whatever else there is, except thee alone, can be conceived not to exist." God is the *only* being whose existence is provable a priori. It was not Gaunilon but St. Anselm himself who first announced the brilliant discovery that neither the existence nor the nonexistence of contingent things follows from our thinking about them; and in offering this as a criticism of St. Anselm, Gaunilon was merely reiterating a point that he could have learned from St. Anselm. The case of the existence of God is unique, however, and St. Anselm simply repeated his earlier insistence on this when he replied to Gaunilon that "whatever exists, except that being than which a greater cannot be conceived, can be conceived not to exist, even when it is known to exist. So, then, of God alone it can be said that it is impossible to conceive of his non-existence . . . ." [11] The fool's problem is that he is unable to tell the difference between a proof of the radical uniqueness of God's existence and a faulty proof of God's existence.

In the second place, the meaningfulness of such expressions as *perfect island* and *perfect devil* may be called into question. No matter how idyllic the island might be, it is still a body of land surrounded by a body of water, the existence of which is contingent on many factors, such as the continued existence of water, of the earth, of the solar system, and so on—or else it is not an island at all. To be an island at all it must be *a part* of the whole of reality. Its shores must be washed by waters that connect it with less idyllic land masses, and its fate must be to some extent bound up with that of its environment. On the other hand, suppose we stretch the meaning of *perfect island* to the breaking point and think of an island that is coextensive with and compassionate toward the whole of reality, that is wise to the point of omniscience and powerful to the point of omnipotence, created by nothing and creating all, self-sufficient and indestructible. Such an "island" would indeed be God, and the proof of its existence would be a proof of God's existence. Similar considerations apply to the notion of *perfect devil*. Is this a meaningful notion? If necessary existence is a perfection, and to be a devil is to be the epitome of imperfection, then either the notion of *perfect devil* is self-contradictory or else a perfect devil is necessarily nonexistent.

OBJECTION 3

Objection 3 is that we do not have a concept of a *perfect being*. Gaunilon and St. Thomas Aquinas were among the first to raise this objection to the ontological argument, and through the ages the meaningfulness of the concept of God offered by St. Anselm has been called into question. There may be many different reasons for questioning the meaningfulness of the notion of "a being than whom none greater can be conceived." For St. Thomas it was a left-handed compliment to God—God is so great that all our thoughts about him are inadequate.[12] We can know the existence of God but not the essence of God, but oddly enough in God himself existence and essence are one. Though the existence of God is self-evident in itself, it is not self-evident to us. In places, St. Thomas leaves the impression that we have no knowledge at all of what God is like, but he is really not content with such total skepticism. It would be more accurate to say that he claims that we have an imperfect knowledge of God, that our concept of God as a perfect being is an imperfect concept. In some sense this must be true, but is this really damaging to the ontological argument? If we agree that we cannot know everything about God, it does not follow that we cannot know anything about him. If the ontological argument requires that our concept of God as a perfect being be a perfect concept, then the argument doubtless falls, for what we know about God, according to both supernaturalism and panentheism, is very abstract and incomplete. In knowing that he knows all, we do not know all that he knows; in knowing that he loves all, we do not love all that he loves; and so on. Yet it seems that this extremely abstract way of conceiving God is all that is required for the validity of the ontological argument, for we can at least see that the notion of a necessary being who might not exist at all is self-contradictory, even if we cannot comprehend the full, concrete richness of such a necessary being. Though our intellects may be weak, it is not beyond us to see that it is self-contradictory to attribute contingent existence to a necessary being.

In earlier discussions we have seen that there are yet other reasons for questioning the meaningfulness of the concept of a perfect being. The logical positivists would certainly want to do so on the grounds that no sense observations are relevant to the claim that God exists. In our discussion of the cosmological argument in Chapter 10, we shall see that they are mistaken in thinking this; but even if they were correct, their objection might not be relevant to the ontological argument at all, for it is an a priori and not an a posteriori proof. The positivists could not afford to reject all a priori truth, for doing so would have involved a rejection of logic itself. As a matter of historical fact, the positivists did recognize both logical and empirical truth, though they insisted that the former was totally uninformative about reality and informed us only about our linguistic conventions. We shall explore the notion that it is all a matter of uninformative, trivial linguistic convention when we arrive at objection 7.

If we are entertaining a notion of *God* that is riddled with paradoxes, if not outright contradictions, it may again be doubted that we have the notion of a perfect being at all. The meaningfulness of "that being than whom none greater can be conceived" may indeed fall if the notion of God is inextricably tied to supernaturalism. In the final analysis, avoiding the charge that the notion of "a being than whom none greater can be conceived" involves self-contradiction may necessitate a total recasting of the very concept of God along lines suggested by the process theologians. The concept of *God* with which St. Anselm and the classical theologians worked may have been a meaningless, self-contradictory notion, and the ontological argument may make sense only within the context of panentheism.

The objection that we do not have a concept of a perfect being might be taken to mean that the notion of *maximal greatness* is meaningless. The critic may maintain that there is no more a concept of *greatest being* than there is a concept of *greatest number*. In one sense he is correct, if the notion of a greatest being is the notion of a being in whom all possibilities are actualized and enjoyed all at once. Contingent existence is competitive existence, as we noted in Chapter 8. But in another sense he is not correct. In this sense it is sheer logic that permits us to know that maximal greatness is being conceived. More specifically, it is the logic of the *omni* attributes. If there are doubts here, they are doubts about the meaningfulness of *all* as a logical quantifier. With respect to greatness in knowledge, there is nothing greater than omniscience, a knowledge of everything that there is to know. With respect to compassion, there is nothing greater than omnicompassion, a compassion toward everything that there is to love, even the fallen sparrow. With respect to presence, there is nothing greater than omnipresence, a presence with all things, from the smallest puff of existence in the most remote corner of space to the man dying on the cross. As Charles Wesley put it in his hymn "Love Divine, All Loves Excelling," God is "*all* compassion, pure unbounded love." With respect to power or influence, there is nothing greater than one who influences all and whose being is a necessary condition for the being of all.

The ontological argument is that if anyone entertains the concept of God, yet denies his existence, he has contradicted himself. This argument certainly may be attacked on the grounds that it is really impossible to entertain the concept of God. It may also be defended by producing and explicating just such a concept. Have we not already done just that?

OBJECTION 4

Objection 4 is that the ontological argument shows only that *if* God exists at all, he exists necessarily, but not that God does necessarily exist. This is commonly assumed to be one of Kant's unanswerable and decisive objections to the ontological argument. Kant compared the claim of the ontological argument that "God necessarily exists" with the claim that "a triangle has three sides." [13] It is true, he said, that I contradict myself in asserting that a certain figure is a triangle but it does not have three sides, but I do not contradict myself in denying that such a figure exists at all. It is logically necessary that *if* the figure exists as a triangle, it must have three sides, but not logically necessary that the figure exist. Similarly, the ontological argument claims only that *if* God exists at all, he exists necessarily, but there is no more logical necessity for asserting that God actually exists than there is for asserting that the triangle actually exists.

What reply can be given to this supposedly definitive objection? In the first place, it should be noted that the comparison being made is between God and a contingent thing, a possibly existent, possibly nonexistent triangle. If the comparison is to hold, only the first form of the ontological argument is involved. The only thing being said is that if God has a merely contingent form of existence, then his existence can be denied without self-contradiction. However, this is nothing new. St. Anselm himself said as much; but he also pointed out that he was not trying to prove the existence of a merely contingent God, that an even greater God was conceivable, and that the denial of the existence of a merely contingent God was not a denial of the existence of this greater, necessary God. The notion of "mere possibility" is applicable to this God only at the price of self-contradiction. In the second place, we might ask, What is the meaning of *if* in the statement, "If God exists at all, then he exists necessarily"? Does it not function to suggest that we are talking only about a merely contingent God, one who might or *might not* exist at all? If so, we are still in the position of the fool who cannot grasp the contradiction involved in saying that "if God is merely contingent, then he is necessary." Norman Malcolm nicely stated this reply to Kant and to Caterus, who raised a similar objection to Descartes' version of the ontological proof:

> I think that Caterus, Kant, and numerous other philosophers have been mistaken in supposing that the proposition "God is a necessary being" (or "God necessarily exists") is equivalent to the conditional proposition "If God exists then He necessarily exists." For how do they want the antecedent clause, "*If* God exists," to be understood? Clearly they want it to imply that it is *possible* that God does *not* exist. The whole point of Kant's analysis is to try to show that it is possible to "reject the subject." Let us make this implication explicit in the conditional proposition, so that it reads: "If God exists (and it is possible that He does not) then He necessarily exists." But now it is apparent, I think, that these philosophers have arrived at a self-contradictory position. I do not mean that this conditional proposition, taken alone, is self-

contradictory. Their position is self-contradictory in the following way. On the one hand, they agree that the proposition "God
necessarily exists" is an a priori truth; Kant implies that it is
"absolutely necessary," and Caterus says that God's existence is
implied by His very name. On the other hand, they think that it
is correct to analyze this proposition in such a way that it will
entail the proposition "It is possible that God does not exist."
But so far from its being the case that the proposition "God necessarily exists" entails the proposition "It is possible that God does
not exist," it is rather the case that they are incompatible with
one another! Can anything be clearer than that the conjunction
"God necessarily exists but it is possible that He does not exist"
is self-contradictory? Is it not just as plainly self-contradictory
as the conjunction "A square necessarily has four sides but it is
possible for a square not to have four sides"? In short, this familiar criticism of the ontological argument is self-contradictory,
because it accepts both of two incompatible propositions.[14]

OBJECTION 5

Objection 5 holds that all existential propositions are synthetic
and contingent. Hume and Kant maintained that all propositions
that assert the existence of something can be denied without self-
contradiction—that is, they are contingent. Kant also held that
they are synthetic, in the sense that they add something new to the
subject of the judgment. To assert that "some cats exist" is to add
something to the thought of *cats*. To put it another way, knowledge
of the existence of some cats does not follow from the mere
thought of *cats* but must be added by our perceptual encounter
with existent cats. So it is with the proposition "God exists," the
critic insists. It can be denied without self-contradiction, and it
adds something new to the thought of *God*. By now we have seen
that Kant was wrong on both these counts, so we may concentrate
on the problem of *how* he arrived at the linguistic thesis that all
existential propositions are synthetic and contingent. Did he
examine *all* existential propositions and just *find* that they were all
like this, or did he examine a representative sample of existential
propositions and *infer* inductively that they were all like this, or
what? If this linguistic thesis was based on an examination of the
ways in which language is actually used, we may wonder why Kant
never took into account the ontological argument or much of the

world's great religious literature. As a matter of fact, this is merely an a priori thesis about language that has no basis whatsoever in actual usage. It is also purely *ad hoc,* since the usefulness of the thesis in "refuting" the ontological argument is the only reason that can be given for adopting it.[15] Malcolm again correctly replied to Kant that

> the view that logical necessity merely reflects the use of words cannot possibly have the implication that every existential proposition must be contingent. That view requires us to *look at* the use of words and not manufacture a priori theses about it. In the Ninetieth Psalm it is said: "Before the mountains were brought forth, or ever thou hadst formed the earth and the world, even from everlasting to everlasting, thou art God." Here is expressed the idea of the necessary existence and eternity of God, an idea that is essential to the Jewish and Christian religions. In those complex systems of thought, those "language-games," God has the status of a necessary being. Who can doubt that? Here we must say with Wittgenstein, "This language-game is played!" I believe we may rightly take the existence of those religious systems of thought in which God figures as a necessary being to be a disproof of the dogma, affirmed by Hume and others, that no existential proposition can be necessary.[16]

It may be anachronistic to attribute the concept of logical necessity to biblical writers, though St. Anselm and many other religious thinkers have clearly entertained the notion. It is not at all out of place, however, to attribute the concept of ontological necessity to biblical thinkers, since they did think of God as beginningless, endless, and self-sufficient.

If this objection is not a wholly arbitrary thesis about the uses of language, it may be even more innocuous than it already appears to be. It may be nothing more than the "empty" claim, with which St. Anselm and all the ontological arguers could wholeheartedly agree, that "all synthetic and contingent existential propositions are synthetic and contingent." St. Anselm knew as well as we do that the existence of contingent things cannot be known a priori and that propositions asserting the existence of such things as perfect islands and devils or imaginary men and money "add something" to the thought of islands, devils, men, and money and can be denied without self-contradiction. The relevance of *this* version of the thesis to the problem of the existence of God has never been explained.

OBJECTION 6

Objection 6 claims that existence is not a predicate. Kant seemed to want to hold that all existential propositions are synthetic in the sense that they add something new to the thought of the thing, and at the same time he wanted to hold that they do not add anything new to the thought of the thing. As he put it, " 'Being' is obviously not a real predicate; that is, it is not a concept of something which could be added to the concept of a thing. It is merely the positing of a thing, or of certain determinations, as existing in themselves." [17] There are no more coins in a hundred possible dollars than in a hundred actual or existent dollars.[18] So it is with the proposition "God exists." Existence is something that a thing must have before it can have any predicates or attributes at all, something that even God must have before he can have any attributes, but it is not itself an attribute.

There has always been an aura of mystery surrounding the claim that existence is not a predicate. What does it mean? Does the claim that the thought of the existence of a thing "adds nothing new" to the thought of a thing mean that there is no difference in saying "God exists" and in saying "God does not exist"? Is not something meaningful being said about God either way? Do these claims not contradict each other? If you had a choice between a hundred imaginary dollars and a hundred existent dollars, would you not opt for the latter? But why should the latter be preferred at all if the thought of existence adds nothing new? Does the doctrine thus interpreted really do justice to the obvious fact that we normally prefer the existent to the imaginary, or that in rare instances, such as concentration camps and atomic wars, we prefer the imaginary to the existent? On the other hand, we must also acknowledge the obvious fact that we cannot normally add to the existent things of the world just by dreaming about them. As Kant put it, the merchant cannot better his financial position "by adding a few noughts to his cash account." [19] Neither can I add to the number of dollars existing in my pocket by merely thinking that the additional dollars exist. Is there any explanation that does justice to all these obvious facts?

First of all, there is a logical difference between the thought of "a hundred dollars" and the thought that "a hundred dollars exist." The former expression may be a definable concept, but it is not a proposition, whereas the latter is a proposition. "Exist" is not contained in the thought of "a hundred dollars," but it is contained in the thought that "a hundred dollars exist." Saying or thinking that "a hundred dollars exist" does not make them exist, obviously, but it is logically quite different from just saying or thinking "a hundred dollars." It is the assertion of a proposition, and the relevant question is whether the proposition has any meaning at all that is not already exhausted by the phrase "a hundred dollars" and that can be meaningfully contradicted. If it does, then "existence" does "add something" meaningful to the phrase, and it is something of a verbal quibble as to whether we wish to call this meaning a predicate. But what does it add? Kant seemed to assume that it would have to add to the *quantity* of that to which it is added, for his argument is that "existence" is not a predicate since its addition would not increase the number of dollars in my pocket or in my bank account. It is certainly true that we cannot increase our financial resources by wishful thinking, but this does not show that existence is not a predicate. I cannot add to the *number* of the hundred dollars in my pocket by thinking that they are *green* dollars or that they are *paper* dollars, but this does not show that "green" and "paper" are not predicates. Why should it be thought that "exist" is not a predicate simply because it does not increase the quantity of the subject to which it is attributed? Perhaps it is not a quantitative predicate but an existential predicate, just as "green" is not a quantitative but a qualitative predicate. Somehow it does make a difference, it does add something new that is worth knowing, to say that the hundred dollars really exist.

However, the defender of the ontological argument is not required to go even this far out on a limb, unless he is defending the first and admittedly indefensible form of the ontological proof; for he is not for a moment committed to the proposition that "existence is a predicate." He *could* hold that in the ordinary case of contingent existence, this formula is perfectly true; and if this accounts for the fact that we cannot ordinarily move from the imaginary to the existent, from the abstract to the concrete, then he can give such an account just as legitimately as anyone else. He *may* be committed to the proposition that "necessary existence is a predicate," though St. Anselm himself did not make use of exactly this vocabulary. St. Anselm claimed only that the assertion of God's possible nonexistence was self-contradictory, but we may wish to analyze this to mean or to imply that necessary existence is a predicate. In the case of God, no analogies with contingent things really hold in every respect, and nothing about the logic of "necessary existence" follows definitively from an examination of the logic of "contingent existence." As Malcolm expressed it:

> Many present-day philosophers, in agreement with Kant, declare that existence is not a property and think that this overthrows the ontological argument. Although it is an error to regard existence as a property of things that have contingent existence, it does not follow that it is an error to regard necessary existence as a property of God.[20]

OBJECTION 7

Objection 7 maintains that although it cannot be denied without self-contradiction that God exists, nothing of any ontological significance follows from this since logic is a matter of purely arbitrary, trivial, and uninformative linguistic convention. This is in part an echo of the positivistic contention that *none* of the a priori conventions of formal logic, to say nothing of conventions that apply to the logic of *God,* inform us in any way about the real world. It is all a matter of uninformative, trivial, arbitrary linguistic convention.

There is so much packed into this objection to the ontological argument that we must examine it bit by bit. First, let us ask what is being suggested by the claim that the a priori principles of logic are merely matters of *convention.* In some sense this must be true, but is it a real threat to the ontological argument? How? If it is thought that conventionality serves to differentiate between the assertions of logic and the assertions of science, this is a delusion; and if there is a danger here, the perils are just as great for natural science as they are for theology. A posteriori assertions have meaning only within the framework of linguistic conventions, just as do a priori assertions. Remove *all* conventionality from the statement "Some cancers are malignant" and no residue of meaning remains. Intelligible discourse and communication take place within a framework of linguistic "givens" and conventionality, and our talk about God is no different from our talk about the world in this respect.

Saying that something is *arbitrary* is quite different from saying that it is conventional. We are often able to give good reasons for having and abiding by our conventions, but saying that something is arbitrary serves to remove it from the realm of rationality altogether. Like the words *illusory* and *unreal,* the word *arbitrary* takes whatever meaning it has from the term with which it is being contrasted. All too often, however, we are not instructed about what the nonarbitrary terms of contrast are like. Even when we are so instructed, things may not be nearly as bad as they seem at first. For example, to suggest that something is arbitrary is often to suggest that it could or should be changed, that there is some workable and more reasonable alternative. The logical positivists often talked as if the whole of logic were arbitrary, but they never really meant it. No doubt there are some logical principles that work better than others, depending on the ends in view, but there are other logical principles to which there are no intelligible alternatives. No one has ever developed a system of logic that dispenses entirely with the principle of contradiction, the principle that an assertion cannot be both true and false in exactly the same respect. At least, no one has ever developed such a system and had much success with it in reasoning about the world, and knowledge of the world is usually the basic purpose of adopting a system of logic. How does all this apply to the ontological argument? It applies because a fundamental principle of logic is involved here, the principle of contradiction. It is alleged that the claim that "God might not exist" is self-contradictory and thus violates this fundamental logical principle. Of course, if the principle is totally arbitrary, if there are intelligible, reasonable alternatives to it, then the option of adopting one of these alternatives is open and the ontological argument need not be accepted. The trouble is, there is no such alternative.

The claim that such logical principles are *uninformative* is often lumped together with the claim that they are conventional, arbitrary, and trivial. Again, this is quite a distinct point, but those who so object to all a priori principles are unable to differentiate between principles that inform us about *everything* and principles that inform us about *nothing*. No wonder the positivists were antimetaphysical: They could not understand certain basic distinctions that lie at the heart of metaphysical thinking. The dogmatic statement that that which informs us about everything is by definition *the same* as that which informs us about nothing is certainly an assertion that needs to be demonstrated, and no adequate demonstration of it has ever been offered. And to maintain at the same time that all definitions are totally arbitrary would seem to leave us perfectly free to adopt some alternative interpretation. Furthermore, another alternative *is* open here, namely that that which informs us about everything is true of everything, true in all possible worlds, whereas that which informs us about nothing is just that. Universal, a priori truths such as those of logic are compatible with all actual states of affairs not because they say nothing at all about such states of affairs, but because they say something true, albeit very abstract, about all such states of affairs. Similarly, the truth expressed by the proposition "God necessarily exists" is very abstract and compatible with all states of affairs because it is a necessary condition for the existence of any contingent thing whatsoever.

There is a grave disadvantage to the view that a priori truths tell us nothing about the world, only about our arbitrarily adopted linguistic conventions. It is that such a complete divorce of logic and reality leaves us without a way of explaining how logic is useful to us in our attempt to know the world. If this divorce is taken with utmost seriousness, the result can only be total skepticism, a skepticism that is as profound and pervasive in the realm of scientific knowledge as it is in the realms of metaphysics and theology. Once logic and the world are totally divorced, they can never be joined together again; but does not the ideal of rational explanation preclude such a divorce? Could there ever be any good *reasons* for such skepticism? Does not the rational ideal of coherence preclude the adoption of arbitrarily disconnected principles, whether they be those of logic, metaphysics, ethics, or theology?

Finally, it is often claimed that the truths of logic are *trivial,* possibly because it is presupposed that they are uninformative. Kant spoke of the tautologies that he believed to be involved in the ontological argument as "miserable." This is stepping out of the realm of logic altogether, for *trivial* and *miserable* are not logical concepts at all. They are merely disparaging, emotionally loaded epithets, negative value judgments disguised as pure, cold, scientific logic. Should we not be free to decide for ourselves whether those assertions that tell us something about everything are important or not? Religiously and metaphysically minded individuals tend to answer "yes" to such a question.

OBJECTION 8

Objection 8 holds that the ontological argument begs the question, since it makes the existence of God true "by definition," and that all that is required for refuting the argument is a rejection of the definition. This objection was developed by Kant, and it is closely related to the preceding one. After all, it is sometimes held, are not definitions matters of convention, just as are the principles of logic? It follows that God necessarily exists only if the definition of God as "that being than whom none greater could be conceived" is accepted in the first place, but if this definition is rejected, is not the ontological argument refuted?

Unfortunately, it is not quite so easy as this. What exactly does one do when one rejects a definition? Declare it to be meaningless? This possibility we have explored and rejected already. Adopt another alternative? It is true that alternative ways of conceiving *God* are available. We may think of God as capable of dying, as do the contemporary "death of God" theologians. We may think of God as the greatest of all contingent beings, as merely a lucky accident, as the defenders of a "finite God" propose. Many alternative ways of defining *God* are available, so why do we not adopt one of these alternatives? By such a simple expedient we should refute the ontological argument, for certainly the existence of God in one of these alternative senses may be denied without self-contradiction. No, such a move would be totally irrelevant. The ontological argument is not designed to prove the existence of God as otherwise conceived, and adopting an alternative definition would only succeed in making our position irrelevant. The ontological argument does not attempt to prove that God as otherwise conceived exists, and a rejection of the existence of God in some *al-*

ternative sense is in no sense a rejection of the existence of God as that being than whom none greater can be conceived. Furthermore, it is only the existence of God in *that* sense that cannot be denied without self-contradiction.

Aside from the fact that neither St. Anselm nor anyone else has ever claimed that God as otherwise conceived could be proved to exist by the ontological argument, there is the further consideration that there are perfectly satisfactory religious reasons for *not* adopting an alternative definition of *God,* namely that some lesser divinity would not be an adequate object of religious worship, devotion, and ultimate concern.

OBJECTION 9

Objection 9 maintains that the ontological argument confuses the necessity of God's existence with the necessity of the proposition "God exists." To what exactly does the predicate *necessary* apply in the context of this argument? It could apply *to God,* as it seems to do in some instances, or it could apply *to the proposition* "God exists." The necessity of the one does not seem to follow from the necessity of the other, and there may be more than one sense of *necessity* involved here.

To this objection it may be replied first of all that it is a matter not of "either–or" but of "both–and." The defender of the ontological argument seems to be committed both to the view that God necessarily exists and to the view that the proposition "God necessarily exists" is a logically necessary proposition, one that cannot be denied without self-contradiction. Furthermore, there *are* two senses of *necessity* involved here: The necessity of God is an *ontological* necessity, and the necessity of the proposition is a *logical* necessity. To say that God is ontologically necessary is to say at least four things about him: that he is everlasting, that he is self-sufficient, that he is indestructible, and that he is unfailing. To say that the proposition "God necessarily exists" is logically necessary is to say that it cannot be denied without self-contradiction. Once all this is admitted, what exactly is the objection? If it is that the *ontological* necessity of God can after all be denied without self-contradiction, then it may be replied that there is still an obvious contradiction in the ontological claim that a being that could not fail to exist does not or might not exist, and that it is the contradiction involved in this *ontological* proposition that makes the opposite claim, that a being that could not fail to exist does exist, a *logically* necessary proposition. If the objection is that there is no such thing as ontological necessity, that *necessity* applies only to propositions and not to things,[21] then it may be replied that this is merely another a priori thesis about language that does not conform to actual linguistic usage. Religious thinkers through the ages have applied *necessity* to God, and this has been an ontological predicate as long as it has been a logical predicate, if not longer. From the fact that *necessity* is at least a logical predicate, it does not follow at all that it is *only* a logical predicate. The truth of this becomes obvious once we realize that *necessary* has more than one legitimate meaning. A necessary proposition is one that cannot be denied without self-contradiction; a necessary being is one that is unfailing, eternal, self-sufficient, and indestructible; a necessary cause or condition is one in the absence of which a given effect cannot occur. No one of these senses of *necessary* has a monopoly on the word. God may be "a necessary being" as well as "a necessary cause of the world," as the cosmological argument would have it. And if the ontological argument is correct, it is true that "God exists" is a logically necessary proposition.

OBJECTION 10

Objection 10 holds that the ontological argument does nothing to differentiate between naturalism and theism, since it does nothing to exclude the naturalistic contention that the sole necessarily existent entity is nature as a whole, or some of the basic constituents of nature. Perhaps when all is said and done, the ontological argument shows that *something* must exist necessarily, that the thought of a necessary being somehow underlies all our thinking about reality; but it tells us nothing whatsoever about the other characteristics of this necessary being. It does nothing to rule out the possibility that what we have here is an ontological proof of the truth of naturalism. Spinoza certainly came very close to using the ontological argument as an a priori proof for a certain variety of naturalism. It does nothing to exclude the possibility, suggested by Hume, that the necessary being is simply nature as a whole as conceived by the naturalist to be eternal, self-sufficient, nonpersonal, nonpurposive, nonintelligent, noncompassionate, and so on. This objection may present the most serious difficulty of all, because the answer to it inevitably involves some highly controversial considerations. We can only examine them for whatever they might be worth. Try to imagine what the alternative to the resolution of the difficulties that is suggested below would be like.

Part of the answer to this objection lies in the fact that the ontological argument makes use of the notion of perfection, worshipfulness, or unsurpassable greatness. The second premise of the argument, as we reworded it on page 227, is that contingent existence (form 1) or necessary existence (form 2) is a perfection. Too little attention has been given to the fact that perfection is a value concept and that in part the ontological argument relies on the adequacy of our value insights as a clue to the essence of ultimate reality. Naturalism is ruled out by the fact that a nonpersonal, nonpurposive, nonintelligent, noncompassionate being is an imperfect being that falls far short of that being than whom none greater can be conceived. But if this is the case, the ontological argument proves far more than that God possesses the one perfection of necessary existence. It proves that God possesses *all* perfections (that is, all consistently combinable perfections), as the first premise of our reworded ontological argument clearly states. If we reserve the expression "ontological argument" for the argument that yields the ontological or existential conclusion, then there is a much broader argument involved here. We might call it "the wider argument from perfection," for it shows that it is self-contradictory to deny that *any* perfection belongs to God. Let us now examine the elements of this argument.

If we use the expression "perfect being" as short for "that being than whom none greater can be conceived," then we must ask about the meaning of the word *perfect*. Obviously this word is as much a value word as it is a metaphysical word. We are confronted here with an integration of axiology and metaphysics in which values provide us with an essential clue to the nature of ultimate reality. Only if we understand what the word *perfect* means will we be able to understand why necessary existence, purposiveness, omniscience, omnicompassionateness, and so on are perfections and why contingent existence, nonpurposiveness, nonintelligence, noncompassionateness, and so on are imperfections. Too little attention has been given to the problem of the meaning of perfection. Etymologically the word means "complete," and it still retains this meaning in such expressions as "perfect stranger" or "perfect imbecile." But in the expression "perfect being," completeness is only part of the story. If God is complete with respect to knowledge and compassion, he is incomplete with respect to ignorance and insensitivity. Some further principle of selection is involved, some judgment that it is somehow *better* to be complete with respect to knowledge and compassion and not with respect to ignorance and insensitivity. The notion of *good* has undergone much analysis in twentieth-century metaethics. We might speculate that definitions of *perfect* or *worshipful* might be constructed that closely parallel some of the analyses of *good* that various recent thinkers have explored. For example, following G. E. Moore, we might regard *perfect* as denoting a simple, nonnatural, nonanalyzable, indefinable property that happens to belong to some things and not to others because of other properties possessed by those things. Or, following Ralph Barton Perry, we might treat it as meaning "any object of most intense positive interest." Paralleling Charles Stevenson, we might take it to mean "I approve of this sort of thing most of all; do so likewise." [22] Paraphrasing R. M. Hare, we might take it as "the most extreme adjective of commendation in the English language." Or, following Robert S. Hartman, we might take it to mean that "this object exemplifies all the characteristics or properties of its *a priori* concept." [23] We do not have space here for a detailed exploration of these alternatives and their advantages and disadvantages, which would involve a review of the whole of contemporary metaethics; but we can at least note that evaluation is involved in the ontological argument, that metaphysics is at this point dependent on axiology.

Of course, it has been clear from the beginning that ideals and evaluations are involved in the ontological argument, even that some wider argument from perfection underlies the argument with ontological conclusions and thus permits us to infer not only that God necessarily exists but also that he necessarily is everything that he ideally ought to be. In the *Proslogium,* St. Anselm uses the expression "that being than whom none *greater* can be conceived" interchangeably with "that being than whom none *better* can be conceived," [24] and he says of this being, "Thou art truly sensible [*Sensibilis*], omnipotent, compassionate, and passionless, as thou art living, wise, good, blessed, eternal; and whatever it is better to be than not to be." [25] Throughout the *Proslogium,* St. Anselm assigns *many* properties to God because it is *better* for him to have them than for him to lack them. Although Descartes usually offered only the first form of the ontological proof, he was at least dimly aware of the wider implications of this general line of reasoning, noting that

> although it may not be necessary that I shall at any time entertain the notion of Deity, yet each time I happen to think of a first and sovereign being, and to draw, so to speak, the idea of him from the storehouse of the mind, I am necessitated to attribute to him all kinds of perfections, though I may not then enumerate them all, nor think of each of them in particular. And this necessity is sufficient, as soon as I discover that existence is a perfection, to cause me to infer the existence of this first and sovereign being . . . .[26]

Charles Hartshorne points out that not only did St. Anselm intend his argument to be a proof of God's necessary existence, but that he "intended also to deduce all the knowable attributes of God from the same definition." [27] Similarly, Norman Malcolm maintains that

> there is nothing we should wish to describe, seriously and literally, as "testing" God's knowledge and powers. That God is omniscient and omnipotent has not been determined by the application of criteria: rather these are requirements of our conception of Him. They are internal properties of the concept, although they are also rightly said to be properties of God. *Necessary existence* is a property of God in the *same sense* that *necessary omnipotence* and *necessary omniscience* are His properties.[28]

Finally, although he rejects the ontological argument, John Hick realizes that *if* it is valid at all, it provides a conclusive answer to those who would reject the traditional philosophical proofs on the grounds that the God of philosophy is not an adequate object of religious devotion, that "the God whose existence each of the traditional theistic proofs professes to establish is only an abstraction from and a pale shadow of the living God who is the putative object of Biblical faith." [29] Hick correctly sees that the ontological argument does not suffer from this defect, that

> if it succeeds it establishes the reality of a being so perfect in every respect that no more perfect can be conceived. Clearly if such a being is not worthy of worship none ever could be. It would therefore seem that, unlike the other proofs, the ontological argument, if it were logically sound, would present the relatively few persons who are capable of appreciating such abstract reasoning with a rational ground for worship.[30]

If this is true, then in some sense the ontological argument is the most fundamental argument of all.

But we have not yet resolved one small point. If metaphysics is finally dependent on axiology, then we can expect agreement on the conclusions of our "wider argument from perfection" only after we have decided that necessary existence is *better* than contingent existence, that intelligence is *better* than nonintelligence, that compassion is *better* than insensitivity, and so on. How can we *show* that this is indeed the case? Are not ideals notoriously relativistic? Does not any argument that depends finally on evaluation rest on extremely shaky foundations? This is an integral part of the much broader question of whether human ideals should ever be relied on in the rational quest for knowledge, and the answer to this *must* be affirmative. The alternative is to give up on reason altogether. It is completely erroneous to hold that in being committed to reason we are thereby committed to something that is valuationally neutral. Every rational quest for knowledge takes human ideas as regulative for knowledge of reality. Being committed to reason is being committed to a set of ideals, and a rational justification of our ideals is never a derivation of an "ought" from an "is," but rather a derivation of a more concrete "ought" from a more abstract "ought." Logic tells us how we *ought* to reason, not how we do in fact reason; but there is more to rationality than mere logic. There is a rational temper, a temper that prizes enlightenment and freedom from bias, compulsion, and irrational persuasion more highly than it prizes the alternatives. It involves a commitment to the normative thesis that only a man of enlightenment, freedom, and impartiality can be a just, accurate, and qualified judge of good and evil, truth and falsity, beauty and ugliness, worshipfulness and idolatry, and all the rest.

What bearing does all this have on the ontological argument? At least this much, that the vast majority of men who do approximate the idea of a qualified judge in such matters, men who have reflected long, hard, and seriously on such questions, do usually conclude that necessary existence is better than contingent existence, that purposiveness is better than nonpurposiveness, that knowledge is better than ignorance, that compassion is better than insensitivity. What better proof could be desired? Even those who reject the ontological argument generally concede that necessary existence would be better than contingent existence *if* there were such a thing—and we have already explored the contradiction inherent in the addition of the "if" clause. Aside from the problem of intelligibility, perhaps there are even adequate grounds for choice here between supernaturalism and panentheism. Is it not *better* that God really be compassionate rather than have no feelings at all, that he be responsive to the world rather than unresponsive, that he be both temporal and timeless in different respects rather than merely timeless, and so on? At last we may have found the place at which this metaphysical argument turns on insight as well as on logic, at least temporarily, at least until a science of evaluation is developed in which the logic of metaphysical and general axiological preference is worked out fully.[31] Philosophies as well as theologies always come to rest somewhere. Everywhere there is believing in order to understand, but some beliefs have greater explanatory power than others, and to some beliefs there are no intelligible alternatives. Even a rejection of the ontological argument on the grounds that contingent existence is really better than necessary existence would still not avoid relying on human ideals as a guide in the rational quest for knowledge. Can such reliance ever be avoided? Of course, it is not all a matter of insight. There is at least one good reason for believing that necessary existence is superior to contingent existence, namely that in the thought of a necessary being, a being that exists neither by chance nor by external causes, our confusion about why there is something rather than nothing is finally resolved.

Suggestions for Further Reading

ON THE ONTOLOGICAL ARGUMENT

ANSELM, ST., *Basic Writings* (*Proslogium, Monologium,* Gaunilon's *On Behalf of the Fool, Cur Deus Homo*), 2nd ed., trans. by S. W. Deane with an introduction by Charles Hartshorne (LaSalle, Ill., Open Court, 1962).

FLEW, ANTONY, and MACINTYRE, ALASDAIR, eds., *New Essays in Philosophical Theology* (New York, Macmillan, 1955), pp. 31–41 and Chapter 4.

HARTSHORNE, CHARLES, *Anslem's Discovery* (LaSalle, Ill., Open Court, 1965). This is Hartshorne's major work on the ontological argument, containing his rejoinder to virtually every important discussion and criticism.

———, *Man's Vision of God* (Hamden, Conn., Archon Books, 1964), Chapter 9.

———, *The Logic of Perfection* (LaSalle, Ill., Open Court, 1962), Chapters 1 and 2.

HICK, JOHN, *Philosophy of Religion* (Englewood Cliffs, N.J., Prentice-Hall, 1963), pp. 15–20.

MALCOLM, NORMAN, "Anselm's Ontological Arguments," *The Philosophical Review,* Vol. LXIX (January 1960).

PLANTINGA, ALVIN, *The Ontological Argument: From St. Anselm to Contemporary Philosophers* (Garden City, N.Y., Doubleday, 1965). This contains most of the important classical and contemporary discussions.

SHAFFER, JEROME, "Existence, Predication, and the Ontological Argument," *Mind,* Vol. LXXI (July 1962), pp. 307–25.

Notes

1   Paul Tillich, *Systematic Theology,* Vol. I (Chicago, University of Chicago Press, 1951), p. 211. See also Tillich, *The Dynamics of Faith* (New York, Harper & Row, 1958), pp. 45–46.

2   *Ibid.,* p. 237.

3   See the Suggestions for Further Reading for major works on the ontological argument by Hartshorne, Malcolm, and others.

4   St. Anselm, *Basic Writings (Proslogium, Monologium,* Gaunilon's *On Behalf of the Fool, Cur Deus Homo),* 2nd ed., trans. by S. W. Deane with an introduction by Charles Hartshorne (LaSalle, Ill., Open Court, 1962), Preface to the *Proslogium,* p. 1.

5   *Ibid. (Proslogium),* pp. 1–2.

6   *Ibid. (Proslogium),* p. 7.

7   *Ibid. (Proslogium),* pp. 7–9.

8   *Ibid.* (Gaunilon's *On Behalf of the Fool),* pp. 149–50.

9   St. Thomas Aquinas, *On the Truth of the Catholic Faith* (Garden City, N.Y., Doubleday, 1957), Book I, p. 82.

10 Anselm, *Basic Writings* (reply to Gaunilon), p. 159.

11 *Ibid.,* p. 161.

12 Aquinas, *On the Truth of the Catholic Faith,* Book I, p. 82. See also the discussion in Anton C. Pegis, ed., *Basic Writings of Saint Thomas Aquinas,* Vol. I (New York, Random House, 1945), pp. 18–19.

13 Immanuel Kant, *Critique of Pure Reason,* trans. by Norman Kemp Smith (London, Macmillan, and New York, St. Martin's Press, 1958), pp. 501–02.

14 Norman Malcolm, "Anselm's Ontological Arguments," *The Philosophical Review,* Vol. LXIX (January 1960), pp. 57–58.

15 On this point see Charles Hartshorne, *Anselm's Discovery* (La Salle, Ill., Open Court, 1965), p. 220.

16 Malcolm, "Anselm's Ontological Arguments," pp. 55–56.

17 Kant, *Critique of Pure Reason,* p. 504.

18 *Ibid.,* p. 505. (Kant used "thalers" instead of "dollars.")

19 *Ibid.,* p. 507.

20 Malcolm, "Anselm's Ontological Arguments," p. 52.

21 Such a position is defended by J. N. Findley and J. J. C. Smart, among others. See Antony Flew and Alasdair MacIntyre, eds., *New Essays in Philosophical Theology* (New York, Macmillan, 1955), pp. 38–39 and Chapter 4.

22 I developed the possibility of such a parallel of Stevenson in Rem B. Edwards, "An Emotivist Analysis of the Ontological Argument," *The Personalist,* Vol. XLVIII, No. 1 (Winter 1967), pp. 25–32. However, I no longer subscribe to the position I developed there, since my earlier objections have been refuted along the lines developed in this chapter.

23 These definitions of *perfect* are paraphrased from the discussions of *good* and *perfect* in the following books: G. E. Moore, *Prin-*

cipia Ethica (Cambridge, Eng., Cambridge University Press, 1959), Chapter 1; Ralph Barton Perry, *Realms of Value* (Cambridge, Mass., Harvard University Press, 1951), Chapter 1; Charles Stevenson, *Ethics and Language* (New Haven, Conn., Yale University Press, 1944), Chapter 9; R. M. Hare, *The Language of Morals* (Oxford, Clarendon Press, 1961), Chapter 5; and Robert S. Hartman, *The Structure of Value* (Carbondale, Ill., Southern Illinois University Press, 1967).

24   Anselm, *Basic Writings,* pp. 20, 24–25.
25   *Ibid.,* p. 19.
26   René Descartes, *Meditations and Selections from the Principles of Philosophy* (LaSalle, Ill., Open Court, 1952), p. 79.
27   Charles Hartshorne, *Anselm's Discovery* (LaSalle, Ill., Open Court, 1965), pp. 30–31.
28   Malcolm, "Anselm's Ontological Arguments," p. 50.
29   John Hick, *The Existence of God* (New York, Macmillan, 1964), p. 14.
30   *Ibid.,* p. 15.
31   Significant progress in developing such a science of axiology has been made in recent years. In my opinion, two of the most significant recent books in this area are Paul W. Taylor, *Normative Discourse* (Englewood Cliffs, N.J., Prentice-Hall, 1961), and Hartman, *The Structure of Value.*

chapter ten

The Existence
of God THE COSMOLOGICAL
ARGUMENT

As we saw in Chapter 9, the ontological argument for the existence of God reasons from the very idea of God to his necessary existence and is thus an a priori proof. By contrast, the cosmological argument attempts to reason from the world or some feature of the world to God as the ultimate ground or necessary presupposition of the world. Since the cosmological proof contains at least one proposition that we know to be true through our experiential encounter with the world, it is often spoken of as an a posteriori proof. As an attempt to reason from the world to the existence of a supreme, intelligent, creative being it is much older than the ontological proof. The earliest version of it appeared in the *Phaedrus* of Plato, and it reappears in such later Platonic dialogues as the *Philebus* and the *Laws*. The version of the argument in Aristotle's *Metaphysics* had a profound influence on many later thinkers about God and the world, especially St. Thomas Aquinas, whose famous "Five Ways" of proving God's existence draw heavily on Aristotle.

The Thomistic Versions of the Cosmological Argument

ALTHOUGH all five of the Thomistic proofs contain cosmological elements, it is the first three that most clearly epitomize the classical attempt to reason from the world to God. Since the other two proofs are mainly teleological rather than cosmological, we shall examine the last one of these separately in the next chapter. We shall not deal with the fourth proof because it is patently invalid. Let us now look at the first three of these Thomistic proofs for the existence of God:

> The first and more manifest way is the argument from motion. It is certain, and evident to our senses, that in the world some things are in motion. Now whatever is moved is moved by another, for nothing can be moved except it is in potentiality to that towards which it is moved; whereas a thing moves inasmuch as it is in act. For motion is nothing else than the reduction of something from potentiality to actuality. But nothing can be reduced from potentiality to actuality, except by something in a state of actuality. Thus that which is actually hot, as fire, makes wood, which is potentially hot, to be actually hot, and thereby moves and changes it. Now it is not possible that the same thing should be at once in actuality and potentiality in the same respect, but only in different respects. For what is actually hot cannot simultaneously be potentially hot; but it is simultaneously potentially cold. It is therefore impossible that in the same respect and in the same way a thing should be both mover and moved, *i.e.,* that it should move itself. Therefore, whatever is moved must be moved by another. If that by which it is moved be itself moved, then this also must needs be moved by another, and that by another again. But this cannot go on to infinity, because then there would be no first mover, and, consequently, no other mover, seeing that subsequent movers move only inasmuch as they are moved by the first mover; as the staff moves only because it is moved by the hand. Therefore it is necessary to arrive at a first mover, moved by no other; and this everyone understands to be God.
>
> The second way is from the nature of efficient cause. In the world of sensible things we find there is an order of efficient causes. There is no case known (neither is it, indeed, possible)

in which a thing is found to be the efficient cause of itself; for so it would be prior to itself, which is impossible. Now in efficient causes it is not possible to go on to infinity, because in all efficient causes following in order, the first is the cause, whether the intermediate cause be several, or one only. Now to take away the cause is to take away the effect. Therefore, if there be no first cause among efficient causes, there will be no ultimate, nor any intermediate, cause. But if in efficient causes it is possible to go on to infinity, there will be no first efficient cause, neither will there be an ultimate effect, nor any intermediate efficient causes; all of which is plainly false. Therefore it is necessary to admit a first efficient cause, to which everyone gives the name of God.

The third way is taken from possibility and necessity, and runs thus. We find in nature things that are possible to be and not to be, since they are found to be generated, and to be corrupted, and consequently, it is possible for them to be and not to be. But it is impossible for these always to exist, for that which can non-be at some time is not. Therefore, if everything can not-be, then at one time there was nothing in existence. Now if this were true, even now there would be nothing in existence, because that which does not exist begins to exist only through something already existing. Therefore, if at one time nothing was in existence, it would have been impossible for anything to have begun to exist; and thus even now nothing would be in existence—which is absurd. Therefore, not all beings are merely possible, but there must exist something the existence of which is necessary. But every necessary thing either has its necessity caused by another, or not. Now it is impossible to go on to infinity in necessary things which have their necessity caused by another, as has been already proved in regard to efficient causes. Therefore we cannot but admit the existence of some being having of itself its own necessity, and not receiving it from another, but rather causing in others their necessity. This all men speak of as God.[1]

It would be easy to spend a great deal of time engaging in textual criticisms and interpretations of these versions of the cosmological argument. For example, it needs to be pointed out that in the third way, the word *possible* means the same as *contingent,* so that the claim that not all beings are merely possible is the same as the claim that not all beings are merely contingent. Moreover, in speaking of necessary beings that are caused by other necessary beings, St. Thomas is merely paying homage to

Aristotle, who spoke of such a hierarchy of necessary beings; but we may easily bypass such a hierarchy by pointing out that the sort of ontological necessity in which we are interested involves self-sufficiency, so that it is self-contradictory to speak of a necessary being that is caused by other necessary beings. St. Thomas finally comes to such a self-sufficient being, and it is *this* being that the proofs are really all about. Finally, it must be pointed out that when St. Thomas denies the possibility of an infinite regress of causes, he is not denying the impossibility of an infinite series of causes *in time,* but rather an infinite series of causes *in "the great chain of being."* Again, he is paying homage to Aristotle's claim that the world coexists eternally with God. St. Thomas himself admitted that his proofs do not prove that the world came into being at some point in the finite past—that is, they do not prove creation *ex nihilo.* They do try to show, however, that the world, which possibly coexists eternally with God, is not self-sufficient. To be ontologically necessary something must satisfy *all three* of these conditions: It must be eternal, self-sufficient, and indestructible. Although the world may satisfy the first of these, it does not satisfy the second and possibly not even the third. This is the whole point of the Thomistic proofs. Even though the world *may* be eternal, it is still contingent, still dependent on God in a variety of ways.

As we did with the ontological argument, let us try to reword these versions of the cosmological arguments, to lay bare their most basic premises. There are many subordinate arguments contained within these proofs, for St. Thomas often gives reasons for accepting the main premises as well as for accepting the theistic conclusions of the arguments. When liberally paraphrased, the most basic premises of the arguments seem to be as follows:

First proof, "from motion"

(1) Some things are in motion.
(2) If anything is in motion, it is moved by another mover.
(3) If there is another mover, then there is a first mover (since it is impossible to regress to infinity in the order of movers and things moved).
(4) This first mover is God.

Therefore, there is a first mover, God.

Second proof, "from efficient causes"

(1) Something is changing.
(2) If anything is changing, there is at least one efficient cause of that change.
(3) If there is at least one efficient cause of change, then there is a first cause of change (since it is impossible to regress to infinity in the order of efficient causes).
(4) This first cause is God.

Therefore, there is a first cause of change, God.

Third proof, "from contingency"

(1) Some contingent things exist.
(2) An extended series of causes on which these contingent things depend also exists.
(3) Either this entire series of causes is contingent, or it is necessary.
(4) The entire series of causes is not necessary.
(5) If the entire series is contingent, then there is a necessary being.
(6) This necessary being is God.

Therefore, there is a necessary being, God.

It is obvious from the way the three arguments have been reworded that they are formally valid. If there is any question at all about whether they prove the truth of their conclusion, it must be a question about one or more of the premises of the argument. The conclusion can be rejected only by rejecting one or more of the premises. We shall thus examine the arguments premise by premise to see whether there are any good reasons for rejecting them. We shall consider the first two proofs together because their structure is so similar, then proceed to the third proof, which is commonly regarded as the most fundamental form of the argument.

THE FIRST AND SECOND WAYS

It should be clear by now why the cosmological argument is called an a posteriori argument. Each version of it contains at least one premise that is known to be true in our experience of the world. Each of them begins with a statement reporting a truth that is confirmed by observation. As St. Thomas puts it, certain things are "evident to our senses," such as that some things are in motion and that some things are changing. Except for the most extreme form of skepticism, these empirical assertions are virtually indisputable. Yet they are thought to have a significant bearing on the question of the existence of God. They also have a significant bearing on the positivistic claim that the metaphysical assertion of the existence of God is meaningless. The cosmological arguments at least have the virtue of showing not only *that* but also *how* observation statements are relevant to the question of the existence of God; and if any statement is meaningful when some observation statement is relevant to its confirmation or disconfirmation, then the assertion of the existence of God is meaningful by the positivist's own criterion of meaning. This also shows the impossibility of erecting an insurmountable positivistic barrier between scientific and metaphysical assertions. Furthermore, it is only an accident of history that St. Thomas made use only of observations of motion and causation in his first two proofs. He could have begun with any observation of *any-thing* in the world and reasoned from it back to God as the ulti- mate ground of its existence. Descartes, for example, reasoned cosmologically from the existence of his idea of God to the exist- ence of God himself as the ultimate cause or ground of the existence of that idea. The third way of St. Thomas begins with observations of birth, growth, decay, and death. We shall see that in its most generalized form, the cosmological argument asserts that all observations of anything in the world ultimately imply the existence of God. If there is a difference between science and metaphysics here, it lies in the fact that unlike the more limited assertions of science, *every* observation of everything whatsoever ultimately counts in favor of the existence of God. The existence of God is confirmed by the existence of anything else whatsoever if all the premises of the argument are true.

What about the more obviously "metaphysical" second premises of the arguments? Can we show that if anything is in motion, it is moved by another, or that if anything is changing, there is at least one efficient cause of that change? St. Thomas argues that the alternative to these principles—that if anything is moving or changing, these motions or changes are *self-initiated*—would itself be absurd. He introduces the Aristotelian principle that nothing merely potential has the power to actualize itself, that changes of any type must be initiated by something already actualized. If we do not like such abstract reasoning, we might ask whether the premises of the argument are known to be true on the basis of some a priori metaphysical intuition or whether they are simply high-order generalizations from experience. It is certainly possible to treat them as the latter and simply to assert that no motions or changes are ever given to us *in experience* that are not initiated by other motions or changes. Can you think of any examples to the contrary? If we believe in some form of "free will," we may think of ourselves as self-initiating causes when we act as agents, but is this really an exception to our principle? Certainly we did not give birth to ourselves; nor did we create the world in which we live, in which only a limited number of options for choice are open to us. Choosing always presupposes antecedent conditions, such as an intelligent reviewing of open alternatives and desires that make some of these alternatives viable for us and some not. If there is a sense in which we are self-initiating causes in our choosing, it could be covered adequately by saying that there are necessary but not sufficient preconditions for self-initiative, and this would still be in keeping with the general metaphysical point that there are necessary preconditions for all change and motion. There is an ambiguity in the notion of *cause* that must be recognized. In saying that all changes have causes, the argument needs to make at least the minimum claim that there are *necessary* preconditions for the occurrence of all changes—that is, conditions in the absence of which the changes cannot take place at all. (Note that here is yet another sense of *necessary*.) It need not make the much stronger and more controversial claim that there are in all cases *sufficient* conditions for the occurrence of these changes—that is, conditions in the presence of which precisely these changes *must* take place. If the second premise of the cosmological argument is given this weaker interpretation, it is perfectly compatible with "free will." Furthermore, this weaker interpretation is all that is required for showing that everything in the world ultimately implies the existence of God. The cosmological argument is an attempt to show that

God is a necessary condition for all the events of the world, but not that he is a sufficient condition for them all. It is not an attempt to prove that in the presence of God evil *must* occur; but it does try to show that in the absence of God neither evil nor anything else would occur.

It is only when we come to the third premise of the first two arguments that we arrive at something really controversial. What is the connection between a mover and a first mover, and between an initiating cause and a first cause? The third premise of these arguments asserts that a first cause is a necessary precondition for all contingent, observable effects within the world, whether they be motions or whatever. The argument from motion is simply a specific instance of a more general argument from causation. To put the matter another way, it is the claim that there can be only a finite number of necessary conditions for the occurrence of any observable event, and its truth involves a denial of the contrary claim that there is or even might be an infinite number of conditions in the absence of which the given effect would not occur at all. St. Thomas argues for the truth of this premise by arguing against the contrary claim that an infinite number of necessary conditions for the occurrence of a given event is possible. St. Thomas recognized something the critics of the theistic arguments are often loath to admit, namely that criticisms of the proofs also involve premises, or commitments, and that if these commitments are indefensible then the criticisms built on them are worthless. In some instances, the strongest defense of a position may involve showing that the alternatives to that position are themselves unacceptable. In no instance is it necessary to surrender a position simply because some critic happens to hold the contrary position. It may always be asked *why* the contrary position is viable, and in some instances it may be shown that the contrary position is untenable. Can this be done with the claim that an infinite number of conditions is possible, in the absence of which a given effect would not occur?

Within the context of Thomism, the defense of the impossibility of a thesis of infinite regress is modified by several factors. It does not involve a denial of every type of actualized infinity, such as an infinite number of points in a line. Neither does it involve a denial of an actualized temporal infinity. It is perfectly compatible, for example, with the Aristotelian thesis of the coexistence of the world and God throughout an infinite past, or with the modernized Whiteheadian version of the same thesis. And since the temporal events in this series are also causes of subsequent events, it is perfectly compatible with the thesis that an infinite number of causes in time is possible. It is in effect the claim that even if there is an infinite number of contingent antecedent temporal causes, they depend ultimately on some noncontingent or necessary cause. Not everything can be capable of not being; at least one being must be self-sufficient, not capable of not being. But why? It is at this point that the first two Thomistic proofs become dependent on the third proof, and we shall attempt to explain why everything cannot be contingent in our discussion of the third proof.

In St. Thomas's version of the first two "ways," the step we have listed in our reworded argument as a fourth premise actually appears in the conclusion. After announcing that a first mover, a first cause, exists, St. Thomas then announces that "this everyone understands to be God." Unfortunately, it is not quite so simple. There are those, such as the naturalists, who refuse to accept the equating of the ultimate causal ground of all events with God, preferring to speak of it as "nature as a whole" or something of the sort. It must be demonstrated that the cosmological argument is more than merely a proof for the truth of naturalism. Why is it *not* the case that the ultimate causal ground of all events is simply nature as a whole—nonintelligent, nonpurposive, noncompassionate, and so on—as David Hume and many of the naturalists have maintained? This vital question cannot be bypassed by simply claiming that everyone gives the name of "God" to the ultimate causal ground of events, because not everyone does. We shall postpone our attempt to show that there are good reasons for ruling out nature as a first cause until we discuss the third proof, the proof from contingency, to which we shall now turn.

THE THIRD WAY

Most interpreters of St. Thomas regard the third proof as the most fundamental of the three, mainly because the first two proofs may be regarded as instances of this even more general argument "from possibility," or from contingency. Contingency of motion ultimately implies a noncontingent mover; contingency of change ultimately implies a noncontingent ground of change. Contingency ultimately implies necessity; nature ultimately implies God; but by what steps? The first two premises of our reworded version of the third proof are both existential premises, and again they are virtually indisputable. It is indeed evident to anyone who has had experience with the world that there are things that are contingent—that is, things that might or might not exist at all and that exist only because of something else. There is generation and corruption. People are born and things are made, and there are parents and makers. Experience shows further that there are lengthy series of such causes and effects. Not only do I have parents, but my parents had parents, and my grandparents had parents, and so on (to infinity?). The stick pushes the stone, my hand pushes the stick, my arm moves my hand, my muscles move my arm, and so on. But how many such preconditions does any natural event have? Where does it all stop (or begin)? Or does it simply never begin at all? Is the entire series of natural conditions itself contingent, or is it necessary? The third premise of the "third way" tells us that it must be one or the other. There are only three possibilities open. The entire series of natural preconditions must be necessary (self-sufficient), contingent (not self-sufficient), or somehow neither the one nor the other. The only defense of this third alternative would be a demonstration of the meaninglessness of the first and second alternatives. Even on positivistic grounds, however, the claim that the entire series of natural events is contingent is experientially meaningful. Certainly the obvious fact that some natural events are contingent is at least relevant to the question of whether the entire series is contingent or not (just *how* relevant we shall see later). And if the second alternative is meaningful, then the first alternative is also meaningful; for the first alternative is but the contradictory of the second. If any statement is meaningful, then its contradictory is meaningful, even on positivistic grounds.

We are thus left with the third premise of our argument: Either the entire series of natural events is necessary, or it is contingent. The naturalist takes the first of these alternatives, and the theist takes the second. The naturalist claims that the entire series of natural events as a totality is self-sufficient. Nature as a whole is necessary; it is eternal or everlasting; and it depends on nothing other than itself for its existence. God is not needed because nature does not need him. Events within the world may be contingent, but the world as a whole is necessary. On the other hand, the theist holds that the entire series of natural events is not necessary, not self-sufficient, and ultimately depends on God. Even though it may be everlasting, it is at least not self-sufficient. It is not itself the bearer of its ultimate *raison d'être*. But how can the theist show that his alternative is true and that of the naturalist is false? Is it merely a matter of irrational faith? On which side?

Theists have sometimes become exasperated at this point and fallen back on faith, but it is not yet necessary to make such a move. Reason has not yet been exhausted. Even St. Thomas gives reasons for rejecting the thesis of the self-sufficiency of the world. Implicit in the "third way" is the insight that if each of the parts of the world is contingent, then the world as a whole must be contingent. If each of the parts of time and space came into being, then the whole of time and space must have come into being. If each of the parts of nature lacks self-sufficiency, then nature as a whole lacks self-sufficiency.

COMPOSITION AND THE COSMOLOGICAL ARGUMENT

At last, the critic will exult, we are able to see where the cosmological argument goes wrong. The argument that nature as a whole is contingent *because* each of the parts of nature is contingent commits the logical fallacy of composition. Thus the cosmological argument falls, and naturalism is triumphant. But not so fast. What is the fallacy of composition, and how exactly does the cosmological argument commit it? As the matter is explained in most introductory logic textbooks, the fallacy of composition is the fallacy of reasoning that a certain whole possesses a certain property because each of its parts possesses that property. Thus it is an obvious mistake to infer that a certain machine as a whole is light in weight because each of its parts is light in weight, or that a play as a whole is artistically perfect because each scene within it is artistically perfect.[2] The critic maintains that it is equally fallacious for the cosmological arguer to infer that nature as a whole must be contingent because each of its parts is contingent.[3]

It is only in recent years that the philosophical world has realized that not every such argument from parts to whole is fallacious. If all the parts of a machine are made of metal, the whole machine must certainly be made of metal. If all the parts of a machine are colored green, the whole machine must certainly be colored green. If all the counties of Tennessee are within the United States, then the whole of Tennessee is certainly within the United States. Thus it seems that in some instances it is fallacious to reason from parts to whole, and in other instances it is not. What exactly is it that differentiates between correct and incorrect inferences from parts to whole? Traditionally it was maintained that the fallacy of composition was a fallacy of ambiguity, that the mistake in reasoning involved here lay in the use of ambiguous terms (such as *smaller, larger, lighter, heavier*). But it is no longer possible to classify the fallacy of composition as a fallacy of ambiguity. There may be ambiguity involved in saying that the whole machine is light in weight because each of its parts is light in weight, but there is no ambiguity involved in saying that the whole machine weighs exactly one pound because each of its parts weighs exactly one pound. Here is an obviously mistaken inference, but the mistake does not lie in ambiguity. Where does it lie?

Recent studies of the fallacy of composition[4] have shown that there is actually no fallacy whatsoever involved in reasoning from parts to whole if *fallacy* is taken to mean that the general *pattern* of reasoning involved is logically incorrect. The difference between correct and incorrect inferences from parts to whole rests entirely on the question of the truth or falsity of the premises of the argument. No fallacious *pattern* of reasoning is ever involved in such inferences from parts to whole. The difficulty is simply that in some such arguments one or more of the premises is false or questionable, and in others it is not. When one or more of the premises is false or questionable, the conclusion will not be proved true; but when the premises are true, then the conclusion will be proved true.

These studies of the fallacy of composition have shown that such inferences from parts to whole are not logical fallacies but logical enthymemes—perfectly valid arguments in which one or more of the premises involved is not explicitly stated. To assess their correctness, we simply need to make everything explicit. Inferences from parts to whole are enthymemes which exemplify the perfectly valid argument form *modus ponens* (plus an instantiation with respect to *this* object), but in some instances the premises are false or questionable and the argument fails to prove its conclusion. In other instances, however, all the premises are true and the conclusion is proved. Each of the following arguments exemplifies this valid pattern of reasoning: p implies q; p; therefore, q. But the second argument fails to prove the truth of its conclusion because one of its premises is false, whereas the first argument does prove the truth of its conclusion because all its premises are true:

(1) If each of the parts of any chair is brown, then the chair as a whole is brown.
Each of the parts of this chair is brown.
Therefore, this chair as a whole is brown.

(2) If each of the parts of any machine weighs exactly one pound, then the machine as a whole weighs exactly one pound.
Each of the parts of this machine weighs exactly one pound.
Therefore, this machine as a whole weighs exactly one pound.

No ambiguity is involved in either of these arguments, and *modus ponens* is unquestionably valid as a pattern of argumentation. If there is an explanation of why these arguments prove or fail to prove their conclusions, it revolves around the truth or falsity of at least one of the premises. The first premise of example 1 is proved true in experience, since in no case do we find a chair not to be brown when all its parts are brown. By contrast, the first premise of example 2 is proved false in experience, since we find or could find many cases in which each of the several parts of a machine weighs exactly one pound while the machine as a whole weighs considerably more than one pound.

What is the relevance of all this to the cosmological argument? For one thing, the critics are simply mistaken in claiming that the argument is a fallacy in the sense that the general pattern of rea-

a fair chance of refuting the cosmological argument, but even here he is in trouble. To contradict the cosmological argument, he must assert that some parts of nature are necessary; and to prove his case he must identify these for us and show us that they do indeed exemplify the predicates of everlastingness, self-sufficiency, and indestructibility. Is not the empirical evidence for the thesis of the contingency of each of the parts of nature literally overwhelming, and is not the evidence for the contradictory thesis virtually non-existent? Where shall we turn to find a self-sufficient part of the natural order of things? Not to mountains, islands, or grains of sand, nor to men, nations, or civilizations, nor to suns, planets, solar systems, or galaxies. The naturalist turns to the utterly minute, to atoms, matter, or energy. Large-scale composite wholes, such as stones, trees, men, and planets, are contingent and come into being and pass away; but the most fundamental parts of nature, such as atoms, matter, and energy, are necessary—that is, eternal, self-sufficient, and indestructible. But is this true, and how do we know it to be true? Earlier naturalists who took matter or the atom to be eternal, self-sufficient, and indestructible have been decisively refuted by modern physics, which has split the atom. The atom and even its most elementary constituents, such as electrons and protons, are subject to generation and destruction, subject to conversion into pure, formless energy and back again. What about pure, formless, natural energy? Is *it* eternal, self-sufficient, and indestructible? Here is where the real problem ultimately lies, and here is where we may have reached the limits of human knowledge, but at least the naturalist is in the same position: Does he *know* that pure, natural energy is self-sufficient? The falsity of such a supposition is at least conceivable. Perhaps no one will ever know whether the claim is true or false, but further investigation of the problem might somehow help. Is it an empirical problem, one that experience would resolve? Is it a conceptual problem? What exactly is energy that is so pure and formless that it is neither atomic energy nor heat energy nor light energy nor any other identifiable kind of energy? Can we not even here develop a strong case against the naturalist? The energy of which he speaks cannot be any definite *kind* of energy—such as light energy, which is contingent on some source of light, or heat energy, which is contingent on the rate of molecular movement, nor atomic energy, which is contingent on the fission or disintegration of subatomic particles, or any other definite or identifiable kind of energy. It can only be pure, formless, sourceless energy per se. Is not the concept of pure, formless energy too amorphous and elusive to be empirically meaningful? What is the difference, when all is said and done, between it and the primordial nature of God, or between it and sheer potentiality? If even the naturalist does not know the answer to these questions, does he have a right to believe in the self-sufficiency of pure, formless, natural energy? Could we not simply be agnostics, abandoning the possibility of a definite answer? But suppose the question were of momentous religious, moral, and metaphysical importance. Would we as religious believers have the right to believe in the contingency of formless, natural energy in order to understand? What introduces form into the formless? Is there not contingency here? Does not the naturalist at this point also believe in order to understand? Must not anyone do so when the limits of human knowledge have been reached? What are the ethics of belief? We might have expected any argument that depends on a posteriori knowledge to flounder when such knowledge itself reaches its limits, but at least we are in a position now to see exactly what those limits are and where we need to concentrate our further investigations. Even if the version of the cosmological argument that we have presented is not totally decisive owing to the presence of empirical premises that are never perfectly indubitable, there is at least the satisfaction of realizing that the claim that the existence of anything in the world ultimately implies the existence of God is not totally irrational, plus the satisfaction of knowing that for once it is the nontheist who has his back to the wall.

Even if we were in a position to show the contingency of natural energy per se, we would still have to reply to the man who admits that nature as a whole is contingent but refuses to look for a further explanation of it. He might hold that the fact is simply there, brute but accidental, and that is the end of the matter. Nature may or not have always been around; but it is here now, and we must simply accept it without explanation. Such an opponent might not understand the meaning of *contingent*. To be contingent is to be dependent, and to be dependent is to be dependent *on something,* and only when this something has been identified is the process of rational explanation complete. On the other hand, the opponent might at this point simply be abandoning rationality, abandoning altogether the attempt to explain—as theologians sometimes do when the going gets rough. If our ethics of belief makes a place for tolerance, we may have to grant him his right to refuse to search for further reasons at this point, but it does not follow that no further reasons exist or that we must follow him in refusing to look for them.

In all three of the Thomistic cosmological proofs, as we reworded them, there is a premise that identifies the first mover, first cause, or necessary being with God. We indicated earlier that the naturalist might resist this move, preferring to identify the necessary ground of our contingent existence with nature as a whole. Is there any way to show that the ultimate ground of our contingent existence is *also* intelligent, purposive, morally perfect, compassionate, and so on? Unfortunately, the cosmological argument alone will not do this, as even St. Thomas realized and expressed in his doctrine that the a posteriori proofs show us only *that* God is, not *what* God is. However, the cosmological proof is only one strand in the rope, only one element in the case; and the case for belief in God does not rest on it alone. When it is supplemented by the ontological argument, the wider argument from perfection, the teleological argument, the moral argument, and the testimony of religious experience, there is a much stronger case for theism as against naturalism.

Suggestions for Further Reading

ON THE COSMOLOGICAL ARGUMENT

AQUINAS, ST. THOMAS, *On the Truth of the Catholic Faith* (Garden City, N.Y., Doubleday, 1957), Book I, Chapter 13. For the classic statement of the "Five Ways," see Anton C. Pegis, ed., *Basic Writings of Saint Thomas Aquinas* (New York, Random House, 1945), pp. 22–23.

BURRILL, DONALD R., ed., *The Cosmological Arguments* (Garden City, N.Y., Doubleday, 1967). Contains selections from many of the important classical and contemporary discussions and criticisms of both the cosmological and the teleological arguments.

FLEW, ANTONY, *God and Philosophy* (New York, Dell, 1966), pp. 82–98.

HARTSHORNE, CHARLES, *Man's Vision of God* (Hamden, Conn., Archon Books, 1964), Chapter 8.

HEPBURN, RONALD W., *Christianity and Paradox* (New York, Pegasus, 1968), Chapters 9 and 10.

HICK, JOHN, *Philosophy of Religion* (Englewood Cliffs, N.J., Prentice-Hall, 1963), pp. 20–23.

HUME, DAVID, *Dialogues Concerning Natural Religion,* Norman Kemp Smith, ed. (Indianapolis, Ind., Bobbs-Merrill, 1962), especially Parts II and IX.

MARTIN, C. B., *Religious Belief* (Ithaca, N.Y., Cornell University Press, 1959), Chapter 9.

MUNITZ, MILTON K., *The Mystery of Existence* (New York, Appleton-Century-Crofts, 1965), Part III.

TAYLOR, RICHARD, *Metaphysics* (Englewood Cliffs, N.J., Prentice-Hall, 1963), pp. 84–94.

Notes

1 Anton C. Pegis, ed., *Basic Writings of Saint Thomas Aquinas,* Vol. I (New York, Random House, 1945), pp. 22–23.

2 These examples are used by Irving M. Copi, *Introduction to Logic,* 3rd ed. (New York, Macmillan, 1968), p. 80.

3 This criticism of the cosmological argument is quite commonplace. See, for example, Sterling Lamprecht, *The Metaphysics of Naturalism* (New York, Appleton-Century-Crofts, 1967), p. 178; J. G. Brennan, *The Meaning of Philosophy,* 2nd ed. (New York, Harper & Row, 1967), pp. 267–68; and Milton K. Munitz, *The Mystery of Existence* (New York, Appleton-Century-Crofts, 1965), pp. 117–19.

4 Such as: W. L. Rowe, "The Fallacy of Composition," *Mind,* Vol. LXXI (January 1962), pp. 87–92; Richard Cole, "A Note on Informal Fallacies," *Mind,* Vol. LXXIV (July 1965), pp. 432–33; Rem B. Edwards, "Composition and the Cosmological Argument," *Mind,* Vol. LXXVII (January 1968), pp. 115–17. My *Mind* article has been criticized by Thomas Mautner, "Aquinas's Third Way," *American Philosophical Quarterly,* Vol. VI (October 1969), pp. 298–304; and I have replied in "The Validity of Aquinas' Third Way," *The New Scholasticism,* Vol. XLV (Winter 1971), pp. 117–26.

chapter eleven

The Existence of God THE TELEOLOGICAL ARGUMENT

The teleological argument is an attempt to reason from the presence of order, design, and purpose in the world to the existence of a supreme orderer, designer, and purposer—that is, to God. With some justification, it is often treated as a subtype of the cosmological argument. The basic cosmological insight is that the existence of any contingent thing in the world will ultimately imply the existence of a necessary being, and if this is so, then the existence of contingent order, design, and purpose in the world will ultimately imply the existence of a necessary ground of this order, design, and purpose. Yet there is something distinctive about the teleological argument that is missed if natural order, design, and purpose are simply regarded as instances of contingency. The point of this argument is that order, design, and purpose not only imply the existence of a *necessary* being but also imply that this necessary being is *intelligent* and *purposive*. Of course, if the ontological argument or the "wider argument from perfection" is sound, this conclusion is already established, and the teleological argument is simply another strand of evidence pointing toward the same conclusion.

The teleological argument is again one of the most ancient of the philosophical proofs for the existence of God, and for some odd reason even its most severe critics, such as Hume and Kant, seem to respect it. It is at least as old as Plato's attempts to show that even if the primordial, formless world stuff does coexist eternally with God, the order of the world as we know it is still contingent on

God's imposition of good form on this formless world stuff. Versions of the argument appear in Aristotle and in the works of most of the great theological thinkers of classical times. As we saw in Chapter 4, the argument from design had its heyday with the theistic rationalists of the eighteenth century. However, the devastating criticisms of the argument by another eighteenth-century writer, David Hume, which we shall examine shortly, are now commonly thought to be a decisive refutation of it; and it is due mainly to Hume's influence that the argument is now unpopular with professional philosophers and theologians. It still has some vogue with the general populace and in very conservative theological circles. It has also had several able defenders in our century who have tried to take account of the Humean critique.[1]

Formulations by St. Thomas Aquinas and Paley

We shall examine two statements of the teleological argument, the classical thirteenth-century statement of it in the "fifth way" of St. Thomas Aquinas, and the familiar statement of it by William Paley in 1802. It is now commonly thought that Paley's version was refuted by Hume a quarter of a century or so before Paley even wrote it.

> *St. Thomas's "Fifth Way"*: The fifth way is from the governance of the world. We see that things which lack knowledge, such as natural bodies, act for an end, and this is evident from their acting always, or nearly always, in the same way, so as to obtain the best result. Hence it is plain that they achieve their end, not fortuitously, but designedly. Now whatever lacks knowledge cannot move towards an end, unless it be directed by some being endowed with knowledge and intelligence; as the arrow is directed by the archer. Therefore some intelligent being exists by whom all natural things are directed to their end; and this being we call God.[2]

> *Paley's Watch–Watchmaker Analogy*: In crossing a heath, suppose I pitched my foot against a *stone,* and were asked how the stone came to be there; I might possibly answer, that, for any thing I knew to the contrary, it had lain there for ever: nor would it per-

haps be very easy to show the absurdity of this answer. But suppose I had found a *watch* upon the ground, and it should be inquired how the watch happened to be in that place; I should hardly think of the answer which I had before given, that, for any thing I knew, the watch might have always been there. Yet why should not this answer serve for the watch as well as for the stone? Why is it not as admissible in the second case, as in the first? For this reason, and for no other, *viz.* that, when we come to inspect the watch, we perceive (what we could not discover in the stone) that its several parts are framed and put together for a purpose, e.g. that they are so formed and adjusted as to produce motion, and that motion so regulated as to point out the hour of the day; that, if the different parts had been differently shaped from what they are, of a different size from what they are, or placed after any other manner, or in any other order, than that in which they are placed, either no motion at all would have been carried on in the machine, or none which would have answered the use that is now served by it. To reckon up a few of the plainest of these parts, and of their offices, all tending to one result:—We see a cylindrical box containing a coiled elastic spring, which by its endeavour to relax itself, turns round the box. We next observe a flexible chain (artificially wrought for the sake of flexure), communicating the action of the spring from the box to the fusee. We then find a series of wheels, the teeth of which catch in, and apply to each other, conducting the motion from the fusee to the balance, and from the balance to the pointer; and at the same time, by the size and shape of those wheels, so regulating that motion, as to terminate in causing an index, by an equable and measured progression, to pass over a given space in a given time. We take notice that the wheels are made of brass in order to keep them from rust; the springs of steel, no other metal being so elastic; that over the face of the watch there is placed a glass, a material employed in no other part of the work, but in the room of which, if there had been any other than a transparent substance, the hour could not be seen without opening the case. This mechanism being observed (it requires indeed an examination of the instrument, and perhaps some previous knowledge of the subject, to perceive and understand it; but being once, as we have said, observed and understood), the inference, we think, is inevitable, that the watch must have had a maker; that there must have existed, at some time, and at some place or other, an artificer or artificers, who formed it for the purpose which we find it actually to answer; who comprehended its construction, and designed its use. . . . Every indication of contrivance, every manifestation of design, which existed in the watch, exists in the works of nature; with the difference, on the side of nature, of being greater and more, and that in a degree which exceeds all computation. I mean that the contrivances of nature surpass the contrivances of art, in the complexity, subtilty, and curiosity of the mechanism; and still more, if possible, do they go beyond them in number and variety; yet in a multitude of cases, are not less evidently mechanical, not less evidently contrivances, not less evidently accommodated to their end, or suited to their office, than are the most perfect productions of human ingenuity.[3]

As we have done with the preceding proofs, let us restate the argument from design as succinctly as possible and then inquire into the truth or falsity of its premises. The basic pattern of reasoning involved here seems to be this:

(1) Anything that significantly resembles the products of purposive intelligence in relevant respects may be inferred to be a product of purposive intelligence.
(2) There is an order of nature.
(3) The order of nature significantly resembles the products of purposive intelligence in relevant respects.

Therefore, the order of nature is a product of purposive intelligence.

The first premise of this rephrased teleological argument may be called the principle of teleological explanation, or the rule that guides us in determining when it is and when it is not legitimate to explain things as resulting in part from conscious design and intent. It has a multiplicity of uses. As a tacit assumption, it undergirds our everyday attempts not only to understand artifacts but also to understand the behavior of our fellow men. It plays a major role in attempts to untangle the philosophical problem of "other minds," for the behavior of perceived human and animal bodies is interpreted as being in part the product of intelligent and purposive planning on just such a principle as this. It plays a major role in psychoanalysis, for the analyst uses it in inferring from the patient's unusual behavior the presence of "unconscious" purposes to which his patient has no direct introspective access. In conjunction with other information about the connection of specific patterns of behavior with specific purposes, our principle of teleological explanation permits us to infer not only that there are purposes, but also specifically what those purposes are. As a matter of fact, the teleological argument is simply the problem of "other minds" writ large, applied to the universe as a whole. Since even at the human level this problem is still largely unresolved and considerations are still highly controversial, we may expect the teleological argument to share these characteristics. The case cannot be conclusive. Skepticism about the existence of other minds can never be conclusively refuted, but a case can be made. The case may show that a teleological explanation of the universe as a whole is permissible, but it probably cannot show that it is required, just as it cannot be shown that a teleological explanation of the behavior of other human bodies is required. It is only when the teleological argument is viewed in light of the ontological argument that the conclusion is required. Kant maintained that both the cosmological and the teleological arguments depend ultimately on the ontological argument (that is, the wider argument from perfection), on the grounds that only within the framework of a concept of a being than whom none greater can be conceived does it make sense to attribute to the necessary being the properties of omnipotence, omniscience, and all-embracing reality. Only within the total context of religious belief does all this make sense, but if within the smaller context of the teleological argument it can be shown that a teleological interpretation of the universe is at least permissible, this will be a worthwhile achievement.

What exactly is covered by the phrase "significantly resembles the products of purposive intelligence in relevant respects"? Under what conditions is it appropriate to say of something that it resembles *the products* of purposive intelligence? This is not quite the same as the question of what it is like *to be* purposively intelligent. St. Thomas wanted to show that the acorn was the product of purposive intelligence, not that it was itself purposively intelligent. Most of us hold that robots are the product of purposive intelligence, but this does not commit us to the view that they are purposively intelligent. It is sometimes mistakenly thought that champions of the teleological argument are defending the view that such natural processes as the development of moths from worms are themselves purposively intelligent, which is easily refuted by showing that in all likelihood worms have no conscious prevision of such distant future ends. But this is not what the theistic teleologist wants to show at all. Without holding that worms are purposively intelligent, he wants to say that their instinctive behavior is the product of God's purposive intelligence. The problem is, how do we ever recognize something as *the product* of purposive intelligence when we come across it? Any answer will be disputable, but we cannot get very far unless we venture a reply. There are at least two and possibly three criteria for deciding the appropriateness of teleological explanation. If we are to regard something as the product of purposive intelligence, we must be able (1) to specify the goals or ends achieved by it, (2) to show that a reasonably efficient means to the achievement of those ends is involved, and (3) to show that it is a specific instance of repeatedly experienced connections between intelligent, purposive planning on the one hand and effective means to specifiable ends on the other hand. The requirement that goals be specifiable is connected with purposiveness, or goal-directedness; the requirement that the means be effective in achieving the ends is connected with intelligent planning; and, ironically, the requirement that repeatedly experienced connections be involved is connected with refuting the teleological argument.

Hume's Criticisms of the Teleological Argument

DAVID HUME had the genius to see that *if* the third criterion of repeatedly experienced connections is accepted, the teleological argument falls to the ground. The theist *may* be able to show that patterns of events in nature as a whole move toward specifiable ends and that the means to those ends are relatively efficient, but what he clearly cannot show is that these are specific instances of repeatedly experienced connections between intelligent, purposive planning and the effectiveness of the means in achieving the ends. What exactly would constitute such an experience? We can not only show that watches, houses, or ships, for example, serve an end and that they involve relatively efficient means to that end, but we can also recognize any particular watch, house, or ship as a specific instance of a general class of things known to be produced by human purposive planning. Could Paley have inferred a watch-maker from the watch he found in the deserted heath if neither he nor any other human being had ever once experienced the connection between watchmaker and watch? Obviously not, Hume would have contended. And since no human being has ever once experienced the connection between Divine Architect and Designed Universe, it is equally obvious that no inference from the latter to the former could possibly be warranted. Hume states his case very well:

> When two *species* of objects have always been observed to be con-joined together, I can *infer*, by custom, the existence of one wherever I *see* the existence of the other: and this I call an argu-ment from experience. But how this argument can have place, where the objects, as in the present case, are single, individual, without parallel, or specific resemblance, may be difficult to ex-plain. And will any man tell me with a serious countenance, that an orderly universe must arise from some thought and art, like the human; because we have experience of it? To ascertain this reasoning, it were requisite, that we had experience of the origin of worlds, and it is not sufficient, surely, that we have seen ships and cities arise from human art and contrivance.
>
> . . . the subject in which you are engaged exceeds all human reason and inquiry. Can you pretend to show any such similarity between the fabric of a house, and the generation of a universe? Have you ever seen nature in any such situation as resembles the first arrangement of the elements? Have worlds ever been formed under your eye; and have you had leisure to observe the whole progress of the phenomenon, from the first appearance of order to its final consummation? If you have, then cite your experience, and deliver your theory.[4]

Hume thus contends that if the analogy of artisan producing arti-fact is to hold, the universe as a whole must be an instance of a class of many universes, which it is not, and I must have been pres-ent at the creation of these many universes by a divine artisan and experienced the connection between the two, which I obviously could not have done. He might have contended further that if I am to differentiate between universes analogous to watches and other universes analogous to stones, I must be in a position to experience both types of universe, compare them, note that there are always specifiable differences in order between designed and undesigned universes, and show that *our* universe exemplifies the characteristics of a designed one. Hume has developed a strong case against the teleological argument, and it is small wonder that philosophers generally take his criticisms to be decisive. Is there any defense?

One possible defense against the Humean critique would be a rejection of the third criterion for deciding on the appropriateness of teleological explanation. Let us call this Hume's criterion. If we are to explain something as resulting from purposive intelligence, must we have repeatedly experienced the connection between it and purposive intelligence? Is this the *only* way that we can tell the difference between a stone and a watch? Is it even a necessary condition for deciding that teleological explanation is appropriate in the latter case but not in the former? It certainly seems to be necessary on the surface, but is it really? On what grounds could a rejection of Hume's criterion be based? We could produce a *reductio ad absurdum* argument against it, showing that *if* we accept it, we are committed to some dreadfully embarrassing conclusions. We can also show that in explaining his own examples, David Hume himself did not accept it! First, what are the embarrassing logical implications of accepting such a principle? They are that the principle rules out the existence of other minds entirely, whether they be human or divine. We experience directly only the *behavior* of other people, never the workings of their minds or their feelings, desires, motives, intentions, or purposes. There is *never* a repeatedly experienced connection between the intelligent purposiveness of *other* human beings on the one hand and the efficient adaptation of their behavior to specifiable ends on the other. Thus if Hume's criterion is accepted, teleological explanation of the behavior of other human beings is never warranted. We can never infer from the seemingly goal-directed behavior of other people that they are engaged in intelligent, purposive planning, that they are anything more than mindless phenomena. If

Hume's criterion for teleological explanation is accepted, it rules out not only God but all other human minds as well. Solipsism is its only consequence. On the other hand, if we use *other* criteria (such as 1 and 2 above) for the identification of other minds, then we might also use them for the identification of the divine mind. At any rate, if one goes, so it seems does the other. Hume's skepticism was even more drastic than he himself knew, and even he does not make use of his own principle in explaining his artisan-producing-artifact examples. If he is not himself the maker of the watch or the ship or the house, if they are the products of other minds, then he has not once experienced the connection between intelligent purposiveness and goal-directed behavior *even in those cases.* He assumes that he is safe in regarding the ship, the house, or the watch as a product of purposive intelligence, but he is not. If a constantly experienced connection between purposive planning and goal-directed behavior is required, Hume has no grounds whatsoever for even regarding the watch as subject to teleological explanation. It is not the teleological arguer who cannot distinguish between designed and undesigned universes; rather it is Hume who cannot distinguish between stones and watches.

Implicitly contained within the Humean critique of the teleological argument is a logical metathesis about the argument, namely that it is an argument from statistical probability and that as such it is invalid, since it cannot satisfy the logical requirements of arguments based on statistical probability. To be sound, it is claimed, the premises of the argument must be confirmed by my experience of many universes, some of which I know to be designed and some I know not to be designed, and by a favorable comparison between *this* universe and those others I know to be designed. Now it is interesting that no defender of the argument has ever advanced this logical metathesis about it, and the actual pattern of reasoning involved here is really quite different from what the critic would require it to be. This is not a scientific argument based on statistical probability, but rather a metaphysical argument from part to whole. We have seen that the naturalist, who asserts the eternity and self-sufficiency of nature as a whole and maintains that order is native to nature as a whole, wishes to draw metaphysical conclusions about nature as a whole, just as does the theist, who asserts nature's ordered contingency; but if the arguments are required to be arguments from statistical probability, they can never be sound, since there are no judgments of probability about this universe based on a statistical comparison of it with other universes. As Hume correctly points out, the universe is unique. As Charles Sanders Peirce put it, "Universes are not as plentiful as blackberries." The metaphysician who wishes to know anything about nature or reality as a whole can never hope to produce probabilistic scientific arguments of the statistical sort to support his conclusions, but this does not mean that he has no arguments at all. His arguments must be such that they permit reasoning from parts of nature or reality to the whole, and we have already examined a readily defensible argument of this sort: the cosmological argument. If we regard the teleological argument as an instance of allowing the parts of reality to inform us about ultimate reality, is the argument here defensible? This will depend in part on the truth of the claims that there is an order of nature and that it resembles the products of purposive intelligence in relevant respects. At any rate, the argument depends not on a comparison of universes but rather on an application of principles of teleological explanation drawn from parts of reality to reality as a whole.

Although the second premise of our reworded teleological argument, which asserts that there is an order of nature, is relatively noncontroversial, the third premise, which asserts that this order significantly resembles the products of purposive intelligence in relevant respects, is highly disputable. We see at this point that Hume's criterion of significant resemblance—that is, repeatedly experienced connections—cannot be accepted if we are unwilling to pay the price of solipsism. We are left with the criteria that an end be specified and that the means to that end be reasonably efficient. Are there other criteria for proving a thing to be the product of purposive intelligence? Try to state them. What price must be paid for them? The teleological arguer must show that somehow the order of nature satisfies these criteria, whatever they are. He must at least show that ends for the patterns of order in nature or for the order of nature as a whole can be specified, and that relatively efficient means to those ends are exemplified in natural processes. This he believes he is able to do. Everywhere we turn there is evidence of natural law and order. The ecological environment of the earth is remarkably well adapted for the development, survival, and satisfaction of a great variety of forms of life, including human life. Bodily parts of living organisms, such as the eye, are remarkably well adapted for seeing and other functions appropriate to the life style of the organism. With no planning of their own, acorns become sturdy oaks. Scientists marvel at the aesthetic value of the objects of their investigation, and scientists and nonscientists alike enjoy the beauty of the earth. The starry heavens above and the moral law within fill us with awe. Even human perceivers and reasoners are a part of the natural order of things, and we confidently believe that our senses and thoughts are effective means to the end of knowing the world. The world is not a dung heap, a torture chamber, or a sand pile, but it might be if only the nonteleological principles of physics and chemistry were involved. The biological principle of natural selection may explain the survival of the fittest, but it cannot explain their arrival. Nor can it explain the origins of living things that somehow must *be* before they can compete or undergo mutations. As F. R. Tennant put it, "Presumably the world is comparable with a single throw of dice. And common sense is not foolish in suspecting the dice to have been loaded." [5]

Here the Humean skeptic interposes the objection that there are many reasons for rejecting the claim that the order of nature significantly resembles the products of purposive intelligence. Hume pointed out that *any* universe will be ordered, whether it be designed or undesigned. This may be true enough, but it is really beside the point. It does not answer the question of why the world has the order that it does have instead of the order of a pile of sand or a torture chamber. Hume held in one of his objections that the universe is *so small and limited* that only a finite cause or ground of it can be inferred, and in another one of his objections he held that the universe is *so immense* that our limited acquaintance with our narrow corner of it will permit no inferences to the nature of the vast whole. Thus Hume's objections to the theistic proofs are inconsistent with each other. The picture of the cosmos available to the eighteenth-century world may have been very small, but today we have the picture of a cosmos of literally astronomical proportions, one that is at least infinite in past time if not in present space. Yet from all that we can discover it is still contingent, as our discussion of the cosmological argument attempted to show. From such a limitless cosmos perhaps *we could* infer the existence of an infinite ground of both contingency and order. When he tries out the hypothesis of the vastness of nature, Hume shifts his objection, now insisting that "A very small part of this great system, during a very short time, is very imperfectly discovered to us: and do we thence pronounce decisively concerning the origin of the whole?" [6] The reply to this is that we must proceed on the basis of whatever evidence we can get. Scientists do it; why not philosophers and theologians? True, skepticism can never be decisively ruled out, but it can never be defended either, since any defense of it involves an abandonment of skepticisms. The fact that there is a great deal that we do not know can never be a good reason for abandoning the great deal that we do know. When it was convenient for him to refute belief in miracles and free will, Hume insisted that the order of nature is absolutely uniform and constant throughout, as if even the magnitude of the universe makes no difference at all. Hume objected that we might be able to account for the world mechanistically, after the fashion of the Greek Atomists and their later Epicurean followers, without appealing to teleological considerations at all; but he did nothing to show that the view, which is at least as old as Aristotle, that mechanistic and teleological explanation are by no means incompatible or mutually exclusive is false. As he presented it, this version of mechanistic naturalism presupposed that the atom was self-sufficient and indestructible, but we have seen that this belief has been refuted by modern science, which in splitting the atom has shown its contingency. Hume also objected that in seeking a ground for the order of nature we could not rule out the possibility of there being many gods who cooperated in making the world, just as many carpenters cooperate in making a house. Hume did not realize that it may be equally difficult to rule out a "multiple personality" explanation of the long-range behavior of each of our fellow men. A full reply to this objection probably would bring us back to the logic of the concept of God expressed in the ontological argument, and Kant may be right in holding that at least here the teleological depends on the ontological argument, while being wrong in holding that he had refuted the latter.

There is one more serious objection to the teleological argument that the Humean skeptic might raise and that we must examine more carefully. Does not the fact of evil in the world count heavily against the hypothesis that an omnipotent, intelligent, purposive, morally perfect, and compassionate God designed the world? How can we rule out the possibility that the world was designed by a feeble, stupid, senile, and even morally corrupt deity? Have not many worlds been attempted and wasted before this incompetent deity luckily hit upon the formula for this one, and does not the evil to be found in this one count decisively against the hypothesis of the deity's moral goodness and compassion? Perhaps the world *does* have the order of a torture chamber after all. The answer to our questions depends in part on our understanding of God's purposes or ends in creation, in part on our understanding of how an ideally virtuous, compassionate, and powerful being could and should relate himself to the world, and in part on how we understand the world itself and ourselves as members of it. Is it God's purpose simply to make all his creatures, or at least all his *virtuous* creatures, happy, with no experience of struggle, frustration, and pain? If so, the hard facts of life decisively refute such a view. There seems to be enough unhappiness in the world to go around. Is there any reason for thinking that a morally perfect, compassionate being could and should be lord of a painless world? There is no good reason for thinking that he *should,* since there may be other values besides happiness, such as freedom, creativity, moral struggle, and achievement, which can be achieved only at the price of some frustration. There is no good reason for thinking that he *could,* since in a pluralistic universe containing a number of individuals with interests of their own, interests are bound to conflict, and the satisfaction of all conflicting interests is bound to be incompossible. Is it God's purpose to produce a world in which everything is merely a means to *human* ends and nothing else is an end in itself, a world in which everything will be directly and obviously useful to human beings? If so, the sometimes brutal facts of life definitely contradict such a view. Many things in the world, such as germs and insect pests, seem to do us more harm than good; but perhaps they have a value of their own, like the lilies of the field or the fallen sparrow. Was the age of the dinosaurs a mere waste, a pointless interlude in our cosmic epoch? Perhaps so, if everything must be directly and obviously useful to human beings, but perhaps not, if worthwhile value was achieved then and there.

If there were many worlds, many cosmic epochs prior to our own, there is no need whatsoever to think of them as wasted unless we make the thoroughly egocentric assumption that unless something is useful to us, it is a total waste. Is the world like a torture chamber? If so, how do we tell the difference between life inside a torture chamber and life outside of one? Is it God's purpose to produce a world in which there is an immense variety of forms of experience, love, loyalty, enjoyment, responsibility, initiative, creativity, achievement, and satisfaction, even at the price of conflict? If so, then the world is a remarkable success.

Psychologistic Criticisms of the Teleological Argument: Feuerbach and Freud

Ludwig Feuerbach in the nineteenth century and Sigmund Freud in the twentieth century developed a psychologistic critique of belief in God that has a special application to the teleological argument. Our view of God, they hold, is merely a psychological projection of our own image of ourselves—perhaps our actual selves, perhaps our ideal selves—on the universe as a whole. The teleological argument, which views the universe as a product of purposive intelligence, is included in this general condemnation. Doubtless a strong case can be made for the view that psychological projection is involved in the development of religious belief. The way in which men conceive of their gods often closely parallels the way in which they conceive of themselves. The image of God as a divine father has strong Freudian overtones. It is men who create God in their own image, not God who creates men in his own image. In reality, God is merely a psychological illusion, an expression of unfulfilled wishes and deep neurotic obsessions.

Unfortunately, the conclusion that is often drawn from such psychologistic reflections is much stronger than the evidence warrants. From the fact that psychologistic projection is involved in our understanding of God, it does not follow that our understanding of God is *merely* a psychologistic projection. It could easily be that plus a great deal more. St. Augustine and innumerable believers have held that God has made us for himself and our hearts are restless until they rest in him, that he has left an imprint of himself on us, that he has made us in his image. If all this is correct, then psychologistic projection is just what we might expect as a result. Such a projection is simply a manifestation of the voice of what Francis Thompson called "the Hound of Heaven," who relentlessly pursues us in every conceivable way until he has found us and we have found him. As John Hick has indicated,

> Perhaps the most interesting theological comment to be made upon Freud's theory is that in his work on the father-image he may have uncovered the mechanism by which God creates an idea of himself in the human mind. For if the relation of a human father to his children is, as the Judaic-Christian tradition teaches, analogous to God's relationship to man, it is not surprising that human beings should think of God as their heavenly Father and should come to know him through the infant's experience of utter dependence and the growing child's experience of being loved, cared for, and disciplined within a family. Clearly, to the mind which is not committed in advance to the naturalistic explanation there may be a religious as well as a naturalistic explanation of the psychological facts.[7]

Suppose for the sake of discussion that the teleological argument originates in what we might call a teleological intuition, a kind of psychological hunch that intelligence and purposiveness lie at the heart of things. Intuitions often result in sound argument and analysis, and it is entirely possible for our arguments to have both a psychological origin *and* a logical forcefulness. We commit the genetic fallacy whenever we hold that a thing is "merely" or "nothing more than" its origins. We cannot prove that a grown man is merely a single fertilized egg cell because he may have originated as such, and neither can we show by the same reasoning that the teleological argument is merely a psychological projection of our own image of purposive intelligence on the cosmos at large, even if it does originate as such. Arguments must be evaluated on their own merits, and psychologisms are irrelevant to the question of logical forcefulness. Incidentally, even psychologists must use arguments to support their psychological theories; and such theories are usually offered to us as the truth, not as illusions without a future. After assessing the logical forcefulness of the cosmological and teleological arguments on their own merits, the phenomenon of psychological projection may become relevant to the question of the existence of God, since even this ordered contingency may ultimately imply the truth of theism.

Suggestions for Further Reading

ON THE TELEOLOGICAL ARGUMENT

BURRILL, DONALD R., ed., *The Cosmological Arguments* (Garden City, N.Y., Doubleday, 1967), Part II. A book of readings.

FLEW, ANTONY, *God and Philosophy* (New York, Dell, 1966), Chapter 3.

HICK, JOHN, *Philosophy of Religion* (Englewood Cliffs, N.J., Prentice-Hall, 1963), pp. 23–26.

MATSON, WALLACE I., *The Existence of God* (Ithaca, N.Y., Cornell University Press, 1965), pp. 87–131.

PALEY, WILLIAM, *Natural Theology,* edited by Frederick Ferre (Indianapolis, Ind., Bobbs-Merrill, 1963).

TAYLOR, A. E., *Does God Exist?* (London, Macmillan, 1945), Chapter 4.

TAYLOR, RICHARD, *Metaphysics* (Englewood Cliffs, N.J., Prentice-Hall, 1963), pp. 94–102.

TENNANT, F. R., *Philosophical Theology* (New York, Cambridge University Press, 1969), Vol. II, Chapter 4.

Notes

1 See the Suggestions for Further Reading for some defenses of the argument from design.

2 Anton C. Pegis, ed., *Basic Writings of Saint Thomas Aquinas,* Vol. I (New York, Random House, 1945), p. 23.

3 William Paley, *Natural Theology* (Boston, Lincoln, Edmans & Co., 1833), pp. 5–6 and p. 13. (Many editions of this work are available.)

4 David Hume, *Dialogues Concerning Natural Religion,* 2nd ed. (London, 1779), pp. 65–66, 70. (Many editions of this work are available.)

5 F. R. Tennant, *Philosophical Theology*, Vol. II (Cambridge, Eng., Cambridge University Press, 1956), p. 87.
6 Hume, *Dialogues Concerning Natural Religion*, p. 63.
7 John Hick, *Philosophy of Religion* (Englewood Cliffs, N.J., Prentice-Hall, 1963), p. 36. Reprinted by permission of Prentice-Hall.

chapter twelve

Religious Language and Experience MYSTICISM

Like love, religious experience has many forms. That is to say, there are many types of experiences that are commonly called religious experiences and that are commonly believed to have religious significance. A religious experience is one that is believed to provide us with a clue to the ultimate nature of things, with access to ultimate being, goodness, and truth, with insight into the ultimate "meaning of life." A partial list of these kinds of experiences would include mystical experiences, personal encounters with the ultimate, revelatory experiences, experiences of the holy, experiences that make us acutely aware of our own finitude, sinfulness, and contingency, and experiences in which we are deeply conscious of the impingement of an ultimate moral demand on our wills. Although many problems arise in connection with religious experience, we shall take the question of the bearing of such experiences on the issue of the existence or nonexistence of God as our basic problem. Is there an argument from religious experience to the existence of God? How strong is the argument? Is it possible to say, "I know that God exists *because* I and/or others have directly experienced him," as it is clearly possible to say, "I know that trees and cows exist *because* I and/or others have experienced them"? Our basic reason for believing in the existence of most physical objects is that we see, hear, taste, touch, or feel them directly. Is there an analogous reason for believing in the existence of God? If so, is some special organ of sense or experience involved? Of course, we believe in the existence of electrons, protons, and neutrons as physical objects even though we do not experience them directly, because we think that their existence is required to explain things that we *do* experience directly, such as meter readings, explosions, and so on. Are there some "religious experiences" in which we encounter God directly, and others in which we indirectly require his existence to explain that which is directly given?

Our view of the world is built up, at least in part, out of experience. We usually have perceptual experience in mind when we make such a statement, and it is possible to hold that we always *ought* to have perceptual experience in mind, that no other type of experience is legitimate and informative. As a matter of fact, however, the world view of most men is built up in part out of some of the types of experiences that we have called religious. Given a world view based on "experience," it is always possible to ask *how* such a view is built up out of experience, whether experience can be *trusted,* and whether we *know* that such a world view is true. Before we discuss some of the types of religious experiences, let us explore these preliminary questions.

Language and Experience

How is a world view constructed from experience? Many answers to this question have been given, but we shall be selective and explore briefly only two of the basic alternatives. In doing so we shall concentrate exclusively on perceptual experience and the language that it generates. We shall then see whether analogous accounts of religious experience and religious language may be given.

VIEW 1: A BUILDING–BLOCK THEORY

If we do concentrate exclusively on perceptual experience, we shall have to abandon temporarily all existing natural languages and construct an artificial "ideal language" in which an entire "scientific" world view is built from the basic building blocks of perceptual experience. In the 1920's and 1930's such philosophers as Bertrand Russell, Ludwig Wittgenstein, Moritz Schlick, and Rudolf Carnap were advocating that we develop such an ideal language, which would be free of all the defects and misleading implications of natural languages. Our ideal language will closely parallel that of the logical atomists. How did we shift so abruptly from talking about experience to talking about language? The shift is actually very natural, for particular beliefs and complicated world views are expressed and communicated in language, and if our world view is to be regarded as *knowledge,* we must not only believe something but also be able to give good reasons for believing it. Not only a *belief* but also a *reason* for belief must be capable of linguistic formulation.

With the possible exception of logical connectives like *and, if–then,* and *or,* and negative words like *not,* all the words in our ideal language will be names. Since we want our world view to be "scientific," they will all be names of things encountered in perceptual experience. Only the names of perceived individuals, qualities, and relations will be meaningful. From perceptual experience we shall learn what there is, and for everything that there is we shall have a name. Perceptual experience will teach us that there are only three kinds of things in the universe: individuals, qualities, and relations; and we shall require a large inventory of names for particular individuals and distinguishable qualities and relations. Ideally, we would have an adequate supply of proper names for every individual thing in the universe, for every quality of those individuals, and for every sort of relation into which those individuals and their qualities might enter. The most important names in our inventory will be the names of utterly simple experienced entities, so simple that they cannot be broken down by analysis into simpler components, and so familiar, clear, and distinct that our experience of them cannot be mistrusted. Perhaps colors like *red* and *brown* and mathematical properties like *line* and *angle* will fill the bill here, and out of these atoms of experience we can build notions of and words for more complex entities, such as *table* and *dog.* These names will be the building blocks of our ideal language, but there is one additional problem. Somehow these building blocks will have to be combined with one another into more complex linguistic units. Not only do we need words like *I, red,* and *patch,* but we also need some way of saying such things as "I see a red patch here now." We need some way of *ordering* our names into meaningful assertions, the most elementary of which we might call "protocol sentences"; but even here we must exercise due caution not to introduce into our language something that is not there in the world itself. We must be certain that our words are ordered in the same way in which things and their qualities and relations are ordered. Even with respect to its order, language should be a picture of the world. The logical structure of our language should be the same as the logical structure of the world. Fortunately, thanks to Russell and Whitehead, we already have at our disposal a formal logical machinery for expressing all this, a logic that has place markers for the names of individuals, such as "x" and "y," place markers for the names of qualities, such as "F," and ways of saying that qualities belong to individuals, such as "Fx." Furthermore, we have an extended logic with place markers for relations, such as "R," and ways of saying that individuals are related to one another, such as "xRy." With this logical language and rules for testing the validity of arguments expressed within it, and with experience to tell us whether or not the propositions and premises expressed within this language are true or false, at least in principle we can know the world, the totality of facts. Now all we have to do is experience the world, say in our ideal language what it is that we experience, and prove the validity of our arguments; we shall then know the truth, the whole truth, and nothing but the truth. Confusions, prejudices, and preconceptions will no longer blind us.

There is a way of looking at how a religious world view can be built up out of religious experience that closely parallels this view of how a scientific world view can be built up out of perceptual experience—and that incidentally, suffers from analogous defects. The claim is that we can arrive at a pure, accurate view of God if we will simply abandon all our confusions, prejudices, and preconceptions and "read off" the truth about God from our experience of him. We must bring nothing to the experience, and everything that we come to believe about ultimate reality must be "read off," or constructed out of, our encounter with the Divine Thou. Religious experience is the beginning and end of all religious knowledge, and it is not rationalistic "proofs" that really count, but rather our immediate acquaintance with God in religious experience. Reluctantly, perhaps, we shall admit that if we are to have beliefs about God and communicate them to others, we shall need a language. Again, all the basic words in our vocabulary will be names, and we shall need names for individuals, such as *Yahweh* and *John Smith,* names for qualities of individuals, such as *holy, omniscient,* and *personal,* and names for relations between individuals, such as *appears to, is present with,* and *loves.* We might allow the word *God* to function at times as a proper name of an individual and at times as a description of a complex of properties belonging to that individual. Thus "God is God" might mean "Yahweh is omniscient, holy, loving, and so on." Ideally, we would have an adequate supply of proper names for God and the other individuals to whom he is related, an adequate supply of descriptive adjectives for all the qualities of God, and an adequate supply of relational words to express the multifarious ways in which God relates to his creatures. The most important names in our inventory will be the names of individuals, qualities, and relations that are given in religious experience and that are so familiar, clear, and distinct to the experiencer that he cannot mistrust his experience of them. As with the building blocks of perceptual experience, we shall have a set of indubitable, self-authenticating experiential elements out of which we can construct a religious world view. Many theologians, such as Buber, Brunner, Farmer, and Baillie,[1] have spoken of religious experience as indubitable and self-authenticating, and presumably they mean that something is given in religious experience that is so clear, self-explanatory, and fundamental that it cannot be doubted and that on it an entire religious world view may be built. Although these theologians have had only a modicum of interest in logic and language, they might easily have insisted that the logical order of religious propositions be the same as the logical order of the Divine Person and that religious arguments be formulated and tested in this ideal language. Then, with the ideal language at our disposal, with rules for testing the validity of arguments expressed within it, and with experience of God to tell us whether propositions and premises expressed within this language are true, we can know God. Now all we have to do is experience God, say in our ideal language what it is that we experience, and prove the validity of our arguments, and we shall know the Truth, the whole Truth, and nothing but the Truth.

Of course, there is a strong tendency on the part of such thinkers as Baillie, Farmer, *et al.* to play down the role of language and propositionally expressed belief. What is known in religious experience is a Divine Thou, not the truth of some proposition, they say. It is entirely a matter of personal acquaintance, of belief in a Person, not a matter of believing propositions to be true. Defenders of such a position can easily be forced to admit that language and propositions are of great importance if religious belief is to be *communicated,* and it can easily be shown that belief *in* a person always involves propositionally expressible beliefs *about* a person, even when these beliefs are not consciously or explicitly expressed—for example, that the person exists, that he is trustworthy, that he is morally knowledgeable and responsible. Similarly, belief *in* God inevitably involves beliefs *about* God, beliefs that he possesses the attributes and relations to the world as interpreted by supernaturalism, panentheism, or some other conceptualization of divinity. It is simply not the case that belief in a person can be separated totally from belief about the person. Problems of language and truth cannot be dismissed so easily.

VIEW 2: A MATRIX THEORY

Now let us look at another view of the way in which world views are built up out of experience. A critique of the "building-block" theory just developed will be contained in our exposition of this alternative account. In some ways our alternative resembles Wittgenstein's later critique of his own earlier logical atomism, and in some ways not. In some respects it is deeply indebted to Charles Sanders Peirce and Alfred North Whitehead. For convenience we might call it the "matrix" view. The basic idea is that, for human beings at least, all experience takes place within a given matrix of beliefs, preconceptions, and interpretations, and that while it is true that experience does modify the matrix, it is also true that the matrix provides an indispensable context for interpreting the experience and for assessing its veracity and noetic significance; and it may even modify the very quality of the experience itself. Is it ever possible to build any sort of world view out of pure experience? Is it ever possible to interpret any type of experience without preconceptions? This is essentially the same as the question of whether it is ever possible to interpret any type of experience without a language—and it is obviously impossible, since interpretation is simply a function of language.

Proponents of the "building-block" view are notoriously reluctant to give examples of pure, atomic, self-sufficient, indubitable, self-interpreting reports of experience, and none of the examples they do give seem to hold up under analysis. "I see a red patch here now" contains the tricky word *I*. Is the *I* simply another thing that I see? If so, with what sense organ do I see it? Is not a complicated theory of selfhood being presupposed here? If we eliminate the troublesome personal pronoun and simply report "Red patch, here, now," this also presupposes a very complicated world view in which the distinction between here and there and between now and then (that is, between spaces and between times) has *already* been made. If I simply say "red patch" and point to what I am talking about, this presupposes that I already know a language in which pointing is a meaningful symbol and in which the redness of the indicated "patch" can be differentiated from its shape, size, weight, solidity, and so on. If I insist that experience teaches that there are only three kinds of things, individuals, qualities, and relations, others will claim that I am simply reading the old Aristotelian metaphysics of substance, attribute, and relation *into* my interpretation of experience and not reading it off experience at all. Perhaps there are more or fewer kinds of things in the universe of experience than are dreamed of in my philosophy. Perhaps there are no substances, only events.

Are there any absolute, indubitable simples in the universe? What exactly are the atomic constituents of experience, and what about them cannot be doubted when we insist that they provide us with infallible starting points for the construction of a world view? Is simplicity a characteristic of the world that we read off experience, or is it relative to human purposes? What are the simplest parts of a chair: the rungs, their molecules, their atoms, their sub-atomic constituents, pure formless energy? Does not the answer depend on human teleology, on what we are trying to do with the chair? Far from being free of assumptions and preconceptions, this quest for the simplest, clearest, most distinct atomic con-stituents is really the empiricist's counterpart of the rationalistic quest for intuitively certain truths or axioms that provide infallible starting points for the construction of a world view that is per-meated with certainty. Why are we so unwilling to face the fact that all knowledge, including empirical knowledge, swims in a con-tinuum of uncertainty? If the history of human thought is to be our guide, we can see that anyone who claims to doubt everything away until he reaches the indubitable is making a phony claim. Let us admit all this and get on with the business of discovering the truth. We always approach experience with a ready-made lan-guage and a ready-made set of beliefs, but experience is still the best teacher. Any scientist will agree that the man who has no pre-conceived theories and hypotheses to test is the man who is *least* likely to learn from experience, not *most* likely to do so.

And what about language? Is not interpersonal communication the basic function of language? If so, does not the very existence of language presuppose a world view, a pluralistic world with many persons in it? If it does, many present-day philosophers insist, then solipsism should be refuted by the sheer existence of language. Is our knowledge of this world entirely built up out of sense ex-perience? Can a knowledge of *other minds* be so constructed? Can a knowledge of *our own minds* be so constructed? Is "mem-ory" the name of a sensation, or of a sense object, or of a sense organ? Even if it is not, would we have much of a world view without it? Is "attention" the name of a sense object? How do we distinguish between appearance and reality, between seeming to experience and really experiencing? How do we differentiate between "veridical" experience and "illusions" and "hallucina-tions"? Is not the former an experience of what is real, and are not the latter experiences of something that is unreal? If so, then we cannot tell the difference between the two unless we *already know* (or think we know) what is real and what is unreal. It is not trustworthy experience that gives us our belief that some things are real and some things are unreal; rather, it is a preconception about what is real and what is unreal that tells us what experiences to trust. Even here, however, there is perhaps a criterion. Some experiences are public, capable of being shared by many minds, whereas some are purely private, belonging to only one mind or to a limited number of minds, as in the case of mass hallucinations. Many of us see the elephant in the circus parade, but only one of us sees the pink elephant prancing on the chandelier. There is a test for what is real and what is unreal after all: Objective reality is what can be experienced publicly by many of us, and subjective appearance is what only one or relatively few of us experience. To put the point in terms of the standard empiricist epistemology, veridical experiences are those that we share with other people (under certain repeatable conditions, of course), whereas illusions and hallucinations are experiences that are essentially private and unshared. If this is the case, however, then we can differentiate between those experiences that are reliable and those that are unreliable only by presupposing the existence of other minds, only by presupposing that the human bodies presented to us in sense experience are more than mere mindless appearances, as the solipsist would have them be. We must assume instead that they are capable of having experiences of their own. The empiricist claim that experience is the sole source of knowledge seems to have its own a priori metaphysical presuppositions. Only if other minds really exist can we tell the difference between veridical and nonveridical experiences, between reality and appearance, and the logical impossibility (that is, the circularity) of constructing a knowledge of these other minds out of pure sense experience now becomes apparent: If my experience of the behavior of other human bodies is evidence for the existence of other minds, I can decide that this very experience is not an illusion only by presupposing the existence of other minds. Is this a case of believing in order to understand? Perhaps it is not simply that the existence of God is knowable a priori. The existence of other minds must also be so knowable, or else the empiricist epistemology itself never gets off the ground. Empiricism presupposes metaphysical pluralistic personalism. Unless I trust what other people say about what they experience, I cannot determine that my experience of their physical behavior is not an illusion or hallucination.

In every case, it seems, our beliefs about how we know and what we know are intimately intertwined with and inseparable from many other beliefs. No item of experience ever stands on its own. Any item of experience will be thrown out as an illusion if we find that other people do not share it, but even here there are unanswered questions. *How many* others must be found to share it? What *conditions* must even they satisfy before we regard them as qualified observers? Must they not be "normal" observers? How do we identify normal observers? Is it merely a matter of statistics? If, say, only color-blind people were permitted to have children for several generations, would not their color-blind descendants then be the normal observers? (Is there such a thing as normal religious experience, or is religious experience always an abnormal phenomenon?) At any rate, it is never *experience as such* that is true or false, but rather our verbal interpretation of it, and no such interpretation stands on its own. Every interpretation stands or falls with an entire world view and must be tested in part by its coherence and consistency with our interpretation of other experiences and ultimately with all else that we believe.

There are other difficulties with the building-block theory that we shall mention only briefly. For one thing, even Wittgenstein finally could make no sense of his claim that the logical structure of language must be the same as the logical structure of the world. Does the world have a *logical* structure or some other kind of structure? Again, if we have a purely empiricist language, one in which all words are names of sensed entities and all sentences are descriptions of empirical states of affairs, we would have a very impoverished language in which many of the language games that we want to play could not be played at all. Incidentally, even the humanistic naturalist who claims to be a strict empiricist normally wants to play most of these games. In this purely empiricist language, we could not praise or commend things by calling them *good, beautiful, desirable;* nor could we influence social behavior by speaking of certain kinds of acts as right or wrong; nor could we give one another advice by saying that certain things should or should not be done; nor could we ever express linguistically our disapproval of anything by using such words as *guilty, reprehensible,* and *irresponsible.* There are numerous language games that simply cannot be played in a purely empiricist language. Read Wittgenstein for a fuller discussion of this whole matter.

Now that we have sketched a matrix theory of how sense experience enters into the construction of a "scientific" world view, let us see whether we can develop a parallel account of how religious experience might enter into the construction of a religious world view. In the first place, we would have to realize that even religious experience occurs within a matrix of beliefs, preconceptions, and interpretations and that while the experience might modify the matrix, it is also true that the matrix provides an indispensable context for interpreting the experience and for assessing its veracity and noetic significance; and it may even modify the very quality of the experience itself. Just as it is never possible to build a scientific world view out of pure sense experience, so is it never possible to build a religious world view out of pure religious experience. Even religious experience must be interpreted, and we must bring to its interpretation whatever language and concepts we happen to have at our disposal. Purely artificial languages are never constructed except by those who have first learned to speak a natural language and who make their plans for such projects within a natural language, and it is likely that such plans will to some extent reflect the ordinary metaphysics of ordinary language.

Many interpreters of religious experience, such as F. R. Tennant and A. E. Taylor,[2] approach the problem as matrix theorists. The matrix theorist never professes to make an absolutely new beginning; nor does he profess to build his world view from absolutely certain starting points in either reason or experience; nor does he claim to approach experience without preconceptions; nor does he claim that an ideal language should be constructed out of pure experience; nor does he claim that every word in his language is or ought to be the name of an experienced object; nor does he claim that every sentence in his language is or ought to be the description of an experienced state of affairs. Nevertheless, he does claim to learn from experience in somewhat the same way as the scientist, despite the fact that he approaches experience with a set of preconceived theories and hypotheses to test. The man who is most likely to find God in a religious experience is the man who already has some conception of God and to some extent knows what he is looking for. It is true that there is a danger involved here: the danger that the interpreter of the experience will read his preconceptions into the experience; but that danger is one that the interpreter of religious experience shares with the interpreter of sense experience. If we demand that the interpreter of religious experience approach the experience entirely without preconceptions, we are certainly making more stringent demands of him than we make of our scientists, and this seems unfair. All we can legitimately demand is that he be open to experience, willing to learn from it and to modify his preconceptions in light of it.

When we examine the language in which religious men attempt to verbalize, describe, and interpret their religious experiences, it becomes even more apparent that the language of religious experience is not constructed out of pure religious experience. To some extent it is borrowed from everyday sense experience, as is fairly obvious with such words as *fire* and *light,* which occur frequently in the literature of mysticism. To some extent also the language is borrowed from our everyday encounters with persons on the human plane of existence, as in *love, thou, personal presence,* and so on. We shall soon see, however, that this language is always qualified in such a way as to make it clear that the religious meanings of these terms are not quite the same as their familiar, everyday meanings—because the object to which they refer is no familiar, everyday object.

As is the case with sense experience, religious experience has to face the problem of how to differentiate between veridical experience and hallucinations and illusions; and we shall explore this problem in more detail when we examine some standard criticisms of mysticism and personal encounter. For now, let us simply note that religious experience is like sense experience in that it also must be interpreted. Moreover, as with the interpretation of sense experience, no single interpretation of a single religious experience stands on its own feet. Religious people must compare notes, just as do scientists. There is a community of religious believers just as there is a community of scientific believers. Every interpretation of religious experience must be tested in part by its own internal intelligibility and in part by its coherence and consistency with our interpretations of other religious experiences and finally with all else that we believe. An interpretation of any experience is only as strong as the entire world view within which it is set. For example, if the rationalistic proofs for the existence of God given in Chapters 9, 10, and 11 are egregiously mistaken, the appeal to religious experience will be exceedingly weak evidence for his existence. But if we can make sense of the existence of God without the appeal to uniquely religious experiences, if we can provide a framework of belief in which it makes sense to think of the existence of a supremely good creative intelligence, then it will not be so far-fetched to think of this God as manifesting himself to men in special ways under special conditions of life and experience. We must be able to relate our experience of God to other experiences we might have, such as birth, growth, death, development, and order. Unless mystics can somehow communicate with nonmystics, in terms even the latter can comprehend, a large measure of skepticism about religious experience may be justified. It should be noted, however, that it is possible to conceive of the relationship between the rationalistic proofs and the argument from religious experience in a variety of ways. We may hold that neither is reliable, that the one or the other is reliable, or that both are reliable. Religious skeptics tend to take the first view. The second view is adopted by people like Buber, Brunner, Farmer, and Baillie, who rely on religious experience and discount the rationalistic proofs, and by thinkers like F. R. Tennant, who come close to discounting religious experience altogether in favor of such rationalistic proofs as the teleological argument. Such thinkers provide us with the important reminder that the rational proofs and the appeal to religious experience do not necessarily stand or fall together. The majority of religious believers and thinkers through the ages, however, have adopted the third alternative, holding that rationalist proof and religious experience can and do cooperate in generating and justifying a reliable religious world view.

We shall now look at some of the varieties of religious experience, and we shall discuss the role of language and interpretation in the construction of world views out of religious experience. First we shall look at the experience of mystical union, then we shall consider the experience of personal encounter in Chapter 13, and finally we shall explore in Chapter 14 the possibility of experiential verification after death of theistic belief.

Mystical Language and Mystical Experience

Let us first tentatively define mystical experience as the all-consuming encounter with what is believed to be the all-encompassing reality. Most mystics would find this definition acceptable, but we must realize that it is tentative and subject to further refinement and interpretation. Experiences thus provisionally characterized are to be found in nearly all the cultures and religions of man. Many questions can be asked about mystical experience, questions that are usually muddled, but well worth attempting to clarify. We may distinguish questions about (1) the *experience* as an experience, (2) the *self* that has the experience, (3) the *conditions and consequences* of the experience, (4) the *object* of the experience, and (5) the *vocabulary* to be used in inducing, discussing, and describing this object. What is the experience itself like? What is it like to be a self undergoing such an experience? Under what conditions is it possible to have such an experience? What are the practical consequences of such an experience? What are the characteristics of the experienced object? What vocabulary best expresses and communicates these characteristics?

In his famous fourfold characterization of mystical experience, William James did not carefully distinguish these questions. As you read the following quotation from *The Varieties of Religious Experience,* ask yourself which question is addressed by each of James's remarks:

1. *Ineffability.*—The handiest of the marks by which I classify a state of mind as mystical is negative. The subject of it immediately says that it defies expression, that no adequate report of its contents can be given in words. It follows from this that its quality must be directly experienced; it cannot be imparted or transferred to others. In this peculiarity mystical states are more like states of feeling than like states of intellect. No one can make clear to another who has never had a certain feeling, in what the quality or worth of it consists. One must have musical ears to know the value of a symphony; one must have been in love one's self to understand a lover's state of mind. Lacking the heart or ear, we cannot interpret the musician or the lover justly, and are even

likely to consider him weak-minded or absurd. The mystic finds that most of us accord to his experiences an equally incompetent treatment.

2. *Noetic quality.*—Although so similar to states of feeling, mystical states seem to those who experience them to be also states of knowledge. They are states of insight into depths of truth unplumbed by the discursive intellect. They are illuminations, revelations, full of significance and importance, all inarticulate though they remain; and as a rule they carry with them a curious sense of authority for aftertime.

These two characters will entitle any state to be called mystical, in the sense in which I use the word. Two other qualities are less sharply marked, but are usually found. These are:—

3. *Transiency.*—Mystical states cannot be sustained for long. Except in rare instances, half an hour, or at most an hour or two, seems to be the limit beyond which they fade into the light of common day. Often, when faded, their quality can but imperfectly be reproduced in memory; but when they recur it is recognizable; and from one recurrence to another it is susceptible of continuous development in what is felt as inner richness and importance.

4. *Passivity.*—Although the oncoming of mystical states may be facilitated by preliminary voluntary operations, as by fixing the attention, or going through certain bodily performances, or in other ways which manuals of mysticism prescribe; yet when the characteristic sort of consciousness once has set in, the mystic feels as if his own will were in abeyance, and indeed sometimes as if he were grasped and held by a superior power. This latter peculiarity connects mystical states with certain definite phenomena of secondary or alternative personality, such as prophetic speech, automatic writing, or the mediumistic trance. When these latter conditions are well pronounced, however, there may be no recollection whatever of the phenomenon, and it may have no significance for the subject's usual inner life, to which, as it were, it makes a mere interruption. Mystical states, strictly so-called, are never merely interruptive. Some memory of their content always remains, and a profound sense of their importance. They modify the inner life of the subject between the times of their recurrence. Sharp divisions in this region are, however, difficult to make, and we find all sorts of gradations and mixtures.[3]

THE MYSTICAL EXPERIENCE AS AN EXPERIENCE

As we discuss some of our questions about religious experience, we shall make references to James's characterizations of mysticism. We shall first ask our questions about *the mystical experience as an experience*. When James speaks of the ineffability of the mystical experience, is he talking about the experience itself, the object of the experience, or the lack of adequate vocabulary for verbalizing and interpreting the experience? Perhaps he is doing all three at once. Perhaps he is saying of the experience that there is no other experience like it, no close analogue to be found elsewhere, and of the object of the experience that it too is utterly unique and radically unlike all more familiar objects, and of our vocabulary for characterizing this object that it is woefully inadequate. For now, let us concentrate on the problem of the experience itself. There are many intelligible statements that can be made about experiences. For example, it can be said that they are datable events in the life histories of persons, that they are sources of knowledge, that they can be remembered and discussed, that they are in some sense private. All these things can be said of mystical experiences, though they are not all equally noncontroversial. Although the mystic is not attending to the feature of temporality in the midst of his experience, he nevertheless can date it before certain other events or experiences and after others: He can say when he had the experience. James discusses the "noetic quality" of the experience, by which he means that the experience is (or at least is regarded as) a source of knowledge, a sort of immediate knowledge by acquaintance rather than an inferential or conceptual knowledge by hypothesis or description. Whether or not it is indeed such knowledge rather than mere illusion will depend in part on whether the object of this experience is in some sense public, but we shall reserve that question for later. For now, let us note simply that mystics certainly regard the experience as involving a sort of direct knowledge by acquaintance with some object supremely worth being acquainted with, and that the transiency of the experience must surely be a serious limitation of its noetic significance. Trying to know all about God on the basis of an hour of mystical experience must be akin to trying to know all about the world on the basis of an hour of sense experience. There is also something private about such an experience, both in the sense that the experience is an event in the "stream of consciousness" or the life history of some mystical individual and in the sense that the only way anyone can fully appreciate the experience is to have it. Of course, mystical experience is not at all unique in this respect. It is also truthfully said of sensory experiences that they are events in the life history of some sentient individual. There is a public and a private aspect to all experience. Both you and I may see the table, but I do not see your seeing of the table, and you do not see my seeing of the table. To say that the *experience* is private in this sense is to say nothing more than that it is mine rather than someone else's, or vice versa; and this type of privateness is perfectly compatible with the publicness of the *object* of experience, which is the thing that really matters as far as the noetic significance of the experience is concerned. Furthermore, sensory experience is also private in the sense that the only way one can fully appreciate the experience is to have it. Music, love, and mysticism are alike in this respect, as James indicates. Closely related to this point is the further consideration that only those who have experienced certain objects or qualities can know directly what the experience of them is like. The congenitally blind man cannot know what color qualities are like directly and concretely, and it is also true that the inveterate nonmystic cannot know what the mystical experience is like directly and concretely. However, colored objects can be known in other ways by the blind man. Although he cannot sense the color of the table, he can sense its shape, size, solidity, motion, and so on, and from what others do and say he can infer that they are able to make discriminations that he is unable to make. He can learn from them that snow is white and blood is red, even though he has no direct knowledge by acquaintance with such facts. Can the nonmystic know the object of mystical experience by using some related sense or some other complicated inferential procedure? Perhaps so. Even if he has never experienced mystical rapture, he may have his own counterpart of the feeling of drastic contingency, or the sense of the unconditioned significance of morality, or a Wittgensteinian sense of being "absolutely safe," or something of the sort that may be interpreted religiously. Even if he has no such experiences as these, he may still be reached through the rationalistic proofs discussed in Chapters 9, 10, and 11, assuming that they hold up under criticism.

THE SELF THAT HAS THE MYSTICAL EXPERIENCE

When we turn to questions about *the self that has the mystical experience,* we find that it is extremely difficult to separate such questions from those about the object experienced. Many mystics have visions, and the envisioned objects almost inevitably reflect the cultural background of the mystic. Protestants never envision the Virgin Mary, but Catholics do; Jews never envision the resurrected Jesus, but Christians do (Was St. Paul on the road to Damascus an exception to this?); Buddhists and Hindus envision divine messengers quite different from those encountered by Western mystics. But there is another level of mysticism besides visionary mysticism, one that is common to all the great world religions and that the mystics of every religion prize more highly than visions. At this level of "pure mysticism," as it is often called, there is the experience of ultimate *union* with an ultimate object of religious adoration, a union so complete that the finite self of the mystic is said to be lost altogether while only the ultimate object remains. Mystics speak of this union in many ways: as absorption into God, reconciliation, self-annihilation, "deep calling unto deep," as the psalmist put it, "an absolute one and I that one," as James put it, "Being's consent to Being" as Jonathan Edwards phrased it, "That art thou" as Hindu mystics express it. Innumerable phrases like this occur in the mystical literature of all the great religions, and such expressions seem to be attempts to focus on a common and significant feature of mystical experience that we shall call mystical union.

Now the problem is, what really happens to the self that has the experience of mystical union? How literally are we to interpret the language of passivity, self-loss, and mystical union? We can be sure about one thing: Whatever self-loss may be involved is never permanent. The mystic trance is transient, and the mystic eventually "returns to himself." Subsequently he remembers the mystical experience as an event in his own history. Unless we can remember experiencing things that we never experienced, in some sense it must be true that even while the experience is taking place, it belongs to someone. Certainly there is an element of verbalization and interpretation involved here. Can we interpret such experiences in a way that will do justice both to the elements of passivity and self-loss and to the fact that the experience belongs to the mystic? No doubt the adequacy of our interpretation can be ascertained only by mystics themselves, but let us try all the same.

Whatever else the mystical experience involves, rapt attention is certainly one element. The mystic encounters and passively responds to something that is of all-absorbing fascination to him. We tentatively defined mystical experience as involving "all-consuming encounter," with the mystic's entire attention focused on the experienced object; but it does not follow from this that nothing else exists, especially that the mystic's own "inner life" does not exist. God is not the only experienced object that catches and holds our attention so completely that we effortlessly attend only to it —and do not attend to our attending. A beautiful woman, the tempestuous sea, a magnificent symphony, may do the same. We are absorbed in such an object, and in no sense are we attending to our own feelings about it or to our own ability to attend to anything. Once we begin to analyze our own feelings and mental activity, the spell is broken, the ecstasy is lost. But from the fact that we were not attending to our feelings and thoughts during the moment of absorption, it does not follow that there were no such feelings and thoughts.

Let us draw another analogy. Often the mystical experience is said to be one of "timelessness." Now this is obviously a matter of interpretation, just as is the matter of "self-loss," and in this situation it is easy to muddle two quite distinct points. Not only in mystical rapture but also in more commonplace moments, it is often said that we encounter "timelessness," as for example when we experience such intense, excruciating pain that nothing else is noticed or when we experience so much love for someone that "time stands still." There is an ambiguity in the concept of *timelessness* or *atemporality* that makes it plausible at first glance that these are experiences of "timeless realities." On the one hand *timeless* may mean "not aware of or attending to time," and on the other hand it may mean "not a datable event in time." Mystics, who frequently lack the ability to make relevant discriminations, often move from the one to the other as if they were identical; but this is not the case. Many people have the experience of concentrating so completely on the book they are reading that they are unaware of time and place, but it does not follow that they are in no place and time. Similarly, it does not follow that an experience of excruciating pain or delirious love or mystical rapture is not a datable event in time simply because the experiencer is not paying attention to the temporal features of the experience. (Incidentally, neither does it follow that the experienced *object* is not temporal simply because the experiencer is not paying attention to its temporal features.) It always makes sense, even to the mystic, to ask *when* the experiences occurred. He knows that the experience took place earlier in time than some of his experiences and later than others, even though he is not attending to the temporality of the experience. Similarly, the mystic may be so completely absorbed in the mystic object that he is inattentive to the fact that it is *he* that is so absorbed, but nonexistence does not follow from inattention.

THE CONDITIONS AND CONSEQUENCES OF MYSTICAL EXPERIENCE

Questions about *the conditions and consequences of mystical experience* could easily be treated as questions about the self that has these experiences. Under what conditions can a person expect to have a meeting with the Holy, are these conditions sufficient for generating such a meeting, and what practical effects on his subsequent behavior can this meeting be expected to have?

There is a regimen of mysticism. The conditions in which the mystic must place himself if he hopes to encounter the Holy form an extensive but closely related set of practices. For example, techniques of meditation, concentration, and prayer are involved. In one way or another, these make possible a withdrawal of attention from the mundane details of nature and everyday life and a redirecting of attention toward something that is more than mundane and familiar. Asceticism and the willful suppression of desire also have a prominent place in the regimen of mysticism. Introspection and self-awareness are often cultivated, for the one who would meet the Holy must learn how to redirect his attention from "things visible" to "things invisible." Contemplation of religious themes, myths, and symbols, sometimes with the aid of devotional literature, is often enjoined; for the one who finds the Holy is usually the one who looks for it and who has some notion of what it is he is looking for. The condition of moral sensitivity, receptivity, and activity is usually regarded as vital for religious awareness because although sinners do meet God, it is the pure of heart who live in constant awareness of the presence of the Holy. All the great world religions have their sacraments, rituals, and "means of grace"; and though these have other functions, such as contributing toward moral growth and solidarity with other believers, they also help to provide an occasion for meeting with the Holy. In many religions the use of "mind-expanding" drugs is a regular part of the regimen of mysticism, though they seem to be most successful within the framework of a much broader discipline of meditation, withdrawal, introspection, purity of heart, and moral activity.[4] Much work remains to be done on the psychological, philosophical, and religious significance of these mind-expanding drugs, but at any rate it may be only a Western prejudice that, as Wallace I. Matson put it, "It is somehow unseemly that the secret of the universe should be unveiled via eating mushrooms." [5]

Although some kind of mystical regimen must be followed if religious awareness is to be generated, these conditions do not guarantee the appearance of the Holy. While drug users may hope to find God or Nirvana, they must also realize that they may have nothing more than a bad trip, or at best an uneventful one. The conditions of religious experience never seem to be quite sufficient in and of themselves to make a meeting with the Holy inevitable. As William James pointed out, not only must the mystic be willing to meet the Holy, but also the Holy must be willing to meet the mystic. It is this unpredictable willingness of the Holy to be encountered that makes the mystic feel "as if his own will were in abeyance, and indeed sometimes as if he were grasped and held by a superior power." [6]

The mystical experience usually has far-reaching consequences for the subsequent life and activity of the mystic, despite the relatively brief duration of the ecstasy itself. It generates a new way of looking at things, an enduring new ability to appreciate the significance and the uniqueness of people and things. It produces an enduring optimism arising from a heightened sense of the goodness and abundance of life. The world to which the mystic returns is in a way a new world, one that challenges creativity in many areas of human activity, which is now seen as having enduring cosmic significance. More often than not, the experience is a stimulus to intense moral concern, involvement, and activity. The experience usually has far-reaching practical implications and consequences only when it is set within a total way of life, which is one of the important differences between religious experiences generated by drugs alone and those generated by drugs within a wider milieu of spiritual and moral discipline. Huston Smith tells us that:

> One thing [drugs] may do is throw religious experience itself into perspective by clarifying its relation to the religious life as a whole. Drugs appear able to induce religious experiences; it is less evident that they can produce religious lives. It follows that religion is more than religious experiences. This is hardly news, but it may be a useful reminder, especially to those who incline toward "the religion of religious experiences"; which is to say toward lives bent on the acquisition of desired states of experience irrespective of their relation to life's other demands and components.
> . . . The conclusion to which evidence currently points would seem to be that chemicals *can* aid the religious life, but only where set within a context of faith (meaning by this the conviction that what they disclose is true) and discipline (meaning diligent exercise of the will in the attempt to work out the implications of the disclosures for the living of life in the everyday, common-sense world).
> Nowhere today in Western civilization are these two conditions jointly fulfilled. Churches lack faith in the sense just mentioned; hipsters lack discipline.[7]

In his penetrating *Treatise Concerning Religious Affections,* Jonathan Edwards attached great significance to the fact that there are outer, visible signs of inner, spiritual graces. (Churchmen have known for generations that inner processes stand in need of outward criteria.) Edwards attempted to differentiate between genuine and spurious religious experiences along those lines. Those who have truly encountered God persevere in godliness and righteousness, and those who do not persevere in godliness and righteousness have not truly encountered God. Edwards wrote that "The difference between doves and ravens or doves and vultures, when they first come out of the egg, is not so evident; but as they grow to their perfection, it is exceeding great and manifest." [8] Although there are many marks of religion, the surest of all, the most difficult to counterfeit, is the perseverance of the saints. It is only reasonable that this should be an effective test of authentic religious encounter, Edwards maintains, for "Reason shows, that men's deeds are better and more faithful interpreters of their minds, than their words." [9] "Herein chiefly appears the power of true godliness, viz., in its being effectual in practise." [10] Try to decide for yourself whether this "pragmatic criterion" of authentic religious experience really is adequate. Is it true that "By their fruits you shall know them"?

THE OBJECT AND VOCABULARY OF
MYSTICAL EXPERIENCE

Questions about *the object encountered in the experience* are the ones that are most interesting philosophically. Is there a real object so encountered, or is it all a hallucination? Does the object really have the characteristics it is said to have? Questions about *the language or vocabulary of mystical experience* are closely related to these, so we shall discuss mystical object and mystical language together. Is there a vocabulary that does justice to the mystical experience? Is it drawn from other, more familiar situations? How can we tell whether it is being applied correctly?

When William James wrote of the "ineffability" of the mystical experience, he certainly meant to suggest that the mystic has great difficulty in verbalizing about the experience, partly because of the uniqueness and unfamiliarity of the object experienced and partly because his vocabulary for verbalizing about this unfamiliar realm of experience is impoverished. Mystics have been notoriously reluctant to try to describe for others the contents of their experience; they retreat into silence and mystery when asked to describe the object encountered. Nevertheless, there is fortunately a vast literature of mysticism of extremely diverse cultural origin. Despite their reluctance to do so, mystics have verbalized loquaciously about their ecstasies. In this respect, mystics are like the supernaturalists who insist that God is so great that no words do him justice, but who nonetheless produce volumes of words about him. Part of the problem is simply to find out what, if anything, the mystics really have to say. After all, if something cannot be said, it cannot be true or false nor believed or disbelieved.

Rudolf Otto's Idea of the Holy

There is widespread transcultural agreement among mystics about one feature of the object of mystic rapture, namely, that it is a thing of fascinating mystery and terrifying magnitude—that it is *holy*. In *The Idea of the Holy,* his classic book on the subject, Rudolf Otto used the word *numinous* for this experience of the holy. Of course, when we speak of fascination and terror, we are speaking about the psychological response of the self that has the experience, but mystics insist that it is *the object* of the experience that is holy, that there is something about this object that makes the human psychological responses of awe, fascination, and fear appropriate and unique. The soul is awed, fascinated, terrified because the thing experienced is uniquely awful, fascinating, terrifying. Sometimes the complaint is made that mysticism has no vocabulary of its own, that it must borrow all its concepts from other areas, such as those of sense experience and personal interaction; but this is not quite the case. The concept of holiness is a rather distinctive religious or mystical category. As Otto put it, " 'Holiness'—'the holy'— is a category of interpretation and valuation peculiar to the sphere of religion. It is, indeed, applied by transference to another sphere—that of ethics—but it is not itself derived from this." [11] Of course, there are analogies to be found elsewhere: there is awe to be found in the encounter with the aesthetically sublime, but there is no awe quite like that which is appropriate to the encounter with the *mysterium tremendum et fascinosum;* there is fear and terror to be found elsewhere, but there is no fear quite like the fear of the Lord; there is fascination to be found elsewhere, but none quite like the fascination with the Holy Ultimate.

The notion of holiness as Otto explicates it turns out to be quite complex. He recognizes in it (1) Self-sufficiency, the complement to our "creature feeling," (2) Awefulness, (3) Overpoweringness, (4) Energy, (5) Wholly Other-ness, and (6) the complement to our fascination—Wonderfulness.

In the subject's response to the holy, there is something like what Schleiermacher called the "feeling of absolute dependence," which is more than just a sense of "personal insufficiency and impotence, a consciousness of being determined by circumstances and environment." [12] There is more than this type of "self-knowledge" involved; there is the givenness of an "other" on whom the subject depends heavily. Schleiermacher thought that this other is *inferred* from the subject's feeling of radical contingency, but Otto insisted that this other is *given* as an integral aspect of the experience of the holy. There is not only the subject's feelings but also the object, which complements these feelings and makes them appropriate. The mystical experience is more than feeling: It is a kind of immediate knowledge by acquaintance with a supreme, self-sufficient religious object. To be sure, the feeling is also there, but it is not the only element. Otto wanted to call this feeling creature-consciousness, or creature-feeling; and he defined it as "the emotion of a creature, submerged and overwhelmed by its own nothingness in contrast to that which is supreme above all creatures." [13] Otto's main emphasis, however, was on the holy object and not on the feelings of the mystic subject. (Incidentally, if the mystic subject has feelings and can later discuss and analyze those feelings, what implications does this have for the matter of self-loss, self-absorption?)

The Holy One encountered in the mystical experience is aweful, and this is to say much more than that the mystic himself is full of awe. The experienced *object* is something tremendous, to which the subjective response of awe is most appropriate. In articulating this aspect of the experience, religious experiencers speak of "the Fear of the Lord," "the Wrath of God," and "the jealousy of Yahweh." Religious experience is disturbing as well as comforting, and the psychologizers who regard religion as merely a projection for receiving cosmic comfort never seem to take full account of this.

The Holy One is overpowering, majestic; and it is this attribute that complements and justifies the subject's feeling of radical contingency. As Otto says,

It is especially in relation to this element of majesty or absolute overpoweringness that the creature-consciousness, of which we have already spoken, comes upon the scene, as a sort of shadow or subjective reflection of it. Thus, in contrast to "the overpowering" of which we are conscious as an object over against the self, there is the feeling of one's own submergence, of being but "dust and ashes" and nothingness. And this forms the numinous raw material for the feeling of religious humility.[14]

Interpretations of this aspect of the mystical experience, along lines we have explored in our discussion of supernaturalism, often take the form of regarding God as an omnicausal agent in relation to whom we are pure effect. However, Otto insists that this *is* interpretation, that this is *not* given in the experience itself. The experience itself simply generates "the consciousness of the littleness of every creature in the face of that which is above all creatures." [15]

The Holy One is encountered as "urgency" or "energy," and, as Otto says, this attribute "everywhere clothes itself in symbolical expressions—vitality, passion, emotional temper, will, force, movement, excitement, activity, impetus. These features are typical and recur again and again from the daemonic level up to the idea of the 'living' God." [16] Ask yourself whether the notion of a living God is easier to incorporate into a supernaturalist world view or whether something like panentheism does it more justice. Otto points out that this aspect of energy is often verbalized in terms of "burning love":

In mysticism, this element of "energy" is a very living and vigorous factor, at any rate in the "voluntaristic" mysticism, the mysticism of love, where it is very forcibly seen in that "consuming fire" of love whose burning strength the mystic can hardly bear, but begs that the heat that has scorched him may be mitigated, lest he be himself destroyed by it.[17]

The Holy One is wholly other, but as Otto describes the wholly other, it has nothing to do with Being "outside space," "before time," or "beyond being," though these interpretations may be applied to it. Otherness is mysteriousness, vastness, radical uniqueness, unfamiliarity. Otto tells us that in its full religious sense, the wholly other is "that which is quite beyond the sphere of the usual, the intelligible, and the familiar, which therefore falls quite outside the limits of the 'canny,' and is contrasted with it, filling the mind with blank wonder and atonishment." [18] In this type of religious experience, "we come upon something inherently 'wholly other,' whose kind and character are incommensurable with our own, and before which we therefore recoil in a wonder that strikes us chill and numb." [19] There is something *positive* about the experienced wholly other that the negative notions of "outside space," "before time," and "beyond being" do not fully capture and communicate.

> These terms "supernatural" and "transcendent" give the appearance of positive attributes, and, as applied to the mysterious, they appear to divest the *mysterium* of its originally negative meaning and to turn it into an affirmation. On the side of conceptual thought this is nothing more than appearance, for it is obvious that the two terms in question are merely negative and exclusive attributes with reference to "nature" and the world or cosmos respectively. But on the side of the feeling-content it is otherwise; that *is* in very truth positive in the highest degree, though here too, as before, it cannot be rendered explicit in conceptual terms. It is through this positive feeling-content that the concepts of the "transcendent" and "supernatural" become forthwith designations for a unique "wholly other" reality and quality, something of whose special character we can *feel,* without being able to give it clear conceptual expression.[20]

The Holy One complements our feeling of fascination. In and of itself the Holy One is wonderful, supremely worthy of our rapt attention and fascination, deserving of our ultimate commitment and concern, and perhaps even fully justified in demanding that we respond to it in love with all our heart, soul, mind, and strength. In the Holy One there is ultimate bliss and beatitude, and in the beatific vision there is salvation. Consider these comments of Otto's:

> The ideals and concepts which are the parallels or "schemata" on the rational side of this non-rational element of "fascination" are love, mercy, pity, comfort; these are all "natural" elements of the

common psychical life, only they are here thought as absolute and in completeness.

· · ·

Widely various as these states are in themselves, yet they have this element in common, that in them the *mysterium* is experienced in its essential, positive, and specific character, as something that bestows upon man a beatitude beyond compare, but one whose real nature he can neither proclaim in speech nor conceive in thought, but may know only by a direct and living experience. It is a bliss which embraces all those blessings that are indicated or suggested in positive fashion by any "doctrine of salvation," and it quickens all of them through and through; but these do not exhaust it. Rather by its all-pervading, penetrating glow it makes of these very blessings more than the intellect can conceive in them or affirm of them. It gives the peace that passes understanding, and of which the tongue can only stammer brokenly. Only from afar, by metaphors and analogies, do we come to apprehend what it is in itself, and even so our notion is but inadequate and confused.

· · ·

. . . the rapture of Nirvana . . . is only in appearance a cold and negative state. It is only conceptually that "Nirvana" is a negation; it is felt in consciousness as in the strongest degree positive, it exercises a "fascination" by which its votaries are as much carried away as are the Hindu or the Christian by the corresponding objects of their worship. I recall vividly a conversation I had with a Buddhist monk. He had been putting before me methodically and pertinaciously the arguments for the Buddhist "theology of negation," the doctrine of Anatman and "entire emptiness." When he had made an end, I asked him what then Nirvana itself is; and after a long pause came at last the single answer, low and restrained: "Bliss—unspeakable." And the hushed restraint of that answer, the solemnity of his voice, demeanour, and gesture, made more clear what was meant than the words themselves.[21]

It would be foolhardy to suggest that *all* myth is generated by mystical experience, but this is no doubt one significant stimulus to myth-making. To the extent that this is so, it is small wonder that religious language is in some sense analogical, metaphorical, or symbolic if it has its empirical ground in religious experience. Although mystics might have tried to create a pure "technical" language of mysticism, they have for the most part failed to do so, choosing instead either to remain silent or to borrow words and expressions that have more familiar and commonplace uses and referents. It is also small wonder that primitive men gave a mythological expression to this experience and that diverse myths reflect the cultural background of the experiencer and are expressed in whatever language he finds available and relevant. We might still inquire, however, what the "literal truth" is in all these analogies, metaphors, and myths. This question cannot be answered piecemeal, but only by developing a thoroughly rationalized world view and by showing how various myths, metaphors, and symbols can be located within this framework. The adequacy of any interpretation depends on the overall adequacy of the world view within which it is set. Although to interpret a myth is to give it a position within a larger conceptual scheme, there may be an "ethics" of interpretation that requires that the intention of the individual or group that generated the myth be discovered and preserved as far as possible and that the myth be allowed to speak for itself as far as possible, in something like the way a work of art is allowed to speak for itself. Not all myths or symbols will be found to be equally appealing and useful to all worshipers. Selection is inevitable, and the selection depends heavily on what best speaks to the religious condition, intuitions, and overall conceptual scheme of the worshiper or the worshiping community. In the final analysis, however, religious symbols stand or fall in accord with the conceptual adequacy of the broad map onto which they are plotted.

Although he often approaches the experience of the Holy as a matrix theorist, there is one interesting comment in which Otto expresses himself as a building-block theorist. He writes that "All this teaches us the independence of the positive content of this experience from the implications of its overt conceptual expression, and how it can be firmly grasped, thoroughly understood, and profoundly appreciated, purely in, with, and from the feeling itself." [22] The main problem here is with the word *understood*. How can anything be understood apart from any conceptual expression? What do you think Otto meant by *understood* in this context?

Criticisms of Mysticism

When we turn to criticism of mystical experience, we find that the foremost accusation leveled at the mystics is that mystical experiences are private, like hallucinations, illusions, and dreams, and that like these "nonveridical" experiences, religious experience is really of no noetic significance at all. Certainly mysticism has to face the problem of how to differentiate between veridical experience and nonveridical experience. The problem of separating appearance from reality is particularly acute here. The naturalistic critic usually admits that mystics have unique and impressive experiences, but he doubts that what they undergo is of any noetic significance because mystical experiences belong to the same general class of experiences as illusions, hallucinations, and dreams— that is, the religious experiencer never *really* experiences anything, but only *seems* to do so. The objects that he encounters are only apparitions, not realities. The naturalist may develop his basic objection in several different ways. He may first insist that mystical experiences are nonveridical because their object is unreal, just as is the case with illusions, hallucinations, and dreams. The mystic only seems to encounter the Holy One, but he does not really do so, for the simple reason that the Holy One is unreal. There is no such thing as the Holy One any more than there are such things as ghosts and gremlins. Of course, putting the objection this way is begging the question, for it presupposes the unreality of the object of religious experience, whereas the reality or unreality of the Holy One is precisely the question at hand, not the answer to that question. There is a second way of putting the matter, however, that is much more to the point and not as obviously question-begging. The naturalist may claim that his reason for classifying religious experiences with illusions, hallucinations, and dreams is that they are essentially private, whereas veridical experiences are public. Experience that we can rely on in our attempt to know the world must be capable of being shared, at least by normal qualified observers. There is one danger that we must guard against in stating this criticism, a danger that the critics themselves are not always careful to avoid: that of confusing the claim that the experience is private with the quite different claim that the object of the experience is private. It is to be suspected that the objection draws much of its strength from just such an equivocation on "the privacy of the experience." Certainly mystical experiences are private, inner events within the mystic's "stream of consciousness," and the mystic has a unique emotional involvement with these events; but it must be recognized that sense experiences are also private in exactly the same way. You may see my sense objects, but you do not see my sensations. Even I do not in any literal sense see my sensations, though I unquestionably do have them. This type of privateness is no more invalidating for mystical experience than it is for any other kind of experience. The real question is whether or not the *object* of the mystical experience is private, and we shall now turn to this issue.

It is really quite difficult to know what the distinction between private and public objects finally comes to. What does it mean to say that an experienced object is public? On the one hand, it might mean that it is an object encountered in normal sense experience, and the further claim that only public objects are real would mean in this case that only objects given in normal sense experience are real. Again this way of putting the matter is question-begging as well as false. The question is whether there are more ways than one to experience reality, and it is not answered by saying without further reasons that there are no more ways than one *because* there is only one way. Furthermore, it is simply wrong to say that there is only one way of experiencing reality. We do not experience having a headache, a toothache, a thought, a memory, anxiety, or jealousy by making use of the "five external senses," despite all the attempts of psychological and linguistic behaviorists to demonstrate that we do.

On the other hand, the claim that an experienced object is public might mean that it is or could be experienced by most qualified observers under specifiable conditions, but even here there are problems. Certainly this presupposes the metaphysical pluralism of persons, which we discussed earlier, but the religious experiencer is seldom interested in quarreling with that presupposition. The problem is, who is to be regarded as a qualified observer? Perhaps there are qualified observers of religious experience. If a qualified observer must be one who approaches experience without preconceptions, then there are no qualified observers of anything anywhere. If a qualified observer is one who sees what most other qualified observers see, then we cannot identify him until we have identified most other qualified observers —that is, until we have said what qualifies them. If qualified observers are those who experience what *many* others experience, then there is the problem of *how* many, for there are such things as mass illusions. If normality is entirely a matter of numbers, then in a world of color-blind men the man who could see colors would be seeing illusions, and it is incorrect to say that color-blind men in such a world would still be abnormal. Even if normality is not a matter of numbers, there is still the danger of writing an entire world view into the very concept of normality. Suppose that a tendency toward mysticism were an inheritable trait, and that only mystics were permitted to have children for a number of generations, so that eventually humanity became a mass community of religious mystics. Would religious experience then be the normal thing for all qualified observers? If being a qualified observer is a matter of having predictable experiences under specifiable conditions, then there is a very close parallel here between religious experience and sense experience. This really seems to be the crux of the matter. In order to see the real shape of an object, the observer must look at it while his organs of vision are "normal": in certain conditions of favorable lighting, from a certain angle of vision, and so on. Before we can see, we must be in a position to see. Similarly, religious believers have insisted that before we can experience things of ultimate religious interest, certain conditions must be met: Techniques of meditation and detachment must be followed, purity of heart must be cultivated, and so on. The Western religions may have a great deal to learn from the Eastern religions about techniques of meditation and detachment, and they may have a great deal to learn from each other about purity of heart.

With respect to having predictable experiences under specifiable conditions, the experience of the Holy seems to be very much *unlike* dreams and hallucinations. Extremely large numbers of people from extremely diverse cultural backgrounds claim to experience the Holy One, and there is a significant amount of transcultural agreement about what these experiences are like and perhaps even about what the experienced object is like. This is not the case with the objects of hallucinations—most hallucinators do not see pink elephants—or of dreams—most dreamers are not embraced by Aphrodite. *Pink elephant* is simply a convenient symbolic abbreviation for the immense variety of weird entities encountered by people having hallucinations, especially alcoholics suffering from *delirium tremens*. The *mysterium tremendum et fascinosum* is weird, no doubt, but it is also an object of transcultural availability to mystics of every historical era and every cultural and geographical milieu who meet specifiable conditions.

The transcultural availability of the Holy is a moot point, of course. Another standard objection to mysticism is that the Holy always seems to assume a localized form—so much so, in fact, that if it proves anything at all, it proves the existence of *all* the gods of all human times and places. It is unquestionable that mystics draw extensively upon their cultural milieu in expressing, interpreting, and communicating their experiences. Local gods, local myths, local vocabularies, have always been involved. Certainly the mystic does not approach his encounter with the Holy without preconceptions, and these preconceptions are inevitably drawn from his own culture. As John Dewey put the objection, "Interpretations of the experience have not grown from the experience itself with the aid of such scientific resources as may be available. They have been imported by borrowing without criticism from the ideas that are current in the surrounding culture." [23] The real question here is whether the point of "borrowing without criticism" is well taken. If it is, then everything the mystic tells us is simply read into the experience, and nothing is read off it. The mystic is never even in part open to the experience and willing to learn from it. Whether this is so or not can be determined only through an intensive comparison of the literature of mysticism with the cultural milieu of each mystic. Such a comparison will doubtless show that the mystic is deeply indebted to his culture, but will it show that he owes *everything* to his culture and *nothing* to his experience? This is very doubtful. Many mystics have emerged from their encounter with the Holy as moral and theological reformers, not as "me-too men." Somehow a vision of better and truer things is generated within the experience, and the power to translate this vision into action and speech is consequent on the experience. Most Western mystics have been brought up in the theological milieu of supernaturalism, but they have not totally written supernaturalism into their view of God. Where the supernaturalists stress the discontinuity of God, world, and man, the mystics emphasize their continuity. Most of them have insisted that the relation between man and God is much more intimate than supernaturalism allows, and they have envisioned a much tighter unity between God and the world than supernaturalism has ever wished to admit. It does not seem to be the case that the mystic's theological preconceptions are totally read into the encounter with the Holy and never modified in light of this encounter. Henri Bergson put the matter nicely in insisting that in some sense the two are mutually influential, which leaves open the possibility of theological growth and development, a possibility that humanity may not yet have exhausted. Of the mystic, Bergson wrote:

> His theology will generally conform to that of the theologians. His intelligence and his imagination will use the teachings of the theologians to express in words what he experiences, and in material images what he sees spiritually. And this he can do easily, since theology has tapped that very current whose source is the mystical. Thus his mysticism is served by religion, against the day when religion becomes enriched by his mysticism. This explains the primary mission which he feels to be entrusted to him, that of an intensifier of religious faith. He takes the most crying needs first. In reality, the task of the great mystic is to effect a radical transformation of humanity by setting an example. The object could be attained only if there existed in the end what should theoretically have existed in the beginning, a divine humanity.
>
> So then mysticism and religion are mutually cause and effect, and continue to interact on one another indefinitely.[24]

Thus, despite all the criticism, the possibility remains that a holy object, and not simply a holy apparition, is given in mystical experience. Let us turn in Chapter 13 to the question of whether something more than sheer holiness is given in mystical experience, of whether the holy one is also a Divine Thou.

Suggestions for Further Reading

ANTHOLOGIES OF THE LITERATURE OF MYSTICISM AND
RELIGIOUS EXPERIENCE

FREEMANTLE, ANNE, ed., *The Protestant Mystics* (Boston, Little, Brown, 1964).

HAPPOLD, F. D., *Mysticism, a Study and an Anthology* (Baltimore, Penguin, 1963), pp. 125–371.

JAMES, JOSEPH, *The Way of Mysticism, an Anthology* (London, Jonathan Cape, 1950).

KEPLER, THOMAS S., ed., *The Fellowship of the Saints* (New York, Abingdon Press, 1958).

O'BRIEN, ELMER, *Varieties of Mystical Experience* (New York, New American Library, 1964).

EARLIER DISCUSSIONS OF MYSTICISM AND RELIGIOUS EXPERIENCE

BERGSON, HENRI, *The Two Sources of Morality and Religion,* trans. by R. Ashley Audra and Cloudesley Brereton, with the assistance of Horsfall Carter (Garden City, N.Y., Doubleday, 1954), Chapter 3.

BROAD, C. D., *Religion, Philosophy and Psychical Research* (London, Routledge & Kegan Paul, 1953), pp. 168–69 and 197–201.

CLARK, WALTER H., *The Psychology of Religion* (New York, Macmillan, 1958), Chapter 12.

EDWARDS, JONATHAN, *Religious Affections,* ed. by J. E. Smith (New Haven, Conn., Yale University Press, 1959).

JAMES, WILLIAM, *The Varieties of Religious Experience* (New York, Modern Library, n.d.).

OTTO, RUDOLF, *Mysticism, East and West* (New York, Macmillan, 1932).

———, *The Idea of the Holy* (New York, Oxford University Press, 1958).

TAYLOR, A. E., "The Vindication of Religion," reprinted in *Essays Catholic and Critical,* ed. by E. G. Selwyn (New York, Macmillan, 1926), pp. 70–80.

TENNANT, F. R., *Philosophical Theology,* Vol. I (Cambridge, Eng., Cambridge University Press, 1956), Chapter 12.

Trueblood, David E., *Philosophy of Religion* (New York, Harper & Row, 1957), Chapter 11.

Underhill, Evelyn, *Mysticism* (New York, E. P. Dutton, 1948).

RECENT DISCUSSIONS OF RELIGIOUS EXPERIENCE AND
RELIGIOUS LANGUAGE

Cobb, John B., *A Christian Natural Theology* (Philadelphia, Westminster Press, 1965). Pages 225–46 of this book present a panentheistic perspective on religious experience.

Flew, Antony, *God and Philosophy* (New York, Dell, 1966), Chapter 6.

————, and MacIntyre, Alasdair, eds., *New Essays in Philosophical Theology* (New York, Macmillan, 1955), especially Chapters 5, 7, and 14.

Lewis, H. D., *Our Experience of God* (New York, Macmillan, 1959).

Martin, C. B., *Religious Belief* (Ithaca, N.Y., Cornell University Press, 1959), Chapter 5.

Matson, Wallace I., *The Existence of God* (Ithaca, N.Y., Cornell University Press, 1965), Part I.

Organ, Troy, "The Language of Mysticism," *The Monist,* Vol. XLVII (Spring 1963), pp. 417–43.

Smith, Huston, "Do Drugs Have Religious Import?" *The Journal of Philosophy,* Vol. LXI, No. 18 (October 1, 1964), pp. 517–30.

Stace, W. T., *Mysticism and Philosophy* (Philadelphia, J. B. Lippincott, 1960).

Notes

1 See the Suggestions for Further Reading at the end of Chapter 13, p. 342.

2 See the Suggestions for Further Reading at the end of this chapter.

3 William James, *The Varieties of Religious Experience* (New York, Modern Library, n.d.), pp. 371–72. Copyright 1902 by Longmans, Green and Company. Reprinted by permission of David McKay Company, Inc.

4 For an excellent review of the world religions that use drugs regularly in the regimen of mysticism, see Huston Smith, "Do

Drugs Have Religious Import?" *The Journal of Philosophy,* Vol.
LXI, No. 18 (October 1, 1964), pp. 518–19.

5   Wallace I. Matson, *The Existence of God* (Ithaca, N.Y., Cornell
University Press, 1965), p. 24. Used by permission of Cornell
University Press.

6   James, *The Varieties of Religious Experience,* p. 372.

7   Smith, "Do Drugs Have Religious Import?" pp. 528–30.

8   Jonathan Edwards, *The Works of President Edwards,* Vol. III
(New York, Leavitt, 1849), p. 64.

9   *Ibid.,* p. 195.

10 *Ibid.,* p. 186.

11 Rudolf Otto, *The Idea of the Holy* (New York, Oxford University
Press, 1958), p. 5.

12 *Ibid.,* p. 9.

13 *Ibid.,* p. 10.

14 *Ibid.,* p. 20.

15 *Ibid.,* p. 22.

16 *Ibid.,* p. 23.

17 *Ibid.,* p. 24.

18 *Ibid.,* p. 26.

19 *Ibid.,* p. 28.

20 *Ibid.,* p. 30.

21 *Ibid.,* pp. 31, 33–34, 38–39.

22 *Ibid.,* p. 34.

23 John Dewey, *A Common Faith* (New Haven, Conn., Yale University Press, 1934), p. 36.

24 Henri Bergson, *The Two Sources of Morality and Religion,* trans.
by R. Ashley Audra and Cloudesley Brereton, with the assistance
of Horsfall Carter (Garden City, N.Y., Doubleday, 1954), p. 239.
Reprinted by permission of Holt, Rinehart and Winston, Inc.

chapter thirteen

Religious Language and Experience PERSONAL ENCOUNTER

Rudolf Otto concluded his discussion of the elements of the Holy One that are given in religious experience on a somewhat controversial note. The Holy One is not merely a nonpersonal or impersonal It, he insisted; rather, it is an intensely personal Thou. As Otto expressed it, the Holy One is a subject in and of himself; but in saying this, he was making a claim to which not all mystics would readily assent. Frequently the mystic seems to encounter the Holy as an all-encompassing It, but not as a personal Thou. Nevertheless, Otto insisted, the Holy is a Thou all the same:

> And so we maintain on the one hand, following the *via eminentiae et causalitatis,* that the divine is indeed the highest, strongest, best, loveliest, and dearest that man can think of; but we assert on the other, following the *via negationis,* that God is not *merely* the ground and superlative of all that can be thought; He is in Himself a subject on His own account and in Himself.[1]

Pluralistic and Monistic Mysticism

Does religious experience show that the Holy One is also a divine person, that the Holy is a Thou and not merely an It? There are really two quite distinct forms of mysticism, one giving a negative answer and the other an affirmative; let us call the first type monistic mysticism and the second type pluralistic mysticism. Each of these types of mysticism seems to generate its own distinctive type of religious world view. For the monistic mystic, the Holy is an all-encompassing It. For the pluralistic mystic, the Holy is also an all-embracing Thou. Two characteristics distinguish monistic and pluralistic mysticism, one having to do with the subject of the experience and one having to do with the object of the experience. It is the monistic mystic who insists most emphatically on the doctrine of self-loss, self-absorption, self-annihilation. For him, the finite self of the mystical experiencer is lost *into* something that is itself not a self. At the climax of the mystical experience, all the finite characteristics of the mystic are said to be lost, and the soul becomes identical with its nonpersonal object—fire consumes fire, being embraces being. By contrast, the pluralistic mystic always retains some sense of self-identity and describes the mystical encounter as one of *communion* with a personal Thou rather than *absorption* into a nonpersonal It. The finite self is transformed, freed, expanded, ennobled, but retains some measure of its identity and unity. The soul of the pluralistic mystic becomes similar to but not identical with its object.

This division between pluralistic and monistic mystics is also a transcultural division. It is not true that most Eastern mystics are monistic and most Western mystics are pluralistic. There are significant numbers of each type of mystic in all cultures. We should also note that there are many degrees of mystical experience, ranging from the ecstatic rapture of the true mystic to the vague, ill-defined sense of the Holy, the feeling that "someone is up there," that is commonplace among even the most mundane of religious worshipers. There is some philosophical significance to the distinction between monistic and pluralistic mysticism. Is the Holy also a Thou, or not? The monistic mystic may insist that the pluralist is simply reading something into the encounter with the Holy that really is not there, whereas the pluralist may insist that the monist simply fails to pay attention to all that really is there, that the lack of Thouness does not follow from the failure to notice it. After all, we cannot reasonably expect to learn everything there is to know about God from one or two mystical encounters with him any more than we can expect to learn everything there is to know about another human person just by glancing at him once or twice. Some mystics may be more perceptive than others, more attentive to features that others might easily ignore. Monistic and pluralistic mysticism might not be mutually exclusive alternatives after all. Rudolf Otto certainly thought they were not, maintaining that the personal and impersonal forms of religious experience "are not different forms of religion, still less different stages in religion, the one higher and better than the other, but the two essentially united poles of a single fundamental mental attitude, the religious attitude." [2] The monistic mystic may be quite correct in speaking of the Holy in impersonal terms, such as *being, light, power, heat, fire,* and *energy,* and the pluralistic mystic may be quite correct in adding that the Holy is also *love, will, wrath,* and *compassion.* Each type of mystic uses a borrowed language that must be qualified somehow before it can do justice to its referent, and the languages are incompatible only when supplemented by the thesis that one or the other tells the whole story. Impersonal mysticism borrows its language from things, and personal mysticism borrows its language from persons, and we may make some progress by asking how we know and talk about persons.

Knowing Persons or Minds: I and Thou

How do we know *other* persons? In the realm of human intercourse there are interesting parallels with monistic and pluralistic mysticism. The behaviorist is like the monistic mystic in that he sees every other person as an "it" and not as a "thou." Other people are simply bodies having certain gross observable properties and relations and more refined physical and chemical properties and relations. Furthermore, they are *nothing more* than this. They are all bodily exterior with no personal interior. The meanings of all words that seem to refer to interior personal attributes can be reduced to external properties that others can observe using only their five external senses. *Thinking* is merely talking silently to oneself; *pain* means nothing more than observable "pain behavior"—crying, grimacing, or the like; *love* is nothing more than the observable ritual of amorous courtship; *anger* is nothing more than observable ranting, teeth-grinding, foot-stamping, fist-clenching, and so on. Not only does the behaviorist regard every other person as an "it," but he identifies himself as an "it." Patterns of explanation that are appropriate in dealing with things are also perfectly appropriate in dealing with persons, the behaviorist himself included. Just as the behavior of billiard balls can be explained perfectly adequately in terms of what is done to them by cue sticks and other billiard balls and in terms of some elementary laws of physics, so also the behavior of persons can be explained perfectly adequately in terms of heredity, environment, and biochemistry. The story of human events is simply the same as the story of things, for human beings are things, dust of the earth indeed. We cannot say, "That are thou," for the simple reason that nothing is really a "thou"; we can only say, "That is that." At some point the behavioristic picture of the person may be complicated by sociological considerations, and men may identify themselves in terms of their social roles. Besides being dust of the earth, a man may also be a carpenter, a father, a lover, a stamp collector, a baseball star, a military hero, and so on. We are still within the realm of the perceptible, for, given an appropriate set of definitions of social roles, we can observe the long-range behavior of a man to see if he plays the roles. If we go no further than this, a person is still an "it," and not a "thou."

The solipsist is very close to the behaviorist in his view of *other* minds, though not necessarily in his view of himself. He may be a person, but other people are never more than things, mere perceptual apparitions. He insists that there is nothing more to them than what is given *to him* in his own perceptions of their bodily structure and behavior. Despite the repeated insistence by more orthodox empiricists that he cannot do so, the solipsist *can* distinguish between normal perceptual objects and dreams or hallucinations without relinquishing the privateness of either, though not in the way usually preferred by less skeptical empiricists. The solipsist can hold that normal perceptual objects are those that his people-like apparitions *claim* to be able to perceive commonly among themselves, whereas they do not claim to be able so to perceive dreams and hallucinations, and the claim is itself only one apparition among others. The less skeptical empiricist wants to go one step further and say that normal perceptual objects are those that other people *really do* perceive commonly among themselves, but the solipsist insists that there is no warrant for making this assertion since I do not perceive their perceiving and since their bodily behavior, including their verbal behavior, is simply another set of perceptual objects, alongside tables, chairs, and baseballs. Another person is simply an "it," simply a set of "sense data" and nothing more. Where do these sense data come from? They are either of "unknown origin," in Hume's phrase, or perhaps of no origin at all if the solipsist applies consistently the Kantian dictum that causal language applies only *within* the realm of appearances.

By contrast, there is another way of thinking about persons that closely parallels pluralistic mysticism, which for convenience we shall call an existentialist view. This existentialist view does see another person as a "thou" and not merely as an "it." There is more to a human being than bodily exterior, biochemical interior, and social role. Although the meaning reference of many of our "person" words may include external properties and patterns of behavior that others may observe using only the "five external senses," this is by no means the whole story. A person is not merely an empty shell. Thinking is more than talking silently to onself; it is the creative manipulation of verbal symbols, and it may take place in private as well as in public. Pain is more than observable pain behavior; it is an inner and in some sense private feeling. Love is more than the ritual of amorous courtship; it is an awareness of the infinite significance of the loved one. Anger is more than external ranting; it is an inner heat and darkness as well. The logic of "person" words is different from the logic of "thing" words; underlying this language is an assumption of the presence of an unseen "I" and an unseen "thou," in the absence of which only behaviorism or solipsism remains. There is an existential story for every person, as well as a sociological and biochemical story. I am not simply the sum total of my social roles; it is I who choose and define these roles, not the roles that define me. My choice, my will to believe, may at some point enter into the construction of a world view, but it enters long before I come to the question of the Divine Thou. Unless I choose to differentiate between normal experience and dreams or hallucinations in the solipsistic way, I must assume that other human bodies really are "thou's" with experiences of their own, even though their sensations are not, and never can be, my sensations. Without such an a priori assumption, I cannot ascertain that my own perceptual experience of their bodily structure and behavior is more than mere private appearance; I must trust that they too are perceivers, that they perceive their own bodies in something like the way I do, and that they usually report truthfully what they perceive, using a public language; only then can I determine that even normal perceptual objects have a public as well as a private side. Language, too, can be private, despite Wittgenstein's insistence to the contrary. I can hold that my people-like apparitions have language rules or habits that I usually choose to follow without conceding that these apparitions are also realities. And if my private memory about using these rules correctly is completely untrustworthy, then the situation is not improved one whit by multiplying bad memories through hypostatizing a "public." The result of multiplying untrustworthy memories is simply a lot of untrustworthy memories. Besides, it is really *my* trustworthy memory that ascertains that *they* are following the same rules today that they followed yesterday.

Perhaps there is an element of disclosure or insight in interpersonal communication that makes solipsism untenable. There seem to be magic moments in which we suddenly realize intuitively that the human "thou" is really there, over against us; but there is no definitive way of ruling out the possibility that such disclosures are merely private psychological quirks with no noetic significance. The look from the other side of the room, the recognition of a long-lost friend, the touch of a lover's hand, the laughter of a child, the verbally expressed demand of another will on my will—all may be occasions for existential insight into the presence of a human "thou"; but solipsistic skepticism may distrust such disclosures all the same. Similarly, the mystical experience of the Holy may provide an occasion for a disclosure of the Divine Thou, of One who is a supreme moral will and love over against me. The insight may be mistrusted. We may be religious solipsists, aware only of an It, mistrustful that the It is also a Thou. On the hypothesis that other human beings are also "thou's," we may develop not only a world view that makes a place for communication and deep existential relations between human persons but also for the standard empiricist's epistemology, which must have the other as a "thou" to effect its distinction between veridical sense experience and hallucination. Are the concessions worth the price of accepting an a priori hypothesis? Similarly, on the hypothesis that the Holy is also a Thou, if that concession is worth the price, we may develop not only a religious world view that makes a place for deep existential relations between men and God but also for a religious epistemology, which must have the Other as a Thou to effect its distinction between veridical religious experience and hallucinations. Religious thinkers insist that there is *self*-disclosure in the encounter with the Holy, that there is in the experience an insight that a moral, loving, intelligent will is over against us and making demands on us, that this will is not entirely at our disposal but chooses to present itself to us in the fullness of time, that we do not entirely choose it but instead it chooses us. Of course, the insight may be mistrusted, in which case something like a naturalistic or solipsistic world view may be generated, depending on which additional insights we choose to mistrust. But if the insight is trusted, a much richer world view is generated, one that religious people find infinitely more interesting, satisfying, and meaningful.

What is a "thou"? Martin Buber seems to have identified being a "thou" with being a Kantian pure noumenal ego, a subject that has experiences of spatiotemporal objects but that is itself somehow "beyond" all space and time and is ultimately identical with all other such transcendental subjects. It is not necessary to espouse such a dubious Kantian metaphysical doctrine in order to give sense to "thouness," however. In attributing to God intelligence, purpose, compassionate feeling, moral integrity, and so on, theologians have usually focused on a more intelligible sense of "thouness." The question of whether God is a person may be interpreted as a question of whether God is uniquely intelligent, sentient, purposeful, compassionate, suffering, morally trustworthy, and so on. And the question of how we know that the Holy is a person is in some sense like the question of how we know that a human being is uniquely intelligent, sentient, purposeful, compassionate, suffering, morally trustworthy, and so on. We may ask and, hopefully, answer such questions without assuming that a human being is beyond all time, for it seems that particular instances of thinking, sensing, choosing, purposing, loving, suffering, and acting rightly are datable events in time. It is not as clear that such events are not somehow nonspatial, though this is a problem that further inquiry into the philosophy of mind may help us to resolve. There does seem to be some inappropriateness in wondering about the size, shape, weight, position, velocity, and so on, of my reasoning from premises to conclusions, or of my act of choice, or of my wanting to be a philosopher, or of my love for my wife and children, or of my resolution to do what is morally right. We need not resolve this difficulty here, however, for our main interest at the moment is in the question of how we know that persons think, feel, choose, purpose, love, suffer, and act from moral principles, not in the question of whether such admittedly temporal occurrences are also in some sense spatial. Being beyond the visible need not be exactly the same as being entirely beyond the spatiotemporal. (From a Whiteheadian point of view, the vital point is that "I" and "thou" not be beyond *time*.)

There are at least four ways in which it has been claimed we can have a knowledge of *human* persons as persons that is grounded in experience. We shall briefly explore these four ways and then see whether they shed any light on the problem of the knowability of the Divine Person. Let us call them knowledge by immediate acquaintance, knowledge by analogical inference, knowledge by criteria, and knowledge by postulate and intuitive sense of presence.

KNOWLEDGE BY IMMEDIATE ACQUAINTANCE

Knowledge by immediate acquaintance was called reflective experience by such traditional empiricists as Locke, Berkeley, and Hume, and in more recent years it has been called introspective experience. Although there are those who deny that there is any such thing, it seems fairly obvious to most of us who are not possessed by the picture of man as a ghostless machine that we can attend directly to and are somehow immediately acquainted with our own thought processes and activities, our own choices between alternatives open to us, our own feelings of repulsion, attraction, love, sympathy, anxiety, frustration, grief, pain, and so on. We can apparently learn some things about ourselves in a different way from the way we learn these things about other people. I can feel my own grief or pain directly, whereas you cannot feel my grief or pain directly. If you know that I am in pain, your knowledge must be some sort of knowledge by analogical inference, by criteria, or by postulate. My body and its behavior, including its verbal behavior, is directly presented to you in sense experience, but not my sensing, thinking, feeling, choosing, and so on. If you know that I do sense, think, feel, and choose, it cannot be in quite the same way in which I know these things about myself.

KNOWLEDGE BY ANALOGICAL INFERENCE

Knowledge of persons by analogical inference has been defended by many respectable empiricists, such as John Stuart Mill. According to this position, I am able to correlate my own "internal" personal states and activities with certain bodily states and activities; and although I can experience only your bodily states and activities, I am able to infer the presence of the correlated inner personal events. Knowledge by analogical inference is based on *experienced* correlations of personal events and bodily behavior. Solipsism is only one step away, however, for the argument from analogy becomes weaker and weaker as my experience of the bodily states and behavior of more and more human beings increases. If A is known to be correlated with B in only one instance, the correlation becomes less and less probable as more B's not known to be correlated with A's are encountered. The solipsist simply holds that since A (inner personal events) is known to be correlated with B (sensed bodily behavior) in only one instance, there are no logical grounds for believing that this correlation ever holds in other cases. There is much sense experience of bodily behavior, to be sure, but in the case of other people's bodies there is no good reason to believe that this sense experience gives us access to inner personal realities. Since the argument from analogy does not really work in the case of other human minds, it is not surprising that it does not work in the case of the universe, as Hume insisted. Yet there *are* other human minds. This problem needs to be entirely reworked, and the teleological argument for the existence of God needs to be reexamined in light of the outcome.

KNOWLEDGE BY CRITERIA

The theory of knowledge of persons by criteria was developed by Ludwig Wittgenstein and his numerous contemporary interpreters as a way of avoiding both the privateness of knowledge by immediate acquaintance and the almost inevitable solipsism of knowledge by analogical inference. How do we learn the language that we apply to persons, and how do we know when this language is being applied correctly? We learn the language of *pain, purpose, feeling, sensing, choosing,* and so on entirely within the context of public, repeatable experiences of the bodily behavior of ourselves and our fellows; and certain features of human behavior are inextricably interwoven with learning the language of "person" words and applying this language correctly. Those public performances that are inextricably bound up with the learning and teaching of the language of "person" words are called criteria. Wittgenstein himself insists that there are criteria, that they are to be found in the workings of ordinary language, that they are identifiable by all native speakers of ordinary language, and that if the criteria are satisfied, no further justification for the application of "person" words is needed. Unfortunately, he never gives any *examples* of criteria. To be sure, he says that "pain behavior" is a criterion of "being in pain," but he never specifies *which* behavior he has in mind in speaking of "pain behavior." His followers have not fared much better in giving examples, in producing noncontroversial instances of criteria. Nor is it very clear what these criteria are criteria of. Is the pain of which pain behavior is a criterion something different from the criterion, or is it just the criterion called by another name? Wittgenstein's answer to this question is equivocal; some of his interpreters can read him one way, and some another; and each side can quote relevant "scriptures" to "prove" its case. If the pain is something different from the criterion, is it something inner and private? If it is the same, then must we not wait until we have screamed or grimaced before we can know that we are hurt? Must we not wait until *after* we have given the waitress our order before we can tell which item on the menu we want to eat? The "refutation" of the solipsistic denial of the existence of *other* minds that is concomitant on such an interpretation is most ironic, for it boils down to the reassurance that things are not so bad after all since in reality *no* minds exist. If the criteria are the mental events, we are left only with public behavior but with no minds. At any rate, the solipsist is not likely to be convinced by the claim that knowledge by criteria is a stronger and more reliable form of interpersonal knowledge than knowledge by analogy. He will recognize the appeal to criteria as the point at which the Wittgensteinian world view simply reaches rock bottom, the point at which its adherents wish to cut off debate. Substantive metaphysical questions cannot be resolved merely by appealing to linguistic conventions, however, no matter how basic these conventions may be. If ordinary language defines *language* as an instrument for interpersonal communication, this shows only that a metaphysical pluralism of persons is embedded in ordinary language, but it does not show that there really is a metaphysical pluralism of persons. If it is a basic convention of language that pain behavior is a criterion for really being in pain, then so much the worse for the basic conventions of language. The solipsist is likely to hold that resolving metaphysical disputes by appealing to linguistic conventions is one of the worst forms of question-begging.

KNOWLEDGE BY POSTULATE AND INTUITIVE SENSE OF PRESENCE

Knowledge of persons by postulate is primarily an account of how we might be said to know other minds, and it is usually combined with the view that I know my own mind at least in part through immediate acquaintance. This is the view that the existence of other minds is a theoretical postulate or hypothesis, reinforced perhaps by a sort of primitive, intuitive "sense of presence" or a prerational "animal faith," a postulate that attempts to account for visible things in terms of deeper, invisible realities. This is not the superficial view that "other minds are mere hypotheses," a view that inexcusably confuses theory and reality. Rather, it is the view that the *proposition* "other minds exist" is a theoretical proposition that has the epistemological status of an explanatory hypothesis, though it is not exactly a "scientific" hypothesis. It is a way of explaining what we can observe about the behavior of other human bodies in terms of deeper, nonobservable realities. It is not in itself a "refutation" of solipsism; it grants to the solipsist the right to develop his view, to explore all its ramifications, and to live with that view if he can endure the solitude. It is, however, an attempt to explore in depth an alternative view. Whitehead wrote that "the true method of philosophical construction is to frame a scheme of ideas, the best that one can, and unflinchingly to explore the interpretation of experience in terms of that scheme." [3] There are always intellectual risks to be taken in the development of a broad explanatory scheme, and calling the statement "other minds exist" a postulate is in part a recognition that there is a risk involved in explaining visible things in terms of invisible things. Analogical inference and criterial certitude make things too easy and involve a refusal to face up to this risk. The attempt to settle substantive metaphysical disputes by appealing to the conventions embodied in ordinary language is often accompanied by a contrived denial that substantive metaphysical issues are involved at all and a naive assumption that one can avoid theorizing simply by speaking "plain English," as if there were no theories encapsulated in ordinary language. At any rate, there are distinct advantages to be gained by postulating the existence of other minds. Not only can we best satisfy our perfectly natural "sense of presence" or "animal faith" with such a postulate, but we can best integrate many focal points of interest thereby. In Chapter 12 we saw that the "standard" empiricist epistemology, which separates appearance from reality in terms of the publicness of real objects of experience, actually *presupposes* a pluralism of other minds that cannot, without circularity, be derived from this empiricist epistemology. Only if other minds exist and have experiences and usually report them truthfully can I tell whether my experience of the bodily behavior of others is reality or illusion. Moral experience, the fact that I have moral duties toward others, also presupposes that other persons with feelings, thoughts, and wills of their own are really there. In his book *The Vocation of Man,*[4] the German philosopher Johann Gottlieb Fichte (1762–1814) was one of the first to develop the view that "other minds exist" has the epistemological status of an explanatory postulate. Fichte may have exaggerated somewhat in saying that it was *only* moral considerations that made the hypothesis appealing, but he was correct in thinking that we can do full justice to the moral experience of having duties to other persons—for example, duties to relieve unnecessary suffering or to respect another person's self-initiative—only by presuming that the other person is really there with all his inner suffering and freedom. More recently, the view that the existence of other minds in all their inwardness has the epistemological status of an explanatory hypothesis, reinforced by an intuitive "sense of thouness," seems to be implicit in Ian Ramsey's insistence that metaphysics is in some sense an attempt to explain the seen in terms of the unseen, and that the word *I* when said both by myself of myself and by another person of himself is a paradigm metaphysical word. Ramsey best develops this position in his essay "On the Possibility and Purpose of a Metaphysical Theology." [5] Here he maintains that metaphysics involves the use of "integrator words," which are logically fundamental in our explanatory "map" of the universe as a whole— words that explain, integrate, and unify experience of every sort, whether it be scientific, moral, introspective, or whatever. These words are not themselves the names of observable entities, but words that name unseen realities underlying visible appearances. *I* when said by myself or by another person is just such a word, and so is the word *God,* which must in Ramsey's view have its logic basically modeled after the logic of *I.* Ramsey does tend to equate "not being verifiable by the external senses" with "not being spatio-temporal" and thus prejudices the case in favor of supernaturalism and against process theology; but if we make suitable allowances for that, he has a great deal to say. For example:

> The consequent cost of a total over-all map, of the kind the metaphysicians seek, is integrator words not native to any of the diverse observational languages of the sciences, yet able to combine with and supplement them: words which, while able in this way to secure a reference to observables by associating with scientific discourse, are not confined within its logical patterns.
>
> . . .
>
> . . . metaphysics, to be genuine metaphysics, must have reference to more than observables, i.e. to the unseen. If our reasoning is

reliable, this is in fact our conclusion. For metaphysical integrators, being not native to any scientific language, must have their grounding in what is more than spatio-temporal, i.e. they must be 'meta-physical' in a more obviously traditional sense. For metaphysics is not merely . . . the construction of some kind of ancillary map—it is . . . the construction of a map in accordance with a vision of the unseen.

.   .   .

But if there is 'more,' where the 'more' cannot be perceptually verified, we return to our question . . .: what is its empirical basis? How do we come to recognize this 'more'? The answer is: In a disclosure, a disclosure in which I come to myself and realize myself as more than the observable behavior I display. The stock example of such a disclosure is that of David and Nathan, when at Nathan's 'Thou art the man!' David comes to himself, the 'penny drops' and the disclosure occurs. What 'I' distinctively stands for, what I am to myself more than I as he is to you, is something which *a fortiori cannot be described*. It can only be evoked in and for each of us, and that means given . . . in a disclosure that justifies our use of 'I' in the extended sense, the sense which belongs to a situation not restricted to the observables in terms of which other people (as well as I) can talk of it.

Here is a word—'I' for each of us—which is, then, not descriptive, and yet it can be united with any number of descriptive words. We may say 'I'm angry' or 'I'm a neurotic' or 'I'm a malaria case' or 'I'm a wage-earner' or 'I'm busy,' and so on. 'I exist' is entailed by assertions such as 'He's a wage-earner'; 'He's a neurotic' in the languages of economics, medicine, psychology; and in so doing it becomes an integrator of these logically diverse areas. Further, what is, in spatio-temporal terms, non-descriptive about 'I exist,' is given in a disclosure situation. Here, then, is a paradigm for metaphysics. Here is a metaphysical integrator, given by reference to a disclosure which transcends the spatio-temporal.[6]

Is the Holy a "Thou"?

Having now explored briefly four possible ways of understanding how knowledge of persons is based on experience, let us now return to the problem of how the Thouness of the Holy One may be given in religious experience. From the literature of mysticism, we may assure ourselves that the Holy is not known to be a Thou through any sort of analogical reasoning. It is not a matter of inference, but of immediacy, the mystics tell us. Although the concept of knowledge by criteria is too new to be available to mystics, it is conceivable that someone *might* develop the view that given the conventions of the language games of mysticism, the experience of the *mysterium tremendum et fascinosum* is a criterion for the Thouness of the Holy One, but such a possibility has yet to be explored in any detail, and religious skeptics are likely to view the position as question-begging in something like the way in which the solipsist regards the metaphysical pluralism of persons made available by the criterial view of interpersonal knowledge as question-begging. As the mystics themselves tell the tale, we might suspect that knowledge that the Holy One is also a Divine Thou is more like immediate acquaintance than anything else. Do not the mystics speak of becoming identical with the Holy One? Unfortunately, however, it is the impersonal, monistic mystics who speak most insistently of total union and identity. The personal, pluralistic mystics, who are most likely to regard the Holy One as a Thou, seem also to insist on *the otherness of the Thou in relation to the I,* not the identity of the I with the Thou. Even if this were not the case, it would be difficult to see how the mystic could be immediately acquainted with the infinite love and inexhaustible intelligence of God in anything analogous to the way in which he is immediately acquainted with his own limited love and intelligence. In mystical union, does the *mystic* become omnicompassionate, omniscient, and so on, and merely see that this is the case by introspection? No doubt the mystic often receives an influx of overwhelming compassion and moral insight and resoluteness in the midst of the experience, but it is difficult to see how all this could be both his and God's at the same time.[7] The most plausible account of how a knowledge of the Divine Thou is based on religious experience may, after all, be something like the view that "Divine Thouness" is an explanatory hypothesis reinforced by the same kind of deep, intuitive "sense of presence" or "animal faith" that we normally have when confronted by another human body, a way of interpreting the experienced by reference to the unexperienced. But interpretation is involved, and the mystical experience must be given a place on a broader theoretical map, which must include the world as we know it in our less mystical moments. The concept of the *Divine Thou* must function logically to unify religious experience, moral experience, scientific experience, and all the rest, and this can be done effectively only when set within the context of some elaborate view of God and the world such as we explored in Chapters 3, 4, and 5 as well as in Chapters 6, 7, and 8.

One further problem remains. If we are to regard "Divine Thouness" as having the epistemological status of an explanatory hypothesis, this presupposes that there is something to be explained. But suppose there were nothing to be explained. Suppose the situation here were analogous to "sensing the presence" of another person in the same room, but the person cannot be found at all when we look around or otherwise try to perceive him and he fails to respond to us in any experienceable way.[8] Examples like this do show that there is really not much of any theoretical or theological significance which can be built on a mere isolated "sense of presence," that this sense of presence must be reinforced by other happenings and interpreted within the framework of a viable world view. The "ordinary believer" has the sense of presence and a poorly rationalized world view to comfort him but even he has some acquaintance with what earlier theologians would have called the divine languages of nature and history. However, the true mystic has something more. He has those "other happenings" in a more immediate and striking form. The situation of the mystic is not at all like the situation of the man who sits alone in his room and tries to establish I–Thou relations with a person who is not really there. That the person is fictional is inherent in the very example, for we have said that he does not respond in any experienceable way. In the situation of the mystic, it is as if "all hell breaks loose" in the lonely room. Perhaps we should parody this expression and say that it is as if "all heaven breaks loose," because such an experience involves much more than feeling a sense of presence where nothing else is happening. In the mystical experience the *mysterium tremendum et fascinosum* is happening, and this calls for an explanation. Which of the explanations discussed in this chapter do you find most plausible?

Suggestions for Further Reading

on "I," "THOU," AND PERSONAL ENCOUNTER

BAILLIE, JOHN, *Our Knowledge of God* (New York, Scribner's, 1939).

————, *The Idea of Revelation in Recent Thought* (New York, Columbia University Press, 1956), Chapter 2.

————, *The Sense of the Presence of God* (London, Oxford University Press, 1962).

BRUNNER, EMIL, *The Divine-Human Encounter* (London, SCM Press, 1944).

————, *Truth as Encounter* (Philadelphia, Westminster Press, 1964).

BUBER, MARTIN, *I and Thou* (New York, Scribner's, 1958).

COX, DAVID, "A Note on Meeting," *Mind,* Vol. LX (April 1951), pp. 259–61.

FARMER, H. H., *Towards Belief in God* (London, SCM Press, 1942), Part II.

————, *The World and God* (London, Nisbet, 1935).

FICHTE, JOHANN GOTTLIEB, *The Vocation of Man* (New York, Liberal Arts Press, 1956).

HEPBURN, RONALD W., *Christianity and Paradox* (New York, Pegasus, 1966), Chapters 3 and 4 and pp. 204–09.

POTEAT, WILLIAM H., "Birth, Suicide and the Doctrine of Creation: An Exploration of Analogies," *Mind,* Vol. LXVIII (July 1959), pp. 309–21.

————, " 'I Will Die': An Analysis," *The Philosophical Quarterly,* Vol. IX (January 1959), pp. 46–58.

————, "God and the 'Private-I,' " *Philosophy and Phenomenological Research,* Vol. XX (March 1960), pp. 409–16.

RAMSEY, IAN, *Models and Mystery* (London, Oxford University Press, 1964).

————, ed., *Prospect for Metaphysics* (London, George Allen & Unwin, 1961), Chapter 10, 11, 12.

————, *Religious Language* (New York, Macmillan, 1957).

————, "The Systematic Elusiveness of 'I,' " *The Philosophical Quarterly,* Vol. V, No. 20 (July 1955), pp. 193–204.

Notes

1 Rudolf Otto, *The Idea of the Holy* (New York, Oxford University Press, 1958), p. 39.
2 *Ibid.*, p. 202.
3 Alfred North Whitehead, *Process and Reality* (New York, Macmillan, 1967), p. x.
4 New York, Liberal Arts Press, 1956. This is one of the few of Fichte's works now available in English translation.
5 Ian Ramsey, ed., *Prospect for Metaphysics* (London, George Allen & Unwin, 1961), pp. 153–77.
6 *Ibid.*, pp. 161, 162–63, 167.
7 Within the context of Whiteheadian metaphysics, this may not be as nearly as difficult to understand as I make it seem here, but a rather elaborate metaphysical scheme is required to make it out. This possibility has been explored in some detail by John B. Cobb, *A Christian Natural Theology* (Philadelphia, Westminster Press, 1965), pp. 225–46.
8 This example is used by William James, *The Varieties of Religious Experience* (New York, Modern Library, n.d.), p. 58.

chapter fourteen

Religious
Language
and
Experience VERIFICATION AFTER
DEATH

Without denying that there are many types of experience that have a bearing on the question of the existence of God, we may ask whether or not it is somehow possible to experience God after death and thus confirm or disconfirm our beliefs about him. Ian Crombie was one of the first recent thinkers to suggest that experience after death might resolve many questions that cannot be decided with much definiteness in our present situation. The question of the existence of a loving God is one issue that cannot be conclusively resolved now, Crombie maintains:

> Since our experience is limited in the way it is, we cannot get into position to decide it, any more than we can get into position to decide what Julius Caesar had for breakfast before he crossed the Rubicon. For the Christian the operation of getting into position to decide it is called dying; and, though we can all do that, we cannot return to report what we find. By this test, then, religious utterances can be statements of fact; that is their logical classification.[1]

Crombie's last remark indicates that the controversy over verification after death takes place within the context of the positivistic attack on the meaningfulness of religious language and various attempts to reply to this attack. Crombie is here claiming that religious language is empirically meaningful after all, but that the really crucial experiences that would verify or falsify religious assertions must be had after death and not before. Such a position has been developed more elaborately in recent years by John Hick, and we shall concentrate on his presentation. Again the main effort is devoted to showing that experience could confirm or disconfirm religious beliefs, albeit experience after death, and that consequently religious assertions are "factually" meaningful after all. In our own discussion, we shall follow Crombie and Hick in concentrating on the problem of the *empirical meaningfulness* of religious belief rather than on the *truth or falsity* of such beliefs, in light of experience after death. Such a narrowing of our frame of reference does not commit us to the position that the verification criterion of meaning is the only adequate criterion and that experience after death is the only relevant and defensible type of religious experience. We shall simply explore this somewhat narrow but interesting perspective for whatever it may be worth, while recognizing its obvious limitations. There are actually two quite distinct questions to be treated: (1) Is the notion of experience after death itself empirically meaningful? and (2) Exactly what experiences might one have after death that would confirm or disconfirm some distinctively Christian form of theism? John Hick addresses himself to both of these questions.

John Hick on the Meaningfulness
of Experience After Death

BEFORE we attempt to deal with the problem of the meaningfulness of a distinctively Christian form of theism in light of experience after death, we must ask whether a religious belief in experience after death is itself empirically meaningful. In developing his view of "eschatological verification," Hick is initially committed to three distinct claims, all of which are essential for the explication of the notion of experience after death. *First* there is the claim that the self persists after death and has experiences. Hick acknowledges that "The idea of an eschatological verification of theism makes sense . . . only if the logically prior idea of continued personal existence after death is intelligible." [2] *Second,* recognizing that in the view of both modern philosophy and biblical anthropology it is unacceptable to think of man as ever being a totally disembodied spirit, Hick insists that the eschatological experiencer is an embodied experiencer, that there will be a resurrection body. In the view of many present-day antireligious thinkers, Hick says,

> there is no room for the notion of a soul in distinction from the body; and if there is no soul in distinction from the body there can be no question of the soul surviving the death of the body. Against this philosophical background the specifically Christian (and also Jewish) belief in the resurrection of the flesh or body, in contrast to the Hellenic notion of the survival of a disembodied soul, might be expected to have attracted more attention than it has. For it is consonant with the conception of man as an indissoluble psycho-physical unity, and yet it also offers the possibility of an empirical meaning for the idea of "life after death." [3]

Third, Hick is committed to the view that resurrected bodies live and move and have their experiences in a space that is totally disparate from present physical space. He speaks of the world inhabited by resurrected persons as "a different world altogether," and he explains that:

> This world occupies its own space, distinct from the space with which we are now familiar. That is to say, an object in the resurrection world is not situated at any distance or in any direction from an object in our present world, although each object in either world is spatially related to each other object in the same world.[4]

Having briefly sketched the elements that enter initially into a view of verification after death, we shall now look at some of the difficulties that arise in connection with such a view. Remember, we are now working only with the problem of the empirical *meaningfulness* of such a view, not with the problem of its *truth.*

Some recent critics have insisted that the whole notion of "life after death" is unintelligible because it is self-contradictory.[5] It is nothing more than the notion of "being alive while not alive," and the difficulties with that should be obvious. Now it is true that if a purely biological interpretation of *life* is involved here, such a notion is self-contradictory. However, the issue is entirely one of semantics. The popular expression "life after death" may be unfortunate and misleading because the word *life* naturally lends itself to a biological interpretation. The real issue is not "life" after death but rather "experience" after death, as H. H. Price has pointed out.[6] Though there is a contradiction in the notion of "being biologically alive while not biologically alive," there is nothing obviously contradictory about the notion of "having experiences in a resurrected body," though there are problems enough with this latter notion, as we shall see.

Hick argues that the notion of having experiences in a resurrected body that exists in a disparate realm of space is an *empirically* meaningful notion, and this is a much stronger claim than that the notion is free from self-contradiction, though it must be at least that. Hick's main argument for this thesis is that the assertion "I am having experiences in a resurrected body existing in a disparate realm of space" could be verified by a surviving eschatological experiencer, just as the claim "I am now having experiences in a biological body existing in physical space" is verified by a this-worldly experiencer. If we assume for the moment that verification is indeed involved in the latter case, the thesis that the former assertion is meaningful because it could be verified after death seems somehow to be decidedly beside the point. Even if we grant that the assertion might be empirically meaningful *then,* the problem is whether it is empirically meaningful *now*—that is, whether the notion of "then" is itself meaningful. Hick comes very close to admitting that the notion is *now* empirically meaningless, in the sense that we could not *now* verify statements about *then,* in his doctrine that in this unique case there is an asymmetrical relationship between the verifiability and falsifiability of statements about *then.* Such statements can never be proved false in experience if they are false, he holds; but they can be proved true in experience if they are true.[7] That is, if it is false that I will continue to be conscious after death, I can never experience its falsity, since I will not be there to experience anything; but if the claim is true, I can experience its truth. The *difficulty* is that the verifying experience could be had only *then,* whereas the *problem* to which Hick addresses himself is whether assertions about *then* are empirically meaningful to us *now*. Since verifying experiences are available *only then,* presumably we must conclude that the whole matter is meaningless to us *now*. As one of Hick's most persistent critics, Kai Nielsen, has put the point, throughout his discussion Hick must "already make reference to the very conceptions whose factual intelligibility is in question. Hick is in effect trying to lift himself by his own bootstraps." [8]

Is there any way at all for Hick to counter this very telling criticism? It might help if we took another look at the verification criterion of meaning, which was discussed in our presentation of logical positivism in Chapter 5. There we formulated the principle of verification as follows: An assertion is meaningful if and only if some sense observation would be directly or indirectly relevant to its confirmation or disconfirmation; an assertion is meaningless if and only if no sense observation would be directly or indirectly relevant to its confirmation or disconfirmation. Now there are many difficulties with this principle, as we indicated earlier. One problem is with the restriction to sense observation. There are other types of experience besides sense experience, and at least some of these nonsensory experiences are of noetic significance. For example, the experience of remembering is not a sense experience, though the object remembered may originally have been presented to us in sense experience. Is it meaningful to talk about remembering as well as about objects remembered? It is difficult to see how it could be as long as we are restricted to sense experience. The experience of having a headache or a toothache or a feeling of grief or anxiety is not a sense experience for the person undergoing such an "inner process," but it is perfectly meaningful to talk about it *experientially*. This sort of difficulty is not the crucial one for present purposes, however. The crucial consideration is that there is a serious ambiguity in the principle as it is formulated. The principle does not say *who* must make the observations, nor does it say *when* they must be made, nor did the earlier versions of the principle make a place for *indirect,* or inconclusive, verifiability. Furthermore, any attempt to answer these questions will appear to be question-begging from someone's point of view, which suggests that the meaningfulness of that point of view logically precedes the application of the verification principle and does not follow from it.

Let us examine in more detail what is involved here. We have suggested that the difficulty with Hick's position is that the experiences that would verify the statement "I experience in a resurrected body in a new world" could be had only *then* and are not available *now*, from which it would seem to follow that all talk *now* about *then* is empirically meaningless. Suppose that someone in remembering his past experiences says, "I once saw a cross," and in anticipating his future experiences says, "I will see a cross." Then suppose that someone with a positivistic bent objected that all such talk about the past and the future is meaningless since those experiences were or will be available only then but are not available now, from which it would seem to follow that all talk *now* about *then* is empirically meaningless. Suppose further that in attempting to reply to this positivistic critic we found that no statements that did not refer to immediate, present experiences were admissible and that when we made use of verbs in past or future tenses we were told that we were merely making use of concepts whose factual intelligibility was in question and thus merely trying to lift ourselves by our own bootstraps.

This hypothetical dialogue is not nearly as far-fetched as it seems, and it certainly was not invented merely to make trouble for the verification theory of meaning. If we review the vast literature of positivism produced from 1920 to 1950, we will find that at times the positivists themselves actually argued this way, that they actually interpreted the principle of verification in such a way that they were in effect committed to a kind of logical solipsism or, even worse, a logical solipsism of the present moment. Such an interpretation always depended on the answers given to the questions of *who* the experiencer must be and *when* the experiences must be had, and these answers were never derived from the principle of verification itself. A review of the history of the interpretation of the verification principle by the positivists themselves[9] shows how diverse interpretations of the principle led various of the positivists to insist on the *meaninglessness* of (1) statements about my own mind, since "I" am not given to myself in sense experience; (2) statements about my own past or future experiences, since these are not given to me in immediate experience; (3) statements about the world before or after my death, since I shall never sense such a world; (4) statements about other minds and their experiences;

(5) statements of scientific law and empirical generalizations that have the logical form of universal propositions; and (6) statements about possible experiences after death. Furthermore, anyone who defended the meaningfulness of *any one* of these classes of statements could have been and often was met with the rejoinder that he was using concepts whose factual intelligibility was in question and that a bootstrap operation was in progress.

The history of the interpretation of the verification principle by the positivists themselves leads one to suspect strongly that instead of producing a criterion of meaning and then deriving from it a noncontroversial list of meaningful statements, they have followed just the reverse procedure. The criterion is always interpreted in such a way that whatever descriptive assertions one *wants* to be meaningful are allowed in under the wire. In other words, first one decides what descriptive assertions one wants to be empirically meaningful, and then one gives an interpretation of the empiricist criterion of meaning that fits. These decisions hidden in the background of positivistic epistemology are the really controversial issues that need to be brought into the open and exposed for what they are. What is at present relevant is that anyone who has not made the same decision we have made will always accuse us of begging controversial questions. Even the positivists were unable to agree on a noncontroversial list of empirically meaningful assertions.

It would be easy for us to say at this point that Hick and his opponents have simply made different decisions about how much is to be let in under the wire, and in some sense this may ultimately be true. If it is true, however, then Hick has been going about defending himself in the wrong way. The lines separating Hick and his critics are too far apart, as Hick has drawn them thus far. The critics insist on verification in this world, and Hick fails to meet them even halfway in replying that verification will come in the next world. The most one can do to reply to the logical solipsist of the present moment is show that in the present moment experiences such as perceptions, introspections, memories, and anticipations are given, out of which intelligible talk about the past and the future can be constructed; but if he insists that it is all unintelligible, not much else can be said. Certainly his demand that we perceptually encounter the past and the future in the present can never be met. Similarly, all the defender of meaningful talk about experience after death can do is show how experiences are given in this world, including perceptions, introspections, memories, and anticipations, out of which intelligible talk about experience after death can be constructed; but if the skeptic insists that it is all unintelligible, not much else can be said except to ask him how he would go about replying to the logical solipsist of the present moment. Certainly the demand that we *now* experience the *then* can never be met.

H. H. Price on Survival After Death

Can we construct meaningful utterances about "another world" without presupposing the present accessibility to experience of that other world? Hick gives only meager hints as to how we might answer this question, but H. H. Price has answered it much more satisfactorily in his essay "Survival and the Idea of 'Another World.'" Price is careful to note that he is addressing his remarks only to the limited question of the meaningfulness of talk about experience after death, not the question of its truth. Although they are not given to us as physical sensations, most of us do not doubt that it is meaningful to talk about memory images and dreams, about the psychological forces that control the development of our dream episodes, about the desires that are fulfilled or frustrated in these dreams, about the impossibility of moving from dream space to the physical space of everyday life, and so on. Some of us even find the notion of mental telepathy meaningful, though this is not the time to launch into a detailed discussion of parapsychology. At least, most of us know from experience what it is like to desire, to remember, to dream, even if we do not know from experience what telepathic communication is like. Furthermore, it is entirely possible to construct an account of experience after death from these elements of present experience, a view that would not be very different from that offered by some of the world's major religions—a view that, moreover, could indirectly make a place for resurrected bodies of sorts. Since Price has already undertaken to construct such a view, let us see how he develops it:

The next world, I think, might be conceived as a kind of dream-world. When we are asleep, sensory stimuli are cut off, or at any rate are prevented from having their normal effects upon our brain-centers. But we still manage to have experiences. It is true that sense-perception no longer occurs, but something sufficiently like it does. In sleep, our image-producing powers, which are more or less inhibited in waking life by a continuous bombardment of sensory stimuli, are released from this inhibition. And then we are provided with a multitude of objects of awareness, about which we employ our thoughts and towards which we have desires and emotions. These objects which we are aware of behave in a way which seems very queer to us when we wake up. The laws of their behavior are not the laws of physics. But however queer their behavior is, it does not at all disconcert us at the time and our personal identity is not broken.

In other words, my suggestion is that the next world, if there is one, might be a world of mental images. Nor need such a world be so "thin and insubstantial" as you might think. Paradoxical as it may sound, there is nothing imaginary about a mental image. It is an actual entity, as real as anything can be. The seeming paradox arises from the ambiguity of the verb "to imagine." It does sometimes mean "to have mental images." But more usually it means "to entertain propositions without believing them"; and very often they are false propositions, and moreover we *dis*believe them in the act of entertaining them. This is what happens, for example, when we read Shakespeare's play *The Tempest,* and that is why we say that Prospero and Ariel are "imaginary characters." Mental images are not in this sense imaginary at all. We do actually experience them, and they are no more imaginary than sensations. To avoid the paradox, though at the cost of some pedantry, it would be well to distinguish between *imagining* and *imaging,* and to have two different adjectives "imaginary" and "imagy." In this terminology, it is imaging, and not imagining, that I wish to talk about; and the next world, as I am trying to conceive it, is an *imagy* world, but not on that account an imaginary one.

Indeed, to those who experienced it an image-world would be just as "real" as this present world is; perhaps so like it, that they would have considerable difficulty in realizing that they were dead. We are, of course, sometimes told in mediumistic communications that quite a lot of people do find it difficult to realize that they are dead; and this is just what we should expect if the next world is

an image-world. Lord Russell and other philosophers have maintained that a material object in this present physical world is nothing more nor less than a complicated system of *appearances*. So
far as I can see, there might be a set of visual images related to
each other perspectively, with front views and side views and
back views all fitting neatly together in the way that ordinary visual
appearances do now. Such a group of images might contain
tactual images too. Similarly it might contain auditory images and
smell images. Such a family of interrelated images would make a
pretty good object. It would be quite a satisfactory substitute for
the material objects which we perceive in this present life. And a
whole world composed of such families of mental images would
make a perfectly good world.[10]

To those who insist that it is unintelligible to talk about a world
constructed mainly of desires and memory images, since memory
and desire cannot exist apart from a physical brain, Price replies
that such a view of the connection between the brain and memory
and desire, "however plausible, is after all just an empirical
hypothesis, not a necessary truth. Certainly there is empirical
evidence in favor of it. But there is also empirical evidence against
it." [11] He reminds us that he is not trying to defend the truth of
such a view, but only its intelligibility:

All I want to maintain, then, is that there is nothing self-contradictory or logically absurd in the hypothesis that memories, desires, and images can exist in the absence of a physical brain. The
hypothesis may, of course, be false. My point is only that it is not
absurd; or if you like, that it is at any rate intelligible, whether
true or not.[12]

To those who are concerned that such a world of images and
desires would not be a "real" world at all, Price replies, somewhat
facetiously, that "if it were true that the next life . . . is a condition of permanent delusion, we should just have to put up with
it." [13] Then, in a more serious vein, he inquires:

What, then, could people mean by saying that a next world such
as I have described would be "unreal"? If they are saying anything intelligible, they must mean that it is different from something else, something else which it does resemble in some respects,

and might therefore be confused with. And what is that something else? It is the present physical world in which we now live. An image-world, then, is only "unreal" in the sense that it is not really physical, though it might be mistakenly thought to be physical by some of those who experience it. But this only amounts to saying that the world I am describing would be an *other* world, other than this present physical world, and yet sufficiently like it to be possibly confused with it, because images do resemble percepts. And what would this otherness consist in? First, in the fact that it is a *space* which is other than physical space; secondly, and still more important, in the fact that the *causal laws* of an image-world would be different from the laws of physics. And this is also our ground for saying that the events we experience in dreams are "unreal," that is, not really physical, though mistakenly believed by the dreamer to be so. They do in some ways closely resemble physical events, and that is why the mistake is possible. But the causal laws of their occurrence are quite different, as we recognize when we wake up; and just occasionally we recognize it even while we are still asleep.[14]

To the critic who insists that such a world would have to be purely subjective and private and in that sense "unreal," Price also has a reply:

"Subjective," perhaps, is a rather slippery word. Certainly, an image-world would have to be subjective in the sense of being mind-dependent, dependent for its existence upon mental processes of one sort or another; images, after all, are mental entities. But I do not think that such a world need be completely private, if telepathy occurs in the next life. I have already mentioned the part which telepathic apparitions might play in it in connection with Mr. [Antony] Flew's contention that "people are what you meet." But there is more to be said. It is reasonable to suppose that in a disembodied state telepathy would occur more frequently than it does now. It seems likely that in this present life our telepathic powers are constantly being inhibited by our need to adjust ourselves to our physical environment. It even seems likely that many telepathic "impressions" which we receive at the unconscious level are shut out from consciousness by a kind of biologically motivated censorship. Once the pressure of biological needs is removed, we might expect that telepathy would occur continually, and manifest itself in consciousness by modifying and adding to the images which one experiences. (Even in this life, after all, some dreams are telepathic.)

If this is right, an image-world such as I am describing would not be the product of one single mind only, nor would it be purely private. It would be the joint product of a group of telepathically interacting minds and public to all of them. Nevertheless, one would not expect it to have unrestricted publicity. It is likely that there would still be *many* next worlds, a different one for each group of like-minded personalities. I admit I am not quite sure what might be meant by "like-minded" and "unlikeminded" in this connection. Perhaps we could say that two personalities are like-minded if their memories of their characters are sufficiently similar. It might be that Nero and Marcus Aurelius do not have a world in common, but Socrates and Marcus Aurelius do.[15]

Price is even able to make a place for the notion of resurrected bodies existing in a totally disparate space, pointing out that we do not have to wait until "after death" to acquire experiences out of which we may construct our meaningful talk about such things. In dream space and memory space we are already acquainted with disparate spaces and times and with bodies that are not integral parts of physical space-time. We have dream images and memory images of our own body, and our "resurrection body" might be so constructed.[16] Something like this might provide an interpretation of St. Paul's insistence that the resurrection body will be a "spiritual body." As for the whereabouts of all this, Price explains that we need not think that it is "in the sky" or "outside space" or related in any way to physical space, and that furthermore we are *already* acquainted with such disparate spaces and times:

> The answer to this difficulty is easy if we conceive of the next world in the way I have suggested, as a dream-like world of mental images. Mental images, including dream images, are in a space of their own. They do have spatial properties. Visual images, for instance, have extension and shape, and they have spatial relations to one another. But they have no spatial relations to objects in the physical world. If I dream of a tiger, my tiger image has extension and shape. The dark stripes have spatial relation to the yellow parts, and to each other; the nose has a spatial relation to the tail. Again, the tiger image as a whole may have spatial

relations to another image in my dream, for example to an image resembling a palm tree. But suppose we have to ask how far it is from the foot of my bed, whether it is three inches long, or longer or shorter; is it not obvious that these questions are absurd ones? We cannot answer them, not because we lack the necessary measurements, but because the questions themselves have no meaning. In the space of the physical world these images are nowhere at all. But in relation to other images of mine, each of them is somewhere. Each of them is extended, and its parts are in spatial relation to one another. There is no *a priori* reason why all extended entities must be in physical space.[17]

If the world of experience after death will be constructed of desires and images and its laws will be those of psychology rather than those of physics, it becomes easy to understand how we might create our own future heaven or hell by what we do, decide, and undergo in the present life. In the most imaginative and exciting part of his presentation, Price explains how some of the claims about the afterlife made by some of the great world religions might make sense after all:

We can now see that an after-death world of mental images can also be quite reasonably described in the terminology of the Hindu thinkers as "a world of desire" (Karma Loka). Indeed, this is just what we should expect if we assume that dreams, in this present life, are the best available clue to what the next life might be like. Such a world could also be described as "a world of memories"; because imaging, in the end, is a function of memory, one of the ways in which our memory-dispositions manifest themselves. But this description would be less apt, even though correct as far as it goes. To use the same rather inadequate language as before, the "materials" out of which an image-world is composed would have to come from the memories of the mind or group of minds whose world it is. But it would be their desires (including those repressed in earthly life) which determined the way in which these memories were used, the precise kind of dream which was built up out of them or on the basis of them.

.   .   .

What could we take out with us, as it were, when we pass from this life to the next? What we take out with us, I suggest, can only be our memories and desires, and the power of constructing out of them an image world to suit us. Obviously we cannot take our material possessions out with us; but I do not think this is any great loss, for if we remember them well enough and are sufficiently attached to them, we shall be able to construct image-replicas of them which will be just as good, and perhaps better.

. . . . .

. . . the next world as I am conceiving it need not necessarily be an agreeable place at all. If arguments about what is good or what is bad did have any relevance, a case could be made out for saying that this conception of the next world is "too bad to be true," rather than too good. As we have seen, we should have to reckon with many different next worlds, not just one. The world you experience after death would depend upon the kind of person you are. And if what I have said so far has any sense in it, we can easily conceive that some people's next worlds would be much more like purgatories than paradises—and pretty unpleasant purgatories too.

This is because there are conflicting desires within the same person. Few people, if any, are completely integrated personalities, though some people come nearer to it than others. And sometimes when a man's desires appear (even to himself) to be more or less harmonious with one another, the appearance is deceptive. His conscious desires do not conflict with one another or not much; but this harmony has only been achieved at the cost of repression. He has unconscious desires which conflict with the neatly organized pattern of his conscious life. If I was right in suggesting that repression is a biological phenomenon, if the "threshold" between conscious and unconscious no longer operates in a disembodied state, or operates much less effectively, this seeming harmony will vanish after the man is dead. To use scriptural language, the secrets of his heart will be revealed—at any rate to himself. These formerly repressed desires will manifest themselves by appropriate images, and these images might be exceedingly horrifying—as some dream-images are in this present life, and for the same reason. True enough, they will be "wish-fulfillment" images, like everything else that he experiences in the next world as I am conceiving it. But the wishes they fulfill will conflict with other wishes which he also has. And the emotional state which results might be worse than the worst nightmare; worse, because the dreamer cannot wake up from it.

. . . . .

To look at the same point in another way: the next world as I am picturing it may be a very queer sort of world, but still it would be subject to causal laws. The laws would not, of course, be the laws of physics. As I have suggested already, they might be expected to be more like the laws of Freudian psychology. But they would be laws all the same, and objective in the sense that they hold good whether one likes it or not. And if we do dislike the image-world which our desires and memories create for us— if, when we get what we want, we are horrified to discover what things they were which we wanted—we shall have to set about altering our characters, which might be a very long and painful process.[18]

Price has done what Hick has failed to do: He has shown how our talk about experience after death can be experientially *meaningful* to us now by showing how a view of experience after death may be constructed out of experiences that are already available to us. Of course, he has not done much to show that any of this is *true,* and about that we may just have to wait and see.

John Hick on Eschatological Confirmation of Christian Theism

WE must turn now to the second main question to which Hick addresses himself: Exactly what experiences might one have after death that would confirm or disconfirm some *distinctively Christian* form of theism? It has always been a commonplace in Christian belief that all our doubts about our religious commitments will be resolved in the "next life" through an immediate experience of God, Christ, and the Kingdom. Following St. Paul, most Christian thinkers have admitted that we now see through a glass darkly, but they have held out the hope that then we shall see face to face. Now our task is to try to decide *exactly what they might see,* and this problem is one to which the literature of Christendom has addressed itself at best only metaphorically, and never with a great deal of clarity and exactitude. True, many Christian thinkers are content to leave it at that; but we cannot do so if we are seriously trying to ascertain whether our talk about experience after death is empirically meaningful. Presumably after death we will not need to speak in metaphors, for they belong to our present situation of seeing through a glass darkly. But if talk about experience after death is to be empirically meaningful to us *now,* we must be able *now* to say with some precision what sort of thing we might experience *then* that would point unequivocally to the truth of Christian theism.

John Hick is quite correct in acknowledging that to establish that it is meaningful to talk about experience after death is not thereby to show that it is meaningful to talk about the verification of Christian theism. The two are quite distinct, as we might have guessed from our review in Chapter 1 of those world religions that think about experience after death in distinctively non-Christian ways. Hicks tells us that

> survival, simply as such, would not serve to verify theism. It would not necessarily be a state of affairs which is manifestly incompatible with the non-existence of God. It might be taken just as a surprising natural fact. The atheist, in his resurrection body, and able to remember his life on earth, might say that the universe has turned out to be more complex, and perhaps more to be approved of, than he had realized. But the mere fact of survival, with a new body in a new environment, would not demonstrate to him that there is a God. It is fully compatible with the notion of survival that the life to come be, so far as the theistic problem is concerned, essentially a continuation of the present life, and religiously no less ambiguous. And in this event, survival after bodily death would not in the least constitute a final verification of theistic faith.
>
> I shall not spend time in trying to draw a picture of a resurrection existence which would merely prolong the religious ambiguity of our present life. The important question, for our purpose, is not whether one can conceive of after-life experiences which would *not* verify theism (and in point of fact one can fairly easily conceive them), but whether one can conceive of after-life experiences which *would* serve to verify theism.[19]

Hick thus hopes to find some experiential situation in the "next life" that would *conclusively* verify the truth of Christian theism, and he must tell us *now* what this might be like in order to establish his point. In an early discussion of eschatological verification, Hick points out that the Christian tradition offers two different accounts of verifying experiences after death: first the expectation of the Beatific Vision, a direct solitary experience of God, and second the expectation of a kind of communal experience of Christ in his Kingdom. Hick doubts that these two accounts can be combined as easily as many traditional thinkers assume, and he also doubts that the Beatific Vision is itself meaningful to us now, "for the expositions of it provide little more than the phrase itself to discuss." [20] He has more confidence in the second form of experience, so much so that in his later essay on "Theology and Verification," he is content to develop only what seems to him to be a "more intelligible possibility. This is the possibility not of a direct vision of God, whatever that might mean, but of a *situation* which points unambiguously to the existence of a loving God." [21] As Hick understands the matter, there would be two elements in this situation which

> would assure us beyond rational doubt of the reality of God, as conceived in the Christian faith. These are, *first,* an experience of the fulfillment of God's purpose for ourselves, as this has been disclosed in the Christian revelation; in conjunction, *second,* with an experience of communion with God as he has revealed himself in the person of Christ.[22]

Hick goes on to explain more carefully why he is skeptical about the possibility of experiencing God directly (in the Beatific Vision) and prefers the indirect route through the Incarnation and the Kingdom of God:

> Several writers have pointed out the logical difficulty involved in any claim to have encountered God. How could one know that it was *God* whom one had encountered? God is described in Christian theology in terms of various absolute qualities, such as omnipotence, omnipresence, perfect goodness, infinite love, etc., which cannot as such be observed by us, as can their finite analogies, limited power, local presence, finite goodness, and human love. One can recognize that a being whom one "encounters" has a given finite degree of power, but how does one recognize that he has *un*limited power? How does one observe that an encountered being is *omni*present? How does one perceive that his goodness and love, which one can perhaps see to exceed any human goodness and love, are actually infinite? Such qualities

cannot be given in human experience. One might claim, then, to have encountered a Being whom one presumes, or trusts, or hopes to be God; but one cannot claim to have encountered a being whom one recognized to be the infinite, almighty, eternal Creator.[23]

In our earlier discussion of mysticism, we noted that even the mystical experience must be interpreted and that alternative interpretations are possible even though some of these may be more appropriate than others. Even if the Beatific Vision after death is a sort of perfected, nontransient mystical ecstasy, it is nevertheless difficult to see how we could get around the necessity of interpreting what is given and thus avoid the possibility of skeptical interpretations. Hick seems to be making precisely this point, but he does offer an alternative that he believes to be considerably less ambiguous than perfected mystical experience. He writes that:

> Only God himself knows his own infinite nature; and our human belief about that nature is based upon his self-revelation to men in Christ. As Karl Barth expressed it, "Jesus Christ is the knowability of God." Our beliefs about God's infinite being are not capable of observational verification, being beyond the scope of human experience, but they are susceptible of indirect verification by the removal of rational doubt concerning the authority of Christ. An experience of the reign of the Son in the Kingdom of the Father would confirm that authority, and therewith, indirectly, the validity of Jesus' teaching concerning the character of God in his infinite transcendent nature.
>
> The further question as to how an eschatological experience of the Kingdom of God could be known to be such has already been answered by implication. It is God's union with man in Christ that makes possible man's recognition of the fulfillment of God's purpose for man as being indeed the fulfillment of *God's* purpose for him. The presence of Christ in his Kingdom marks this as being beyond doubt the Kingdom of the God and Father of the Lord Jesus Christ.[24]

Without claiming that experience could prove certain Christian religious beliefs to be logically necessary and in that sense conclusively established, Hick nevertheless does want to claim that such experiences as he has described could remove Christian theism from the realm of reasonable doubt. However, this claim presents difficulties that must be faced.

In the first place, there are difficulties with the matter of observing Christ in his Kingdom. Hick is not very specific about exactly what one would have to be looking at in order to see Christ in his Kingdom. Would one be observing a resurrected Jesus presiding over a society of subjects who themselves were living Jesus-like lives? If so, how would this differ, in an epistemologically relevant way, from the situation of Jesus and his disciples during his "earthly sojourn"? After all, the New Testament says that Jesus was presiding over a society of subjects who were themselves living Jesus-like lives before his crucifixion, and very few people then or since, Christians included, believed that what could have been observed would have removed belief in God, the Sonship of Christ, the Trinity, and so on, from the realm of reasonable doubt. The New Testament insists that even during the earthly life of Jesus the Kingdom of God was in our midst. However, it does distinguish between the Kingdom simply being present and the Kingdom being present in *all its glory;* presumably an eschatological verifier would see the Kingdom in all its glory, but exactly what would he see? What could one *see* to remove reasonable doubt about the doctrine of the Trinity or the Incarnation? Presumably the eschatological view of Jesus in his Kingdom would have to be radically different *in kind* from the earthly view of Jesus in his Kingdom, for the latter certainly did not remove Christian theism from the realm of reasonable doubt. The eschatological view would have to be so different in kind as to make impossible the sort of *interpretation and faith response* that Christians in this world have forged so painstakingly and quarreled with one another about so heatedly. But if it must be so completely different from what the disciples of Jesus were able to observe, is this not tantamount to admitting that we do *not now* know what observations we could make, even in heaven, that would substantially confirm a distinctively Christian form of theism?

There are also problems about the connection between Jesus and God, and it is difficult to see how eschatological *observation* could establish the doctrine that "Jesus was the Christ, the Son of God" any more than this-worldly observation could. After all, the "God" part of the expression is admittedly unobservable even in heaven, according to Hick. Why would these claims not still be matters of interpretation, rather than matters of observation, even in heaven? Neither Hick nor any other Christian thinker seems to have done very much to answer this question. Is it that on earth and in heaven as well, Jesus can observe God, whereas the rest of us cannot? If Jesus is our ultimate authority on God, how does Jesus know? What does he see? What makes him an authority? Does he have superior powers of observation, or is something besides observation involved even here?

The crucial difficulty with this emphasis on eschatological verification seems to be that it makes the question of the existence of God a question of "scientific fact," whereas God's existence and essence may be neither factual nor scientifically observable even in principle. Finite observers presumably must always observe only finite situations, not total reality, and the finite situations that we are able to observe constitute for us the realm of scientific facts. God is not located in such a *limited* region of space, whether it be the space of this world or the space of another world. If self-identity is preserved, then even in the other world we would still be finite observers perceiving finite states of affairs. Although God might be an omni-observer, *we* could never be; and our problem is whether or not we could observationally verify the existence of an omnipresent omni-observer. We can observe only contingencies, but God is the necessary being. As such, the question of the existence of God is not like the question of the existence of factual states of affairs, as St. Anselm repeatedly insisted. This is not to say that the expression "God exists" is false or totally meaningless or that no experiences could have a bearing on the question of its truth or falsity, but it is to say that it belongs to the realm of metaphysical rather than factual discourse. God's existence is a matter of metaphysical rather than scientific truth, but it is a matter of truth or falsity all the same, and there are reasons that count for or against it.

Another difficulty with the emphasis on verifiability is that it does not do full justice to the doctrine that God is a spirit. It is true that spirits must reveal themselves to one another through bodies and things, but it is also true that the spiritual depths of personhood are not given in sense observation even in this world. And it is difficult to see how they could be or even why they should be so given in the next world. Suppose we asked whether solipsism could be made *observationally* untenable even in heaven (or in hell). Could we simply *look* at the resurrected Jesus and tell that he compassionately loved us or that he was intensely grieved by our misfortunes and misdeeds? How could we rule out the possibility, on observational grounds alone, that the Kingdom of Heaven as well as its King are only apparitions, like the dream world envisioned by H. H. Price? More than observation goes into the development of any world view; conceptual construction must be present as well. It is difficult to imagine how even in heaven an observed fact or set of such facts could ever generate a completely noncontroversial world view for interpreting the total significance of those facts. According to one motif in Christian theology, it is not God who consigns sinners to hell but rather sinners who consign themselves to eternal separation from God because they still will not believe even after they have eschatologically observed all that there is to see.

The final truth about the matter seems to be that it is difficult to understand how our reasons for believing in God in heaven could be radically different *in kind* from our reasons here on earth. To be sure, there might be significant differences in *degree* of completeness, clarity, logicality, consistency, and closeness to experience in our eschatological world view; but if there are radical differences in kind, we can only admit that it does not make sense *now* for us to talk about them or to place any confidence in them. In other words, as far as we are able to tell, our evidence for theism in heaven would not be radically different from or superior to the evidence that we now have. However, this is not necessarily a negative or pessimistic conclusion. Even in the Kingdom of God in all its glory we would still be finite and contingent, and most if not all of the other things and persons that we encountered in that world would be the same. We might still have most if not all of the existential anxieties of finitude. There would still be cosmological and teleological intuitions that would prompt us to reflect on our situation and develop total world views, and we might still find that the concept of a necessary, intelligent, and benevolent God best unifies and explains it all. It would still be self-contradictory to entertain the thought of a being than whom none greater can be conceived but who yet might not exist at all. And our mystical and intuitive powers as well as our sensitivity to other persons might be greatly enhanced, though the predicament that even these must be interpreted and put to the test in thought and in action would not be transcended. What all this boils down to is the conviction that even in the realm of experience after death, a reasonable belief in God and total devotion to him could not be had effortlessly, which is not to say that they could not be had at all.

Suggestions for Further Reading

ON VERIFICATION AFTER DEATH

BEAN, WILLIAM, "Eschatological Verification, Fortress or Fairyland?" *Methodos,* Vol. XVI (1964), pp. 91–107.

DUFF-FORBES, D. R., "Theology and Falsification Again," *The Australasian Journal of Philosophy,* Vol. XXXIX, No. 2 (August 1961).

HICK, JOHN, *Faith and Knowledge* (Ithaca, N.Y., Cornell University Press, 1957), pp. 150–63.

———, *Philosophy of Religion* (Englewood Cliffs, N.J., Prentice-Hall, 1967), pp. 100–05.

———, "Theology and Verification," *Theology Today,* Vol. XVII (April 1960), pp. 12–31. Reprinted in John Hick, ed., *The Existence of God* (New York, Macmillan, 1964), pp. 252–74.

MARTIN, C. B., *Religious Belief* (Ithaca, N.Y., Cornell University Press, 1959), Chapter 6.

MAVRODES, GEORGE I., "God and Verification," *Canadian Journal of Theology,* Vol. X (1964), pp. 187–91.

MITCHELL, BASIL, "The Justification of Religious Belief," *Philosophical Quarterly,* Vol. XI (July 1961), pp. 213–26.

NIELSEN, KAI, "Eschatological Verification," *Canadian Journal of Theology,* Vol. IX (October 1963), pp. 271–81.

———, "God and Verification Again," *Canadian Journal of Theology,* Vol. XI, No. 2 (1965), pp. 135–41.

PRICE, H. H., "Survival and the Idea of 'Another World,'" *Proceedings of the Society for Psychical Research,* Vol. L, Part 182 (January 1953), pp. 1–25. Reprinted in John Hick, ed., *Classical and Con-*

temporary Readings in the Philosophy of Religion (Englewood Cliffs, N.J., Prentice-Hall, 1964), pp. 364–86.

SCHMIDT, PAUL F., *Religious Knowledge* (New York, Free Press, 1961), pp. 58 ff.

Notes

1 Ian Crombie, "Arising from the *University* Discussion," in Antony Flew and Alasdair MacIntyre, eds., *New Essays in Philosophical Theology* (New York, Macmillan, 1955), p. 126.

2 John Hick, "Theology and Verification," *Theology Today,* Vol. XVII (April 1960), p. 20.

3 *Ibid.*, p. 21.

4 *Ibid.*, p. 23.

5 This is suggested by Antony Flew in his essay "Death," in Flew and MacIntyre, eds., *New Essays in Philosophical Theology,* pp. 267–72. See also Antony Flew, "Can a Man Witness His Own Funeral?" *Hibbert Journal,* Vol. LIV (1956), pp. 242–50.

6 H. H. Price, "Survival and the Idea of 'Another World,'" *Proceedings of the Society for Psychical Research,* Vol. L, Part 182 (January 1953), p. 6.

7 Hick, "Theology and Verification," p. 16.

8 Kai Nielsen, "God and Verification Again," *Canadian Journal of Theology,* Vol. XI, No. 2 (1965), p. 137.

9 An excellent critical review of this sort will be found in Brand Blanshard, *Reason and Analysis* (London, George Allen & Unwin, 1962), Chapter 5.

10 Price, "Survival and the Idea of 'Another World,'" pp. 4–5.

11 *Ibid.*, pp. 17–18.

12 *Ibid.*, p. 18.

13 *Ibid.*, p. 14.

14 *Ibid.*, pp. 14–15.

15 *Ibid.*, p. 16.

16 *Ibid.*, p. 8.

17 *Ibid.*, pp. 11–12.

18 *Ibid.*, pp. 17, 18, 21, 24.

19 Hick, "Theology and Verification," pp. 25–26.

20 Reprinted from John Hick, *Faith and Knowledge,* p. 157, © 1957 by Cornell University. Used by permission of Cornell University Press.

21 Hick, "Theology and Verification," p. 26.
22 *Ibid.*, pp. 26–27.
23 *Ibid.*, p. 28.
24 *Ibid.*, p. 29.

chapter fifteen

The Future
of Reason
and Religion

What has it all come to? Where are we now? Where shall we go from here, and how shall we get there? What is the future of religion? What is the future of reason?

Let us first try to summarize the general conclusions to which our discussions have pointed. If humanity survives its own technology of destruction, there is no doubt that religion has a future. But this depends, of course, on what we mean by *religion*. It is fairly safe to predict that a respectable number of individuals in every generation will be men and women of deep feeling, deep concern, intense involvement, and ultimate commitment. What they will be concerned about, involved with, and committed to, however, is considerably less predictable. It is in this highly uncertain area that the really interesting questions about the future of religion are to be found. What we want to know is whether the traditional forms of religious belief, ceremony, and practice are alive today and will be alive tomorrow. Which of the traditional family traits of religion do we still seriously reckon with? Has the secularization of modern society completely killed our interest in metaphysics, including our wonderment about a supernatural or supreme intelligent being or beings? Do we no longer need to develop complex world views that make a place for the significance of human life, or has our preoccupation with science and nature provided us with adequate answers that totally bypass traditional religious answers to such questions? Do we no longer require a metaphysical foundation for morality? If so, is this because we no longer even require morality? Have we outgrown the problem of evil? Have we become so thoroughly scientific in our understanding of methodology that we are disgusted by metaphysical reasoning as well as by all claims to revelation from on high? Have we relegated worship, prayer, ritual, scripture, and sacred things, places, and institutions to the realm of superstition? Have we become so prosaic that we have lost our propensity for mysticism?

If we were to conduct a survey of the ways most Westerners would answer the foregoing questions, such a study would probably find the majority of us giving antireligious answers, at least in the way that we live and behave if not also in explicit verbal rejection of religious views and values. God may not be dead, but there is much evidence that in our time traditional religion is at least senile if not deceased altogether. If these are the facts, and it seems that they are, how might we react to the present religious situation? Once the sociological question of where we are now has been settled, the normative question of whether or not we are now well off remains to be treated. On the one hand, we may rejoice and proclaim that our generation is the first to live in the adulthood of the world, the first to outgrow the infantile mythological, theological, and metaphysical phases of human development, the first to become a truly free, sane, scientific, empirical, and mature generation. On the other hand, we may not view the death of religion with such euphoria. If religion, morality, and idealism are dead, then so much the worse for us, so much the worse for our era, so much the worse for mankind, we may judge. There is such a thing as gaining the world and losing the soul. Scientism, empiricism, positivism, and materialism may not be enough after all. The latter judgment becomes philosophically interesting, however, only when we state and defend our reasons for making it. Most of the chapters of this book have been devoted to stating and exploring just such reasons. The general thrust of the book has been proreligion rather than antireligion—not in the sense that the old religious *answers* have been reiterated uncritically, but in the sense that the old religious *questions* have been treated with healthy respect. Hopefully, some new answers have also been explored, which in the long run may hold up better under critical examination.

The Future of Religion for Men of Reason

As philosophers, we must finally move away from a sociological assessment of where we are now and deal with the question of what the future of religion *ought* to be for men of reason and good will. Serious men who press hard for a reasoned world view have had many reasons for rejecting traditional religious answers, but these antireligious reasons themselves must sooner or later be subjected to scrutiny. How well do antireligious world views hold up under examination? They too are controversial and must meet rational criteria of consistency, clarity, comprehensiveness, coherence, simplicity, logicality, closeness to experience, and so on. There may be some religious world views that are not really so bad when compared with some of the alternatives, but this is not enough. We want the *most reasonable* world view we can find, but in order to arrive at it we must look at the options and finally judge for ourselves. In this book we have explored some of the options that are open to us today, but the individual must make the final judgment for himself.

We have shown, however, that many of the standard objections to theistic metaphysics can be bypassed, especially given the panentheistic alternative to supernaturalism. Is our talk about God and his relation to the world intelligible? Some of it may be so riddled with paradox that whether it makes sense or not is at least open to question, but we are now in a position to realize that other insights into the nature of God and his relation to the world have been developed or may be developed that may make good sense after all. It is not just naturalists and process philosophers who are discontented with traditional supernaturalistic ways of thinking about God and the world. A great many eminent church thinkers today are united in their rejection of classical supernaturalism, and it seems likely that the influence of this churchly antisupernaturalism will increase rather than diminish in years to come. Even within organized religion, there is a rapidly growing consensus that the concept of God is desperately in need of revision. Traditional supernaturalism is dead, even within the church; and prominent churchmen are united at least in what they reject.

Unity is lacking, however, in the alternatives they offer to traditional supernaturalism. Where can we go from here? If supernaturalism is dead, does this mean that naturalism wins the day after all? Certainly the crucial problem for religious antisupernaturalists is that of offering a well-developed alternative to traditional religious belief and showing how this new alternative differs significantly from that naturalistic humanism which is as old as the pre-Socratics and Greek Atomists and as viable as the scientific passion for knowing the world. This problem becomes especially acute in light of the fact that there are many present-day naturalists who have studied depth psychology, who have encountered "the depths of being" in their own personal experience, and who are *not* lacking in existential seriousness or moral integrity. As most present-day religious antisupernaturalists will admit, the present situation is very unstable because no very clear-cut alternative to classical supernaturalism has been arrived at. When Paul Tillich rejects the notion that God is *a being* among other beings that he created and instead identifies God with "being itself," how is this "being itself" different from "nature as a whole" as conceived by the naturalists? And when he shifts his position and identifies God with the *ground* of being rather than with the *whole* of being, why is this ground not just *a being* or a *part* of reality and consequently less than ultimate? When Rudolf Bultmann identifies myth with talk about transcendent (that is, supernatural) reality and insists that such talk be demythologized—be replaced by verbal and symbolic expressions of man's existential concerns and anxieties— could this not be done perfectly well within the framework of a thoroughly naturalistic world view, even if Bultmann himself is not interested in naturalism or in metaphysics? When Dietrich Bonhoeffer insists that in a world that has come of age men will no longer need to appeal to the "religious hypothesis" (supernaturalism), why is he not telling us that all mature, modern human beings are thoroughgoing naturalistic humanists? When Karl Barth develops what has been called his "unitarianism of the second person of the Trinity," why is he not telling us that we should use our religious words to refer not to metaphysical entities but to historical personages, events, and situations and to the ideals that they inspire—which could easily be done within the framework of naturalism? When the death-of-God theologians insist that the God of supernaturalism is no longer alive and that we are entirely on our own in the world, are they not telling us that nature is all, that man is a part of nature, and that man must create his own ideals and values and actualize them as best he can given his natural intelligence, motivation, and available resources? Are there any significant differences between thoroughly "secularized religion" and "naturalistic humanism" at its best? Are not the Christian antisupernaturalists simply naturalists in disguise, naturalists who do not have the courage of their own deepest convictions, who disguise their total naturalism by expressing it in "the language of Zion" and lack the integrity to admit it even to themselves?

Of course, many of our contemporary religious antisupernaturalists fail to think of themselves as naturalists and believe themselves to be in pursuit of some third alternative that cuts through the old dilemma of naturalism versus supernaturalism. But what is this third alternative? To hold with Santayana that "there is no God, and Mary is His mother" is not to provide a clear-cut alternative to anything, but merely to reflect the confusion that characterizes much present-day religious thought. Although the religious antisupernaturalists are united in what they reject, they have no clear conception of where they are going or what may emerge as a positive alternative to supernaturalism and naturalism. Nevertheless, a third alternative is available, one that has been quite thoroughly worked out; and there is some likelihood that those religious antisupernaturalists who do not move further in the direction of thoroughgoing secular naturalism will move further in the direction of panentheism. Naturalism and panentheism are the viable alternatives for our age.

Can reason help us to choose between naturalism and panentheism? In the chapters on the arguments for the existence of God and in our later discussions of religious experience, we attempted to show that reason can help us. No one argument for the existence of God does the whole job, but this does not mean that our conclusion in favor of theism is the cumulative result of a series of bad arguments. On the contrary, they are very good arguments, no one of which says everything that needs to be said. We need not repeat the arguments here, but we can remind ourselves that they are not stupid arguments and that many if not most of the standard objections to them have been stupid objections. Very few of the critics of the ontological arguments have even read

St. Anselm, much less realized that there are *two* ontological arguments to be found in the *Proslogium*; and the second of these has been virtually untouched by criticism until very recently. We are now in a position to see that the cosmological argument at least does not commit the logical fallacy of composition and that in many instances it is perfectly proper to argue from parts to whole. And it may be suspected that, if we are really hard-headed about applying them, any principles that are used to refute the teleological argument will also imply the nonexistence of all other minds, even those on the purely human plane of existence. When all is said and done, any set of epistemological principles that generates a non-solipsistic world view will probably generate a theistic world view.

How much can we safely claim for our proofs for the existence of God? We can say that belief in God is at least not totally irrational, that there are many good reasons for believing in God, and that such a belief is highly defensible; but can we claim to have finally settled the question? No, but this is not a peculiarity of the philosophy of religion. As long as the human mind is creative, as long as new logics and techniques of analysis are produced, *no* important philosophical question can be claimed to be settled conclusively. Most of the seemingly serious objections to the rationalistic proofs for the existence of God really apply to the entire enterprise of rationality and are not at all peculiar to the philosophy of religion. For example, it may be possible to state all the classical theistic proofs in a logically valid form, but even then the theistic conclusion can be avoided by rejecting one or more of the evidential premises. It is often argued that the theistic proofs do not really prove anything, or that they prove that God exists only to those who already believe and thus need no proofs, because if one does not accept the premises of an argument, no matter how valid, one is not logically obliged to accept the conclusion. Furthermore, it is usually assumed that the theistic proofs are unique in this respect, but the truth is that the entire rational enterprise suffers from this defect, if it is a defect at all. There are no philosophical conclusions, whether in epistemology, metaphysics, ethics, aesthetics, the philosophy of mind, the philosophy of religion, or what have you, that may not be avoided by rejecting the reasons given to support them. No noncircular argument ever proves its own premises. Thus it may be said of the entire enterprise of rationality that *nothing* ever gets proved or that things get proved only to those who already believe and thus need no proof. If the philosophy of religion runs in a circle, then the whole of philosophy and even of natural science does the same.

Human rationality must function somewhere between the extremes of absolutely conclusive proof and no proof at all. Granted that, in Peirce's phrase, all our knowledge "swims in a continuum of uncertainty," we still want the most reasonable view of things that is available to us, and it is possible to determine that some of the options are more reasonable than others. This may not exempt us from simply appealing to our own most basic insights and intuitions when argument reaches the end of its road; but it is a long road, and we can at least try to guard against bringing it to a premature end and against establishing unnecessary roadblocks that might prohibit others with more vision from traveling farther than we have been able to go. Given such modest expectations of human reason, belief in God is just about as reasonable as any major world view available to us. In the first few centuries of the modern period, theologians did attempt to block the path of scientific investigation; but in our own century we may yet come to thank them for keeping pathways open that might have been closed prematurely by an excessively dogmatic scientific empiricism or positivism.

Of course, the man who attempts to construct a viable rational world view is at a disadvantage. He must assemble all the pieces into a complex whole, and his critics can usually get away with tearing down his structure piece by piece without considering where their own principles of criticism lead when put together into a coherent and comprehensive view of things. Metaphysics and the philosophy of religion will always be at a disadvantage in an age of piecemeal philosophizing, not because there is something irrational about them, but because in such an age the rational ideals of coherence and comprehensiveness of explanation are not properly functioning. This century has so far been an age of piecemeal philosophizing, and analysts and existentialists alike have been guilty of this. The problems of metaphysics have been avoided to a certain extent because philosophers have been willing to allow their opponents to attack their programs by offering piecemeal alternatives, being themselves in no position to object. Very few have been willing to put all the pieces together again to find out where it all leads, but we may be seeing the end of such an era. It is easy enough to avoid the problem of God as long as no responsibility is assumed for producing a comprehensive, coherent, viable alternative. It is considerably more difficult to avoid the problem of God when one has to put together again all the pieces of human experience, including sense experience, moral experience, existential experience, mystical experience, our primitive animal faith in the existence of other minds, and all the rest.

Naturalism and panentheism both attempt to see life and human existence whole, and it is to their credit that neither of them is content with fragmented perspectives. However, it is highly questionable that either world view is built exclusively on the application of "scientific method" narrowly conceived, and it is to the advantage of the panentheists that they explicitly maintain that reason is richer in function than naturalists can consistently allow. There are many rational methodologies, science using one, mathematics and logic using another, and metaphysics and ethics using still others. Scientific method will not yield a belief in other minds but instead presupposes it, for scientific method is not grounded simply in *my* experience but in *our* experience of the world. Without a metaphysical pluralism of persons there is no science. Whether logic and mathematics inform us about anything other than themselves is still a matter of debate, but there is no question that they are extremely useful to us in our attempt to know the world and that their methodology is not one of observation and generalization from experience. As our earlier remarks about the nature of metaphysics have indicated, rational methodology in metaphysics is very complex. It involves a conceptual analysis of the basic assumptions and categories of thought that underlie all our thinking about everything, as for example in St. Anselm's analysis of the concept of God. It includes a critical dialectic of the sort proposed by Plato and Hegel, carried out in public by many minds reasoning together, beginning with our present standpoint and subjecting it and some of its alternatives to intensive scrutiny in light of the ideals of coherence, comprehensiveness, completeness, simplicity, and so on. It contains a creative vision of how all the pieces of the puzzle fit together to form *one* whole. It involves reasoning from parts to whole, choosing models from finite structures as aids to understanding the ultimate structure of our world, and arguing for some preferred models and against others. It incorporates an attempt to integrate the diverse factual and normative languages of science and philosophy into a total explanatory scheme in which logic, ethics, aesthetics, and science are not arbitrarily disconnected from one another. It involves explaining things visible in terms of things invisible—something that even naturalism must finally do, if it makes a place for other minds and if it can be driven to that corner in which it must treat pure, formless, mindless, sourceless energy as the basic, necessary stuff of the world order. In some respects, theism is even better supported by arguments than is naturalism. There are many rational proofs for theism, but where has the naturalist attempted to *prove* the eternity and self-sufficiency of pure, sourceless, formless, mindless energy?

It is possible to develop theistic world views that are highly intelligible and defensible, but what shall we men of reason do with them once they are available? We can, of course, write them off as sheer poetry, as an attitudinal stance, or as a psychological "blick" that is somehow useful in allaying our existential anxieties. We can hold that for all their beauty, they are somehow "cognitively meaningless" and only "psychologically meaningful," mere feeling with no noetic significance whatsoever. Unfortunately, reason and feeling are not so easily and totally separated. Nor is it easy to draw a noncontroversial line between the cognitively meaningful and the psychologically meaningful. We still have the urge to find the "right blicks." Even poets might wish to protest an emotivistic interpretation of the notion of *poetry,* for to many of them even poetry is of noetic significance and not merely a matter of cognitively irrelevant feeling. Even poets often regard themselves as having reliable insights into the way things are, in addition to having complex feelings about these things.

If we cannot in good conscience dismiss metaphysical and theistic world views as mere poetry and do regard them as capable of telling it like it is, then we are confronted with the problem of deciding which of the many alternatives open to us is the most reasonable. At this point, the future of religion, or at least of the philosophy of religion, is inextricably intertwined with the future of reason. Why are there so many competing world views? Why is there such bewildering diversity in the products of human creative reason? Is the dream of finding the *most* reasonable world view available to us an idle one? It is possible to hold that the limitations of human knowers prevent the decisive victory of one world view over another. There is so much to include in a world view, so much logical order to arrange, and so many different ways of arranging it, that no one world view can ever expect to win a decisive victory.

Is Reason Dead?

THIS sort of pessimism about human knowers is easily transferred, however, to a pessimism about reason itself. It may be not the limitations of human reasoners, but the limitations of reason itself, that produce such metaphysical diversity. It may be possible, for example, to develop *several* world views that satisfy *equally well* the rational criteria of logicality, comprehensiveness, consistency, coherence, and so on. Of course, philosophers have traditionally lived by the hope that this would never be the case, and we may still have to live by such hope, recognizing it for just what it is. Throughout, we philosophers have hoped that only *one* world view could possibly fit the ideals of rational excellence and explanation, that there is only *one* world view on which all competent rational authorities are ultimately destined to agree, that whenever any two or more world views *seem* to satisfy all criteria of rational adequacy, there is always something in at least one of them that does not quite fit or work. Yet, after so many centuries, we must finally face up to the fact that there is neither an empirical nor an a priori guarantee that all rational investigators are ultimately destined to end up in the same place or even to move in the same general direction. Have we expected too much of reason all along? We must also face up to the fact that in any philosophy, argument finally runs out, and some sort of basic intuition takes over. Who has produced an infinity of proofs of proofs of proofs of proofs . . . ? Perhaps there are diverse fundamental intuitions that generate different world views, with little or no hope of crossing over or communicating or moving in a common direction. The difficulty, in other words, may be more with reason than with religion.

The least we can say is that there is something problematic in being committed to reason, that unavoidable risks are built into any decision to pursue a rationalistic world view. There is no guarantee that men of reason and good will are destined ultimately to agree. There is no final proof or disproof of the possibility that several equally rational world views may be produced, each of which is somehow self-contained and self-confirming. However, any proof or disproof of such a thesis would have to make use of rational criteria of adequacy in explaining and justifying its case. Reason is in some sense able to transcend its own limits each time it recognizes those limits. The very notions of "true belief," "justified belief," and "what there is" are meaningful *only* insofar as they are given some definite position within the context of a rationalistic world view. And philosophers, too, are men who are entitled to some measure of faith and hope. Walking by faith and not by sight, we may decide to keep the traditional faith and believe that finally truth is one and that reason is the best of all possible approaches to it. If we abandon reason, even with all its inherent risks laid bare, what do we have left? Could not mankind do worse than uphold reason? After all, having faith in reason is not quite like having faith in God. There are *prima facie* rational alternatives to the latter, but not to the former. And the limiting question "why be rational?" presupposes that the inquirer is rational, and thus his own question needs no answer.

To say that there are no *prima facie* rational alternatives to reason is not to say that there are no alternatives to it at all. There are many violent, nonrational techniques available to us for resolving our disagreements, and these are often employed. We men have a serious practical problem—we often disagree with one another. Parents and children disagree, and there is a generation gap; nations disagree, and there is a war; religious men disagree, and there is an inquisition or a proliferation of religious sects and denominations. The trouble with disagreement is that it is deeply disturbing. If we could only ignore it there would be no great problem, but those with whom we disagree force themselves on us, and we cannot ignore them. There is a real sense in which the problem of disagreement is a moral problem and in which reason is a moral solution to it. For one thing, disagreement is genuinely disturbing to us only when our opponent is important to us, either because we fear him or because we respect him. If a "nobody" disagrees with us, we hardly seem to mind or to notice; but if someone we deeply respect or fear disagrees, then we are deeply disquieted. And the degree of our disquietude is in direct proportion to the degree of our respect. In cases where respect rather than fear is involved, being disturbed by disagreement is often a moral response to a moral predicament; for it is indicative of concern for, interest in, and respect for the one with whom we disagree. Disagreement is not a problem for those who do not care; it is a problem for those who respect others as ends in themselves. But moral problems do not always find morally correct solutions. How can we bring a dissenting person into agreement with us without doing violence to his integrity as an individual? Certainly there are many techniques available to us for resolving disagreement that are often used but that do cheapen, degrade, demoralize, and even destroy the opposition. Social ostracism, political exile, subtle and not so subtle threats and intimidations, emotionalistic appeals, torture, inquisition, brainwashing, bombastic rhetoric, Madison Avenue advertising, and so on, are always available to those who would remove the discomfort of disagreement by nonrational means. Reason, by contrast, is a moral solution to a moral problem. We can reason with a man without compelling, degrading, or destroying him. The question of the future of reason is thus intimately connected with the question of the future of morality.

If we look at the question of the future of reason from the historical or sociological standpoint, the situation may be even bleaker for reason than for religion. There are varying degrees of commitment to and development of the human capacity for reason, and the great majority of men, not excluding philosophical analysts and existentialists, have always scored very low on the scale. Being reasonable involves more than thinking logically; it involves a comprehensiveness of vision and enlightenment, fairness and impartiality of judgment, and freedom from external and nonrational pressures, all of which only God ideally possesses and men can at best only approximate. But how many of us are seriously interested in approximating these conditions? How many "thinking men" are there today? If Jonathan Edwards was correct in suggesting that

Index

A
B
C
D
E
F
G
H
I
J